Television Trends,
2016–2020

Television Trends, 2016–2020

Authenticity, Diversity, Sexual Candor, and Retrospection

Yvonne D. Leach *and*
Nicholas J. Natalicchio

McFarland & Company, Inc., Publishers
Jefferson, North Carolina

This book has undergone peer review.

Library of Congress Cataloguing-in-Publication Data

Names: Leach, Yvonne D., author. | Natalicchio, Nicholas J., 1986– author.
Title: Television show trends, 2016–2020 : authenticity, diversity, sexual candor, and retrospection / Yvonne D. Leach and Nicholas J. Natalicchio.
Description: Jefferson, North Carolina : McFarland & Company, Inc., Publishers, 2024. | Includes bibliographical references and index.
Identifiers: LCCN 2023050697 | ISBN 9781476689227 (paperback : acid free paper) ∞
ISBN 9781476652269 (ebook)
Subjects: LCSH: Television series—United States—History—21st century. | LCGFT: Television criticism and reviews.
Classification: LCC PN1992.3.U5 L346 2024 | DDC 791.45/7509730905—dc23/eng/20231031
LC record available at https://lccn.loc.gov/2023050697

British Library cataloguing data are available

ISBN (print) 978-1-4766-8922-7
ISBN (ebook) 978-1-4766-5226-9

© 2024 Yvonne D. Leach and Nicholas J. Natalicchio. All rights reserved

No part of this book may be reproduced or transmitted in any form or by any means, electronic or mechanical, including photocopying or recording, or by any information storage and retrieval system, without permission in writing from the publisher.

Front cover: (left to right) Hunter Schafer and Zendaya
in Season 1 of the 2019 TV series *Euphoria* (HBO/Photofest)

Printed in the United States of America

*McFarland & Company, Inc., Publishers
Box 611, Jefferson, North Carolina 28640
www.mcfarlandpub.com*

To our wonderful students
at Drexel University,
who have taught us so much

Table of Contents

Introduction	1

I. Authenticity

1. *Euphoria*: Raw Portrayal of Adolescence in a Teen Drama	8
2. *Normal People*: Slice of Life Approach in a Coming-of-Age Miniseries	30

II. Diversity

3. *Atlanta*: First-Person Comedy-Drama on the Black Experience	52
4. *Ramy*: First-Person Comedy-Drama of an Arab Muslim Community	74

III. Sexual Candor

5. *Vida*: Sex-Positivity in a Drama	92
6. *I May Destroy You*: Overcoming Sexual Harm in a Drama	111

IV. Retrospection

7. *Stranger Things*: Exploring the Eighties Through Genre TV	138
8. *Lovecraft Country*: Exploring Our Racist Past through Genre TV	157
Chapter Notes	193
Bibliography	213
Index	233

Introduction

Whether it is in print, on the stage, or on the screen, fiction is about exploring the human condition. People choose to engage with fictional stories for two general purposes: entertainment and enlightenment. Lovers of fiction are also looking for emotional responses to the material, which often lead to catharsis, the release of strong, repressed emotions. In terms of fictional stories on the screen that are live action, the involvement is in many ways increased because a viewer is seeing and hearing actual people in tangible environments. For a television viewer, as opposed to a film viewer, the involvement is further intensified because of the sheer number of hours a viewer invests, sometimes binging a whole season in one sitting, or alternatively, viewing material in shorter sessions as episodes are progressively released over weeks, months, or years. In addition, for shows that have continuing characters (as opposed to anthologies), the division of content into episodes, whether stand-alone or serial, offers the opportunity for differences in tone and narrative purpose, which adds a certain richness to an ongoing saga. TV viewers not only form relationships with the characters on such shows, but with the shows themselves. Some shows they may simply find interesting, whereas others they may come to adore. A good TV show can be likened to a friend you've invited into your home, again and again, because you want to spend quality time with them. And sometimes it's more than friendship, and then there is heartbreak when the show is over. It's not just the characters that the viewers will miss, but also the voice of the storyteller, who often provides nuanced insights about their characters and a profound understanding of life itself.

By way of introduction, we are full-time faculty in the Cinema & Television Department at Drexel University in Philadelphia, Pennsylvania, and are writing from an American perspective. We are both filmmakers who became academics, who developed a passion for teaching film and television studies to undergraduates who plan on entering the industry as filmmakers, television creators, screenwriters, and media producers. Therefore, in our television studies courses, we not only examine shows historically, thematically, and critically, but also from business and production perspectives. We encourage our students to study the shows as accomplished narratives that address the human condition as well as works of art that employ cinematic language and style to support the storytelling. Our students often gravitate toward discussions about cinematography, sound, direction, performances, production design, editing, special effects, and other production elements.

This book is based on a course, "Recent TV Trends," that we designed together and continue to teach in separate but synchronous sections. The initial idea was to introduce the field of television through an examination of what is current, rather than through the history of what is past, with one of the advantages being that recent shows could deliver more diverse and inclusive content. We decided that we would only choose the shows for the first half of the course and that the students (through a series of surveys) would collectively choose the shows for the second half and then present on them. We were excited to launch the course in the spring quarter of 2020 as a brand-new requirement for our First-Year Film & Television majors, when suddenly the pandemic hit. We had to quickly retool the course for remote teaching and found (somewhat ironically) that the new framework using Zoom and an online teaching portal was beneficial for the course. In large part, this was because it allowed for greater discussion than would have previously been possible in the classroom because students were doing all of the viewing on their own. We also instituted multiple ways for students to engage in determining the trends we were witnessing as the course progressed. The result was that we had a substantially different teaching experience than we had previously. The students learned from us, and we learned from them. Although we began screening material in the classroom once again when we returned to face-to-face instruction, we have continued to leave ample time for discussions. Through this transformative teaching experience, we have found that a trend, which can be defined as a general development or change toward something new and different, can be amorphous at first but ultimately can reveal itself and become more specific. In addition, over time, we have accepted that some of the trends may end up being merely fads. But we believe that other trends have the possibility of becoming part of the mainstream and therefore are important to identify early on, especially for students who wish to embark on careers in the industry.

Having distilled what we've learned from teaching multiple sections of this course over the past three academic years and from doing the necessary research, we arrived at four trends: Authenticity, Diversity, Sexual Candor, and Retrospection. To support each trend, we have chosen two representative shows, resulting in extensive discussions of eight noteworthy, live-action, fictional television shows in the five-year period from 2016 to 2020. Although the four trends are intended to be distinct and separate from each other, it is also the case that some of the shows reflect more than one trend.

Starting with ***Authenticity***, the first word that students often use to describe the shows that they like is "relatable." If one digs deeper, one soon gets to a designation of "authentic." This doesn't mean that the show must be realistic in that there are sci-fi, fantasy, horror, and superhero shows that students feel are authentic because the metaphors employed in the shows resonate as emotionally true. Authenticity simply implies that the students perceive that a show comes from a "no bullshit" place that they respect. Not only is authenticity something that students and other viewers seek, but it is also something that show creators aspire to provide.

As for ***Diversity***, the students, as well as most viewers, want to see themselves and their communities reflected in the shows they watch, although they are also curious to learn about people and communities that are different from them. If dominant characteristics include being white, straight, cisgendered, non-disabled, and male, then diverse characteristics include being BIPOC (Black, Indigenous, People of Color), LGBTQ+ (Lesbian, Gay, Bisexual, Transgender, Queer, plus others), disabled, and/or female or non-binary. In addition, there are many other ways that diversity can be present in a show that are related to ethnicity, religion, economic class, age, and body type. Although a typical way of including diversity in a show is to have an ensemble cast that includes characters from a variety of diverse groups, we believe that one of the most substantive ways that diversity can be explored in fictional TV shows is when a member of a diverse group provides a first-person perspective on their particular community.

As for ***Sexual Candor***, this trend tends to be more female-centered and includes sex-positivity, which originates from sex-positive feminism for both straight and queer women. In this trend, we also address the topic of sexual activity that furthers the story, rather than sex as a romantic interlude or a titillating add-on to a story. Another aspect of sexual candor is approaching sexual assault from a survivor's perspective, rather than through the lens of police procedurals or courtroom dramas. This challenging endeavor of frankly examining what happens to survivors trying to regain their lives is an important aspect of this trend.

Finally, ***Retrospection*** deals with our propensity to look backward in order to understand where we are now. Retrospection can lead to a nostalgic stance in some cases and to a critical stance in other cases. Examining society's past flaws presents a particular conundrum since history can't be pinned down, in large part because it depends on both the vantage point and the motive of those exploring the given history. The art of paying homage to media of past eras also becomes a significant aspect of retrospection. In looking at the past, this trend encompasses reminiscing about positive aspects of it, critiquing negative aspects of it, and using it to make points about the present.

In this book, we have chosen the eight shows based on the qualities of the shows themselves and how they fit the trends and not because they are from a specific streaming service, network, or premium channel. Nonetheless, there is a wide variety of platforms that are represented. Primarily, the shows are from America, with the exception of *Normal People*, which is from Ireland (a BBC Three/Hulu collaboration), and *I May Destroy You*, which is from the UK (a BBC One/HBO collaboration). The streaming channels represented are Netflix and Hulu, with *Stranger Things* and *Ramy*, respectively. The premium channels represented are HBO with *Euphoria* and *Lovecraft Country* and STARZ with *Vida*. There is just one show that didn't begin on a premium channel or a streaming platform, and that is *Atlanta*, which originated on FX, although later it also became available on Hulu. In our explorations of the shows, we are hoping to convey the essence of the shows themselves and to provide new insights on them. We will address business aspects as well as themes, narrative approaches, and cinematic styles. The chapters are written to contain only a few spoilers at the start, but as you keep reading, there will be increasingly more. The hope is that if you like what you read in the beginning, you may begin watching more of the show before you finish the chapter. Please be advised that there will be discussions of sexual assault, physical assault, death, racism, sexism, homophobia, and other forms of bias as they pertain to certain shows. There is also some discussion of mental health issues as well as quoted dialogue that includes explicit language and offensive comments.

Beyond the specific trends we have chosen, we also need to acknowledge some overall trends during this time period. First, there were many effects of the pandemic in 2020: production was halted and then resumed with Covid-19 restrictions; some shows were canceled after their first season and never got the chance to go to a second season; and some shows changed their planned stories in order to comply with production methods conducive to Covid-19 safety precautions. One of the overall trends that has affected these five years can be summed up as "shorter is better." From 2016 to 2020, there were many more miniseries, as well as many more half-hour dramas, both of which describe *Normal People* and *I May Destroy You*. In addition, there were often half the number of episodes per season (or less) as compared to the traditional 22-episode American season. This trend of fewer episodes emulates British narrative television and is evident in all eight of the shows we've chosen. In terms of content, another overall trend is the incorporation of a singular voice, which is the case for *Ramy*, *Atlanta*, and *I May Destroy You*. These show creators work from their own experiences and choose to tell the story from a main character's perspective that resembles theirs, rather than from a more omniscient point of view. A final overall trend is an interest in mental health issues, which includes diagnoses such as ADHD (Attention-Deficit/Hyperactivity Disorder), bipolar, depression, anxiety, and addiction as well as an examination of trauma, whether it's childhood trauma or trauma from assault. We would also like to note that for other TV shows mentioned (outside of the primary eight shows), we provide the platform, dates, and show creators (or developers if derived from source material), and for films mentioned, we provide the distributor, date, and director.

Finally, we would like to make it clear that we are white, straight, cis-gendered, non-disabled Americans—one female and one male. So, when we write about people who are trans, or lesbian, or Black American, or Egyptian American Muslim, or disabled, or Latinx, or Black British, etc., this is not our lived experience. In both our Recent TV Trends course and this book, we have desired to present a wide range of content that reflects experiences that are different from our own. In order to do this in an informed and respectful way, we were fortunate to receive feedback on specific chapters from the following sensitivity readers: Prof. Annette Fierro, Dr. Erin-Lee Hairston, Ms. Jacquelyn Mendoza, Dr. Kadian Pow, and Mr. Ola Shokumbi, all of whom we would like to thank wholeheartedly for their time and their insight.

I
Authenticity

CHAPTER 1

Euphoria
Raw Portrayal of Adolescence in a Teen Drama

Euphoria is an American teen drama that premiered in 2019 on HBO and was produced by the production company A24. It is set in the suburbs of Los Angeles and is primarily about a high school student, Rue (Zendaya), who has just returned from rehab and meets someone new, Jules (Hunter Schaffer). The viewers are introduced to Rue's mother, Leslie (Nika King), and younger sister, Gia (Storm Reid), as well as many teenagers in Rue's social group at East Highland High School. The show is based on an Israeli, Hebrew-language TV show that was also called *Euphoria* (2012–2013), created by Ron Leshem, which was set in the 1990s and followed a group of teenagers who spent their time doing drugs and having sex. Sam Levinson, the creator and executive producer of the current *Euphoria*, which has a present-day setting, is the son of famed film and television director and producer Barry Levinson, who directed *Diner* (MGM/United Artists: 1982), *Good Morning, Vietnam* (Buena Vista Pictures Distribution: 1987), and *Rain Man* (MGM/UA Communications Co.: 1988) as well as executive-producing the TV shows *Homicide: Life on the Street* (NBC: 1993–1999, Paul Attanasio) and *Oz* (HBO: 1997–2003, Tom Fontana). Before creating *Euphoria*, Sam Levinson co-wrote *The Wizard of Lies* (HBO: 2017, Barry Levinson) with his father and then wrote and directed the film *Assassination Nation* (Neon: 2018).

    Euphoria enjoyed a successful first season, premiering on June 16, 2019, and ending on August 4, 2019. Less than a month later, it was renewed for a second season. Because filming was delayed by the pandemic until April 2021, however, the second season didn't premiere until January 9, 2022, almost two and a half years after the first season had ended. In the interim, Levinson created two *Euphoria* specials that could be filmed within Covid-19 restrictions. The first special on Rue was released in December 2020, "Trouble Don't Last Always," consisting primarily of a long Christmas Eve conversation that Rue has with her Narcotics Anonymous (NA) sponsor, Ali (Colman Domingo). The second special on Jules was released in January 2021, "Fuck Anyone Who's Not a Sea Blob," consisting of an extended session that Jules has with her new therapist. This chapter will cover the first season and the two specials. It is worth noting that Sam Levinson was the sole writer for the first season and the director of Episodes 2, 3, 4, 7, and 8. He was also the writer and director of both specials. The other directors for Season 1 were Augustine Frizzell (Pilot), Jennifer Morrison (Episode 5), and Pippa Bianco (Episode 6).

One of the reasons that *Euphoria* stands out is because it was HBO's first teen drama and it seemed like an odd fit for a premium channel that catered to adults and not teens. The fact that the show included the graphic sexual and violent content to be expected from HBO, as well as the depiction of extensive drug use, led some to believe that the approach taken in *Euphoria* was inappropriate for a teen show. The very placement of the show on HBO raised the question as to whether young bodies were being put on display for the consumption of an older audience. The criticisms levied at the show included that the nudity was gratuitous, such as the male frontal nudity in the locker room scene in "Stuntin' Like My Daddy" (S1, E2), and that the show bordered on being both sensationalist and prurient. Despite the fact that many were shocked by the content of *Euphoria*, there were similar explorations in the 1990s, such as the film *Kids* (Shining Excalibur Films: 1995, Larry Clark, Harmony Korine), a controversial depiction of teen skaters having sex, doing drugs, and spreading HIV in New York City.[1] In her *Vox* article, Emily Todd VanDerWerff explains, "But too much of the *Euphoria* pilot feels like leftover 'What the kids are getting up to today—it might *shock* you! More at 11!' paranoia from the '90s, reheated for today's viewers."[2] She goes on to make the argument that the intended audience of *Euphoria* are those who were teens in the 1990s, who are now parents themselves.

To sort out whether *Euphoria* was intended for an adult or a teen audience, it's worth establishing what the targeted audience was initially and what the outcome was over time. The most reasonable assumption is that *Euphoria* was initially intended for adult viewers, especially parents, because of its placement on HBO. The figures for the show's debut, however, hint at an early development involving younger viewership. There were 577,000 viewers for the initial screening, but the first-night total came close to one million viewers with replays and streaming.[3] To tease out what portion of this was streaming on HBO Now (and not replays on the cable channel), Rick Porter, in his article "TV Long View: HBO's 'Euphoria' Audience Is Extremely Online," first makes the point that streaming figures are hard to substantiate because they come from the companies themselves, and then states, "[HBO] did say that the number of people who watched the premiere Sunday on HBO Now was the most for a series debut since *Westworld* in 2016.... Its outsized streaming figures are not a huge surprise, given what's known about the way young adults consume media."[4] Further background on HBO will clarify how *Euphoria* increasingly became available to a teen audience through streaming.

HBO (Home Box Office) has the distinction of being the longest-running pay television service in the United States, having started in 1972 as a joint venture between Charles Dolan's company, Sterling Communications, and Time-Life. A year later, however, Dolan's struggling company was bought out by the parent company, Time Inc. In 1990, Time was merged with Warner to create Time Warner, a sizeable corporate conglomerate, which nonetheless largely left HBO alone. In 2010, HBO launched its first streaming service, HBO Go, which was only available to existing cable subscribers of HBO, and in 2015, it launched HBO Now, a stand-alone streaming service. In October 2016, it was announced that HBO was acquired by AT&T as one of three major divisions of the renamed WarnerMedia, although the deal wasn't finalized until June 14, 2018, because of an anti-trust lawsuit filed by the Justice Department. AT&T's influence then led to the May 2020 launching of HBO Max, which subsumed HBO's previous two streaming services, and most significantly, offered content beyond that which was produced by HBO. Surprisingly, on May 17, 2021, AT&T announced its plan to spin-off WarnerMedia for a merger with Discovery,[5] a deal which was completed on April 8, 2022. This led to HBO Max becoming Max in May 2023 to acknowledge the combination of the HBO Max library with the Discovery+ content and to protect the HBO brand from being associated with "not-so-prestige TLC reality shows."[6] An important milestone in these corporate changes is that on June 19, 2018, just five days after the AT&T deal was completed, John Stankey, the newly-named CEO of WarnerMedia (and a long time AT&T executive), addressed HBO employees, calling for a substantial increase in subscribers as well as more shows and more types of shows. Even though Netflix wasn't addressed by name, the understanding was that HBO would need to successfully compete with Netflix and establish one of the major streaming services in the near future.[7]

What is relevant for this discussion is that *Euphoria* was then ordered to series on July 30, 2018, just six weeks after Stankey's remarks. This appears unusual because the pilot was still in the beginning stages, having been ordered on March 13, 2018, and cast by June 5, 2018. Alison Herman wrote on June 14, 2019, in *The Ringer*, "Even if the decision [to order *Euphoria* to series] were not a direct result of HBO's new evolution, the pursuit or at least centering of a new demographic certainly feels in line with it."⁸ Within two years, it became apparent that HBO was indeed pursuing a teen audience. Kalea Martin noted on March 30, 2021, that HBO Max offered 15 teen shows, including popular shows that originated elsewhere, such as *The O.C.* (Fox: 2003–2007, Josh Schwartz) and *Pretty Little Liars* (ABC Family/Freeform: 2010–2017, I. Marlene King), as well as HBO originals, such as *We Are Who We Are* (2020, Luca Guadagnino, Paolo Giordano) and *Betty* (2020–2021, Crystal Moselle), and HBO Max originals, *Generation* (2021: Zelda Barnz, Daniel Barnz) and the new *Gossip Girl* (2021–2023, Joshua Safran), based on the popular 2007–2012 series on The CW.⁹ It's safe to say that HBO's ability to attract a teen audience started with delivering teen content via *Euphoria* in 2019. The salient point is that even though the show was made for a premium channel with an adult audience in mind, it became immensely popular (through streaming) with a teen audience seeking an edgier authenticity.

When asked the question "Is *Euphoria* authentic?" the students in our Recent TV Trends course overwhelmingly believe that it is. Some of them allowed that it reflected their college experience more than their high school experience, but others believed that it reflected their high school experience accurately. Many of them were drawn to the frank depiction of sex (which felt uncensored to them), the critical view of romantic relationships (which felt accurate to them), and the portrayal of mental health issues (which felt relevant to them). They also resonated with the zeitgeist of the show, best expressed in Rue's statement from the Pilot, "And I know it may all seem sad, but guess what? I didn't build this system, nor did I fuck it up." This line expresses a frustration that is emblematic of how the young generation feels, especially regarding societal problems they inherited from previous generations: racism, sexism, homophobia, transphobia, classism, etc. Added to that are more recent issues like the rise of mental health issues, the opioid epidemic, cyber bullying, and the diminishing possibilities of attaining a financially comfortable life. To an older audience, the show may seem unnecessarily depressing, but to many young viewers, the show simply mirrors their particular stressors and concerns.

As a general observation, the teen television genre is a fitting vehicle for exploring authenticity because it concerns an individual's search for identity, a social group, romantic relationships, and happiness, all of which are essential drivers at the core of human beings, even as they get older. Sharon Marie Ross, in her 2008 co-edited book with Louisa Ellen Stein, *Teen Television: Essays on Programming and Fandom*, starts her essay, "Defining Teen Culture: The N Network," with the following question: "What is an 'authentic' teen voice in the new millennium of the United States, and what role does television play in the creation and maintenance of such a voice?"¹⁰ Within her essay, Ross provides a thorough discussion of the Canadian teen drama *Degrassi: The Next Generation* (CTV: 2001–2015, Linda Schuyler, Yan Moore), which explored a wide array of issues facing teenagers and which aired in the U.S. on Noggin within the nighttime teen block called "The N." Another teen drama that concentrated on prevalent issues was the earlier American show *Beverly Hills, 90210* (Fox: 1990–2000, Darren Star), which typically highlighted a societal problem for an episode or two before moving on to the next one. In the first season alone, there were topical storylines that included the AIDS epidemic, gambling, teen pregnancy, date rape, breast cancer, and affirmative action, among many others.¹¹ Both *Beverly Hills, 90210* and *Degrassi: The Next Generation* are prime examples of the desire to teach lessons to young people about a myriad of societal problems they may face. And even though *Euphoria* also presents some notable issues, it substantially differs from earlier offerings in that it does not provide solutions. Sam Levinson states the following about *Euphoria*: "It's not a cautionary tale, it's not an after-school special."¹² Rather than teaching lessons, Levinson is interested in demonstrating the enormity of primary, on-going issues in revelatory ways. It's important to recognize, however, that striving for authenticity is not the same as striving for verisimilitude. *Euphoria*, with its overdramatized storylines, evocative music, subjective camerawork, and glamorous stars, is clearly not a fictional show that aims to be a naturalistic slice of life. But it does aim for emotional realism, which it often achieves. The point is that the show's creator aspires to authenticity in *Euphoria*, and viewers seek authenticity in it.

An important point that Ross makes about authenticity, which also applies to *Euphoria*, is that *Degrassi: The Next Generation*'s authenticity is demonstrated "through acknowledging the role that diversity is playing in millennial teens' lives."¹³ The students in our Recent TV Trends course acknowledged that *Euphoria* has the diversity that they have come to associate with TV shows that feel realistic and current. Beyond white, straight, and cis-gendered characters, the show includes main characters that are Black, Latinx, queer, and trans. The show also includes teenage characters that run the gamut from rich to middle class to working class. Even though the show addresses sexual behavior and gender expectations in both straight and queer relationships, it doesn't typically foreground the impact of race and ethnicity on the characters and their stories. For example, Rue is biracial with a Black mother and a white father, and yet race doesn't appear to play a large part in her life. As if to acknowledge this, in the special "Trouble Don't Last Always," when Rue is confused about Ali changing his name when he converted to Islam, he says, "What am I, your first Black friend?" The same holds true for the Latina character,

Chapter 1. Euphoria

Maddy, played by the Mexican American actor Alexa Demie, in that we are only given rare glimpses of her Latinidad.[14] With the other Latina character, Kat, played by the Brazilian American actor Barbie Ferreira, it is only her last name of Hernandez that lets us know that she is Latina. It is also worth mentioning that Ali is played by Afro-Guatemalan actor Colman Domingo, who was born and raised in Philadelphia, although the character of Ali is not identified as Afro-Latino. We finally see how race impacts a storyline in "The Next Episode" (S1, E6) when McKay (Algee Smith), a Black character, is confronted with bigotry as a child and is then lectured by his father on the importance of not losing his temper. In the present timeline, we see him as a freshman football player in college assaulted by white fraternity brothers, who fake-hump him as part of a hazing ritual. The prevalence of this kind of assault in real life came to the public's attention in the summer of 2023 with the news of the Northwestern University football scandal. In "Abuse and Racism Accusations Bring '#MeToo Moment' to Northwestern," *The New York Times* reported, "Former players described hazing rituals, including a practice known as 'running,' in which athletes, typically freshmen who had made mistakes on the field, were held down by older players who simulated sexual acts on them while the rest of the team watched."[15] As for McKay, he breaks down afterward and cries in the bathroom (and then has aggressive sex with his girlfriend, making her cry in the bathroom). But he then brushes the incident off and continues to bottle up his emotions in order to fit in.

Ultimately, it is the raw and unfiltered tone of *Euphoria* that heralds the show's realness. Sam Levinson states, "and the one comment that we consistently get from young people is, 'This feels so real.'"[16] Another contemporary "no holds barred" teen show, especially in regard to its explicit sexual content, is *Sex Education* (Netflix: 2019–2023, Laurie Nunn), in which the teen protagonist functions as a sex therapist for his classmates at school. After discussing the similarities between *Euphoria* and the sometimes comedic *Sex Education*, Tim Goodman states in his review, "The difference with *Euphoria* is that there's nothing remotely funny about it, as Levinson steers unflinchingly into what many adults and particularly parents will be triggered (and maybe outraged) by while most teens will probably agree it's one of the few accurate visual interpretations of their life."[17] In this way, *Euphoria* is also somewhat similar to the British version of *Skins* (E4: 2007–2013, Jamie Brittain and Bryan Elsley), which shocked some viewers with its frank depiction of teenagers doing drugs and having sex but which enchanted other viewers with its unapologetic portrayal of characters navigating complicated lives. Another similarity that *Skins* has with *Euphoria* is that most of its episodes are devoted to particular characters, even though storylines for other characters are present within these episodes. A quick (and admittedly reductive) overview of *Euphoria*'s Season 1 episodes, characters, and issues is as follows: Ep. 1—Rue (Drug Addiction), Ep. 2—Nate (Toxic Masculinity), Ep. 3—Kat (Body Image), Ep. 4—Jules (Gender Dysphoria), Ep. 5—Maddy (Abusive Relationship), Ep. 6—McKay (Setbacks to Success), Ep. 7—Cassie (Love Addiction), and Ep. 8—All (Relationships). Although *Euphoria*'s episodic structure is similar to that of *Skins*, it goes further in its deep and intense exploration of interrelated issues. The two salient aims of *Euphoria* that enhance its authenticity are (1) the reflection of the grim nature of mental health issues, particularly drug addiction, and (2) the dismantling of the fantasy surrounding romantic and sexual relationships, including the dynamic of masculine/feminine constructs and the effects of explicit photos and videos. It's important to note that the two main characters are emblematic of these two preoccupations of the show in that Rue is tied more to the first and Jules more to the second.

The depiction of mental health issues, in and of itself, is a major component of the authenticity that our students appreciated in *Euphoria*. This emphasis is made clear in the opening sequence of the Pilot, which Rue narrates over a montage of scenes from her childhood. The first sign that Rue came into the world in anxiety-ridden times is that she was born three days after 9/11. As her parents first held her in their arms, they were watching the constant coverage of the terrorist attack on television. Then, when she was four years old, a health professional said to her parents, "I'd say she's suffering from obsessive compulsive disorder, attention deficit disorder, general anxiety disorder, and possibly bipolar disorder. But she's a little young to tell." Despite the first season validating the usefulness of therapeutic drugs in later episodes, we see in the Pilot that Rue was given an alarming array of medications as a child and as a result she hardly remembers anything between the ages of eight and 12. Later in the Pilot, we find out that when she was 11 years old, she was given liquid valium in a hospital after a panic attack. Rue comments, "This is the feeling I have been searching for my entire life, for as long as I could remember. Because suddenly, the world went quiet. And I felt safe, in my own head." Sam Levinson confirms that this sequence mirrored something that happened to him as a child.[18] Much of the authenticity found in the portrayal of Rue's addiction comes from Levinson's own experiences with drug use, addiction, and recovery.

Since we are in a culture rife with people that suffer from chronic addiction, whether to street drugs or prescription drugs, many viewers are familiar with the life-long battles that addicts wage against addiction. It's significant that the 2019 World Drug Report, released by the United

Chapter 1. Euphoria

Nations Office on Drugs and Crime, revealed that "the adverse health consequences of drug use are more severe and widespread than previously thought. Globally, some 35 million people are estimated to suffer from drug use disorders."[19] Because *Euphoria* depicts Rue mostly using opioids, as well as experiencing an overdose, it is also worth examining statistics relating to opioid overdoses. In "The Epidemiology of Drug Use," Martha J. Ignaszewski states, "In 2017, the US Department of Health and Human Services declared the US opioid epidemic a public health emergency following an increase in opioid overdoses that accounted for more than 42,000 deaths in 2016—a record high."[20] That number then rose to 47,000 in 2017.[21] In terms of teen drug use, the National Center for Drug Abuse Statistics reports that "by the time they're in 12th grade, 46.6% of teens have tried illicit drugs."[22] In addition, in a *TIME* article on *Euphoria*'s depiction of drug use and addiction, the following is stated: "In the U.S., about 1.6 million kids ages 12 to 17—6.3% of the adolescent population—had substance use disorder in 2020, according to the Substance Abuse and Mental Health Services Administration (SAMHSA)."[23] These statistics elucidate the reality that is reflected in the teen world in *Euphoria*.

In the present action in the show, Rue has just returned from a summer in rehab after having had an overdose that put her in a coma. But instead of continuing to be clean, she seeks out drugs as soon as possible. One of the memorable sequences from the Pilot is when Rue gets high at a party and emerges from the bathroom, disoriented. The hallway begins to turn, and in a seamless way, she is shown walking on the wall, then the ceiling, and then back down the other wall, although the other partygoers remain with their feet on the ground. This sequence captures Rue's subjective experience while high in a way that demonstrates her lone perspective as well as the feeling that there's no judgment here. Viewers understand early on that *Euphoria* is not going to assert that an addict can easily fight temptation with the right intervention and soon be on the triumphant road to recovery. In a voice-over in Episode 2, Rue states, "I know you're not allowed to say it, but drugs are kind of cool. I mean, they're cool before they wreck your skin. And your life. And your family. That's when they get uncool. It's actually a very narrow window of cool." In this narration, the show acknowledges the damage that drugs can cause but offers no easy solutions. During the first season, viewers watch Rue steal money from her mother; traumatize her younger sister, Gia, who found Rue when she overdosed; lie to everyone at her NA meetings about being clean; and even threaten her mother with a piece of glass to force her way out of the house. These scenes, as well as many others, present a believable picture of addiction.

Rue also has significant moments with her drug dealer, Fezco, that illustrate the realities of drug addiction. In a pivotal scene between Rue and Fez toward the end of "Made You Look" (S1, E3), Rue comes to his house to get drugs and he won't give her any because he cares what happens to her. After he closes the door on her, she begins screaming at him, accusing him of being the one who sold her drugs in the first place and making it clear to him that he has ruined her life. Then, she belittles him and yet she still begs him to open the door. Although it's heart-wrenching to hear the pain in Rue's voice, Fez doesn't give in, even when she threatens to hate him until the day she dies. Immediately after this, in the final shot of the episode, we see Rue in an alleyway calling Ali, who offered to help her after one of her NA meetings. In a bold camera move marking an important moment, there is a long dolly back from Rue until she becomes small in the frame. It's worth noting that in "The Next Episode" (S1, E6) when Rue starts taking NA seriously, she does take responsibility for her actions and apologizes to Fez, who tells her, "I don't take nothin' a drug addict says personally because I don't believe nothing a drug addict says." He goes on to explain that whether it's "I love you" or "I hate you," it's simply an angle that an addict uses to get drugs. Although Rue sometimes speaks of Fez as being clueless, there is often wisdom in what he says.

As *Euphoria* progresses, the despondency generated by Rue's story is soon balanced by the buoyancy that Jules brings to the show. One of the refreshing aspects of *Euphoria* is that Jules is not introduced as the transgendered character but rather as the cool new girl in town. She is beautiful, stylish, cheerful, and fun, and when threatened by Nate at a party in the Pilot, she also proves to be courageous. In this scene, Nate focuses his rage randomly on Jules because she's the only one left in the kitchen after he tells everyone to clear out. He uses the fact that no one at the party knows who she is to get in her face and scream, "Somebody better speak up—or this bitch is gonna get fucked up." Jules suddenly grabs a kitchen knife and screams, "You wanna fuckin' hurt me?" Nate backs up quickly, afraid of what she's about to do. She stops advancing on him, and in a surprise move, she cuts her own arm. Nate is shocked and thinks she's crazy. In regard to this scene, Levinson confirmed that when he was young, something similar happened to him and he chose to hurt himself first so he wouldn't be hurt worse by his aggressor.[24] Again, this demonstrates that the stories that come from Levinson's life ring true, providing the surprise and nuance needed to make drama feel authentic. Just as the audience is impressed by this scene, so is Rue. She follows Jules out to her bicycle, introduces herself, and asks if she can ride home with her. The following bike-riding sequence is the first of many beautiful, lyrical sequences of Rue and Jules riding bikes, either together or separately. And yet, isn't it odd that in the suburbs of L.A., the land of cars, that the two main characters ride bikes? Nonetheless, these scenes prove that riding bikes provides much more evocative visuals than riding in a car. When they arrive at Jules' house, Rue bandages Jules' arm in her bedroom. She then asks Jules if she wants to get high, which ends the Pilot. It's only in the next episode that the audience sees the full extent of the transcendent experience they have while high, complete with images of glitter dripping from their faces and the distorted sound of Rue saying how happy she is. Interestingly enough, there are some images from this experience interspersed throughout the Pilot, chronologically out of sequence, which foretell their bond. The relationship between Rue and Jules deepens, and at first, it is in the territory of friendship (talking, laughing, hanging out after school, and having sleepovers), but later that changes.

It turns out that Jules has some mental health issues of her own, which are established in "Shook Ones Pt II" (S1, E4). (In regard to the episode title, the joke is that there is no "Pt I" previous to this episode.) In the beginning segment that explains Jules' backstory, we find out that she was depressed as a child, hating both her mind and her body. When she was 11, her mother left her at a psychiatric unit (having gotten her there under false pretenses), where she slit her wrists. After a lengthy stay, she returned home somewhat better, but her mother's issues got worse (which we later find out were related to addiction), and then her mother went away. After her parents' subsequent divorce, Jules was raised by her loving father, David. By 13, she transitioned, and by 16, she began having sex with adult men who were cis-gendered and either married to women or in long term relationships with women. This is presented as risky behavior for a minor and yet understandable in terms of Jules' desire to prove her femininity. The prime example of this pattern within the present action of the show is in the Pilot when Jules decides to hook up with "Dominant Daddy," who turns out to be Nate's father, Cal (Eric Dane). It ends up being an upsetting encounter for Jules, and for the audience, a disturbing scene of violation and statutory rape that establishes the show's shock value early on. There are also other moments in the show that demonstrate Jules' experience of being a trans teenager. For example, in "Made You Look" (S1, E3), when Rue expresses concern about Jules planning to meet ShyGuy118 (known to her as Tyler at this point) in a secluded spot at night, Jules gets frustrated and says to her, "This is the difference between, like, you and me. Like, I don't always get the privilege of meeting people in front of a fucking audience or something." In these tell-tale moments, Jules' approach to her personal life is presented as a logical extension of the realities she faces in being trans. It is also an important reflection of our current culture for *Euphoria* to have a main character who is trans. According to a report that is based on CDC health surveys from 2017 to 2020, the "number of young people who identify as transgender has nearly doubled in recent years."[25] This depiction makes *Euphoria* appear up to date and relevant.

For the most part, Jules' journey into gender exploration is presented as a creative endeavor. This is especially apparent in "The Trials and Tribulations of Trying to Pee While Depressed" (S1, E7) when Jules is visiting her L.A. non-binary friend, TC, played by non-binary actor Bobbi Salvör Menuez and meets TC's roommate, Anna, played by non-binary, femme actor Quintessa Swindell.[26] It is worth noting that part of the authenticity of *Euphoria* is in casting a trans actor, Hunter Schafer, in a trans role as well as in casting non-binary actors in the non-binary roles of TC and Anna. In the scene where Anna is applying makeup to Jules' face as they prepare for a night out, Jules tells Anna about buying her first pair of heels and then continuing her transformation with clothes, makeup, and hormones. Jules ends her account by saying, "I just kind of kept leveling up." Anna asks, "So what level are you at now?" Jules replies, "I don't know. But I definitely haven't reached my full power." They both laugh. Jules then tells Anna that her relationship to men is weird and says, "In my head, it's like, if I can conquer men, then I can conquer femininity." Anna asks, "Why do you need a guy to make you feel more feminine?" When Jules hesitates, they kindly let the moment pass. Hunter Schafer, who plays Jules, echoes this discussion in the extra, *Euphoria Unfiltered* "Sn1/Ep4," when she says that her character, Jules, is "wanting to be treated a certain way by a man in order to feel like a woman [from] this binary vantage point." In the special "Fuck Anyone Who's Not a Sea Blob," which Schafer co-wrote, Jules tells her new therapist, "Basically, I feel like I've formed my entire womanhood around men. When, like, in reality, I'm no longer interested in men. Like, philosophically. Like ... like, what men want." She then goes on to express that she built her body, her personality, and her soul around what men desire and now she finds all of that embarrassing. This forthright expression of trans experience is a rarity on television and contributes to *Euphoria*'s authenticity.

In a more subtle way, Rue is presented as having a masculine expression in her manner and choice of clothing. At the beginning of "And Salt the Earth Behind You" (S1, E8), Jules is dressing Rue for the winter formal in a feminine way, contrary to her usual look. When Rue expresses that she's uncomfortable, Jules says that she looks hot. Later at the dance, Jules confesses, "I like the way I dressed you, but I'm worried I fucked with your gender expression." This demonstrates that Jules is aware that the hoodie and sweats that Rue usually wears constitute a deliberate choice to not appear feminine. This is followed by Jules asking Rue why she doesn't "kiss-kiss" her. Rue asks her if she wants that, and

Chapter 1. Euphoria

Jules' reply is that she wants Rue to want to do it so much that she doesn't ask. It substantiates that Jules wants Rue to take the dominant role in their burgeoning romance because that is what she is accustomed to from her sexual experiences with men. But Rue, with her limited sexual experience and her uncertainty about her desires or the role she wants to play, isn't sure how to proceed.

Establishing this discourse on feminine, masculine, and non-binary gender expression is an aspect of *Euphoria* that makes it feel current to many viewers. In particular, the dynamics of the primary straight couples (Nate and Maddy and Cassie and McKay) exaggerate elements relating to traditional feminine and masculine roles throughout the first season in order to provide a backdrop for the flexible gender roles that later become apparent in the queer relationship of Rue and Jules. But early on, there is also an intriguing and troubling romantic connection presented between Nate and Jules. In "Made You Look" (S1, E3), we witness an impressive moment as the camera pulls back from Rue in the corridor of her high school and then turns a corner, revealing Jules leaning against a wall texting with ShyGuy118, her mystery guy, ending on a wipe to a split screen of Nate texting her back, revealing that ShyGuy118 is actually Nate. A visual comparison of Jules and Nate is then offered in successive shots, culminating in a side-by-side split screen shot, demonstrating an arresting feminine/masculine dichotomy. And yet, one is also struck by how much Jules and Nate look alike. It makes one wonder, "What exactly is gender?" If one accepts that gender presentation is learned by both osmosis and self-aware invention, and is subsequently performed, then taking a deep dive into how gender is constructed through the means of drama can comprise an authentic journey. In the extra segment *Euphoria Unfiltered*: "Sn1/Ep2," Jacob Elordi, the actor who plays Nate, says that his character is afraid of Jules, not only because she represents the problem his dad has (in that she could ruin his father's life by revealing the statutory rape), but also because she challenges Nate's idea of masculinity.

And Nate's idea of masculinity is presented as the same toxic masculinity of his father. *Euphoria* shows us that from an early age, Nate has wanted to be strong like his father, and indeed, his macho stance is presented as the product of his father's upbringing. In the Pilot, during the statutory rape scene with Jules, the viewers can readily see that Cal's game is power, control, and dominance. At first, Jules likes being praised by Cal and goes along with what he wants. But when they progress to having sex, it quickly becomes aggressive and is clearly painful to Jules. Later in the Pilot, Nate's threatening of Jules at the party poses a counterpoint to Cal's behavior. Whereas Cal offers champagne and flattery to Jules at the beginning of their encounter and then dominates her at the end,

Nate approaches Jules with aggressive bullying in the beginning and then capitulates to her at the end. Throughout the series, there is an odd duality in that both father and son harm Jules and yet also compliment her. Cal's flattery is largely superficial since it's mostly about her body, whereas Nate seems to genuinely believe that out of everyone in their high school, Jules is the most likely to lead a remarkable life. A major difference in how father and son treat Jules, however, is demonstrated in how they respond once they feel threatened by her. After his transgression, Cal begs Jules not to destroy him, whereas Nate chooses to entrap her. When Jules unwittingly meets Nate by the lake, expecting him to be ShyGuy118/Tyler, he threatens her with being charged for creating and disseminating child pornography because she sent erotic photos of herself to "Tyler," which he has put in an account that can't be traced to him. After weeks of texting and sexting, Jules feels like she has fallen in love with Tyler, and ironically, Nate seems genuinely moved by Jules at times.

In many ways, Tyler can be seen as an alter ego for Nate: the imagined sweet, sensitive boy who gets to be with Jules, rather than the "alpha male quarterback dating a cheerleader" persona that he is stuck with. The show suggests that Nate's discovery as a young boy of Cal's hidden sexual life (through the DVDs that Cal makes of his sexual encounters) has shaped him to believe that he can't openly explore his own sexuality and that, in general, he must keep his true feelings hidden. Many of the moments when Nate is provoked by Maddy are when she questions his sexuality. For example, in the Pilot scene at the party when Maddy is in the pool with Tyler Clarkson (who is the real Tyler), and Nate calls her a whore, she replies, "Suck my dick!" He seems to be not only triggered by Maddy stepping out but also by the way in which her phrase seemingly comments on his own sexual preferences. In "'03 Bonnie and Clyde" (S1, E5), Cal talks to a random hook-up, Minako, about his two sons in a motel room, saying, "Do you think this stuff affects them even if they don't know it?" and then adds, "Do you think hiding it creates the same thing in them?" There is also a strange moment just a short while later when Cal is pulling his truck out of the dark motel parking lot and Nate is pulling his truck in so that he can meet Maddy in a motel room. Father and son don't see each other, but when Nate gets out of his truck, Minako happens to be sitting on the steps and says to Nate, "Hello, handsome." This scenario linking father and son through Minako prompts us to think more about Cal's effect on Nate overall. Ultimately, it is left up to the viewer—Nate can either be seen as a psychopath of his own making or a tortured soul who is the product of his upbringing.

To complement the toxic masculinity portrayed in the story, there are two characters, Maddy and Cassie (Sydney Sweeney), who are emblematic of throwback femininity from a different era. Although both Maddy and Cassie had other interests in childhood, pageantry and ice-skating, respectively, those activities were replaced in adolescence by their pervasive efforts to attract boys. In addition, they are both presented on the show as over-sexualized. Depending on one's point of view, this can either be seen as sex-positive or demeaning. To take the case of Maddy first, she knows that she's in a toxic, abusive relationship with Nate, and yet she goes along with it in part because she likes being pampered, showered with gifts, and being promised an easy life. In the short narrative about Maddy, we see her realize as a child that her mother's pedicure clients are rich women who don't work, planting the idea that she should become a lady of leisure herself. So, yes, Nate, as a rich kid, could be seen as solely a means to an end for her. Unfortunately for Maddy, she happens to love Nate and finds that she can't completely break the bond even when she knows that she should. In Episode 5, Rue's narration tells us that Maddy's totem animal is Sharon Stone in *Casino* (Universal Pictures:1995, Martin Scorsese), who plays Ginger, a hustler and former prostitute. Maddy lets Nate know that she wants the same fur coat as Ginger in the movie, and indeed, he buys it for her. Through this and other telling moments, Maddy seems like a caricature of a woman from a time gone by. In the window of her bedroom, Maddy is seen modeling the lingerie that Nate bought her so that she can make him feel good, even though her response to it initially is "Ewww." She also watches porn to learn about poses and reactions that will enhance Nate's enjoyment and confidence when they have sex, so he, in turn, will be more likely to do things for her. But as much as Maddy appears to be an outdated portrayal of a male-pleasing woman, the point is made that today's teenage girls still find themselves indulging male partners' desires to the exclusion of their own.

Given Maddie's exaggerated femininity, one expects her to crumble into passivity when Nate becomes abusive to her, especially when he chokes her at the carnival in "Shook Ones Pt II" (S1, E4). But one of the interesting facets of Maddy's character is that even though Nate has a pronounced physical advantage over her (since she is petite and Nate is a behemoth in comparison), she is never cowed by him. In that instance, she stands up to him, immediately asking him why he has dick pics on his phone, which oddly gets him to calm down. Her unabashed response to his abuse seems similar to Jules' reaction to Nate's aggression at the party in the Pilot. The point seems to be that innate courage lies beyond traditional feminine and masculine assumptions stemming from physical weakness and strength. In the Season 1 finale, "And Salt the Earth Behind You" (S1, E8), Maddy and Nate have broken up once again and yet he convinces her to dance with him at the winter formal, his date having already been reduced to tears.

As they slow dance, with her head resting on his chest, Maddy makes the following pronouncements, with him saying "I know" each time: "Y'know, I really fuckin' hate you.... You're abusive, psychopathic. Most of the time, I really hate the way you make me feel.... It's not good for us.... Meaning, like, we shouldn't be together." This conversation is so honest that the audience believes that Maddy is completely done with him. But just before this, Kat tells their group of friends, "I guarantee you that Maddy and Nate are gonna get married and probably, like, get divorced three times, and in some strange way, live a pretty happy life." Everyone at the table finds themselves nodding in agreement. This unexpected insight has the ring of truth to it and serves as an example of what makes the show feel real.

Cassie, on the other hand, presents a milder version of throwback femininity. She falls whole-heartedly in love with her boyfriends, with fewer expectations than Maddy of what they will give to her or do for her. Her tendency, however, is to go along with whatever her male partners demand of her. She is charmed when Christopher McKay becomes interested in her. As previously mentioned, he is the football player, who is now a freshman at a nearby college. But unfortunately, Nate gets to McKay before the party in the Pilot (which is at McKay's house) and shows him explicit photos and videos of Cassie that she made for previous boyfriends. From this knowledge, McKay gets the wrong impression of Cassie, and when they hook up later, he chokes her, thinking she would like it. She protests and immediately he says that he's sorry. A pertinent question is where McKay falls on the scale from sensitive to toxic male. The answer is that he seems to be somewhere in between, just like Cassie (in comparison to Maddy) is somewhere in between being her own person and being a female that caters to males. In Episode 4, when McKay and Cassie go to Cal's chili tent at the carnival, he tells everyone that he and Cassie are just chillin.' He listens politely to Cal Jacobs' lecture about football's relationship to success in life, which comes off as a perversion of Coach Taylor's uplifting speeches to his football players in *Friday Night Lights* (NBC: 2008–2011, Peter Berg). The outcome of this scene is that Cassie is offended because McKay doesn't publicly acknowledge their relationship. At first, McKay says that it's because he's worried about what Nate will do with that information, but then he refers to the explicit photos and videos of Cassie that he's seen, which leaves her feeling betrayed. Similarly, in a later episode, McKay is shown criticizing Cassie's Halloween costume of Alabama Worley from *True Romance* (Warner Bros.: 1993, Tony Scott) because he thinks it's too revealing, and he makes her change into a staider football jersey. He tells her that he'll never hear the end of it if she goes to the party at his college dressed in a provocative way. Looked at another way, it is a sign of insecurity on his part. He simply doesn't want to deal with other guys wanting his gal. The hypocrisy of it all is that later in the first season, McKay asks Cassie to photograph herself so he can get off on it, providing exactly what she has provided other boyfriends in the past—for which he has judged her. This contradiction between being shamed for past photos and videos and yet being pressured to provide them again in a new relationship is a situation that many teens find familiar.

A significant moment happens when Cassie and Maddy end up doing Molly together at the carnival in "Shook Ones Pt II" (S1, E4) that comments on whether these two straight female characters will be able to attain meaningful agency in their lives. When they are in the house of mirrors and gazing at different reflections of themselves, Cassie says to Maddy, "We should just pick the hottest, most confident, bad bitch version of ourselves and be that for the rest of the school year." And yet, after this telling moment, Maddy decides to get back at Nate (for criticizing her sexy outfit earlier) by dumping Cal's prize-winning chili and cursing out Nate's mom, leading to Nate becoming enraged and choking her. We can readily see that her life is intolerable either way—when she accommodates Nate's every whim and when she retaliates against him. As for Cassie, after feeling rejected by McKay, she ends up coming on to Daniel (Keean Johnson), leading to her climaxing while riding a horse on the carousel and embarrassing herself in front of onlookers. Their "house of mirrors" plan clearly doesn't work out well for either of them. The show's message appears to be that Maddy and Cassie are not allowed to have positive outcomes from being the "most confident, bad bitch version" of themselves. In "The Next Episode" (S1, E6), when Cassie is once again disenchanted with McKay, she wears the Alabama Worley costume to another Halloween party, this time at Daniel's house when she's back home. Daniel is clearly waiting for a chance to make his move. When they are alone at the party, Cassie tells him that they can't have sex because she would feel too guilty because she has a boyfriend. Daniel then lets loose with a lengthy, venomous diatribe that ends with "Like, every time you start talking, I think, who the fuck does this girl think she is? You are so fucking boring. Hey, I'm going to be honest with you, because no one else will. Any guy who says he's interested in you beyond just fucking you is full of shit." The trap for Cassie is that she feels pressure to be sexy and yet she is punished for it as well.

Yet another teenage girl affected by a leaked sex video is Kat. In "Stuntin' Like My Daddy" (S1, E2), Kat's story comes to the foreground when she is horrified that the video of her having sex for the first time (with a St. Mary's student, Wes, at McKay's party in the Pilot) is being circulated online. The next episode, "Made You Look" (S1, E3), focuses on Kat and the short narrative in the beginning shows how her friends were hurtful to her when she was 11 after she gained 20 pounds while on vacation. In the present timeline, she gets busy trying to undo the damage of the video since everyone is now staring at her and making comments at school. Within this episode, Rue's voice-over provides the following commentary: "I know your generation relied on flowers and father's permission, but it's 2019, and unless you're Amish, nudes are the currency of love. So stop shaming us." It's interesting that in this voice-over, Rue is directly addressing the older generation (which is more evidence that the show was primarily intended for an adult audience). Luckily for Kat, she can't be clearly seen on the video and so she gets Troy (Tyler Timmons), one of McKay's younger twin brothers, to spread the rumor that it wasn't her. She then denies it to the principal, telling him that just because it's a fat girl in the video, that doesn't mean it's her. She follows that with "You know, it's one thing for my classmates to body shame me, but for you, Principal Hayes, that's just a whole other thing. It's degrading. It's discriminatory. And it just goes to show how insidious and systemic body terrorism truly is in this country." After she quells the gossip, however, she feels differently about the video when it gains substantial popularity online. Having already experienced some notoriety as an author of erotic fan fiction, she makes the decision to become a cam girl.

Ostensibly, Kat becomes empowered by displaying her body for paying clients, albeit with a mask on. As part of her transformation, she blackmails Troy into buying her clothes and makeup, threatening him with the repercussions of disseminating child pornography. In this case, we're supposed to see this as reasonable payback for Troy not stopping his twin brother, Roy (Tristan Timmons), from initially posting the video. Kat soon adopts a sexy new look in everyday life and dives into a string of casual hook-ups. Ironically, in "The Next Episode" (S1, E6), after Daniel has finished denigrating Cassie for not having sex with him at his Halloween party, he happens to run into Kat, who *is* interested in having sex with him. When Kat says afterward, "I always thought I was going to lose my virginity to you," he is confused, at first thinking that this had been her first time. It is then that we recall (from three episodes before) that Daniel is the boy who broke up with her in the sixth grade. It turns out that teenage Daniel has no recollection of their five-month relationship as children. Kat is taken aback by this, a chink in the armor of her now–super-cool persona. Other examples of more direct fallout from Kat's transformation are that she is often understandably skeeved by what she encounters as a cam girl. She also ends up hurting her friends with the hardened demeanor she has adopted (to go along with her new look) and then they hurt her back.

It is worth asking at this juncture, "Are there missteps in *Euphoria*'s pursuit of authenticity?" And yes, there certainly are. For one, the weaponization of sexting and the unwanted sharing of explicit photos and videos on *Euphoria* seems overplayed to the exclusion of other aspects of current interconnectivity. To recall the instances of this prevalent motif, we see Nate blackmail Jules with the explicit photos she sent to the fictitious Tyler, and then we see Nate himself made to feel uncomfortable about the dick pics on his phone when Maddy shares the information with friends and rumors are started. We also see Cassie slut-shamed by Nate and the other football players for the explicit photos and videos of her. And we see Kat, at first a victim of a leaked video and then a cam girl, who finally experiences an online encounter that goes further than she would like. Kat, in turn, threatens Troy with charges of disseminating child pornography to get what she wants from him. Although in part this motif makes *Euphoria* seem more current, upon closer examination, it makes the show seem unnaturally skewed toward a menacing aspect of interconnectivity. Reggie Ugwu states in his review in *The New York Times*: "But there is more to online community than the hungry eyes of perverts and frauds (usually), and it's surprising that a show that goes to such pains to wrap itself in the political and aesthetic banners of contemporary youth culture would adopt such a retrograde posture."[27] Emily VanDerWerff also points out that there is a surprising absence of characters in *Euphoria* who are on YouTube or on social media.[28] As a way to summarize this discussion, it feels like the characters on the show are not operating within the same digital reality as the rest of us, and this impairs its aura of authenticity.

Another impediment to authenticity in *Euphoria* is the problematic use of twenty-something actors to portray teenagers, which is an almost ubiquitous issue in the teen genre. For example, Ben McKenzie was 25 years old in the year he began playing 16-year-old Ryan on *The O.C.* (Fox: 2003–2007, Josh Schwartz) and Cole Sprouse was also 25 years old in the year he began playing 15-year-old Jughead on *Riverdale* (The CW: 2017–2023, Roberto Aguirre-Sacasa). In 2019, the ages for the primary actors playing high school students in Season 1 of *Euphoria* were as follows:

- 23 years old   Zendaya (Rue)
- 20 years old   Hunter Schafer (Jules)
- 22 years old   Jacob Elordi (Nate)
- 25 years old   Alexa Demie (Maddy)
- 22 years old   Sydney Sweeney (Cassie)
- 23 years old   Barbie Ferreira (Kat)

With the exception of Hunter Schafer, these ages are a far cry from the 17- to 18-year-old characters that the actors are playing. The issues caused by older actors playing teen characters can be summarized as follows (as gathered from years of student discussions in a Teen Television course at Drexel University). The first is that body issues can arise when teen viewers seek to emulate the adult actors playing teenagers because they come to believe that their own bodies are underdeveloped. In addition, because the twenty-something actors seem so natural in their pursuit of adult activities (often related to sex and drug use), teen viewers can feel like those activities should come naturally to them as well. Finally, in a more fundamental way, teens don't move in the world with the same aplomb and sophistication as adults, causing an odd disjuncture in their behavior when they try to imitate the seasoned stars from their favorite teen shows. In contrast to the mainstay of teen dramas, the creators of the many iterations of the *Degrassi* shows took a stand on this issue and did their best to cast actors who were the same ages as the characters.[29] They also cast actors who weren't model-beautiful but instead had a wide range of body types and looked like typical teenagers. Conversely, *Euphoria*, which strives so hard for authenticity, is filled with strikingly good-looking, twenty-something actors. Ironically, Drake, who acted in *Degrassi: The Next Generation,* is one of the executive producers of *Euphoria*. He clearly wants to now be associated with a different kind of teen show. There is another issue as well in the case of *Euphoria*, which is the fact that the twenty-something actors somewhat absolve the viewers because they can tell themselves that they aren't really watching underaged kids being sexually assaulted and harmed. It's false comfort, however, because within the story of *Euphoria*, these characters are indeed teenagers in high school.

Another detour on the road to authenticity is the use of Rue's narration. There is a tension created in the show between Rue as the main character and Rue as the omniscient narrator. It makes sense for Rue to narrate her own story, but it doesn't make sense for her to narrate the stories of all the other characters. It feels both confusing and forced. In the interview with Sam Levinson, he says that when his mother was looking at one of the scripts in its early stages, she threw it in the trash at the point when McKay chokes Cassie. When Levinson explained to his mother that McKay was acting on his preconceptions about Cassie, based on the photos and videos of her, and was also influenced by the impact of pornography on the culture, his mother asked him how she was supposed to know that.[30] As a result, he came up with the idea of having Rue continue to narrate the story. This demonstrates that changes to fix one narrative problem can often cause other problems to occur within the larger story. Another oddity with the narration is that from the beginning,

Chapter 1. Euphoria

Rue is telling us the story after the fact. In the Pilot, she is already referring to what Nate did to Jules and yet it hasn't happened yet on the show. And then she tells the audience, "This is where it gets weird" about an event that she didn't witness. Since it was Jules who saw the photo of Cal and his family on his phone in the motel room, why is Rue telling us that it gets weird when the same photo is up on the wall in Nate's home, thereby revealing that Cal is Nate's father? It's interesting to note that there are a few places where the show tries to explain away the inconsistencies caused by Rue as an omniscient narrator. The first one is in the Pilot during the party when Rue says in voice-over, "Now, there's a couple versions of what happened that night. It all depends on who you ask. And to be honest, I'm not always the most reliable narrator." And then at the beginning of Episode 2, Rue's voice-over is "Sometimes when I get really high, I kind of think I'm psychic," which offers a loose explanation for why she appears to know everything about other people.

There is also a tension in the show between the genuine explorations of teen relationships versus the rapid unfolding of the plot, which can be seen as a succession of falling dominoes that force the next thing to happen. For example, in the Pilot, Cal's sexual exploitation of Jules propels his son, Nate, to entrap Jules in a fake romance and then blackmail her. Also in the Pilot, Maddy's decision to get back at Nate by screwing Tyler Clarkson in the pool causes Nate to beat Tyler up (threatening him with a statutory rape charge if he goes to the police) and then later coerce him into taking the blame for something Nate did. In a strange nod to self-awareness, all of the confusing twists and turns of the plot are then investigated in Episode 7 when we see Rue acting like a detective unraveling the secrets of the show, evoking Morgan Freeman's character, Somerset, from the film *Se7en* (New Line Cinema: 1995, David Fincher). Even though Rue as a detective has its fun moments from a performance perspective, it renders a muddled understanding of what should be taken as real and what should be taken as fantasy on the show. For example, how much is Lexi (Maude Apatow), as Rue's sidekick, actually participating in the ruse and how much is further embellished by Rue's imagination? The point is that despite all of the effort put into the intricate plot, the most memorable parts of the show are those teen experiences that ring true as well as the depiction of the deepening relationship between the two main characters.

By the end of Season 1, the relationship of Rue and Jules emerges as the only one with the promise of real love. The other romantic relationships in *Euphoria* are either significantly marred, such as the toxic relationship of Nate and Maddy or the fraught relationship of Cassie and McKay, or feel unrealistic, such as Kat's blossoming relationship with Ethan (from biology class), which gives off rom-com vibes that don't seem in sync with the ethos of the show. In Episode 3, Rue explains what real love should be: "Real love is when you can't exist without someone, when you'd rather die than be apart, and the whole world goes dark and nothing else matters but the person standing in front of you." The audience then sees clips of characters from TV shows that many viewers know well: Lorelai and Luke on *Gilmore Girls* (The WB: 2000–2007, Amy Sherman-Palladino), Sookie and Vampire Bill on *True Blood* (HBO: 2008–2014, Alan Ball) and Olivia and Fitz on *Scandal* (ABC: 2012–2018, Shonda Rhimes). Interestingly enough, these are all examples of adults in love, which again points to the intention of making the show for an adult audience. For what it's worth, there are many examples of romantic love in classic teen dramas that could have been used in this particular sequence, such as the relationship between Joey and Pacey in *Dawson's Creek* (The WB: 1998–2003, Kevin Williamson) or, if an example of human/vampire love was desired, between Buffy and Angel on *Buffy the Vampire Slayer* (The WB/UPN: 1997–2003, Joss Whedon). Later in Episode 3, however, an acclaimed teen show is indeed referenced when Rue sees her younger sister watching *My So-Called Life* (ABC: 1994–1995, Winnie Holzman). Rue comments that she never wants Gia to be interested in someone like Jordan Catalano. But the apt comparison of *My So-Called Life* with *Euphoria* is not with Angela and Jordan, but with Angela and her new best friend, Rayanne, with whom Angela is quite smitten. In *Euphoria*, the tale of new best friends goes further, and Rue and Jules become the ones who have a chance of attaining real love.

To be fair, the relationship between Rue and Jules is also fraught with problems, such as Rue's struggle to stay clean and Jules' growing sense of responsibility to keep her clean. There is a significant moment in "Made You Look" (S1, E3) when Jules takes Rue back to her house after Rue was made to take fentanyl by Fezco's drug supplier, Mouse (Meeko), and Jules tells her that she can't be around her unless she quits doing drugs. This proves to be enough of an incentive for Rue to take NA seriously and begin a process with Ali, who becomes her sponsor. But it is Ali who points out that Jules has become Rue's new addiction. Given these complex dynamics, the relationship still demonstrates genuine caring and tenderness. In VanDerWerff's article, she makes the point that *Euphoria* is actually two shows put together, the bad one about teenage antics that will alarm parents and the good one about "two girls who find each other right when they need to."[31] Even Doreen St. Félix, in her highly critical review of *Euphoria* in *The New Yorker*, states, "Rue and Jule's relationship is the jewel of 'Euphoria.' I'll keep watching because I desperately want to protect them."[32] It is also refreshing that Rue and Jules don't want to define what they have. In "'03 Bonnie and Clyde" (S1, E5), Jules' father, David, asks Jules, "Are you two, like, a thing?" and Jules' answer is "No, we're not a thing. I don't know what a thing is." Throughout the first season, Jules' dream of living in New York with her female best friend, with whom she would curl up in bed each night, is presented as another way to love someone. The implication is that Jules could still have hook-ups with men as she pleased. This dream of course becomes increasingly complicated by the blossoming romance between Rue and Jules, beginning with a quick kiss by Rue and deepening into something more in the virtuoso ending sequence in "Shook Ones, Pt II" (S1, E4). While the two of them embrace, the bed turns over from side to side with endearing moments of their interactions intercut, giving us the sense that their world is joyfully spinning on its axis because of this monumental change. Since their connection defies typical expectations for relationships and goes to rarely explored places, the viewers feel like they're figuring out the relationship along with the characters. The fact that the two specials released after the first season are devoted to Rue and Jules, filling in many of the details that fans crave, is a testament to the fact that Rue and Jules are at the heart of this show and are an essential part of its authenticity.

CHAPTER 2

Normal People
Slice of Life Approach in a Coming-of-Age Miniseries

Normal People is a coming-of-age miniseries set in Ireland that premiered in 2020. It was a collaboration between BBC Three and Hulu, in association with Screen Ireland, and was produced by Element Pictures. The Irish broadcast service RTÉ did not have the financial resources to develop the series but did acquire it and air it.[1] When the miniseries was released, the numbers showed that it was "a hit among RTÉ viewers" and that BBC Three "had the best week ever."[2] The drama was adapted from Sally Rooney's highly successful 2018 novel of the same name, which begins with the relationship of two teenagers in County Sligo: Marianne (Daisy Edgar-Jones) and Connell (Paul Mescal). The two main characters, their friends, and their families are all white Irish, although from different socioeconomic classes. *Normal People* was executive produced by Ed Guiney, known for executive producing *Ripper Street* (BBC One: 2012–2016, Richard Warlow) and *Dublin Murders* (BBC One/STARZ: 2019, Sarah Phelps). Sally Rooney was both an executive producer and a co-writer of six episodes with Alice Birch, who is the award-winning playwright and story editor of *Succession* (HBO: 2018–2023, Jesse Armstrong). Birch also wrote five more episodes on her own, and Mark O'Rowe wrote the last remaining episode to complete the 12 episodes. In an unusual arrangement, the show had two different director/cinematographer teams: Lenny Abrahamson and Suzie Lavelle for the front half and Hettie Macdonald and Kate McCullough for the back half. This chapter will only examine the front half (six episodes), which comprises the work of the Abrahamson and Lavelle team. Abrahamson's recent directing work includes *Room* (Elevation Pictures, StudioCanal, A24: 2015), *Chance* (Hulu: 2016–2017, Kem Nunn, Alexandra Cunningham), and *The Little Stranger* (Pathé Distribution, 20th Century-Fox: 2018). Lavelle's recent work as a director of photography includes *Ripper Street*, *Sherlock* (BBC

One: 2016, Mark Gatiss, Steven Moffat), *Vikings* (History: 2013–2020, Michael Hirst), and *His Dark Materials* (BBC One/HBO: 2019–2022, Jack Thorne). In 2020, *Normal People* was nominated for four Emmy awards, including Best Actor in a Limited Series or TV Movie for Paul Mescal and Best Directing for a Limited Series for Lenny Abrahamson.

One of the ways that *Normal People* sets itself apart from mainstream television is evident in its first three episodes, which comprise the teen years of a larger story, in that it runs counter to most teen dramas in its palpable realism. *Normal People* presents a nuanced examination of the complexities of human beings during the stage of adolescence as opposed to presenting us with familiar teen archetypes within recognizable tropes. In an interview clip, Catherine Magee (producer) says, "I think the tone of it is I would say authentic, raw, intimate, and I think all of those things are what possibly distinguishes it from other shows."[3] Again, just like with *Euphoria*, achieving authenticity was a goal for those who created this show. In short, *Normal People* aims to render a realistic portrayal of young love rather than furthering a fantasy of it. Through carefully selected everyday scenes and moments, the miniseries establishes the psychological makeup of both Marianne and Connell and from there demonstrates the resulting dynamic of their relationship. More importantly, *Normal People* explores the ethics of romantic love, centering on the notion that many straight teenage girls give themselves completely to teenage boys with whom they are in love. In turn, the teenage boys are often unable to express their feelings well or even understand how to behave in a relationship. The show asks basic questions. As teenagers, how do we learn what is fair in love? And how important is it to publicly acknowledge someone with whom one is involved? There is a clear universality in this story. The students in our Recent TV Trends course, most of whom are American, easily related to this story set in the Republic of Ireland. Many of them discovered that the dynamics of the teen love relationship resonated with their own experiences. Jen Chaney in her *Vulture* review states, "There's a tendency to dismiss high-school relationships as temporary, meaningless connections that fade once we grow up.... While Rooney's series acknowledges that individuals evolve as they grow older, it also does something that only the best coming-of-age stories do: it treats young adults with respect and takes their relationships, especially first loves, seriously."[4] An important facet of the show's authenticity is that the story continues beyond adolescence in its later episodes and charts the repercussions of the teen events on the adult lives of Marianne and Connell.

Also essential to *Normal People*'s authenticity is its format and directing style. The miniseries is notable for the half-hour format of its 12 episodes, which do an uncanny job of packing in drama while still feeling low-key in their everyday rhythms. Abrahamson states, "It used to be that only sitcoms were half an hour and if you wanted to tell a dramatic story, it had to be an hour. But we really liked the idea of short episodes because it allows you to be single-focused.... You couldn't have had that density of focus over an hour."[5] It's this dense texture that allows for the subtle unfolding of the teen relationship between Marianne and Connell, which explores both the private and public spheres of their lives. Suzie Lavelle says in a *Variety* interview, "In the half hour there's so little plot to move forward that you can really get into mood and tone and it starts feeling like chapters, like the book."[6] Although the brilliance of Sally Rooney's novel cannot be overstated, the translation of a successful novel to the screen is no easy feat. James Poniewozik in his review for *The New York Times* states, "Rooney precision-mapped her self-aware characters' psychological states in cool, piercing prose. Here, much of that interior work falls to the direction ... which renders the story warmer, dreamier, more tactile."[7] Since the audience no longer has access to the characters' thoughts but is instead only seeing their actions and hearing their dialogue, the director must do everything possible to reflect the characters' inner world.

In addition, the naturalistic visual and aural style of the series, which Abrahamson and Lavelle established so well in the first six episodes, is vital to the authenticity of the show. One of the delights is seeing how the cinematographer, Suzie Lavelle, discovered unscripted additions to the story. She explained how Lenny Abrahamson wanted her to shoot "studies" of characters, which he thought of as small moments showing what happened right after a scene concluded. These studies were inserted throughout the show to reflect moments of everyday life, which in turn enhanced the authenticity of the miniseries.[8] When Lavelle was invited into rehearsals eight days before shooting began, she realized that she needed to be in closer to see everything, from eyes dilating to nostrils flaring, and so she did all the hand-held camerawork herself. "We never blocked the scene too much either because of, you know, wanting to capture authenticity and making it feel real and fresh."[9] Lavelle goes on to say, "The main thing that working with Lenny taught me was, like, checking: 'Is it real?' 'Do I buy it?'"[10] It's so important for directors and cinematographers to be agile and to be able to make decisions fluidly on the set. Developing an instinctual feel for whether something is playing correctly, as well as establishing a set culture that encourages that kind of internal process, is necessary for creating authentic work.

Beyond the directing style and naturalistic cinematic approach, it is the true-to-life story that has been so effectively brought to the screen that makes *Normal People* such a good example of this trend

Chapter 2. Normal People

toward authenticity. Just like memorable lines from Marcel Proust's writing, or the characters' thoughts in Leo Tolstoy's work, or the world building of Octavia Butler's books bring a profound understanding of the human condition to the reader, so too does Sally Rooney's novel deliver a particular kind of truth. Her art is on a personal scale and excels at articulating what happens when two people come together. But achieving this in a miniseries takes a myriad of well-imagined decisions along the way. One of the most captivating aspects of the story is how the psychological issues of the two protagonists collide to form the recipe for a harmful relationship. But when a work is adapted for the screen without the crutch of voice-over thoughts, the motivations and confusions of the characters must be demonstrated through the actors.

Thus, it was essential that the characters of Marianne and Connell be performed to feel real, fully formed, and distinctive. From the beginning of the story, set in the fictional town of Carricklea, it's clear that Marianne doesn't conform to expectations. In Episode 1, Mr. Kerrigan, her teacher, says, "If you're staring out the window daydreaming, then you're not learning, are you, Marianne?" She replies, "Don't delude yourself. I have nothing to learn from you." She then goads him into giving her detention. This is one of many moments in the first episode that establishes Marianne as both confident of her intelligence and unbothered by being a social outcast. In an interview clip, Emma Norton, one of the executive producers, says this about casting Marianne: "Finding Marianne was harder because Marianne, she can be fairly vulnerable, but she can be really defiant and kind of, a little bit obnoxious. It was really hard to find someone who could be all of those things and bring them together in one unified person."[11] Daisy Edgar-Jones, who was cast late in the process, was able to do this, seemingly effortlessly. Episode 1 also establishes Connell's qualities, which include his academic excellence, his prowess as an athlete, and his popularity within the school. Again, the casting of Paul Mescal was fortunate. He is quintessentially Irish and well suited for the role. He also manages to embody both physical strength and mental confusion at the same time. One of the book critics at *The New York Times*, Jennifer Szalai, remarks, "Because Rooney's novel is so interior, so much of the performance rests on how the actors manage silences, minute changes in expression, furtive looks—all of that was incredibly well done on the part of Edgar-Jones and Mescal."[12] The actors do a remarkable job of embodying the characters to the extent that the smallest expression, gesture, or movement communicates what they're thinking.

Their class differences, which are part of the realistic fabric of the story, are made plain in the Pilot when Connell first comes by Marianne's house to pick up his mother, Lorraine (Sarah Greene), who cleans for

Marianne's family two to three days a week. Marianne's family, the Sheridans, have a large house on a hill within a lush landscape. In her *Vulture* review, Jen Chaney brings up a Bono quote: "In the United States, you look at the guy that lives in the mansion on the hill, and you think, you know, one day, if I work really hard, I could live in that mansion. In Ireland, people look up at the guy in the mansion on the hill and go, one day, I'm going to get that bastard."[13] The implication is that regular people in Ireland resent the rich because they believe that the rich use their wealth to lord over others. That explains how being wealthy is a social handicap for Marianne in Sligo. Typically in teen shows, the rich girl is at the social pinnacle, not the poor boy. For example, in *Veronica Mars* (UPN: 2004–2007, Rob Thomas), we see rich kids dominate the social scene, whereas those with modest means, including Veronica, comprise the outcasts. Jen Chaney states, "In pretty much all the John Hughes movies as well as *Heathers*, *Clueless*, and *Mean Girls*, not to mention TV shows like *Beverly Hills, 90210* and *Gossip Girl*, members of the in crowd tend to come from money, while the socially outcast (and not-so-secretly cooler) kids often live on the wrong side of the tracks."[14] For example, in *Gossip Girl* (The CW: 2007–2012, Josh Schwartz, Stephanie Savage), Dan, who is merely middle class, is on the outside looking in on the lives of the fabulously wealthy. It's a paradigm we often see in American teen shows. Here, it is the reverse. In Episode 2, Connell's friend, Rob, initiates an awkward conversation about Connell's mother working in the Sheridan house, asking, "What's Marianne like in her natural habitat?" Connell replies, "I don't know. I don't see much of her, so…." Rob says, "So she thinks of you as her butler, does she?" Connell keeps his cool and says simply, "I doubt that." It's a useful bit of dialogue to establish the inherent class differences.

And yet, it must be understood that Connell has the social advantage over Marianne, and that in their initial interaction, it is Connell who predominates. In Episode 1, when Connell comes by Marianne's house to collect his mother, he asks Marianne for confirmation that she likes him as more than a friend, which he gathered from an earlier conversation they had at school. He says to her, "See, I'm just a little confused about what I feel. I think it would be awkward in school if something happened with us." She pauses before deciding to accommodate his concern. She says, "No one would have to know." And this is the heart of their negotiation. He indicates that he may be interested, but he has a condition that must be met. She agrees to that condition and the deal is concluded with a kiss, the first kiss she's ever had. Connell then says to her, "Don't tell anybody in school about this, all right?" to which Marianne replies, "Like I talk to anyone at school." On yet another visit to her house, this time when his mother isn't there, he starts kissing her again. Revealing her naiveté, she then asks, "Can we take our clothes off?" He sheepishly says, "No, not here." They sit down. Connell offers, "I've got a free house on Saturday. You could come over then if you wanted to." They now have an agreed-upon plan. Some reviewers, who saw only the first two episodes, mistakenly believed this was the beginning of a generic teen romance. But it wasn't. It's the specific story of one person in a relationship needing to keep it a secret and the other person being harmed by that requirement. Another reviewer suggested that it was Marianne's wish to keep the relationship secret. It assuredly was not. Connell was the one dictating terms and she acquiesced in order to seal the deal.

By the second episode, when Marianne comes over to the modest row house that Connell shares with his mother, it could still appear as a typical girl-meets-boy teen drama. And yet, in the ensuing scene, it begins developing into something non-generic, in large part because of Marianne and Connell's frankness and ability to listen to each other. When they are talking in his bedroom, Connell says, "You think I'm shy? Just because I don't give my opinion on everything all the time?" Marianne replies, "You never give an opinion about anything, ever." Connell says, "You just always know what you think. I'm not like that." She says, "You must know what you feel, though." He replies, "No. I struggle with that, actually." And this is a character trait that becomes part of the developing issue between them. He doesn't know what he thinks and feels. When they begin to undress and she gets caught in her clothing, it's a humorous moment. Daisy Edgar-Jones says that she loves that scene, adding, "It's so awkward. For me, it is the most representative love scene I've ever seen. Connell is so kind and giving and safe with her that it's a very healthy depiction of what first-time sex can look like."[15] And indeed, Connell makes sure that this is what she wants. He tells her, "It's just that if you want to stop or anything, we can obviously stop." She says, "I doubt I'll want that." Connell continues, "I know, but if it hurts or anything ... we can stop. It won't be awkward. You can just say." This is a good example of how the sexual interactions in the miniseries further what is happening in the story between the two characters, rather than functioning as pauses in the dramatic action. Sally Rooney told one interviewer, "When I hear the phrase 'sex scene,' I think about a dialogue scene.... What do these characters want to say to each other?"[16] This is echoed by Suzie Lavelle, who comments, "[Lenny Abrahamson's] main note was that the sex should feel like a continuation of the dialogue, so that nothing changes camera-wise."[17] With this approach to the sex scenes, the viewer understands exactly what's happening and what it signifies emotionally. In addition, Daisy Edgar-Jones noted that there was equal representation of both her and Paul Mescal's nude bodies.[18] After they make love in Episode 5, there's an arresting shot of Connell, naked and lying on his side across the bed with his head on her stomach. Marianne says, "It's not like this with other people." He says, "I know. I think we'll be fine." And indeed, this verbal interchange seems like a continuation of the sex they've just had.

To capture this kind of realistic intimacy, it is essential for the production environment to be a supportive one. In order to achieve this, the decision was made to hire an intimacy coordinator, Ita O'Brien, who is credited with making everyone on the set feel comfortable with the sexuality in the show. Abrahamson notes, "But what's brilliant is that she would come in and talk to the whole crew and production about simple things like not using euphemisms, about getting explicit consent every time you're about to do something and finding a language to talk about lovemaking, and the shapes and moods of it, that is empowering for the people involved."[19] In Anna Russell's article in *The New Yorker*, the actors remember funny moments which included Mescal needing to hold himself over Edgar-Jones and freeze while the crew worked on production details, with sweat dripping from his nose, which Edgar-Jones joked was just great.[20] In the same article, Mescal says about O'Brien, "There was this wonderful thing where she would use her hands.... She'd be like, 'So, Paul, I need you to give more *thrust!*'"[21] In the interview, when Edgar-Jones mirrors Mescal's gesture, they both laugh. In *The Guardian* article by Claire Armitstead and Johanna Thomas-Corr, Edgar-Jones comments further about O'Brien, "The sex scenes were a joy to us because it was her job to worry about how it would work and we just turned up, did the choreography and carried on. We just had to think about the emotional beats."[22] And it's the emotional beats that are at the heart of the story and what actors should be free to concentrate on.

After the first scene of Marianne and Connell making love, it seems as if they will soon become a publicly acknowledged couple. But this proves to not be the case and this is where the story becomes distinctive, rather than commonplace. The book is better at explaining Connell's desire for secrecy: "In total he had only had sex a small number of times, and always with girls who went on to tell the whole school about it afterward. He'd had to hear his actions repeated back to him later in the locker room: his errors, and, so much worse, his excruciating attempts at tenderness, performed in gigantic pantomime. With Marianne it was different, because everything was between them only, even awkward or difficult things. He could do or say anything he wanted with her and no one would ever find out."[23] In the series, it's more difficult to decipher Connell's reasons for secrecy. Even though he seems to ignore her at school, he can't help but steal glances now and then, demonstrating that he is genuinely interested in her. So, at first, it seems like the secrecy is perhaps titillating for both of them and is part of the excitement of a new relationship. Because they have a tangible rapport, it also seems like they will move beyond this initial stage of secrecy. In Episode 2, after they have sex at her house, Marianne talks about seeing him play in a recent Gaelic football game, "I was watching you play. And, honestly, you looked so beautiful. I kept thinking how much I wanted to watch you have sex. I mean, not even with me, with anybody. How good it would feel. Is that really weird?" Connell replies, "Yeah, that's really weird, Marianne. But I think I understand it." The fact that they can be so open with each other is enchanting. In their intimate moments together, it's admirable how precisely they share their feelings and how attentively they listen to each other. For him as a budding writer, this articulation process seems to come out of the fact that he's not sure what he thinks and therefore he goes from one simple truth to another to build to a greater truth, which becomes its own form of poetry. Edgar-Jones comments, "They have this way of communicating with each other that's really honest and raw, which I think is so beautiful."[24] But soon, their complete honesty when they're alone, contrasted with their utter of lack of acknowledgment when they are in public, demonstrates that there is something off-kilter in their relationship.

As they continue to hide their relationship, we slowly become aware of Marianne's lack of self-worth. She is often shown searching for signs of Connell's interest in her. In Episode 2, it's somewhat of a relief to see them at the beach, finally out in the open air with each other, although it's clear that this only works because there is no one around who knows them. She talks about the upcoming fundraiser at the night club and says, "I hope you don't find it too hard trying to resist me." Connell says, "Sure, don't I always?" Marianne says hesitantly, "Do you?" He nods and she puts her head on his shoulder. In this scene, she is telling him straight out that she doesn't know how he feels about her, and yet he doesn't seem to comprehend how unsure she is of his affection. Later in the episode, when they are in bed after having sex, Marianne asks, "Is there anyone you have a crush on at school?" He laughs and says, "What? I'm literally still inside you." Marianne continues, "What about Rachel?" Connell replies, "Why do you say that?" Marianne continues, "She's pretty. She clearly likes you." Connell says, "I wouldn't have strong feelings either way on it." Even though it seems odd that she would casually talk about his potential interest in someone else while they are making love, it serves to illustrate her gnawing feeling of inadequacy. She is also demonstrating that she has no idea how a relationship would typically progress. The issue of private vs. public in love relationships (often involving extramarital or taboo affairs) has a long history in storytelling, with this story being a worthy entry into that pantheon. Obviously, there are many reasons why society benefits from the public declaration of private feelings and why the individuals involved benefit as well. But when relationships are not made public, what are the advantages or disadvantages for the participants? There is also the question of timing. At what point in a relationship do the individuals benefit from a public declaration? And what are the repercussions when that point has long passed?

At this stage of the story, we see that Connell's unwillingness to acknowledge Marianne has become harmful to her, and yet we understand that this hesitancy is fed by his own psychological issues. After the scene when Marianne asks him about Rachel, Connell goes to the pub to be with his friends and ignores her text. She is, like usual, at home alone. It is unclear whether Connell is being oblivious or callous or both. One wonders if this scene is in the series because Connell judges himself or because we, as the viewers, are invited to judge him. This is followed by a scene where Marianne is humiliated at school as Connell stands by. His group of friends is gathered around the lockers in the hallway and Eric asks in a half-joking way if Marianne will go with him to the Debs (the equivalent of a prom). When she doesn't answer in the affirmative, Eric says, "Oh, you think you're too good for me, do you?" Marianne replies, "Yeah, pretty much." The exchange continues, ending with Eric calling her an "ugly, flat-chested bitch" as she walks away. Connell is there for the entire interaction and does nothing. She is humiliated and yet he is the one who feels anxious. It makes one wonder what his inner rules are regarding his relationship with Marianne. Why can't he defend her in front of his friends? Why can't he admit that they are involved? In the book, it's made plain that he suffers from social anxiety to the extent that he second guesses everything he is about to do or say. One can surmise that he is usually so agreeable because he fears what might happen if he isn't. On the other hand, Marianne is seen as damaged by her classmates. And yet she is the one who often has the courage to speak her mind and stand her ground.

The miniseries feels realistic enough that it evokes questions in the viewers' minds as if they were observing reality. And one of those questions is, why does Marianne let Connell treat her this way? Part of the answer is that she has given herself completely to him. In Episode 2, there is a demonstration of this when Marianne asks Connell to take her to the "Ghost House" where his school chums go to hook up, just so she can see it. When they are standing outside in the daylight, Marianne says to him, "I would lie down here, and you could do anything you wanted to me. Do you know that?" Connell's reply is "Do you enjoy making me feel uncomfortable?" As the conversation continues, Marianne says, "You don't mind that I'm ugly and flat-chested, then." Connell says, "I'm sorry they said that to you." Marianne says, "Is that what you think of me?" Connell tells her that it isn't even what Eric thinks of her because if he thought he had a chance with her, he would change his tune. In Episode 3, we see another scene of her looking for reassurance from him when they are in his bedroom. When Marianne asks if he slept with Rachel, he replies, "I did. Once, like, last year. But it wouldn't be the kind of thing where, like, feelings would be involved." Marianne asks, "'And what about with me?' Would you say your feelings are involved?" Connell says, "Obviously." Confused, Marianne asks, "Who is it obvious to?" This reveals that one of the functions of publicly acknowledging a relationship is that there are witnesses to attest to its very existence. Marianne realizes that she would benefit from others knowing about her intimacy with Connell because it would demonstrate that it is meaningful.

An excellent example of how *Normal People* subverts what would happen in a typical teen drama and instead takes a more realistic approach occurs in Episode 3. Marianne is pleased to have been invited to participate in the fundraiser for the Debs, which is being held at a night club. At first, she is having fun, dancing with Karen, who is one of the few in the group who is nice to her. As she moves to the music, we can see that Connell's eyes are on her. And in a typical teen drama, this would be the moment that the ugly duckling would turn into a swan (for surely Marianne looks gorgeous in her slinky black dress) and the guy would finally demonstrate his love for her in front of everyone. But this is not what happens here and the moment passes. Later, when they are all standing around, an acquaintance of the group, Pat, comes over and tries to get Marianne to dance with him in exchange for 10 raffle tickets. She is put off and says no. He apparently knows her older brother, Alan (Frank Blake), and everyone else seems to feel comfortable with him. He then roughly grabs her breast. She pulls away, clearly upset, and runs out of the club. The others come outside to see Marianne crumpled against a wall, crying, and Karen goes to comfort her. Rachel says, "We were all laughing a minute ago." Connell says, "No, we weren't." He then turns to Marianne and says, "You okay?" Rachel says, "You want to kiss her better now, do ya?" Unexpectedly, Connell turns to her and says, "Rachel, would you ever just fuck off?" We see that he is finally driven to action by the need to protect Marianne from harm. He then offers to give her a lift home. Again, this seems like it could be another turning point—the moment when he reveals to his friends that he and Marianne are in a relationship. But that doesn't happen, primarily because their dynamic is that she is too insecure to demand that he acknowledge her and he is too afraid to go against popular opinion about her. When Connell and Marianne are in his car, he asks if she wants to go back to his house instead of hers, and she indicates that she would like that. After a conversation about her feeling like an idiot and Connell reassuring her that she did nothing wrong, Marianne says that his mother must be proud of him. She continues, "You've turned out so well as a human being." With doubt in his voice, Connell asks, "How did I turn out well?" Marianne replies, "You're such a nice person. Do you know how rare that is?" This seems like an odd thing for her to say in light of how he has treated her over the course of their relationship. And yet because he came to her rescue this one time, she is immensely grateful. Later, when they are in bed, Connell tells her that he loves her, and he does so in a sincere way. In the book, however, there are underlying currents that are explained thusly: "It wasn't the first time he'd had the urge to tell Marianne that he loved her, whether or not it was true, but it was the first time he'd given in and said it. He noticed how long it took her to say anything in response, and how her pause had bothered him, as if she might not say it back, and when she did say it, he felt better, but maybe that meant nothing. Connell wished he knew how other people conducted their private lives, so that he could copy from example."[25] This notion, of wanting to learn from the way that other people conduct their lives, is important to the overall message of both the book and the miniseries.

What follows the scene of Connell telling Marianne that he loves her is a sequence of events that allows the viewers to make up their own minds about the behavior they observe, just as they would in real life. After the weekend, when they are back at school, his friends want to know if he "shifted" her. They tease him while he keeps his head in his locker. As he walks down the hall, Rob shouts, "I think you should ask her to the Debs." This is when Connell heads to the bathroom, his anxiety getting the better of him. In the book, this is how it is described: "When he got to the bathroom, he locked himself in a cubicle. The yellow walls bore down on him and his face was slick with sweat. He kept thinking of himself saying to Marianne in bed: I love you. It was terrifying, like watching himself committing a terrible crime on CCTV. And soon she would be in school, putting her books in her bag, smiling to herself, never knowing anything. *You're a nice person and everyone likes you.* He took one deep uncomfortable breath and then threw up."[26] In the miniseries, we see Connell briefly panicking in the bathroom, but since we don't hear what he's thinking, it is hard to know if he is ashamed about the possibility of his friends guessing at his involvement with Marianne or if (like in the book) he is horrified at having told Marianne that he loves her and letting her think that he's a nice person. After leaving the bathroom, he has a smoke and then finds Rachel. First, he apologizes to her for telling her to fuck off, then he denies that there's anything between him and Marianne, and then he inquires if he can ask her something, which we later find out is whether Rachel will go to the Debs with him. It's a short bit of handiwork to counteract the shame he felt about his secret possibly being exposed. His ability to outright lie to Rachel about his involvement with Marianne, however, is somewhat astonishing, because up to this point, he has been able to circumvent divulging his secret, a sin of omission, as it were. Being evasive is quite different from being a liar. The scene with Rachel ends with a wide shot of them laughing and smoking, with the rest of the gang slowly sauntering up and joining them. The viewers clearly see that this is what he traded Marianne for, the security of being embraced by his social group.

What happens from that point onward is expertly supported by the cinematic approach that communicates the meaning of the details that the audience is observing. Connell comes to Marianne's house and says casually, "So I asked Rachel to the Debs today, not a big deal or anything. Thought you should know and, yeah, just wanted to let you know. It's not romantic or anything. Just friends." Marianne says quietly, "Like we're just friends." Connell says, "No, that's ... that's different." Part of the pathos of this scene is that when she hears the doorbell ring, we see her in close-up and then in a wide shot in her bedroom, straightening her school outfit in anticipation. We see her walk down the hall, happy and smiling, and then we see her look at Connell waiting for her on the other side of the door. His beginning lines are in voice-over during this sequence, and then he we hear him finish his statement over her close-up in her bedroom. From her expression walking down the hall, we can intuit that she is anticipating something quite different. In her interpretation of previous events, no doubt she would remember the climactic moment at the nightclub when he stood up for her and then offered to take her home in front of all his friends, which by now might have led to him revealing his relationship with her to them. That night, he even told her that he loves her. And in the morning, when his mother, Lorraine (Sarah Greene), saw them, she seemed pleased. We can see from her deadened expression in her bedroom, however, that she quickly realizes that this is not going the way she expected. It is worth pointing out that the shot was deliberately cut off when Connell is about to ask Rachel his question. The viewers, like Marianne, only find out that he asked Rachel to the Debs when he shows up at Marianne's house and tells her. Therefore, this sequence is clearly from Marianne's point of view, which makes the viewers feel her shock more acutely. As a general rule of thumb, films and television shows unfold in a certain order, resulting in some information being revealed and other information being withheld, and the expertise with which that is done determines how well the story is told. This sequence continues from Marianne's point of view when she is in her bedroom talking to him and we see her response to his actions change. From somewhere inside of her, she accesses some resilience, some kernel of self-respect. After they exchange a few more words, she tells him that he should go. When he doesn't heed her the first time, her resolve hardens, and she is more emphatic the second time. After he leaves, she covers her face with her hands (symbolically effacing herself) and begins to cry. After cutaways of him walking to his car, we see her sobbing in her bed with her back turned to the camera, a relatable moment for many teen girls who have had their hearts broken.

Both the book and the miniseries expose a truth about the human condition, which is the way in which ignorance of what's fair in love can lead to hurtful outcomes. It is Connell's mother, Lorraine, who spells it out for him and in so doing articulates the condemnation that many of the viewers are feeling. In Episode 3, after he has had the interchange with Marianne, he is driving in the car with Lorraine, and he tells her that he has asked Rachel to the Debs. She immediately tells him to pull the car over, and then asks, "Who's Marianne going to the Debs with?" Connell says, "Don't know." She continues, "So maybe no one will ask her, and she just won't go." He says, "Yeah. Maybe. I don't know." Lorraine says, "And you don't think maybe you should have asked her? Seeing as how you fuck her every day after school." Under his breath, he says, "Vile language to be using." She retorts, "Well, feel free to explain in your own words, Connell. What exactly is the arrangement? Marianne comes over to our house, you have sex with her, and then she's not allowed to tell anyone, is that it?" The conversation continues in this vein and finally Lorraine says, "What are you afraid of? What people would think of you if they found out you liked her? I'll say what I think of you. I think you're a disgrace and I'm ashamed of you." She gets out of the car to take the bus home, afraid she will say something that she will later regret. Lorraine is a welcome voice of emotional intelligence on the show.

At this point in the story, the questions mount. Should Connell be forgiven for the way he treats Marianne? Is his social anxiety to blame? Do her insecurities contribute to what has happened? Is society to blame for how teenagers treat each other? Should young people be taught about the ethics of sex and romance? Most people, whether they are presently adolescents or seasoned adults, are confused by at least some of their adolescent romantic relationships. As a teen, you're often adrift with no one to guide you, especially when the relationship is secret. This is a show that invites viewers to think about these issues, at first through the lens of Conner and Marianne's relationship but then within a broader discussion of our societal customs and norms.

Once Marianne breaks off her association with Connell, there is an understated way of showing that she doesn't go back to school but stays home. For an American audience, it's hard to understand how she's able

Chapter 2. Normal People 43

to get away with this, but it soon becomes clear that attendance isn't mandatory and all she needs to do is study for her exams. The "everyday texture" of these scenes demonstrates the naturalistic style of the miniseries well. We see the back of Connell's head as the teacher calls her name in class and there's no answer. We see Marianne in bed at home, first just lying there, but then sitting up and studying. Within this tapestry of realistic moments, the essence of what is transpiring is conveyed. Essentially, we see one slice of life followed by another and we're free to surmise what's important. Small vignettes make it clear that Marianne is ignoring his texts and following her own path. This demonstrates that she is no longer under his spell and is moving forward with her own plans.

Something that one wouldn't see in typical teen shows is that Connell's mother continues to side with Marianne. In fact, one can rightly say that Lorraine becomes Marianne's sole comfort. In Episode 3, Lorraine says, "My son tells me you're ignoring his messages." Marianne says, "Well, I am. I suppose." Lorraine says, "Good for you. He doesn't deserve you." And then she gives Marianne a hug. It's a shame that Marianne's own mother, Denise (Aislín McGuckin), doesn't seem to care about her as much as Lorraine does. And, in Episode 3, when Connell is at home watching TV with his mother and asks if Marianne is doing all right, Lorraine only tells him that he hurt Marianne's feelings. When he says that she's overreacting, Lorraine says, "Marianne's a very vulnerable person and you did something really unkind. And you hurt her." Connell says, "You know, um, you could just try being on my side." Lorraine replies, "I don't want to be on your side on this one. I don't think it's a bad thing that you're feeling bad about this." This demonstrates a wonderful parenting lesson: don't shield your child from feeling the pain associated with their actions because it's all part of their journey of developing into an empathetic human being with a conscience.

Marianne's family, on the other hand, is revealed to be strikingly cold and abrasive. Her brother, Alan, criticizes her, and her mother, Denise, often expresses disdain. Without telling the audience what to think, the show gradually presents the evidence, so viewers can draw their own conclusions. In Episode 1, we see Alan making Marianne get out of the car in the pouring rain, simply because he decides to heed a sudden request from a friend for a ride. Later in Episode 1, we see Denise come home from work, ignore Marianne's offer of dinner, and then snap at her for having the heat on high without closing the curtains. Then, in Episode 3, Marianne tells Connell that her late father would hit her mother when she was growing up. When Connell asks if her father ever hit her, she says no. But in the book, she replies, "Sometimes."[27] Over the course of the miniseries, the evidence of Marianne's harsh treatment by her family gradually increases to acts of aggression on the part of her brother, with her mother simply standing by. This ill treatment is carefully woven into the story and explains how Marianne developed her sense of worthlessness that plays into the relationship dynamic with Connell. The fact that the audience can piece this together adds to the veracity of what they're witnessing.

Connell's enlightenment about his own behavior is finally prompted by a conversation he has in Episode 3 with his friend Eric when they are taking a cigarette break at the Debs. Eric says to him, "A shame Marianne didn't come in the end…. What was going on there?" Connell is still feigning indifference, but Eric isn't having it and says, "You think we don't know you were riding her? Sure, everyone knows." So his friends knew all along. Connell leaves the Debs abruptly and drunk as he is, he calls Marianne, leaving yet another message for her, which ends with "I can't really talk to anyone the way I talk to you or anything like that. And, um, yeah, um, I don't really know what to say other than the fact that I miss you and I really love you, Marianne, and, um, I'm sorry." He crouches on the sidewalk and sobs. He finally understands what he has been doing to her all this time. And now, he regrets losing her.

In Episode 4, we then experience the brilliance in continuing the story beyond secondary school as we see Connell and Marianne at Trinity College. Seeing them change as they get older reflects reality in that one stage of life leads to another. We already know that it was Marianne who changed the course of Connell's life because of their interaction in secondary school. In Episode 2, when they are talking in Connell's bedroom, she suggests that he pursue the only subject he's interested in, which is English, rather than pursuing something practical like law. She also encourages him to apply to Trinity. He ribs her about being sure that she'll get in. Connell says, "Then we'd be in college together. I bet you'd pretend not to know me if we bumped into each other…." She takes a long pause and looks directly at him, saying, "I would never pretend to not know you, Connell." And we know this is true. She would never do to him what he is doing to her. Once again, the story offers enough evidence for viewers to figure this out for themselves. When an audience can make connections that aren't explicit in the material, it makes what they experience feel more authentic.

Episode 4 begins by showing Connell's everyday actions at Trinity College. He gets a place to live and he attends classes. After several months, he is talking to fellow students about the debate club and then one of them, Gareth, invites him to a party that he's having that night. At the party, Gareth introduces Connell to his girlfriend, who turns out to be Marianne. She is now stylish and sophisticated. She smoothly tells him to come with her and she'll get him a better drink. When it's just the two of them, Marianne says, "I've missed you." Connell says, "Yeah, you too. I was a bit worried when you left school and I was pretty down about it." Marianne says, "Well, we never hung out much during school hours." Then they engage in an honest examination of their past, which is gratifying for viewers. Most coming-of-age shows don't tend to linger on the verbal analysis of events long after the fact. And yet, there is something satisfying about it, and it mimics what people do in real life. When Marianne explains that what happened between them wasn't really why she left school, but only a "last straw sort of thing," he says, "Yeah, I was wondering if that was what it was." She then says, "Hmm. Maybe you're telepathic." He says, "You know, I did think I could read your mind at times." She says, "In bed, you mean?" He says, "Yeah, and afterwards. But I don't know, maybe that's normal." She says, "It's not." So this theme comes up again—that it's different for them than it is with other people. By Episode 5, they even revisit the debacle of the Debs. Connell asks if Marianne would be embarrassed if her friends found out they were together in school. Marianne replies, "Yes, it was humiliating." Connell confirms, "You mean the way I treated ya?" Marianne says, "Yeah. And just the … just the fact that I put up with it. Did you ever think about asking me to the Debs? I know it's such a stupid thing. But, uh, I'm curious whether you thought about it." Connell says, "Uh, to be honest, uh, no. I wish that I did. Yeah. Would you have said yes?" Marianne replies, "Yeah. Fuck's sake." She then gets choked up. But Connell's recollection isn't strictly true. In school, after his friends were teasing him about shifting Marianne the night of the Debs' fundraiser, Rob clearly shouted after him, "I think you should ask her to the Debs." So it did come up as an idea, although not one he wanted to act on. It would have been more accurate for him to say that he was incapable of asking her because he was too afraid of his friends finding out about them. But now, he feels differently. Connell says, "I'm really sorry. Apparently, everybody knew about us, anyway." He continues, "I feel really guilty about all that stuff I said to you about, uh, how bad it would be if people found out. Like, obviously, that was just what was going on in my head and there'd be no reason why anybody would care, I just…. I think I just suffered from anxiety with those sorts of things." He again says that he's sorry and she forgives him. It is as if the show is granting him clemency for his misdeeds.

At Trinity College, class differences come into play again in the social arena, but in reverse. We soon find out that she fits in well, and he doesn't. At the end of the previous conversation, Marianne asks Connell, "Finding it hard to meet people here?" He says, "Uh-huh. It's a bit different from home, I suppose." Marianne says, "Probably why I'm good at it. I have some girlfriends I could introduce you to." He says, "Oh, yeah." She says, "I have those now." And we see her with Joanna having wine at her place and then with Peggy in class. Peggy later says that Marianne annihilated another student when he made an indefensible point. So Marianne now has friends as well as respect in class. Conversely, we see that Connell has challenges. We see him working in a convenience store, which is juxtaposed with her going out with friends. In addition, she is staying in her mother's comfortable flat, where she can easily entertain friends, whereas he rents a room that he shares with his new roommate, Niall (Desmond Eastwood). In various sequences, it's shown that he's at a disadvantage as compared to Marianne in several ways: in his modest living situation, in having less time for studies because he needs to work, and in his discomfort with the social manners that Marianne and her well-off friends demonstrate. In Episode 5, when he questions the actions of her friends, she repeats his sentiment back to him (which he said to her in secondary school in Episode 1): "And at the end of the day, they're my friends. It's different for you." It is worth mentioning that in Episode 8, when Connell and Niall come to visit Marianne at her family's villa in Italy, Connell has a realization about all that he's been able to experience because his financial situation has improved. He remarks that it's money that makes it all real: foreign countries, famous artwork, and remnants of the Berlin Wall. Marianne goes on to say that she's aware that they got to know each other because his mother works for her mother. When they finally have a discussion about their class differences, Marianne wonders why they hadn't talked about it before. Even though Connell is at an economic disadvantage at Trinity, it's clearly established that he is at the top of his class in English, and, in fact, like Marianne (in history and political science), he becomes one of Trinity's scholars after his second year, awarded five years of waived fees and free accommodations. But being academically accomplished isn't enough to make him feel like he fits in, especially his first year. He tells Marianne that he feels like he's trying on a hundred different versions of himself and that he can't connect this life and his life back home. In essence, he feels lost when he comes to Trinity, whereas she comes into her own. It is made apparent that she has been raised to fit in with life among the wealthy elite.

In Episode 5, when Marianne suggests to Connell that they should be friends, they try that for a short while. Later in the episode, after Marianne breaks up with Gareth, she gets drunk at a party and says to Connell, "I want you to fuck me." He says, "Not tonight. You're wasted." One can't help but wonder if this is believable behavior or wishful thinking about how young men should act in situations like this. If the sole point of this is to model good behavior for others, then that may be a good enough reason for writing the scene that way. But it may also be that the show's developers wanted to make sure that the audience would still be able to like Connell, even after everything he has put Marianne through, and so it was vital that his sexual behavior be without blemish. When we see Connell pick up Marianne from the party the next morning, he takes her back to her place. She showers while he makes the coffee. When she comes into the kitchen in her robe, that's when they make love.

If one were looking for a flaw in the overall authenticity of the show, this is the aspect that one might question: the believability of Connell's sensitivity in the sexual arena in contrast to his cluelessness in the social arena. During their first time having sex, he overtly and repeatedly makes sure it's what Marianne wants. He demonstrates that he fully understands consent and that he is genuinely caring when it comes to sex. But would a guy who treats her so poorly socially be that solicitous about sex? There is another possible explanation for this aspect of the story being accentuated in the miniseries, which is that it engendered a better set climate. Lenny Abrahamson states, "The sex was a big challenge and we took it really seriously from the beginning [in] what we would aim to show, but also literally [in] how we would do the sex in a way that was positive, safe and healthy for everyone involved both in front of and behind the camera."[28] Several critics have noted how the series was sanitized in many ways as compared to the book, so this could be seen as yet one more way. One of the book critics at *The New York Times*, Parul Sehgal, makes the comment, "[Marianne's] character has been cleaned up. She's such a good girl now, and so legible, whereas in the book she is much more complicated and confusing, even to herself. Connell isn't spared either; the show omits what was for me the most charged moment in the novel: when he contemplates Marianne's submissiveness toward him and feels revulsion and a terrifying urge to hurt her."[29] In examining the differences between the novel and the miniseries, one must acknowledge, however, that it's easier to write about something that is disturbing than it is to make actual human beings, both actors and crew, go through experiences that are upsetting.

The authenticity of the show comes to the fore again when we see the intricate underpinnings of how Marianne and Connell break up in Episode 6. It seems at first to be a break-up that is inadvertent and without real cause. The episode starts with a broken glass in the kitchen sink and Marianne's sad close-up. There is then an intertitle: "Six Weeks Earlier." She's in the same spot in her kitchen, smiling. Connell tells her that she's his best friend and they make love. But what follows is Connell denying to Niall that Marianne is his girlfriend. There is some memorable dialogue in a subsequent phone conversation with his mother, Lorraine, about how he treated Marianne in school. Conner says, "Like, how would you feel if I kept going at ya about some stupid teenage mistake that you made?" Lorraine replies, "Sweetheart, you are the stupid teenage mistake I made." Later, Peggy looks for confirmation that Marianne and Connell are together when they are all sitting in the living room: "Everyone's speculating even though you, like, never actually touch each other." When Peggy suggests a threesome, Marianne says that she would be much too self-conscious and adds that there's something unappealing, unlovable, and cold about her, a self-assessment which we know comes from her experiences with her family. Afterward, Connell confirms that he could never have a threesome as Peggy suggested. Marianne says that she wouldn't want to, but if he wanted to, she would do it to make him happy. He tells her she shouldn't do things she doesn't want to. In other words, underneath their seeming bliss, they still have the same issues as they did in school. They still aren't public about their relationship; Connell still denies that Marianne is his girlfriend; Marianne still believes that she's unlovable; and Connell is still unable to demonstrate his commitment to her. From this perspective, the break-up is not random at all, but rather inevitable.

In this same episode, Episode 6, the class difference between them is again a barrier. Connell loses his job at the café because they will be closed June and July for renovation, and he needs the money to pay for a place. His pride keeps him from asking if he can move into her place. Niall doesn't understand why Connell doesn't stay with Marianne while he looks for a job. The dialogue and the scenes are telling us straight out what the situation is, but the naturalistic performances and shots make it seem so fluid and every day that it's easy to overlook the mounting pressures. Later, Connell reacts to Marianne's friend, Jamie, putting his hand on her knee: "The lads you hang out with, they always have their fucking hands all over you." Marianne replies, "You don't want to touch me, but you get to dictate who else does." Connell defends himself. "I touch ya." Marianne sets him straight: "Yeah, as long as there's about six closed doors between us and another person who might fucking witness you demonstrating some level of affection towards me." To be fair to Connell, he has a breakthrough at Sophie's pool party when he swims over to Marianne sitting on the edge of the pool and then sits next to her, putting his arm around her and kissing her shoulder. She holds his hand on her hip. But then they break up after that pool party because of their "misunderstanding." At the beginning of the next episode, Episode 7, we see Connell with Rob at a pub in Sligo and then we see Connell's version of what happened. The intertitle comes up, "Six Weeks Earlier," and Connell is in Marianne's kitchen telling her that he isn't going to be in Dublin for the summer because he can't pay the rent. Marianne says, "You'll go back to Sligo then." After a short scene of Connell and Rob dancing at the Sligo

Chapter 2. Normal People

pub, we come back to the scene and hear Connell say, "I guess you want to see other people." Marianne replies, "I guess so, yeah." After the next quick scene of Connell at the pub, we see Marianne lying on a blanket in front of her house in Sligo, remembering Connell say, "So, I guess we should see other people," and then we hear Marianne's reply, "I guess so." The misunderstanding is that she remembers it as "we" which implies that *he* wants to see other people. He remembers it as "you" which means that he was asking her if *she* wants to see other people. But why did he ask her this in the first place? The answer is because he is lacking in self-confidence as well. Connell is unsure if Marianne truly wants to be with him.

How does this feed into the authenticity of the show? So often one hears things wrong and doesn't understand what one's partner is actually saying. And people often hear what they think will hurt them the most, because that is evidence that their partner isn't treating them right. Since they already feel hurt, this gives them reason to be more upset and fits into a narrative of being "done wrong." In other words, insecurity can lead to poor communication and assuming that others don't want you. Often, we look for reassurance from our lovers that they do really love us, while at the same time seize upon clues that they don't really love us. This contradiction is part of the human condition. In Episode 7, we see Connell and Marianne deconstructing what occurred between them. Connell says he doesn't know what happened last summer and he had hoped she would have let him stay here, at her flat. Marianne replies, "You said you wanted to see other people." Connell says, "No." Marianne says, "I thought you were breaking up with me. You never said anything about wanting to stay here. I … that would have been…. Always. Obviously." So they do clear up what happened between them. But they still have so much more to go through before they actually start believing in their love for one another.

To conclude, this miniseries stands out from many other coming-of-age stories in terms of its authenticity. First, it aims for reality rather than fantasy in how the story progresses. Second, it has a naturalistic style that seamlessly supports its authentic story. Third, it goes beyond secondary school in a successful way, something that many teen dramas have had trouble doing effectively. Fourth, it delivers a deeper message about the effects of romantic love in our lives, not just for adolescents, but for everyone. Not to spoil anything in the second half of the series, but by Episode 12, Connell says, "I wouldn't be here if it wasn't for you," and Marianne replies, "No, that's true. I mean, you'd be somewhere else entirely. You'd be a different person. And me, too. But we have done so much good for one another." The note that the show ends on is that they have profoundly affected each other's lives and who they are as people.

II
Diversity

CHAPTER 3

Atlanta

First-Person Comedy-Drama on the Black Experience

Atlanta is a comedy drama that premiered on FX in September of 2016 and was created by Donald Glover. The show explores the Black experience and is about a twenty-something man named Earnest Marks (Donald Glover), Earn for short, who manages his cousin Alfred Miles (Brian Tyree Henry), Al for short, who has found success as a rapper under the stage name "Paper Boi." Despite Al's success, Earn struggles to catch a break, is periodically without a place to live, and frequently disappoints his parents and his sometimes girlfriend, Van (Zazie Beetz). Still, Paper Boi seems to be on the verge of stardom and Earn is determined to be there when it happens. Prior to the premiere of the second season on FX in 2018, the first season of *Atlanta* became available for streaming on Hulu, and subsequent to that, all seasons were available on Hulu after their run on FX.[1] The third season premiered in 2022 after several delays caused by Covid-19. The fourth and final season, which began production before the third season was completed, was also released in 2022. This chapter will primarily discuss the first two seasons.

Donald Glover, who grew up in Stone Mountain, Georgia, originally came up with the idea to make *Atlanta* because he wanted to show white people that they didn't know everything about Black culture.[2] He is often characterized as a man of many talents. In 2006, he graduated from the New York University Tisch School of the Arts with a degree in Dramatic Writing. He first gained notoriety as a member of the sketch-comedy group Derrick Comedy, and his first big break came when he was hired to write for the sitcom *30 Rock* (NBC: 2006–2013, Tina Fey), which he did from 2006 to 2009. Glover went on to play a main character named Troy on the comedy series *Community* (NBC, Yahoo! Screen: 2009–2015, Dan Harmon), leaving part way through Season 5, even though the show continued through Season 6. Glover was featured on the stand-up comedy show *Comedy Central Presents* (Comedy Central: 1998–2011, Paul Miller) in 2010 and had his own one-hour comedy special, *Weirdo* (Comedy Central), in 2011. Soon after he left *Community*, Glover launched his music career under the name Childish Gambino by releasing several mixtapes (an independently released album usually free of charge). His debut album, titled *Camp*, was released in 2011 by Glassnote (Childish Gambino, Ludwig Göransson). To date, Gambino has four studio albums and is considered one of the biggest names in hip hop. Most notably, Gambino's song "This Is America"[3] became the number-one song in America and won four Grammy Awards. Notable film roles include young Lando Calrissian in *Solo: A Star Wars Story* (Walt Disney Studios Motion Pictures: 2018, Ron Howard), a musician named Deni in *Guava Island* (Amazon Prime Video: 2019, Hiro Murai), and the voice of adult Simba in the remake of *The Lion King* (Walt Disney Studios Motion Pictures: 2019, Jon Favreau). From his stand-up comedy to his music, much of his work offers commentary on the Black experience. In particular, the music video for his song "This Is America" made waves for its striking visual metaphors on Black culture, gun violence, and white consumption of Black tragedy. Though often praised for his candor, Glover has also faced a fair amount of criticism. In the past, he has poked fun at rape and AIDS and jokingly encouraged white people to use the N-word. He has also been accused of, among other things, fetishizing Asian women in his lyrics.[4] All that being said, it's undeniable that Glover has evolved through the years, as is evidenced by *Atlanta*.

As for a brief history of FX, it was originally launched by Fox as a broadcast channel in June of 1994, making the transition to cable in 1997. It ultimately tried to compete with premium channels like HBO and Showtime, although it continued to remain part of basic cable. In the early 2000s, after several iterations, FX emerged as a major player with the success of shows like *The Shield* (2002–2008, Shawn Ryan) and *Nip/Tuck* (2003–2010, Ryan Murphy). In 2007, FX Productions, an in-house television production company, was created, and in 2013, FXX was launched as a partner channel to FX, primarily catering to an 18–34 male demographic. Throughout the years, FX garnered a reputation for taking risks and pushing the envelope with its often violent and raunchy content. Other hit shows include *It's Always Sunny in Philadelphia* (2005–present, Rob McElhenney), *Sons of Anarchy* (2008–2014, Kurt Sutter), *The League* (2009–2015, Jeff Schaffer, Jackie Schaffer), *Justified* (2010–2015, Graham Yost), *American Horror Story* (2011–present, Ryan Murphy, Brad Falchuk), *The Americans* (2013–2018, Joe Weisberg), and *Legion* (2017–2019, Noah Hawley). In December of 2017, the Walt Disney Company announced its acquisition of 21st Century Fox, and, along with it, FX Networks, LLC.

The deal was finalized in March of 2019, making FX a subsidiary of Walt Disney TV. The deal also included National Geographic and ESPN, among other entities, and gave Disney a majority stake in Hulu, which now offers FX programming.

John Landgraph, who currently serves as chairman of FX, has been an executive at the network since 2004. In recent years, he has been praised by many for his willingness to identify his own privilege as a white, cisgender, heterosexual male, and to use his position of power to work toward a more inclusive television industry. Under his supervision, FX has ushered in many more diverse shows, including *Atlanta*. Landgraph was featured in the documentary film *This Changes Everything* (Good Deed Entertainment: 2019, Tom Donahue), which explores gender and race discrimination in the television and film industry and the detrimental effect they can have on viewers. In it, Landgraph is candid about how FX originally fell short under his leadership in terms of diversity. He says, "I thought of myself as an enlightened person. I would have described myself as a feminist.... I started to inquire much more deeply into the kinds of unique challenges faced by women, by African Americans, by people who are not gender normative.... I had this unconscious bias that we would have to be making sacrifices to hire people with less experience and maybe that the talent wouldn't be there.... I'm here to say it's there. The minute we open our door, and we say, 'come express it here,' the work got better."[5] In 2020, FX announced that "diverse and female" directors would be at the helm for 63 percent of their productions in 2021.[6] That same year, Michaela Jaé Rodriguez made history by becoming the first transgender lead to be nominated for an Emmy in the Outstanding Lead Actress in a Drama Series category for her role in the FX series *Pose* (2018–2021, Ryan Murphy, Brad Falchuk, Steven Canals). It's worth noting that changes at FX were put into motion after a study, conducted by the Directors Guild of America, revealed that 88 percent of the network's episodes in the 2014–2015 season were directed by white men.[7]

Before *Atlanta* can be fully analyzed, a brief history of Black representation in television is in order. The first sitcom with a Black cast was *The Amos 'n' Andy Show* (CBS: 1951–1953), which was created by white actors Charles J. Correll and Freeman F. Gosden who based it on their radio show (1928–1960) for which they voiced the Black main characters. They relied heavily on minstrel traditions, which included using racial stereotypes for comedic effect. While some applauded the TV show for having an all-Black cast, others dismissed it for presenting racial stereotypes. In fact, when the show first aired, the National Association for the Advancement of Colored People (NAACP) labeled it as "a gross libel of the Negro and distortion of the truth."[8] By the 1960s, more shows featuring Black cast members, such as *East Side West Side* (CBS: 1963–1964, David Susskind), *I Spy* (NBC: 1965–1968, David Friedkin, Morton Fine), and *Julia* (NBC: 1968–1971, Hal Kanter), were able to break through. Although these 1960s shows were regarded as a step forward in some respects, there was also criticism, including that *Julia* inaccurately depicted the Black experience in America. By the 1970s, a myriad of sitcoms featuring more nuanced Black characters became immensely popular. These shows included *Sanford and Son* (NBC: 1972–1977, Bud Yorkin), *Good Times* (CBS: 1974–1979, Norman Lear), and *The Jeffersons* (CBS: 1975–1985, Don Nicholl, Michael Ross, Bernie West). Even though all three shows could be termed color-conscious in many respects, there were still problems with certain depictions, such as the criticism that *Sanford and Son* furthered the stereotype of the lazy Black man. There were also noteworthy developments in other television formats, such as the miniseries *Roots* (ABC: 1977, Alex Haley, David L. Wolper), which focused on the history of enslaved Black people in America, and the musical variety show *Soul Train* (Syndicated: 1971–2006, Don Cornelius), which introduced audiences to a plethora of soul, R&B, and hip-hop artists. In 1984, *The Cosby Show* (NBC: 1984–1992, William H. Cosby, Jr., Ed. Weinberger, Michael J. Leeson), which is about an affluent Black family living in Brooklyn, became the number one show in America for five consecutive seasons. Shows like *A Different World* (NBC: 1987–1993, William H. Cosby, Jr.), which was a spin-off of *The Cosby Show*, and *Family Matters* (ABC/CBS: 1989–1998, William Bickley, Michael Warren) carried the Black sitcom into the 1990s, with *Family Matters* eventually becoming one of the longest-running Black sitcoms ever, second only to *The Jeffersons*. In the 1990s, when hip-hop culture in the U.S. was becoming more mainstream, the Black sitcom experienced a resurgence with shows like *The Fresh Prince of Bel-Air* (NBC: 1990–1996, Andy Borowitz, Susan Borowitz), *Martin* (Fox: 1992–1997, John Bowman, Martin Lawrence, Topper Carew), and *Living Single* (Fox: 1993–1998, Yvette Lee Bowser). Each of these '90s shows was considered progressive at the time.

In the 2000s, there was a new approach termed post-racial TV, which affected the development of television shows in regard to race. In her 2018 book *Latinas & Latinos on TV*, Isabel Molina-Guzmán addresses the post-racial TV era, which she dates as lasting from 2007 to 2016, stating, "post-racial productions operate under the assumption that audiences no longer see racial difference and are past racial discrimination—subscribing to the post-racial belief that TV's comedic texts and the audiences who watch them are now colorblind."[9] An apt example of a show that carries on the post-racial TV idea, but which is from the time frame we're examining, would be *The Good Place* (NBC: 2016–2020, Michael Schur), about a group of strangers who bond while navigating the afterlife. The show boasts an ensemble cast that is both racially and ethnically diverse, but race and ethnicity rarely add to the complexity of the characters or the story being told.

A further development of this post-racial notion (that audiences no longer see racial difference in shows written to include characters of different races) was the "colorblind casting" concept, in which roles would be written to be independent of race and therefore could be filled by auditioning actors of any race. In her 2015 book *The Cultural Politics of Colorblind Casting*, author Kristen J. Warner argues that colorblind casting, also referred to as blindcasting, is detrimental to both the TV show and the viewer.[10] According to Warner, colorblind casting is often used to increase diversity on a given show but creates a world that reflects white ideologies and protects white privilege.[11] Warner writes, "Blindcasting became a useful tool because it allowed showrunners and television writers to avoid explicitly writing race into the script with the confidence such actions could create equal opportunity for actors of diverse backgrounds. *Grey's Anatomy* (2005–) showrunner Shonda Rhimes receives much of the credit for reintroducing the discourse of blindcasting back into mainstream consciousness."[12] An example of a show that aligns closely with colorblind casting in the 2016–2020 time period that is executive produced by Shonda Rhimes is *Bridgerton* (Netflix: 2020–present), which was created by showrunner Chris Van Dusen. To understand the context, Rhimes is a lauded show creator and a Black woman, and Van Dusen is someone who has worked extensively on Shondaland shows and is a white man. *Bridgerton*'s historical fiction romance was derived from Julia Quinn's novels about white aristocrats in Great Britain from 1813 to 1827. What makes the show notable is that it has a diverse cast of both BIPOC and white actors. While race doesn't necessarily add to the complexity of the characters in the series, there is nonetheless a bold statement being made by the presence of BIPOC British aristocracy within this historical period. In addition, the character of Queen Charlotte (Golda Rosheuvel), who is Black, is based on the actual Queen Charlotte, who ruled Great Britain and Ireland from 1761 to 1818 and who some claim had African ancestry, although others dispute this.[13] While some have lauded *Bridgerton* for its approach to race, others have accused the show of whitewashing racism and/or misrepresenting history.[14] Warner continues her critique: "While on the surface [blindcasting] may seem a laudable practice, the problem with blindcasting is that it forces minority actors to portray characters who are often written as white."[15] Although there may be times when colorblind casting makes a worthwhile statement, Warner's critique raises salient points.

Chapter 3. Atlanta

Warner continues to investigate representation in television in her 2017 *Film Quarterly* article titled "In the Time of Plastic Representation." She states, "An operational definition of plastic representation can be understood as a combination of synthetic elements put together and shaped to look like meaningful imagery, but which can only approximate depth and substance because ultimately it is hollow and cannot survive close scrutiny."[16] In other words, roles that aren't specific in regard to race tend to be written as white and therefore result in plastic representation when acted by non-white actors, causing "synthetic malleability."[17] In the last chapter of Warner's 2015 book, "Is There Hope? Alternatives to Colorblind Casting," she turns her attention to color-conscious shows such as *Homicide: Life on the Street* (NBC: 1993–1999, Paul Attanasio) and *The Wire* (HBO: 2002–2008, David Simon).[18] She explores these two shows as positive developments in that they include cultural specificity and the pain of race in American society.[19] In her article on plastic representation, Warner goes further and calls for change, writing, "For this industry, actual progress would involve crafting a more weighted diversity, one generated by adding dimension and specificity to roles, and achieved in tandem with diverse bodies shaping those roles at the level of producing and writing."[20] In many ways, one can see this as having been accomplished in *Atlanta*.

When looking at the television landscape in 2019 and 2020, it is clear that Black representation has continued to evolve. According to UCLA's "Hollywood Diversity Report: 2021 Television," Black lead actors surpassed proportional representation on scripted cable television in the 2019–2020 season. Specifically, 16.4 percent of scripted cable shows featured at least one Black lead while 12.4 percent of the U.S. population identifies as Black.[21] While scripted broadcast television hasn't quite reached the same level of Black representation as scripted cable television, the numbers show that progress is still being made. In the 2019–2020 season, when it comes to overall cast diversity, Black actors came in at 18.4 percent.[22] According to a 2020 report issued by Nielsen, "Being Seen on Screen: Diverse Representation & Inclusion on TV," which looked at the top 300 most watched shows in 2019, SVOD (Subscription Video on Demand), which includes Netflix, Amazon Prime Video, Hulu, etc., boasted the most overall diversity compared to broadcast and cable.[23] Black actors also had 18.9 percent screen time, which was a close second behind broadcast television, where Black actors had 24.78 percent of screen time.[24] Across cable, broadcast, and SVOD, Black actors had the highest total share of screen time among people of color with 18 percent.[25] It should be noted that the numbers for Black female actors tell a very different story. Across cable, broadcast, and SVOD, the majority of Black lead roles were played by men.[26] Perhaps most importantly, the study revealed that all audiences, regardless of race, prefer to see diversity in the shows they watch.[27] As illustrated by both studies, significant disparities in television representation in terms of race, gender, and sexual orientation still exist. Furthermore, some of the biggest disparities are behind the camera, making shows like *Atlanta* even more notable.

If one believes that having more color-conscious American TV shows is both a desirable development and a better way to showcase diversity, then one can celebrate that this is exactly what has happened in the five-year period, 2016–2020, which we are examining. *Atlanta* is a clear example of this trend toward greater diversity in that the creator of the show is Black; the primary characters, their families, their friends, and their communities are Black; and the aim of the show is to authentically explore the Black American experience. One could make the argument that this goes beyond color-conscious to color-centric. Not only does the show make no adjustments for white characters or viewers, but according to Glover, *Atlanta* goes one step further at times by trying to make white viewers feel uncomfortable. In a *New Yorker* article, "Donald Glover Will Not Save You," Tad Friend quotes Glover as saying, "I don't even want them laughing if they're laughing at the caged animal in the zoo.... I want them to really experience racism, to really feel what it's like to be [B]lack in America."[28] *Atlanta* covers a wide range of topics related to the intersectionality of its Black characters, including racism, sexism, hair discrimination, culture appropriation, colorism, transphobia, homophobia, transracial identity, intra-race prejudice, internalized racism, and toxic masculinity. *Atlanta* also pokes fun at white pseudointellectuals (and university professors) who offer commentary on the Black experience.

The starting point of *Atlanta* is when Earn convinces his rapper cousin, Al (a.k.a. Paper Boi), to hire him as his manager. Al supplements his successful rap career by selling drugs, which, at times, proves to be dangerous. Al must also navigate unexpected changes in his life due to his new-found stardom and issues that arise when his rap persona clashes with who he feels he is as a person. Al is reluctant at first to let Earn manage him, but Earn, who dropped out of Princeton University for initially unknown reasons, slowly proves his value. In addition to Earn, Alfred's closest friend and confidant is Darius (LaKeith Stanfield). Unlike Al, who can be hotheaded and short-tempered, Darius is exceedingly even keeled and mellow. He is also at times kindhearted and is as bright as he is eccentric and mysterious. Earn is in an on-again, off-again relationship with Van, who is a schoolteacher when she is first introduced in Season 1. She is also the mother of their young daughter, Lottie (Mia Atehortua). As the title would suggest, the show takes place in Atlanta, Georgia. The show is both commercially successful and critically acclaimed, winning two Primetime Emmy Awards for Outstanding Lead Actor in a Comedy Series and Outstanding Directing for a Comedy Series, and two Golden Globe Awards: Best Television Series—Musical or Comedy and Best Actor—Television Series Musical or Comedy. *Atlanta* also has a 98 percent average rating among critics on the aggregate site RottenTomatoes.com.[29]

As previously noted, *Atlanta* tackles an array of complex social, political, and cultural issues related to race. Yet it does so in a way that is oftentimes seamless to the viewer. In other words, *Atlanta* excels at talking about race without being didactic. Transgressions range from large to small and are presented in an authentic, straightforward manner that is never at the expense of plot, character development, or the sheer entertainment value of the show. *Atlanta* trusts the viewer to pick up on the transgression and move on. It often does not attempt to find a solution, nor does it linger on Black suffering (though Earn is often down on his luck) or pander to non–Black viewers.[30] In the first season of *Atlanta*, there are several examples of this approach. In "Nobody Beats the Biebs" (S1, E5), Alfred agrees to participate in a celebrity basketball game for charity. One of the other celebrity participants, who goes by the name Justin Bieber (Austin Crute), is immature, arrogant, and rubs Al the wrong way almost instantly. There is no mention of the actual Justin Bieber, who, in real life, is a multi-platinum recording artist. It's important to note that the real Justin Bieber is white, while *Atlanta*'s Justin Bieber is Black. Soon after we first meet *Atlanta*'s Justin Bieber, he brazenly urinates in public. The actual Justin Bieber did the same in 2013 when he urinated into a mop bucket at a restaurant. Afterward, he sprayed a photo of former president Bill Clinton with cleaning solution while saying, "Fuck Bill Clinton." Bieber later apologized to Clinton over the phone. By simply changing the race of *Atlanta*'s Bieber from white to Black, but having their antics remain the same, Glover forces the viewer to imagine a world in which Bieber is stripped of his white privilege. Does the excuse "he's just trying to figure it out" (often applied to white men) all of a sudden seem absurd? Glover challenges the viewer to answer this question and more.

The episode also explores how Al is unable to escape being typecast as a villain in the eyes of the media. At the beginning of the episode, he urges a reporter to do an interview with him, but she only knows him as "the guy who shot someone." Al insists on being interviewed so people can get to know the real him, but she remains uninterested because her audience "isn't into the whole gangster thing" and neither is she. Later in the episode, Bieber delivers an absurd apology after he and Al fight at the basketball game. As Al watches the apology get eaten up by the media, the reporter from earlier offers him some free advice. She says, "Play your part. People don't want Justin to be the asshole. They want you to be the asshole. You're a rapper. That's your job." In other words, Al has a role to play, and they expect him to play it. It's worth noting that the real Justin Bieber used to live in a 5,500-square-foot mansion in Atlanta and has also been accused by many of cultural appropriation.

The viewer is confronted with several other instances in Episode 5 in which race plays a factor. Earn decides to tag along to the celebrity basketball game with Al and quickly gets misrecognized by a white agent named Janice (Jane Adams) who mistakes him for an agent she used to work with named Alonzo. Earn decides to play along and assumes the identity of Alonzo, which gets him into a networking event that's happening in conjunction with the celebrity basketball game. After all, there is no doubt that Earn has repeatedly been put at a disadvantage due to his race. In the rare instance that he can benefit from a microaggression, why would Earn not take advantage? Everything goes according to plan at first. Earn, pretending to be Alonzo in front of Janice, is making important contacts that may help him down the line. Things fall apart soon after when Janice reveals that she knows it was Alonzo, who Earn is pretending to be, that betrayed her and ruined her career. Also in the episode, Darius, who is a gun enthusiast, goes to a shooting range. His target of choice depicts a dog, which offends some of the other patrons, all of whom are white. When one asks Darius if he's "psycho" for shooting at an image of a dog, he responds, "the dogs in my neighborhood, they're crazy." When the white patron objects further, Darius responds, "Well, why would I shoot a human target?" As the argument continues, a third patron, seemingly of Middle Eastern descent, comes to Darius's defense, saying to the white patron, "You shoot at your racist target with no problem. I saw you shoot at that one with a Mexican holding a knife. It's shameful." Things take a comedic turn when the third patron implicates Darius in a "revolution that will rise from within" and concludes by saying, "blood will spill." Clearly, the white patrons cannot relate to Darius's perspective but are willing to overlook their own racist aggressions.

"Juneteenth" (S1, E9) is another example of the seamless approach *Atlanta* takes when addressing issues of race. In the episode, Earn and Van are invited to a Juneteenth party, which celebrates the date (June 19, 1865) when enslaved people in the United States were freed. Earn describes the party as a "Spike Lee–directed *Eyes Wide Shut*," complete with themed cocktails like "Juneteenth Juice," "Emancipation Eggnog," "Plantation Master Poison" and "Forty Acres and a Moscow Mule." Since Van is using the party to network with Atlanta's social elite, Earn agrees to pretend that he and Van are married and downplays his involvement in the rap

Chapter 3. Atlanta

industry. The party is being hosted by a well-off Black acquaintance of Van's, Monique (Cassandra Freeman), and her white husband, Craig (Rick Holmes), who immediately takes a liking to Earn. Craig expresses his affinity for African and African American history and culture to Earn, who is taken aback when Craig shows him his den, which is filled with African artifacts and framed photos of Black icons. As Craig, an optometrist, pours Earn a glass of Hennessy (a drink that is considered popular in the Black community), he tells him about one of his own paintings that was inspired by a Malcom X quote and goes on about his trip to Africa, or "the motherland," for atonement. He's surprised that Earn doesn't know more about his own ancestry. Earn responds by saying, "This spooky thing called slavery happened and my entire ethnic identity was erased." Later on, Craig insists that Earn be front and center as he recites his poem about Jim Crow to the entire party. In a conversation with Van, Monique admits that her husband's "Black people as a hobby shit" is inappropriate but views their relationship as more of an economical exchange. She says, "I get the big-ass house, and he gets the Black wife he always wanted." The party takes a turn for the worse when it is revealed that Earn represents a rapper, who was involved in a shooting, which draws the ire of Monique. Earn loses his cool and points out the absurdity of the party to Monique and Craig before storming off. He later tries to apologize to Van, and the two end up having sex in her car. Earlier in the episode, Craig is enthusiastic about Earn's career, stating, "Music is such an integral part of African American culture ... and it's been stripped from you. Black music artists are products for white American consumption and appropriation." Craig is oblivious to the fact he is also appropriating Black culture, similar to what he is accusing the music industry of doing.

At face value, the episode may seem to only be about a white party host guilty of culture appropriation. On a deeper level, the episode comments on how some feel that white people have co-opted Juneteenth and other similar holidays. Many advocates fought tirelessly to have Juneteenth declared a federal holiday and it finally was in 2021. In a *Salon* article, "This Juneteenth, 'Atlanta' will give you all the insights you need on how America co-opts a holiday," Melanie McFarland asserts that, like Martin Luther King, Jr., Day, Juneteenth is at risk of becoming a day in which white people enjoy a paid day off from work, which they use to hunt for holiday discounts.[31] There is also the risk of the day being twisted to reflect one's own ideology. For example, in 2019, Vice President Mike Pence, on the eve of Martin Luther King, Jr., Day, compared President Donald Trump to Dr. King in an attempt to sell the border wall to a democratic-controlled House of Representatives.[32] Others have used Juneteenth, a day of celebration, to dwell on Black suffering. For example,

National Geographic scheduled the premiere of *Rise Again: Tulsa and the Red Summer* (Dawn Porter) for Juneteenth 2021.[33] And then you have those like Craig, who, at a glance, seem to be doing a lot right. He has put in the legwork to educate himself about Black culture and history. He sees nothing wrong, however, with lecturing Earn about the plight of the contemporary Black man. Even Monique realizes the absurdity of Craig telling her 95-year-old grandmother she was "cooking her collard greens wrong." *Atlanta* expresses some of the genuine concerns surrounding cultural appropriation.

While other shows would need an entire episode, or even several episodes, to cover the ground that *Atlanta* covers, Glover is able to pack an astounding amount of social commentary and humor into a single half-hour episode. A prime example of this is "Money Bag Shawty" (S2, E3). Finally doing better financially, Earn decides to treat Van to a night out where they act as if money is no object. Their first stop is a movie theater, where Earn attempts to use a hundred-dollar bill. The theater employee informs Earn that a bill that large cannot be accepted. When Earn tries to pay with his debit card, he's informed that his card and driver's license need to be photocopied each time he uses it. Earn expresses concern over his information being stolen, for which the theater "would not be responsible," and the two decide to go somewhere else. Right before they leave, a white patron pays with a hundred-dollar bill with no questions asked. When Earn approaches him about the witnessed hypocrisy, the white patron causally flashes a gun strapped to his person. A little later on, Earn says what they experienced was "racist," while Van maintains it was "weird." Earn insists, claiming that he caught the theater employee "red-handed." Van then feigns outrage over Earn's use of the term, claiming it came from the stereotype that Native Americans "are always stealing." After revealing that she's only teasing Earn, she admits that she's not sure if that's where the term comes from. On a side note, the term "red-handed" comes from 15th-century Scotland and has nothing to with Indigenous peoples. The next stop for Earn and Van is a hookah lounge. After being thoroughly patted down by the bouncer at the door, Earn pays the entry fee with his hundred-dollar bill, which is accepted. As Earn and Van decide what flavor hookah they want, two uniformed police officers approach Earn and ask if he paid with a hundred-dollar bill. The owner, who is Black, insists the bill is fake and Earn and Van are forced to leave. As they are escorted out, one of the police officers admits that the bill was real and apologizes. This time, Van confirms that what they experienced "was definitely racist." Earn wants to go somewhere that will appreciate his money and decides that a strip club would be the best choice. They meet up with Al, Darius, and Al's friend, Tracy (Khris Davis). Things don't quite work out for Earn, as he finds out that the strip club has all sorts of upcharges and hidden fees. After hearing about Earn's disappointment, Al gives him some advice. He says, "There's a reason that a white dude dressed just like you can walk into a bank and get a loan and you can't even spend a hundred-dollar bill, man." To Al, it's not enough to just have money, you need to act like you have it too. With Earn's quest to spend his hundred-dollar bill, *Atlanta* floats between issues like racism (white movie theater employee), Indigenous stereotypes (caught "red-handed"), intra-race prejudice (Black hookah lounge club owner), and racial double standards (white patron carrying a gun). On a side note, the episode ends in hilarious fashion with former football star Michael Vick challenging club-goers to race him in the parking lot and taking bets on the outcome. A very cocky Earn likes his chances and challenges Vick to a race. While the viewer never actually sees the race, we are treated to cheesy inspirational eighties music and a freeze frame of Earn at the starting line. It's only after the race that we find out that Earn lost. In the back of the limousine they rented for the evening, Van turns to a dejected Earn and deadpans, "It's Michael Vick." He was foolish to think he could beat him.

Much has been made about *Atlanta* as a form of high art, rivaling even the most artistic of films and raising the level of what viewers have come to expect from television. In his *New Yorker* article, author Tad Friend quotes Jordan Peele, director of the films *Get Out* (Universal Pictures: 2017), *Us* (Universal Pictures: 2019) and *Nope* (Universal Pictures: 2022), as saying, "For [B]lack people, 'Atlanta' provides the catharsis of 'Finally, some elevated [B]lack shit.'"[34] Some of *Atlanta*'s most critically acclaimed episodes are the result of Glover not being afraid to experiment with format. An early example comes in "B.A.N." (S1, E7), in which the entire episode is formatted as a talk show on the fictional Black American Network that mimics what viewers might see on public programming. Glover wrote and directed the episode but is noticeably absent from the cast. Al is a guest on the show *Montague*, hosted by Franklin Montague (Alano Miller), along with Dr. Debra Holt (Mary Kraft), who is head of the fictional Center of Trans-American Issues. The topic of the show is "the growing outlook of accepted sexuality and its effects on Black youth and culture." Al seemingly agreed to do the show after some blowback for a vulgar and derogatory tweet he made about Caitlyn Jenner, who is a transgendered woman. The show is complete with faux commercials throughout that are aimed at Black consumers, all of which offer a slice of social or cultural humor and commentary. The commercials also get more outlandish as the show progresses. For example, viewers see a recurring Dodge Charger commercial in which a Black man confidently drives around town. The voiceover says, "The Dodge Charger. The official car of making a statement without saying anything at all." The third time around, we see him pull into a gas station and quickly pump gas while naked from the waist down. One mechanic turns to another and says, "That's Victor Wallace. His wife left him for his brother. Long court battle. Kids, house, it got messy. He ain't said one word the whole trial. But then, at the end, he just stood up and said, 'Leave me my Dodge Charger.' He's been driving around this neighborhood in circles for a week, just waving." The voiceover then changes to "The Dodge Charger. Keep it in the divorce." Clearly, Glover is willing to experiment with format and garner laughs in the process.

The episode is a rollercoaster of topics that includes gender, sexuality, homophobia, transphobia, and masculinity in the Black community. Dr. Clark, who is white, takes Al to task for his offensive remarks, while Al resents her for lecturing him on the Black community. At first, Montague seems to be thoughtful and intellectual, but he begins to play the role of instigator as the show progresses. The show really goes off the rails when Montague pivots to a segment on Antoine Smalls (Niles Stewart), a teenager born Black who identifies as white in a case of transracial identity. Antoine, who likes to go by Harrison, talks about missing Colorado and his job as a systems engineer for Coca-Cola, even though it's later revealed by his mother that he is unemployed. Adding to the absurdity, Harrison is shown practicing saying "What IPA do you have on tap?" and "Did you see *Game of Thrones* last night?" in the mirror. Harrison, who hopes to get a surgical procedure to make him appear white, also comes across as "racist" when he walks up to two officers talking to a Black man and says, "This is definitely the guy. He doesn't even live in the area. I've never seen him before." The Black man responds, "I called them." Later on, Harrison, wearing what is clearly a blond wig, joins the show via Facebook video chat. After Al mocks him and calls him "Drake Malfoy" (referring to the musician Drake and Draco Malfoy from the *Harry Potter* series) and "Felon DeGeneres" (referring to the actor, comedian, and daytime personality Ellen DeGeneres), Harrison proclaims, "the Black community, they just aren't accepting of racial diversity or anyone different, for that matter." Just as Al is unwilling to accept Caitlyn Jenner as transgendered, he is also unwilling to accept Harrison as transracial.

It's easy to draw comparisons between Harrison and Rachel Dolezal, who legally changed her name to Nkechi Amare Diallo. Diallo served as a chapter president for the National Association for the Advancement of Colored People (NAACP) and taught Africana Studies at Eastern Washington University while keeping up the deception that she was born Black even though she was born white. In the aftermath of the 2015 controversy, she resigned her position at the NAACP and was dismissed

Chapter 3. Atlanta

from her teaching position. She now identifies as transracial. In a *Vanity Fair* article titled "Rachel Dolezal's True Lies," author Allison Samuels quotes her as saying, "I don't know spiritually and metaphysically how this goes, but I do know that from my earliest memories I have awareness and connection with the [B]lack experience, and that's never left me. It's not something that I can put on and take off anymore."[35] Diallo has been roundly criticized both for her deception and her claims of transracial identity. In an NPR article titled "Why Rachel Dolezal Can Never Be Black," author Denene Miller writes, "like diamonds, [B]lackness is created under extreme pressure and high temperature, deep down in the recesses of one's core."[36] After laying out all the cultural experiences, both good and bad, that have defined her as a Black individual, she continues, "it is the ultimate in white privilege, really, for a white woman to see that diamond, all shiny and hard and unbreakable, and pluck it for her own, like it's a gift from Tiffany's, with seemingly zero regard for the pressure, the heat, the pain it went through—that *we* went through—to earn that shine."[37] Miller also points out that Diallo choosing a first and last name from two separate African languages is indicative of her attempt to claim an identity that is not hers to claim.[38]

As Season 1, Episode 7 continues, Dr. Clark attempts to tie transphobia in the Black community to prejudice toward Harrison. She poses the question, "Don't you think the rap community and its treatment of trans people and homosexuals is indicative of a larger problem in the Black community, one that makes your lifestyle unacceptable?" The big twist comes when Harrison reveals that he is homophobic and transphobic, calling gay marriage "gross" and transgendered people "unnatural." Throughout the episode, the question is posed, if your gender can change, can your race change as well? The question is never really answered. However, Al does get to the heart of the issue when he says, "It's hard for me to care about [transgendered people] when nobody cares about me as a Black man.... Caitlyn Jenner is just doing what rich white men been doing since the dawn of time, which is whatever the hell he want." It should be noted that Al repeatedly misgenders Caitlyn Jenner throughout the show. Dr. Clark assumes that since Al is part of a marginalized community, it is his responsibility to identify with other marginalized communities. Al sees that as an unfair burden. In a *Los Angeles Times* article titled "Setting the scene in 'Handmaid's Tale,' 'Atlanta' and more: Writers explain the draw of nominated episodes," Stephen Glover, bother of Donald Glover and story editor of the episode, explains the approach taken for the episode. Author Randy Dawn quotes him as saying, "First and foremost, it's just funny. But it helps frame the Caitlyn Jenner conversation.... It's never about being 'preachy' to an issue, it's more so about seeing how the world actually operates when dealing with these issues, and letting viewers decide what that means."[39] That is not to say all questions go unanswered. When pushed, Dr. Clark and Al agree that freedom of speech is to be protected and respected. Also, the episode poses that when politically incorrect comments are made, perhaps the best approach is one of listening and understanding instead of swift condemnation.[40]

It should be noted that attitudes toward transgendered individuals in the Black community, like any community, can be a nuanced and complicated issue. It should also be noted that Black transgendered individuals face some of the toughest challenges within the LGBTQ community. According to the National LGBQ Taskforce, 26 percent of Black transgendered people are unemployed, 34 percent have a household income of less than ten thousand per year, 41 percent have experienced homelessness, and 20.23 percent are living with HIV.[41] Furthermore, several high-profile hip-hop artists have made transphobic statements similar to Paper Boi. After Caitlyn Jenner transitioned to female, veteran hip-hop artist Snoop Dogg posted on social media, "Shout out to Akon! He is about to supply 600 million Africans with solar power. I'm really upset that this isn't major news but that science project bruce jenner [sic] is."[42] By having an episode of *Atlanta* in the format of a talk show, complete with over-the-top personalities and faux commercials, the show is able to tackle and demystify many culturally relevant topics in a way that is comedic, informative, and digestible to the viewer.

Not everyone is on board with how Glover handled the episode. Some felt that its mocking tone attempted to make a false equivalency between transgendered and transracial.[43] In a *Washington Post* article titled "An 'Atlanta' episode and Dave Chappelle's Netflix special show what has—and hasn't—changed in five years," author Bethonie Butler quotes transgender writer and activist Raquel Willis, who says, "Because [*Atlanta*] ticks off maybe one box in particular around affirming an expanded portrayal of a marginalized group—i.e., Black people—it gets a pass when it missteps on portraying other marginalized experiences…. And that's not okay."[44] Still, it is clear that *Atlanta*'s approach brought transgender issues to the forefront, and that conversation continues today. It's worth mentioning that, as the title of the above article suggests, Black comedian Dave Chapelle heightened the relevancy of the episode by causing controversy with his Netflix comedy special *The Closer* (2021), in which he mocked transgender and queer communities. While some have defended his stand-up as "anti-cancel culture," others have criticized him as tone-deaf and incendiary at best, transphobic and homophobic at worst. On a side note, Donald Glover has long been a critic of cancel culture. In an

Chapter 3. Atlanta

IndieWire article titled "Donald Glover: Fear of 'Getting Cancelled' Is Resulting in 'Boring' Films and TV," Zack Sharf quotes Glover as saying, "We're getting boring stuff and not even experimental mistakes because people are afraid of getting cancelled.... So they feel like they can only experiment with aesthetic."[45] Clearly, Glover is willing to take risks with *Atlanta*.

"Teddy Perkins" (S2, E6) once again experiments with format and delivers what is perhaps the most critically acclaimed episode of *Atlanta* to date. This time, the show takes on the horror genre in what some have called a wink to Jordan Peele's *Get Out*. In it, Darius travels to a mysterious mansion in the middle of nowhere to pick up a piano that was posted online. While Donald Glover's character Earn only briefly appears in the episode, Glover plays Theodore Perkins, a strange and eccentric man and brother of famed piano player Benny Hope (Derrick Haywood). Teddy explains that his brother, who lives with him, developed a rare skin condition that requires him to stay out of the sun. The house doesn't have a single light turned on, and while Perkins is Black, his skin is light. Moreso, based on old photos, we can surmise that Teddy went through some sort of physical transformation. On a phone call to Al, Darius describes Teddy as "somebody left Sammy Sosa in the dryer." To add some context, Sammy Sosa was a professional baseball player who had a 19-year career with the Texas Rangers, Chicago Cubs, and Baltimore Orioles, whose skin became noticeably lighter after he retired, which he attributed to his use of a skin bleaching cream.[46] It's important to note that skin bleaching is an $8.6 billion industry.[47] Many have pointed out the physical and psychological damage that can be caused by these products and how they promote colorism within the Black community. Even though it is unclear what has caused Teddy's appearance to change so dramatically, his transformation is similar to the physical changes that the "King of Pop," Michael Jackson, went through starting in the mid-1990s. Jackson said he had vitiligo, which, according to the Mayo Clinic, is "a condition in which the skin loses its pigment cells (melanocytes)."[48] Jackson was suspected of bleaching his skin in order to hide the effects of the disease. This was in addition to his plastic surgery procedures, which altered his appearance further. If the comparison of Teddy to Michael Jackson is apt, then Teddy's transformation can be seen as a manifestation of the pressure put on him to conform to a white-dominated society. He also reflects that Hollywood has long been accused of colorism, favoring lighter skinned actors to fill diverse roles. In fact, Zazie Beetz, who, as previously mentioned, stars in *Atlanta*, was recently criticized for her role in the Netflix western *The Harder They Fall* (2021, Jeymes Samuel), which Netflix touted as "the biggest, poppiest, and most star-studded Black Western ever made."[49] In it, she plays Stagecoach

Mary, who is based on a real person and whose skin was much darker as compared to Beetz's.[50]

Returning to the episode, the tone begins to change when Teddy stalls in giving Darius the piano. First, he reveals that he is converting the mansion into a museum. He shows Darius a part of the museum dedicated to "great fathers," including Joe Jackson (father of Michael Jackson), Marvin Gay, Sr. (father of musician Marvin Gay, Jr.), Earl Woods (father of golfer Tiger Woods), and Richard Williams (father of tennis players Venus and Serena Williams), all of whom have been accused of emotional and/or physical abuse toward their children. In many cases, they justified their abuse by claiming it helped to push their children toward greatness. Marvin Gay, Sr., is in a category all his own, having shot and killed his son, Marvin Gay, Jr., in 1984. Teddy throws in "the father that drops off Emilio Estevez in *The Breakfast Club*" for comedic effect. By way of explanation, in *The Breakfast Club* (Universal Pictures: 1985, John Hughes), high school student Andrew Clark (Emilio Estevez) attributes his toxic behavior to his domineering father. Teddy also includes his own father, who ruthlessly doled out physical punishment if his and his brother's piano playing wasn't up to snuff. According to Teddy, he and his brother were their father's "sacrifice." The strange encounter becomes even more bizarre when Darius discovers Benny in a wheelchair, covered from head to toe, in the basement. Darius had assumed that Teddy was Benny and that he had constructed the story of taking care of his brother as a coping mechanism. Benny scribbles on a chalkboard that Teddy will kill them both and implores Darius to get Teddy's gun. Darius ignores Benny's plea and finally brings the piano outside, only to find that he's blocked in by Teddy's car. When Darius confronts Teddy about his car, Teddy pulls a shotgun on him and informs him that he has been chosen as his "sacrifice." While handcuffed to a chair, Darius tells Teddy that he disagrees with his philosophy that great things can only come from great pain. Referencing an earlier conversation, he says that Stevie Wonder saw love through his music. The twist comes when the elevator doors open to reveal Benny, who picks up the shotgun and shoots Teddy. Badly injured from Teddy's earlier attempt to kill him, Benny asks Darius for the fire poker he grabbed earlier for protection. He then puts the shotgun to his head and uses the poker to pull the trigger. Darius is left still handcuffed to the chair with the bodies of Teddy and Benny around him.

"Teddy Perkins" is beautifully shot and was originally presented without commercial interruption. In fact, the episode won Emmy Awards in 2018 for Outstanding Cinematography for a Single-Camera Series (Half-Hour) and Outstanding Sound Editing for a Comedy or Drama (Half-Hour) and Animation. It was also nominated for Outstanding Production

Design for a Narrative Program (Half-Hour), Outstanding Directing for a Comedy Series, and Outstanding Single-Camera Picture Editing for a Comedy Series. The high production value in the episode, as well as the whole series, is another reason why it is considered to be high art. The episode also functions as an effective piece of horror. Glover and director Hiro Murai accomplish this, in part, by drawing on classic horror films like *The Invisible Man* (Universal Pictures Corporation: 1933, James Whale), *Psycho* (Paramount Pictures: 1960, Alfred Hitchcock), *Whatever Happened to Baby Jane?* (Warner Bros. Pictures: 1962, Robert Aldrich), and *Misery* (Columbia Pictures: 1990, Rob Reiner).[51] As previously mentioned, *Get Out* is also a major influence. Stanfield, who plays Darius, had a supporting role in the film as Andre, a man who is kidnapped and has a white man's consciousness put in his body. A camera flash briefly brings Andre out of his stupor, and he warns Chris (Daniel Kaluuya), the main protagonist of the film, to "get out" before the procedure can be done on him too. In *Atlanta*, Darius is blinded by a camera flash when Teddy takes his photo. Darius responds by saying, "I'm not a big photo person" as a clear nod to *Get Out*.[52] Similar to *Get Out*, Glover uses horror in "Teddy Perkins" to help illustrate the Black experience to viewers. In a *Vulture* article titled "In Its Second Season, Atlanta Used Horror to Explore Black Identity," Angelica Jade Bastién writes, "so much of [B]lackness in America carries an undercurrent of dread, in which the prosaic points of everyday life—wearing a hoodie to run an errand, attending church, passing a huddle of cops while walking through your own neighborhood—are fraught with meaning and reminders of the potential for violence."[53] *Atlanta* has also used horror on other occasions to illustrate feelings of dread related to racism. For example, in "Alligator Man" (S2, E1), Darius tells Earn about the "Florida Man," who is basically a boogeyman.[54] According to Darius, "Florida Man shoots unarmed Black teenager. Florida Man bursts into ex's delivery room and fights new boyfriend as she's giving birth…. Florida Man found eating another man's face." Darius says that Florida Man is in cahoots with the state government "to prevent Black people from coming to and/or registering to vote in Florida." It's a wink at the steady stream of articles highlighting the shocking actions of unidentified white men from Florida.

The use of horror in "Teddy Perkins" to comment on racism is a bit different from earlier uses on the show because it is more concerned with specific issues like internalized racism, inherited trauma, the cost of celebrity, cyclical violence, white privilege, the absurdity of blackface, and the dangers in losing one's own Blackness. Bastién writes, "As Teddy and Darius speak about familial tragedies, rap music, Stevie Wonder, and abusive fathers, the titular character synthesizes into something more than his various influences and monstrous visage. He becomes a horrifying emblem of what happens when [B]lack people resent their [B]lackness and seek to obliterate it."[55] Some have even posed that Benny is the physical manifestation of the part of Teddy's identity that he wishes to destroy.[56] On a side note, Glover was so unrecognizable as Teddy Perkins that he decided to play a trick on Stanfield, who plays Darius, and pretended to be another actor hired to play the part. It wasn't until a crew member let the secret slip that Stanfield realized it was Glover.[57] The character, Perkins, even made an appearance at the 2018 Emmy Awards, though he was not played by Glover or Stanfield. To this day, the identity of the person playing Perkins remains a mystery.

Most of the episodes of *Atlanta* mentioned so far in this chapter have one thing in common: they all have elements of the surreal. Merriam-Webster defines surrealism as "the principles, ideals, or practice of producing fantastic or incongruous imagery or effects in art, literature, film, or theater by means of unnatural or irrational juxtapositions and combinations."[58] *Atlanta* transitions from the real to the surreal without offering any explanation to the viewer. Furthermore, *Atlanta*'s use of the surreal is another reason why the show is considered to be high art. From the very first episode, "The Big Bang," Glover lets the viewer know that the surreal will be an integral part of the show. The episode starts with Al's mirror getting knocked off his car, and an altercation follows. As the tensions escalate and guns are drawn, Darius says, "I'm getting crazy déjà vu right now. Okay. Where's the dog...." Spotting the dog, he says, "There he is. That's a trip, man." The episode then uses discontinuous editing to create a circular structure so that it ends with nearly the same scene with which it started. Although new information is introduced the second time around, the viewer experiences the same scene twice. This causes Darius to have déjà vu and thus sets him up as a supernatural character.[59] Later on in the episode, Earn is riding on the bus with his young daughter sitting in his lap. A well-dressed man says to Earn, "Your mind's racing. Tell me...." Earn responds, "I just keep losing.... Some people just supposed to lose? For balance in the universe?... Are there just some people on earth who supposed to be here just to make it easier for the winners?" The man, who is making a sandwich on the bus, replies, "Resistance is a symptom of the way things are. Not the way things necessarily should be. Actual victory belongs to things that simply do not see failure. Let the path push you like a broken branch in a river's current." Earn responds, "I'm not going out like that, but thanks for the advice." The man then commands him to "bite this sandwich." When Earn refuses, the man becomes threatening. A siren distracts Earn and he looks away. When he turns back, the man is gone. He then sees him disappear into the forest with his dog, who was not with him before. On a side note, he appears again briefly in the "B.A.N." episode and is revealed to be a self-help guru named Ahmad White (Emmett Hunter).

Many of the surreal events that are incorporated in the show also provide humor. For example, in "Streets on Lock" (S1, E2), Al and Darius order wings with fries from one of their favorite restaurants. As Darius lifts the lid of the container to reveal the "lemon pepper joints" with "the sauce on them," a faint golden glow can be seen coming from the box. This is done for comedic effect, but is also nostalgic, as it harkens back to the glowing briefcase in *Pulp Fiction* (Miramax Films: 1994, Quentin Tarantino).[60] Another example of the surreal for comedic effect is an invisible car owned by fictional NBA player Marcus Miles (Jason Simon), which the viewer gets to "see" in "The Club" (S1, E8). After gunshots go off at a club, the invisible car presumably speeds away, plowing through pedestrians, who go flying into the air. Prior to the shooting, Al tells Darius he doubts the invisible car is real.

The surreal is also used in the show to articulate the unpredictable nature of being Black in America.[61] For example, in Season 1, Episode 7, as previously mentioned, the faux commercials that break up *Montague* on B.A.N. become more surreal as the show progresses. One commercial in particular depicts a cartoon wolf attempting to eat a breakfast cereal but gets thwarted because "only kids can have Coconut Crunch O's." The commercial is reminiscent of other cereal commercials, such as Trix, with the catch phrase "Silly rabbit. Trix are for kids." The audience reasonably infers that the wolf is Black, and the children watch in shock as a white police officer tackles the wolf and proceeds to rough him up while arresting him. Events escalate when the children, all of whom are Black, object to how the wolf is being treated and one starts recording the interaction on his cell phone. Glover's commentary on police brutality is clear.[62] Other moments of the surreal are harder to decipher, even though they can still offer the viewer a glimpse into the Black experience. They include a giant alligator walking down a residential street in "Alligator Man" (S2, E1), one of Van's Black students in "white face" in "Value" (S1, E6), and the strange man Al encounters while lost in the woods in "Woods" (S2, E8). In a *Slate* article titled "*Atlanta*'s Surrealism Is What It Feels Like to Be Black," Evan Higgins writes, "Like its precursor *Twin Peaks*, *Atlanta* cultivates its surreal atmosphere by grafting bizarre moments onto everyday ones. But where *Twin Peaks* used those details to evoke the danger hidden in small-town America, *Atlanta* employs them to replicate the fear, anguish, and unpredictability constant in the daily lives of lower- and middle-class black Americans."[63] Donald Glover himself has been candid about the influence that *Twin Peaks* (ABC: 1990–1991, David Lynch, Mark Frost) has had on *Atlanta*. In a *TV Guide* article, Malcom Venable quotes Donald Glover as saying, "I just wanted to make *Twin Peaks* with rappers."[64]

Some scholars have described *Atlanta* as an example of Afrosurrealism, and there is a case to be made for doing so. Afrosurrealism can be defined as "a literary and cultural aesthetic that is a response to mainstream surrealism in order to reflect the lived experience of people of color."[65] The term was first coined by author, activist, and Black Arts Movement founder Amiri Baraka in 1974. Baraka specifically used the term Afro-surreal expressionism, but it was expanded upon by author D. Scot Miller in 2009. Miller is thought to be the founder of the Afrosurreal Arts Movement. How does Afrosurrealism differ from surrealism? In his video essay, Thomas Flight says, "*The Sopranos* and *Twin Peaks* utilized traditional surrealism, but they do so to explore dreams, psychology, and metaphysical reality. They're using surrealism to get at a reality that exists beyond reality, but Afrosurrealism doubles back on this and presents a reality again, but it's a reality that is itself inherently real for marginalized people."[66] No matter the term used, *Atlanta* challenges what viewers have come to expect from television, creating a more dynamic and engaging viewing experience and adding tremendous value to the show. On a side note, other recent shows like *Reservation Dogs* (2021–2023, Sterlin Harjo, Taika Waititi), also on FX, have experimented with having the real exist alongside the surreal. Some even view it as a successor to *Atlanta*.[67]

At this point, the question must be asked, is *Atlanta* funny? Our Recent TV Trends students overwhelmingly believe that it is. Not only is the show funny, but Donald Glover has also cultivated a brand of comedy that is uniquely his own. He doesn't strive to have the viewer fall out of their chair laughing at every at scene. Rather, he peppers authentic, slice-of-life moments with comedic ones. A prime example is the cold open of "Go for Broke" (S1, E3). Down on his luck, Earn discretely tries to order a kids meal at a fast food restaurant. He is informed by the day manager that one must be 14 years old or younger to order the kids meal, to which Earn responds, "Do you have to be Evander Holyfield to get the champ? Do you have to be fucking Chubby Checker to get the Chubby Decker? Do you need to have a long foot to…. That one doesn't translate." Earn eventually gives up and asks for a cup for water. The manager's cheery disposition returns, and she hands Earn a cup. Earn slyly fills the cup with soda instead but is spotted by another employee who is mopping the floor, who just stares at him. Earn puts his finger to his lips, making a shushing gesture, and slowly walks backward out of the restaurant. The humor, along with surreal storytelling techniques, all contribute to making a show that tackles serious issues more digestible to the viewer. Unlike its contemporaries like *The Chi* (Showtime: 2017–present, Lena Waithe), which presents a sobering look at the harsh realities of living on the South Side of Chicago, *Atlanta* keeps the audience amused and surprised enough to make it bingeable. At the same time, the show maintains its authenticity, superior quality, and social relevance. In an era when bingeable content is at a premium, but too often comes at the cost of overall quality, *Atlanta* is in a league of its own.

Despite the role that comedy, especially satire, has historically played in advocating for social justice, Glover has warned against putting that kind of weight squarely on the shoulders of shows like *Atlanta*. In a profile of Glover published by *Vulture*, "Donald Glover's Community: The comic turns his eye to his hometown—and [B]lack America—in Atlanta," Glover says, "The No. 1 thing we kept coming back to is that [*Atlanta*] needs to be funny first and foremost. I never wanted this shit to be important. I never wanted this show to be about diversity; all that shit is wack to me. There's a lot of clapter going on."[68] The term "clapter" was allegedly coined by comedian, writer, producer, actor, and television host Seth Myers several years earlier. It can be defined as what happens when audiences agree with the politics of a joke and, in turn, respond positively to it (often by clapping) but do not find the joke itself to be funny.[69] While some might accuse Glover of downplaying what the show is trying to accomplish, Glover has achieved his goal of making *Atlanta* funny. As previously mentioned, the show is also authentic and innovative in its effective articulation of the Black experience in America. This is accomplished by Glover taking risks and being bold.

CHAPTER 4

Ramy

First-Person Comedy-Drama of an Arab Muslim Community

The American comedy-drama television series *Ramy*, created by Ramy Youssef (along with Ari Katcher and Ryan Welch), premiered on the streaming service Hulu in 2019 with A24 as the production company. The show takes place in a New Jersey neighborhood and is about a twenty-something Egyptian American Muslim named Ramy Hassan (Ramy Youssef) who struggles to balance his religious convictions with the pressures of being a millennial. As Ramy juggles work, family, friends, and his dating life, he embarks on a journey to discover what kind of person and Muslim he wants to be. He has many people to guide him, tempt him, or present obstacles along the way, including his mother, Maysa (Hiam Abbass); his father, Farouk (Amr Waked); his sister, Dena (May Calamawy); his Uncle Naseem (Laith Nakli); and his best friend, Steve (Steve Way). Season 2 of *Ramy* was released in 2020 and Season 3 was released in 2022 after production was delayed due to Covid-19. Youssef announced that there will be a Season 4 and that it will be the last.

Born in the Queens borough of New York City and raised in Rutherford, New Jersey, Youssef launched his acting career by playing a main character named Kevin on the Nick at Nite show *See Dad Run* (2012–2019, Tina Albanese, Patrick Labyorteaux). He has also made a name for himself as a stand-up comedian, and in 2017, he appeared on *The Late Show with Stephen Colbert* (CBS: 2015–present), where he delivered his stand-up routine. He made his HBO stand-up comedy debut a few years later with his special *Ramy Youssef: Feelings* (2019). *Ramy* hasn't quite reached the same level of popularity as other Hulu original programming such as *The Handmaid's Tale* (2017–present, Bruce Miller) or *Little Fires Everywhere* (2020, Liz Tigelaar), both of which have held the title for most watched Hulu original series. Still, the show has a devout following, has received much critical acclaim, and overall has generated positive buzz for Hulu.

Chapter 4. Ramy

Youssef, who is partial to self-deprecating humor, poked fun at *Ramy* for being under the radar when he accepted the Golden Globe in 2020 for Best Actor in a Television Series—Musical or Comedy, stating in his acceptance speech, "Look, I know you guys haven't seen my show...."[1] Youssef was also nominated for two Emmy Awards in 2020 for Outstanding Directing for a Comedy Series and Outstanding Lead Actor in a Comedy Series but did not win. Mahershala Ali was nominated for Outstanding Supporting Actor in a Comedy Series for his portrayal of Sheikh Malik in Season 2 but also did not win.

Youssef attributes the creation of *Ramy* to the rise of streaming platforms, stating that, 10 years ago, the show would not have been made.[2] In general, the rise of streaming has led to more diverse representation in television. In the 2020 report "Being Seen on Screen: Diverse Representation and Inclusion on TV," Nielsen looked at the top 300 programs from 2019 across broadcast, cable, and SVOD (Subscription Video on Demand), which includes Netflix, Amazon Prime Video, Hulu, etc. The report found that about 92 percent of shows had at least one recurring character who is female, a person of color, a member of the LGBTQ community, or some combination of the three.[3] Furthermore, the report found that SVOD supplied the widest range of shows featuring diverse characters.[4] When looking at SVOD compared to broadcast and cable, SVOD had the highest rate of female, LGBTQ, Hispanic/Latinx, East Asian, MENA (Middle Eastern/North African), and Native American characters.[5] The study also found that broadcast television had the highest rate of Black characters, with SVOD coming in second.[6]

According to Youssef, Hulu was interested in *Ramy* from the start.[7] Creatively, he felt it was a good match for him as well.[8] In her *GQ* article "Ramy Youssef Is Upending the First-Generation Narrative," Jaya Saxena quotes Youssef as saying, "[At Hulu] I feel like we got the most room to play at a place that was really excited and hungry to start fresh, as opposed to walking into a place that is an establishment ... as a new creator that's a perfect match."[9] In a *Daily Bruin* article titled "Actor draws from Muslim-American identity in show exploring challenges of dual cultures," Youssef elaborates further. Umber Ghatti quotes him as saying, "Hollywood is at a spot where they're trying to be on the right side and get ahead of things ... because people care and want to humanize people who are being dehumanized.... This is a story that people were excited to tell and it's an exciting time for [narratives] that haven't been told."[10] Clearly, streaming has opened its doors to new ideas and perspectives that viewers weren't seeing elsewhere. Hulu gave Youssef the tools he needed to tell his story, and both have greatly benefited because of it.

Originally owned by NBC Universal and News Corporation, Hulu launched to the public in 2008 with 220 television shows and 148 feature films.[11] In April of 2009, at the urging of Providence Equity (which owned a 10 percent stake), the Walt Disney Company joined Hulu as a stakeholder, with plans to offer content from ABC and the Disney Channel. At this point, three of the four major networks (ABC, NBC, and Fox) had interests in Hulu. In December of 2017, Disney announced that they would acquire 21st Century Fox, including its 30 percent stake in Hulu. The sale was completed in March of 2019 and resulted in Disney having a controlling 60 percent interest in Hulu. Comcast's NBC Universal is currently the minority stakeholder with plans to either sell to Disney or buy them out by 2024.[12] In 2020, eight months after Disney took over, Hulu CEO Randy Freer stepped down and the CEO position was dissolved. Hulu was then overseen by chairman of direct-to-consumer and international operations Kevin Mayer, who stepped down soon after to become CEO of TikTok. He was replaced by Rebecca Campbell, who previously served as Disneyland Resort president. Today, Hulu offers a large catalogue of streaming content, original programming, and a live television option for its 41.6 million subscribers.[13] Disney also owns the streaming service Disney+, which launched in 2019. In addition to *Ramy*, Hulu has several other shows that feature diverse characters. For example, *PEN15* (2019–2021, Maya Erskine, Anna Konkle, and Sam Zvibleman), *Woke* (2020–2022, Keith Knight, Marshall Todd), and *Reservation Dogs* (FX on Hulu: 2021–2023, Sterlin Harjo, Taika Waititi) all feature at least one main character who is BIPOC.

Despite having successful shows that feature BIPOC characters, it's important to note that Hulu recently came under fire for its lack of diverse programming by Zoë Kravitz, who starred in the Hulu comedy series *High Fidelity* (2020, Veronica West, Sarah Kucserka). After the show was cancelled by Hulu, Kravitz posted on social media, "It's cool. At least Hulu has a ton of other shows starring women of color we can watch. Oh wait."[14] Furthermore, the success of *Ramy* and similar shows should not undercut the fact that there are tremendous inequities in the television industry, both in front of and behind the camera. According to UCLA's "Hollywood Diversity Report: 2020 Television," about 32 percent of studio chair and CEO jobs are held by women and about 8 percent are held by people of color.[15] A year later, in their 2021 report, which looks at the 2019–2020 television season, they report that 24.3 percent of episodes were directed by people of color and 23.3 percent of shows were written by people of color.[16] These numbers leave much to be desired. When minority writers have managed to break through, they often feel viewed as a "diversity hire" by their white colleagues and are asked to represent their entire race in the writers' room. In her *Washington Post* article, author Sonia Rao quotes *The Good Place* writer and executive story editor, Cord Jefferson,

Chapter 4. Ramy

who says, "people will just populate the room with people of color or queer people or women but not really respect those people's voices or pay attention to what they're saying.... It feels like you're diversity decoration a little bit, as opposed to a valuable member of the team."[17] As previously mentioned, in front of the camera, BIPOC individuals have fared a little bit better. However, problems still persist. According to the 2021 UCLA report, when looking at scripted leads in the 2019–2020 television season across broadcast, cable, and digital, Latinx and Asian leads were underrepresented and Native American leads were nonexistent.[18] When looking at broadcast only, MENA leads were also nonexistent, further underscoring the significance of shows like *Ramy*.[19]

As established in the previous chapter on *Atlanta*, a much preferable alternative to colorblind shows are color-conscious shows, in which race shapes the nuances of both the show and its characters.[20] *Ramy* is one such color-conscious show because it authentically explores Ramy, his family, his friends, and his community members, all of whom are Arab American, and was created by Youssef, who is also Arab American. Again, one could consider this show as going beyond color-conscious to color-centric. In addition to diversity in terms of people of color and ethnicity, the show also portrays diversity in terms of religion. Ramy is devoutly Muslim, and from the first episode, he prays, goes to mosque, and abstains from drugs and alcohol. More importantly, he continuously looks for ways in which his faith can evolve. This can range from small acts, like wearing a *jellabiya* (a traditional garment) to the mosque during Ramadan, to larger acts, like traveling to Egypt during a crisis of faith. Despite his religious convictions, much of the show centers on Ramy's difficulty in following Muslim customs, resulting in Ramy being portrayed as flawed, conflicted, and complex. Ramy is caught between the Muslim world, which is grounded in tradition and provides a path to spiritual salvation through adherence to a strict moral code, and the secular world, where Ramy can open himself up to new experiences and live his life free of judgment. As one can imagine, these two worlds are often at odds with one another. As Youssef put it in an NPR interview, "I'm a Muslim-American, and I feel most like the hyphen between these two words."[21] In *The New York Times* article "Ramy Is a Quietly Revolutionary Comedy" by Sophan Deb, Youssef elaborated further, saying, "I do believe in God.... I realized that there was this void in entertainment of someone talking about that genuine construct.... I want to pray, and then, I also go out, and I have a girlfriend."[22] "Do the Ramadan" (S1, E5) perfectly encapsulates how Ramy's faith is often at odds with the world around him. The episode opens with Ramy and a group of other Muslims praying before the sun rises as part of Ramadan. An old acquaintance, Shawn (Gus Halper), spots Ramy and tells him that his mother is ill. After

Ramy assures him that he will pray for her, his friend insists that he "do the Ramadan" and pray for her right then. What follows is an awkward yet humorous sequence in which Ramy prays in front of his friend in Arabic, while occasionally interjecting "Shawn" and the name of his friend's mother, "Jackie." Often, Ramy's faith is a square peg, and the world around him is a round hole.

As Youssef is a stand-up comedian, it makes sense he would choose an approach for *Ramy* that incorporates an authentic portrayal of a diverse community that comes from personal experiences. After all, the primary job of a comedian is to convey their singular thoughts and experiences to the audience in a humorous way. Much of Youssef's stand-up routine is deeply personal and goes back and forth between the spiritual and the profane. One minute, he can be talking about how he believes in God, and the next, about having sex without a condom.[23] Similar to his stand-up, *Ramy* is in equal parts an intimate and an irreverent look at one man's journey through life. And yet, there is a universality present in *Ramy*, much like his stand-up. The problems that the main character faces, both as an adult and as a child, are the same problems that many people grapple with, regardless of race, ethnicity, or religion. In that way, *Ramy* is similar to other shows like *Girls* (HBO: 2012–2017, Lena Dunham) and *Insecure* (HBO: 2016–2021, Issa Rae, Larry Wilmore).[24] Ramy must navigate work, dating, friendships, and his family just like everyone else. An example of *Ramy*'s universality is "Strawberries" (S1, E4), which focuses on Ramy's childhood. In it, young Ramy (Elisha Henig) has his world turned upside down in the wake of the terrorist attacks in the United States on September 11, 2001. And yet the episode is just as much about Ramy's inability to "jerk off" like other boys his age and his acute embarrassment about this when talking with his friends. The juxtaposition of these two storylines is no coincidence. One stems from Ramy being Muslim, while the other stems from a universal desire to conform in a group. Yet they are both equally devastating to young Ramy. When discussing the episode on the podcast *The Last Laugh*, Youssef said, "A big part of this show is trying to say, 'Hey, we're humans, and so, what is the most human thing that could be happening under one of most devastating headlines? And what would it look like if those things happened at the same time?'"[25] In Derek Lawrence's *Entertainment Weekly* article "A golden match: Ramy Youssef and Mahershala Ali are each other's biggest fans," Youssef talks about how people belonging to different faiths can relate to Ramy's quest for spiritual fulfillment. He says, "I got an email from this guy in Nebraska, like, 'I'm an evangelical Christian, and I am Ramy'... I couldn't believe it. I feel really proud when people say, '[*Ramy*] made me think about my spiritual practice and want to connect to it more.'"[26] Ramy's experiences, aspirations, and

Chapter 4. Ramy

struggles, though deeply personal, often transcend culture and religion, allowing viewers the chance to relate to Ramy in a meaningful way.

In order to fully appreciate the significance of *Ramy*, a brief history of Arab and Muslim representation in television is needed. After 9/11, a "war on terror" was declared in the United States and has continued up to the present day. This has led to television shows depicting Muslims as terrorists, misogynists, sex fiends, and/or dictators, such as in *24* (Fox: 2001–2010, Joel Surnow, Robert Cochran), *Sleeper Cell* (Showtime: 2005–2006, Ethan Reiff, Cyrus Voris), and *Tyrant* (FX: 2014–2016, Gideon Raff).[27] Negative depictions of Muslims were prevalent long before 9/11, however, and in the late 1970s, scholar Jack Shaheen emerged as the leading voice on Arab and Muslim representation in television and film. In his 1984 book *The TV Arab*, Shaheen analyzed more than 100 shows and their depictions of Arabs and Muslims. He concluded that "television tends to perpetuate four basic myths about Arabs: They are all fabulously wealthy; they are barbaric and uncultured; they are sex maniacs with a penchant for white slavery; and they revel in acts of terrorism."[28] These depictions clearly had an impact on the public's perceptions of Arabs and Muslims as evidenced by a poll conducted in 1980 that Shaheen cited, in which Muslims were characterized as "cunning," "unfriendly," and "anti-American."[29] A later Gallup poll conducted in 1993, shortly after the first terrorist bombing at the World Trade Center, concluded that 32 percent of Americans had an unfavorable view of Arabs.[30] After 9/11, with a few exceptions, negative depictions of Arabs and Muslims went into overdrive. Out of all the post-9/11 shows that depict Arabs and Muslims in an offensive and stereotypical manner, *Homeland* (Showtime: 2011–2020, Howard Gordon, Alex Gansa) is often cited by critics as the most egregious offender. In her *Washington Post* article titled "'Homeland' is the most bigoted show on television," Laura Durkay writes, "The entire structure of 'Homeland' is built on mashing together every manifestation of political Islam, Arabs, Muslims and the whole Middle East into a Frankenstein-monster global terrorist threat that simply doesn't exist."[31] Once again, these negative portrayals seem to have contributed to many Americans having a negative perception of Islam. According to a report issued in 2017 by the Pew Research Center, 41 percent of all U.S. adults thought Islam encourages violence and 50 percent thought Islam is not part of mainstream American society.[32]

Ramy combats these stereotypes. In an interview on *The Daily Show with Trevor Noah* (Comedy Central: 2015–2022), Youssef stated, "We haven't really had any chance at seeing ourselves onscreen in a story that doesn't involve explosives or national security.... This is just the story of this family and we're really going to kind of humanize them by watching them deal with their problems in the way that everyone does."[33] Youssef is also quick to point out that *Ramy* isn't meant to represent all Muslims everywhere. In *The Wrap* article "Why Ramy Youssef Doesn't Intend 'Ramy' to Represent Every Muslim Experience," author Omar Sanchez quotes Youssef as saying, "I didn't want to claim at any point that I was speaking for anyone other than myself.... This is just one type of Arab Muslim family. We have different food and different experiences from other Arabs."[34] In a *Shondaland* article, "Ramy Youssef Isn't Trying to Represent All Muslims, He Just Wants to Be Himself," Youssef expands on this further. He's quoted by Alya Mooro as saying, "there's not a lot of content, especially coming from, let's say, English language content, that's trying to even authentically speak to these experiences. So the audience is put in this weird situation, because a show like mine gets talked about like it's *the* Muslim show."[35] Cleary, Youssef is telling a story that reflects his unique perspective and experiences. Given that there are roughly 1.8 billion Muslims in different communities all around the world,[36] it is impossible for one show to speak for them all.

To be fair, *Ramy* is not the only post–9/11 show to counter negative Muslim stereotypes. *Grey's Anatomy* (ABC: 2005–present, Shonda Rhimes) introduced surgical resident Dr. Dahlia Qadri (Sophia Ali) in Season 14. Dr. Qadri is not only Muslim but she is also the first major character to wear a hijab on the show. *Grey's Anatomy* doesn't just stop at having Muslim representation. There are several instances where Dr. Qadri's faith is put on full display. For example, in "You Really Got a Hold on Me" (S14, E13), while treating a patient, Dr. Qadri removes her hijab and uses it as a tourniquet to prevent a patient from bleeding to death. Dr. Hunt (Kevin McKidd), who is her attending physician, later asks her why she took off her hijab. She replies, "It's a symbol of my faith. And my faith is about service and compassion." Following the episode, Iman Zawahry, filmmaker and lecturer in the Department of Media Production, Management, and Technology at University of Florida, took to social media to express her gratitude toward the show. She stated, "Two years ago when I first taught 'Islam, Media and Pop Culture' I couldn't find one good example of positive portrayal of Muslims in television and definitely not a hijabi on camera.... This minor, simple line and character shows humanism, understanding and unity in our community."[37] Another example is CIA director James Greer on the political action thriller *Tom Clancy's Jack Ryan* (Amazon Prime Video: 2018–2023, Carlton Cuse, Graham Roland). Based on characters from the book series written by Tom Clancy, *Jack Ryan* could be accused of falling into the same traps as shows like *Homeland* and *24*. In season 1, the main antagonist is an Islamic terrorist named Mousa bin Suleiman (Ali Suliman), who Ryan (John Krasinski) must stop before he commits another terrorist attack. Ryan's

Chapter 4. Ramy

boss and confidant is CIA director James Greer (Wendell Pierce), who also happens to be Muslim. Greer's faith is notable, in part, because of his occupation. As CIA director, Greer is integral in protecting American values both at home and abroad. Put simply, episode after episode, Greer's patriotism is on full display.[38] When the show brings up his faith, its juxtaposition with his career is no coincidence. In "The Wolf" (S1, E4), Greer and Ryan partner with French authorities to track down Suleiman's brother Ali (Haaz Sleiman), who they believe is in southern France. Greer finds himself being driven by a French police officer, who confides in Greer that Islam means "submission" and then proceeds to complain that Muslims are taking over France "from the inside" and warns that it may be "*Sharia* for all of us." Not missing a beat, Greer pulls out his *Tasbih*, or Muslim prayer beads, and begins to pray, saying he uses them "when I'm unable to pray or when I need Allah to grant me restraint." It's important to note that Greer is not Muslim in Clancy's original book series. The character shift was the result of creators Carlton Cuse and Graham Roland wanting to have a variety of Muslim characters represented, including some that are heroes.[39] The trend is clear. Show creators are putting more thought into how Muslim characters are represented now than ever before.

While shows like *Grey's Anatomy* and *Jack Ryan* contain examples of post–9/11 characters that actively work against Muslim stereotypes, it's worth noting that these and other examples are typically recurring or supporting characters, not the star of the show. Examples of shows in which Muslim characters are front and center are exceedingly rare. There are a few, however, that we can point to other than *Ramy*. The show *Mo* (Netflix: 2022–present) deserves special mention, as it is co-created by Ramy Youssef and Mo Amer, who also plays a supporting character on *Ramy*. Amer stars as the title character, who is a Palestinian refugee living in the United States. Another such show is the Netflix comedy drama *Master of None* (Netflix: 2015–2021, Aziz Ansari, Alan Yang) that stars Aziz Ansari as Dev, a 30-year-old actor living in New York City. Dev was raised in a Muslim household but does not consider himself to be religious. Some of the show's humor even centers on Dev pretending to be a more devout Muslim in front of his family than he actually is. For example, in "Religion" (S1, E3), much of the humor derives from Dev trying to hide his pork-eating habits from his parents. The show *Chad* (TBS/Roku: 2021–present, Nasim Pedrad) takes a similar approach. Chad, a 14-year-old boy played by the 39-year-old actress Nasim Pedrad, will do almost anything to be popular. In the pilot episode, when Chad's mom Naz (Saba Homayoon) starts dating a Muslim man, Chad admits that he is embarrassed to be Muslim and sees it only as a deterrent to him fitting in. On a side note, Pedrad, who created the show, insisted on playing the title character because she felt it would add to the show's comedic sensibility.⁴⁰ As we have established, the characters in *Master of None* and *Chad* are in stark contrast to Ramy, who doesn't distance himself from his Islamic roots. Rather, he fully embraces aspects of Islam. When Ramy is confronted with a crisis of faith, he faces it head-on, making *Ramy* rather unique.⁴¹

Another way in which *Ramy* differentiates itself from other shows like *Grey's Anatomy*, *Jack Ryan*, *Master of None*, and *Chad* is Youssef's willingness to take on controversial issues. In Episode 4, the stress of young Ramy becoming a social outcast overnight due to 9/11 leads him to dream that Osama bin Laden (Christopher Tramantana) is in his kitchen eating strawberries. What follows is one of the most memorable monologues from the series. Speaking to Ramy, bin Laden explains that Egyptians were forced to turn their wheat fields, which provided bread for Egyptians, into strawberry fields because their country "owes money to men in suits." He goes on to explain that the strawberries are for Westerners, not Egyptians. Youssef is able to pull off this nuanced look at 9/11 because, once again, he stays true to his experiences. Ramy's house on the show is even modeled after Youssef's childhood home, complete with pictures of him as a kid on the walls.⁴² Youssef has been candid about the profound impact 9/11 had on his life. In a *Bustle* article titled "Why Ramy Youssef Says 9/11 Made Him 'More Muslim,'" Rebecca Patton quotes Youssef as saying, "I was told it was my fault. I was told that the most horrible thing that I had ever seen happen, to this day, was because of who I was, where I came from, the language that I speak, and my faith.... I realized, not only was that not true, but [being Muslim] was something that I really wanted to be a part of my life."⁴³ Youssef isn't afraid to show the events of 9/11 from the perspective of a Muslim American kid and the complex emotions felt in its aftermath.

Although much of *Ramy* dispels Muslim stereotypes, it also pokes fun at those stereotypes while acknowledging prejudices that exist within Muslim communities. This is reminiscent of *Atlanta*, which uses humor to critique flaws within Black communities. This brings us to Ramy's Uncle Naseem, who is the brother of his mother and Ramy's employer. In many ways, Uncle Naseem can be sexist, bigoted, crude, violent, and antisemitic. He seems to be tolerated by Ramy and his immediate family only because they are related. In "Uncle Naseem" (S2, E9), the focus shifts to Ramy's uncle and it is revealed that he is gay. To Ramy's father, Farouk, there are few things worse than being gay. His homophobia was revealed earlier in "Saving Mikaela" (S1, E8) when he finds out about Ramy's affair with the wife of his friend and concludes "at least you're not gay." This homophobia also extends to other Muslim characters in the show. For example, in the Pilot, Ramy's date, Nour (Dina Shihabi), tells him about her father giving the sex talk, which consisted of "Girls, no boys. Boys, no boys." Insensitivity is also shown later on in Season 2 when Ramy's mother, Maysa, misgenders a transgendered person. In many ways, Uncle Naseem is the embodiment of a Muslim stereotype, but his sexuality also reveals skeletons in the closet that those within his community would prefer not to acknowledge. *Ramy* tackles these topics head-on.

As previously stated, *Ramy* takes the time to show various perspectives within Ramy's community, including back-to-back episodes in Season 1 that focus on Ramy's sister and mother, respectively. At times, these episodes may lack the same level of authenticity the show has when Ramy is front and center, but Youssef's efforts to present the female Muslim perspective still offers a great deal of value to the viewer. At this point, it's important to emphasize that some Muslim stereotypes are reserved solely for women. In the BBC article "How Muslims Became the Good Guys on TV," author Mohammad Zaheer points out that, historically, Muslim women are often viewed as "exotic" and "subservient."[44] Dr. Margreet van Es, assistant professor of religious studies at Utrecht University, takes it one step further. In an essay published by Palgrave Macmillan, she says, "the 'oppressed Muslim woman' stereotype does not only deprive women with a Muslim background [of] their individuality, but also positions them as outsiders to the society they live in."[45]

In "Refugees" (S1, E6), the focus shifts to Ramy's sister, Dena, as she contemplates dating a white, non–Muslim man named Kyle (Jake Lacy) and grapples with the fact that she is a 26-year-old virgin; she attributes the latter to her strict and overprotective parents. In the episode, Dena dreams that her parents walk in on her and Kyle having sex. Uncle Naseem walks in soon after, followed by Ramy, who is on his way to "hang out with this girl." While their response to Dena having sex is shock and disgust, they all collectively revel in Ramy's sexual prowess. Dena's grandmother comes in next and Dena is informed by her father that she came all the way from Egypt to watch her have sex. The sequence culminates in a refugee telling her, "Instead of praying for us, you have sex." Clearly, Dena's nightmare was caused by stresses that Ramy, even as a fellow Muslim, has trouble relating to. Later on, Dena's actual date with Kyle ends badly after he confesses to fetishizing her ethnicity. This episode reveals that Dena doesn't possess a "hall pass" like Ramy does to test the boundaries of Islam. Her path to a moral life is expected to be a straight line, while Ramy is permitted to take twists and turns along the way.

In "Ne Me Quitte Pas" (S1, E7), the focus shifts to Ramy's mother Maysa. In the episode, Maysa is depicted as being unhappy with various aspects of her life. Her discontent leads her to start driving for Lyft, a job that she hopes will be liberating because she can meet new people. She eventually meets a charming Frenchman named Jacques (Jean Brassard), a reference to Jacques Brel who wrote the song "Ne Me Quitte Pas" (Don't Leave Me),[46] for which the episode is named. Maysa bonds with Jacques by speaking French with him and quickly becomes infatuated, agreeing to give him subsequent rides. When Maysa realizes Jacques is romantically involved with someone else, the evening ends with her washing off her make-up in the restroom of a fast-food restaurant. Much of Maysa's discontent stems from her feeling ignored by her husband and children and, once again, her husband and Ramy are unable to empathize.

The most common way in which Ramy challenges his own religious convictions is through his romantic relationships, particularly through not abstaining from sex (at least not for long). In the very first scene of the Pilot, "Between the Toes," Ramy's mother encourages him to meet a nice Muslim woman at the mosque. A little later, despite his Muslim friends warning him that "white girls suck," we learn that Ramy is involved with a Jewish woman named Chloe (Anna Konkle). After Ramy and Chloe have sex, Chloe discovers Ramy checking the used condom for holes by filling it with water in the bathroom. Visibly shocked and "kind of offended," Chloe explains to Ramy that if she did get pregnant, she would "do the responsible thing" and get an abortion. Ramy responds that he's "pro women getting to choose what to do with their bodies," but since he's Muslim, he's "pro us not having to make that choice." Chloe responds by saying, "You're Muslim, I thought, in the way that I'm Jewish. Like, it's a cultural thing. I didn't know that you were Muslim-Muslim." Clearly, Ramy was not up front with Chloe about his beliefs, nor about the fact that she would not be fully embraced by Ramy's family and friends. Ramy has initiated a relationship that, deep down, he knows cannot continue. Later in that episode, Ramy asks his mother to set him up with a Muslim woman (much to her delight), and she arranges the date with Nour. Everything is going well, until Nour attempts to have sex with Ramy. Initially shocked by her forwardness, Ramy ends the sexual encounter after she asks him to choke her. Nour is quick to point out Ramy's hypocrisy, saying that he would have no problem having sex on a first date if she were a non–Muslim. She accuses Ramy of putting her "in this little Muslim box" and says, "I'm supposed to be the wife or the mother of your kids, but I'm not supposed to cum." Just as some might stereotype Ramy for being Muslim, he was stereotyping Nour for being a female Muslim. Much like the character Ramy, Youssef admits to having limited experience when it comes to dating Muslim women. In his *Vulture* article "There's Never Been a Show Like Ramy—How a weird, personal, sexually complicated, and yes, Muslim-American comedy, made it to TV," Gazelle Emami quotes Youssef as saying, "In my own life, I was probably pushing away experiences with

Muslim women because of some of these barriers.... Because we don't talk about sex in our communities, we don't have sex with each other."[47] On a side note, Youssef has also admitted to his own limitations when it comes to writing female characters, which is a problem exacerbated by the show's creators all being men. According to Youssef, he has attempted to remedy this by diversifying the show's writers' room with new hires, including three Muslim women.[48]

There are other romantic relationships that further affect Ramy's efforts to stay within the boundaries of his faith. In "A Black Spot on the Heart" (S1, E3), Ramy becomes involved with a non–Muslim woman named Sarah (Molly Gordon). Once again, she is Jewish, making a lasting relationship unlikely. Not only is Ramy dating outside of his faith, but he also is drawn to relationships that many would consider taboo. Ramy meets up with Sarah at a party she's hosting and she encourages him to take ecstasy with her. Ramy tells her that he's never done drugs before and decides not to do it. She ends up hooking up with another guy and Ramy leaves the party soon after. Before he leaves, Sarah tells him, "I feel so bad for Palestine," alluding to tensions between Muslims and Jews. His failing relationship with Sarah ultimately leads him to test his faith-based morality further by taking some of Steve's medical cannabis. Similarly, in Season 1, Episode 8, the first time Ramy drinks is when he is on a quest to help Steve have sex, though this time he's a wingman. In "Do the Ramadan" (S1, E5), Ramy's next relationship begins with good intentions. He meets a married woman named Salma (Poorna Jagannathan), whose car is blocked in at the mosque. Ramy offers to carry her son home and the two strike up a conversation afterward. She expresses dissatisfaction with her marriage, and in short order, the two have sex. They continue to meet for sex in secret thereafter. Unlike Chloe and Sarah, Salma is Muslim. The fact that she is married, however, makes her forbidden to Ramy. Once again, he chooses to enter into a relationship that cannot have a future and his morality is further eroded by having sex with a woman who is married and who has a child. Salma eventually ends the relationship and confesses her infidelity to her husband.

Ramy's affair with Salma then causes him to have a crisis of faith. In "Dude, Where's My Country?" (S1, E9), Ramy travels to Egypt in hopes of finding himself. This proves to be difficult for Ramy, as his Americanized cousin Shadi (Shadi Alfons) is much more interested in partying than praying. Ramy was expecting everyone in Egypt to be spiritually enlightened, once again proving that he is susceptible to stereotyping those within his own community. Ramy also starts hanging out with his cousin Amani (Rosaline Elbay). Similar to Ramy, Amani is trying to figure out her life (in her case because of a recent divorce) and the two have an instant connection. They end up kissing after Amani takes Ramy to pray. In Season 2, we learn that they had sex while Ramy was in Egypt. Amani is Muslim, but the fact that they are cousins makes the relationship taboo. Later, in "You Are Naked in Front of Your Sheikh" (S2, E10), Ramy is finally set to marry Zainab (MaameYaa Boafo) a Muslim woman that he has a meaningful connection with, but he sabotages the relationship by sleeping with Amani again. In Season 1, Episode 9, before having sex with Amani, Ramy makes an important realization about himself. When talking to Amani about his dating life, he says, "I've dated women who think it's crazy I believe in God. Like, God God, not yoga.... I've dated Muslim women and I feel like the problem's really that I just don't know what kind of Muslim I am." Until Ramy figures out what kind of Muslim (and person) he wants to be, his relationships will leave him with more questions than answers and he will continue to hurt people along the way.

It's important to note that not everyone is on board with how women, specifically Muslim women, are represented on *Ramy*. Some may feel that, despite Youssef's intentions, female characters aren't given enough agency. In her article in *The Atlantic*, "What 'Ramy' Gets Wrong About Muslim Women," Shamira Ibrahim writes, "the frame of reference for *Ramy*'s female Muslim characters is rather limiting, one that denies the significant power they hold within their own faith systems."[49] On the popular blog *Muslim Girl*, writer Nailah Dean vents her frustration about dating men like Ramy, who dive headfirst into relationships without considering the implications. She says, "The Ramy Man never wants to choose. He wants to have his cake and eat it too."[50] According to Dean, "The Ramy Man" uses relationships to explore his own moral boundaries and faith with a certain reckless abandon, giving little thought to those he hurts along the way.

Another source of diversity on *Ramy* comes from Ramy's best friend Steve (Steve Way), who has a rare form of muscular dystrophy, both on the show and in real life. In Way's case, he has Ullrich congenital muscular dystrophy, which according to him, is so rare that only one other person is known to have his specific genetic mutation.[51] As a result, Steve makes use of a wheelchair and needs assistance with most daily tasks. Ramy and Steve are best friends in real life as well as on the show. Similar to on-screen representations of Muslims, depictions of disabled characters have a long and troubled past. Historically, disabled characters on television, especially recurring characters, were exceedingly rare. If a show does attempt to accurately portray a character with a disability, there are still several pitfalls that the show can fall into. Often times, characters with disabilities are defined by their disability and are either meant to be pitied or exist as a tool to educate viewers. In her *IndieWire* article "Disability in

Chapter 4. Ramy

Television: Who Was the First Disabled Person You Saw on Television?" Kristen Lopez points to an episode of *Saved by the Bell* (NBC: 1989–1993, Sam Bobrick) as an example. In "Teen Line" (S4, E6), high school student Zach Morris (Mark-Paul Gosselaar) goes on a blind date with a girl named Melissa (Jennifer Blanc-Biehn) without knowing beforehand that she is in a wheelchair. When discussing the episode, Kristen Lopez writes, "more often than not, these characters weren't actual people, just conflicts meant to give a teachable moment to the able-bodied main leads."[52] Often, disabled characters are denied the complexity and nuance that other characters are given. A study conducted by Nielsen and the nonprofit organization RespectAbility revealed another troubling trend. Approximately 95 percent of disabled characters are played by actors who do not have said disability.[53] At this point, it should be noted that Jennifer Blanc-Biehn was able bodied when she played the disabled character on *Saved by the Bell*. Steve Way has been candid about his inability to land roles prior to being cast as Steve. In an interview conducted by Michael Stahl titled "How a Lifelong Friendship Led to Steve Way's Ramy Role," published in *Vulture*, Way stated, "I can't tell you how many times I've auditioned for a disabled person's role and I was the only disabled actor, and I still didn't get it."[54] On *Ramy*, Steve is not defined by his disability nor is he routinely pitied for it. Rather, Steve is a nuanced character who is funny, profane, and, at times, reprehensible. At the same time, the show doesn't hide the harsh reality of Steve's muscular dystrophy, such as in "Princess Diana" (S1, E2) when Ramy helps Steve clean himself in a public restroom. Even then, Steve adds some levity to the situation by telling Ramy, "Don't half ass it. I know when your heart's not in it."

Ramy also doesn't rob Steve of his sexuality, as is often the case with disabled characters. When we are introduced to Steve in the pilot episode, he is heckling Ramy for swiping no on women with burqas on his Muslim dating app. He then muses that he loves it when "they're covered head to toe like that" because "the mystery is sexy." In "Saving Mikaela" (S1, E8), Steve strikes up a relationship with a girl named Mikaela he met online through a video game. They decide to meet in person and Ramy agrees to come along. When they arrive, Mikaela and her friend get drunk and Ramy realizes that they are both 16 and in high school. (Steve points out that the age of consent in New Jersey is 16.) Steve pursues a sexual interaction with Mikaela despite Ramy's warnings, which ends in total disaster. In "Authentically Casting People with Disabilities and Talking About Sex: Why You Should Watch 'Ramy,'" Maria Maddux discusses the importance of Steve's sexual agency. She writes, "'*Ramy*' offers a window into the sexual needs of people with disabilities in a way that is rarely seen by mainstream audiences. Because sexual agency is a hallmark of adulthood, the idea that people with disabilities do not or should not be interested in sex reinforces the patronizing stereotype that disabled people are child-like and asexual."[55] Steve has autonomy over his life and his sexuality and Ramy supports his decisions, even when he disagrees. A perfect example of Steve's agency occurs in this episode when Ramy expresses concern about Steve smoking a blunt with Mikaela because he uses a ventilator. Steve replies, "I use a ventilator so I can live ... for this." Later, in "Atlantic City" (S2, E7), Ramy and Steve share an equal parts tender and cringeworthy sexual experience together as Ramy helps Steve have an orgasm at Steve's urging.

The good news is that, over this past decade (and especially within the past five years), on-screen representation of both physical and mental disabilities have changed for the better. According to the Nielsen/RespectAbility study, the number of film and television characters with disabilities this decade increased by more than 175 percent compared to the previous decade.[56] In their annual "Where We Are on TV" 2020 study, GLAAD (Gay & Lesbian Alliance Against Defamation) found that the number of television shows that regularly feature disabled characters had risen to a record-high 3.5 percent, which was a 0.4 percent increase from their 2019 study.[57] What do these studies demonstrate? The needle is indeed moving toward increased representation of characters with disabilities. However, given that there are 61 million Americans who have a disability that impacts major life activities,[58] the numbers still aren't where they need to be. Also, the way in which disabled characters are depicted, and who depicts them, continues to be an issue. On a side note, it should be pointed out that Steve is white. As Ramy's best friend, he fills a role that a Muslim character might typically be relegated to in a group of white friends. This role reversal is no mistake. In his *Daily Show* interview, Youssef said, "So many times in sitcoms you see an ethnic best friend, and, in this show, we're predominantly with an Arab cast ... and we're like, 'all right, I guess we're going to have to have the white best friend.'"[59] Youssef is currently working on a new show for Apple TV in which Way will star.

At this point, the question must be asked, is *Ramy* funny? To be clear, if the humor doesn't resonate, it undermines the diversity and authenticity of the show. Our Recent TV Trends students overwhelmingly said yes. But it is also true that *Ramy* is decidedly darker than its comedic predecessors like *The Office* (NBC: 2005–2013, Greg Daniels), *30 Rock* (NBC: 2006–2013, Tina Fey), *Parks and Recreation* (NBC: 2009–2015, Greg Daniels, Michael Schur), and *Community* (NBC: 2009–2015, Dan Harmon). The same can be said for its contemporary counterparts, such as *Fleabag* (BBC Three/BBC One: 2016–2019, Phoebe Waller-Bridge), *Barry* (HBO: 2018–2023, Alec Berg, Bill Hader), and *Dead to Me* (Netflix: 2019–2022, Liz Feldman). It

Chapter 4. Ramy   89

also relies on awkward, situational humor that often focuses on the taboo. In the first two seasons, topics covered include sex, incest, prostitution, masturbation, sending "dick pics," drinking, drug use, and gambling. In Season 1, Episode 3, Ramy's irreverent brand of comedy is on full display. As previously mentioned, Ramy decides to take drugs for the first time. He then goes to dinner with Steve and Steve's mom, Mrs. Russo. Visibly high, Ramy launches into a monologue about how Mrs. Russo's life "sucks" because of Steve and how she must feel guilty because when Steve was born, she "didn't give him enough body." He concludes that she'll outlive Steve and have to pick out a coffin but assures her that the baby coffin will be cheaper. On its face, the scene is heartless and needlessly cruel. However, between Ramy's earnest delivery, Mrs. Russo's uncomfortable reaction, and Steve's insistence that Ramy "shut the fuck up," the monologue works comedically. In an interview conducted by Matt Grobar and published *by Deadline*, Youssef discusses the show's brand of humor. He says, "genuine awkwardness has to come out of showing stuff that you don't want to show, in a real way.... I think it's actually genuinely awkward, because of what we get into, and I think that's what excites me with the show."[60] Ramy has an overabundance of awkwardness, which leads to some truly hilarious moments.

With shows like *Ramy* becoming more prevalent, there is a growing debate about the role comedy should play in public discourse. In addition to *Ramy*, shows like *Transparent* (Amazon Prime Video: 2014–2019, Joey Soloway), *Insecure*, and *Atlanta* have been lauded by critics for sparking national dialogues on topics like gender, race, and religion. In their book *A Comedian and an Activist Walk Into a Bar: The Serious Role of Comedy in Social Justice*, authors Caty Borum Chattoo and Lauren Feldman argue that the current state of the television industry and society's renewed focus on social issues have set the stage for socially critical comedies to thrive. In addition, they believe these shows play a role in bringing about social change. They write, "As a far reaching projector of cultural values and narratives, contemporary mediated comedy can serve as a site of cultural resistance.... Dominant shared norms are fluid, and popular culture both reflects and shapes societal values and beliefs."[61] In regard to *Ramy*, however, Youssef has at times been wary of putting the weight of social justice on the shoulders of comedy shows like his. In a *New York Times* interview conducted by David Marchese, titled "Ramy Youssef Is Not Using Comedy to Teach You About Muslims," Youssef says, "It's like there's this weird role reversal in what society wants. They want comedians to have every talking point be *on* point and every piece of art equally represent this and that. That's what politicians should do—and now our politicians are a joke."[62] He goes on to call this the "'Daily Show' effect" and concludes by saying, "don't get [the news] from me."[63] This echoes similar comments made by *Atlanta* creator Donald Glover, which were discussed in the previous chapter. Still, the positive impact that *Ramy*, and other similar shows, have had on public discourse is undeniable. Even Youssef acknowledges that *Ramy* has started conversations on sexuality and religion that weren't being had prior.[64] *Ramy* is a show that explores the nuance and complexities of a community that, historically, has only been seen through a narrow lens. At the same time, Youssef stays true to himself and his story, making *Ramy* a truly remarkable feat.

III

Sexual Candor

Chapter 5

Vida

Sex-Positivity in a Drama

Vida is a drama set in Los Angeles that premiered in 2018 on STARZ and ran three seasons. The central characters are two Mexican American sisters in their twenties, Emma (Mishel Prada) and Lyn (Melissa Barrera), who have returned home because their mother, Vidalia (Rose Portillo), has died. They must decide what to do with Vidalia's apartment building as well as the bar on the ground floor. What they find is Eddy (Ser Anzoategui), their mother's grieving widow, as well as old loves they left behind. As with *Normal People*, *Vida*'s half-hour format was greeted as refreshing by critics, although by Season 3, there were longer episodes that reached 40 to 50 minutes. In January 2016, STARZ announced *Vida* as one of three shows from Latinx creators as part of its "programming strategy of seeking diverse voices,"[1] according to Chris Albrecht, the CEO of STARZ at the time. It is noteworthy that Chris Albrecht was the former Chairman and CEO of HBO who brought in shows like *The Sopranos* (1999–2007, David Chase), *The Wire* (2002–2008, David Simon), *Six Feet Under* (2001–2005, Alan Ball), and *Deadwood* (2004–2006, David Milch). Lesley Goldberg, in a review in *The Hollywood Reporter*, notes, "While *Vida* has struggled to pull a large audience on the premium cable network, it ranks as a poster child for critical darlings. Seasons one and two both carry a rare 100 percent rating among critics on aggregate site RottenTomatoes.com."[2] *Vida* received this critical acclaim not only because of its distinctive Latina voice but because it was striking in many other ways as well.

Vida's creator, Tanya Saracho, first had a career as a playwright in Chicago, writing 16 plays and directing 14 of them. She then wrote for such shows as *How to Get Away with Murder* (ABC: 2014–2020, Peter Nowalk), *Looking* (HBO: 2014–2016, Michael Lannan), and *Devious Maids* (Lifetime: 2013–2016, Marc Cherry). When former STARZ executive Marta Fernandez reached out to her in 2016, Saracho assumed that it was about another writing job. She was stunned when she was offered a

Chapter 5. Vida

chance to create her own show.³ Saracho states, "They wanted a female millennial show about *gentefication*, which is the gentrification of a Latinx space.... The queerness came from me. I identify as queer, and it had to be there."⁴ Saracho assembled an all-Latinx writers' room, with all but one identifying as female and half identifying as queer.⁵ By the second season, Saracho decided to hire all Latina directors. In addition, all the production department heads were women, and the casting director, composer, and editor were all Latina. In "How Starz's 'Vida' Created a Safe Space to Explore Latinx and Queer Stories," Pilot Viruet states, "This all adds up to a series that feels free of the male gaze, every step of the way. It makes for queer sex scenes featuring women, and genderqueer people, that aren't filmed from the perspective of a straight man."⁶ One of the directors that Saracho hired, Catalina Aguilar Mastretta, comments, "Tanya's in a position of power, and she's empowering other people that are like her."⁷ In many interviews, Saracho has emphasized how important it is to have more Latinx shows and more Latinx creative professionals involved in every aspect of the industry, and she has done her utmost to help make that a reality.

Vida is an apt example of both trends we've already established, "Authenticity" and "Diversity," in terms of its up-close-and-personal perspective of Latina protagonists, one who is queer and one who is straight, as well as its insider view of Latinx culture in Boyle Heights. It's important to note that those identifying as Latinx (or Hispanic) comprise 18.5 percent of the population of the United States and yet Latinx representation in the television industry is at roughly one third to one quarter of that across a variety of positions and delivery platforms. To clarify, "Latinx" is the gender-neutral term describing those in or from Latin America, including Portuguese-speaking people such as Brazilians, whereas "Hispanic" refers to speakers of Spanish. An article from *Variety* in October 2021 uses UCLA's "Hollywood Diversity Report: 2021 Television" to report the following: "the share of total cast roles in television for the 2019–2020 season for Latinx actors stood at just 6.3% for broadcast, 5.7% for cable and 5.5% for digital.... Furthermore, the UCLA report's analysts estimated that Latinx directors were responsible for only 5.4% of the episodes in broadcast, 3.5% in cable and 3% in digital. Latinx representation amongst credited writers remained just as bleak, with just 4.8% in broadcast, 4.7% in cable and 4.3% in digital."⁸ The article continues with "Representation in the writers' room matters. You could say, 'Well, it's simple, let's just multiply the Tanya Sarachos and Gloria [Kellett] Calderóns,'" said NALIP (National Association of Latino Independent Producers) executive director Benjamin Lopez, referring to the success of the *Vida* and *One Day at a Time* showrunners. "It's not as simple because most of the next generation in line haven't been able to access a writers' room in the first place."⁹ Melissa Barrera, who plays Lyn, comments, "I mean, there have been other Latinx shows on TV, but … I think you can count them with one hand, and to sort of be like the frontrunners of this new movement of inclusion on television and telling these stories and giving these voices, like, a platform is so important."[10] Tanya Saracho is quoted as saying, "There's so much TV and we get five shows? That's the crime right there. Hopefully we will start to reflect how much space we take up in this country."[11] But it's not enough to just put representation on the screen; it must be done in an authentic and resonant way in order to draw viewers in.

Something that was important to Saracho was to show variations and differences within the identities highlighted on the show. Tracy E. Gilchrist in "Vida Boldly Tackles Identity Policing Among Queer People" states, "And counter to early shows like *The L Word* and *Queer as Folk* in which the characters embraced a kind of sameness in their LGBTQ circles, *Vida* continually pushes at the margins of queer identity."[12] The article is referring to *The L Word* (Showtime: 2004–2009, Ilene Chaiken, Michele Abbot, Kathy Greenberg) and *Queer as Folk* (Showtime: 2000–2005, Ron Cowen, Daniel Lipman), which was based on the British version of *Queer as Folk* (Channel 4: 1999–2000, Russell T. Davies). In the same article, Saracho is quoted as saying, "I wanted people's real perspectives to happen, and it's not all *Kumbaya* because we're all queer. It can't be."[13] Saracho also explores differences that come up within the Latinx community. In *The New York Times* article on colorism, Tanya Saracho talks about encountering what she calls the authenticity police: "You're not brown enough, you're not light enough, you're not Mexican enough. Your Spanish is not good enough."[14] This is highlighted on the show when Lyn is frequently reminded that she never learned to speak Spanish properly, whereas Emma decided to do so. Both of them, however, consistently use Spanglish, as do most of the other Latinx characters on the show. Jared Richards, in his *Guardian* article, notes, "The result is Vida … a show that makes no apologies for trading in specificity to create a refreshing, lived-in world. Which, yes, means that unless you're Latinx and queer, you'll probably miss a few references or jokes. You may, say, not be able to follow as characters code-switch into LA Spanglish, sans subtitles."[15] The point is that the show is skillfully enough written to make it easy for those viewers who aren't in the know to figure out the intended meaning from the context. Part of the delight of *Vida* is that viewers can become so immersed in the characters' lives, culture, and community that they can readily understand what's relevant to the story.

Another important aspect of the show's accurate representation is its central theme of *gentefication*, which is gentrification done by upscale Latinxs moving into traditional Latinx neighborhoods. Ludwig Hurtado writes, "Boyle Heights is experiencing unfettered and unprecedented transformation. The Mexican American neighborhood, located just east of Downtown Los Angeles, was once characterized by its taquerías and quinceañera shops. Today, the barrio is glittered with new boutique coffee spots, bars, and record stores.... Recently, the barrio has seen an influx of upwardly mobile, college-educated, Mexican Americans."[16] The term *gentefication* was created in 2007 by Guillermo Uribe, the owner of the wine bar Eastside Luv as a positive way to describe what was happening in the neighborhood. He said in a 2014 interview with *Los Angeles Magazine*, "If gentrification is happening, it might as well be from people who care about the existing culture. In the case of Boyle Heights, it would be best if the *gente* decide to invest in improvements because they are more likely to preserve its integrity."[17] But the community group Defend Boyle Heights (DBH) and affiliated groups do not agree with this position and make it their mission to fight all gentrification, including *gentefication*. Within the show, it is the character of Mari (Chelsea Rendon) who belongs to the Vigilantes (similar to DBH) that is the face of the movement against *gentefication*. When Lyn sees Mari in the pilot, Lyn tries to diffuse a tense situation by telling Mari to say hi to her brother, Johnny, for her. Mari replies, "Uh, nah, sorry. I won't be doing that. You're persona non grata around here, Lyn Hernández. Everyone always knew you were a fucking *puta* [whore]. Both of you *whitetina* bitches." With the second insult, Mari is commenting on the fact that both Emma and Lyn have been immersed in white worlds, Emma in Chicago working in a high-powered job and Lyn in San Francisco dating white men who have funded her free-spirited lifestyle. Now that the sisters are back in Boyle Heights, their fashion choices (a corporate look in Emma's case and a hippie look in Lyn's case) stand out. Emma makes light of it by saying, "It isn't a homecoming until someone calls you a *puta*." Julia Barajas, in her *Los Angeles Times* article, makes the point that it's odd that three of the precious few Latinx shows are set in L.A.'s Eastside. Besides *Vida*, those shows are *Gentefied* (set in Boyle Heights) and *On My Block* (set in the fictional community of Freeridge, modeled on Lynwood in East L.A.).[18] The *gentefication* of this specific area of Los Angeles is a major theme of both *Gentefied* and *Vida*, although clearly, *gentefication* occurs in other major cities around the country as well. This topic could potentially be a difficult one to dramatize, but Saracho has found a worthy vehicle for this through the characters of Mari and others in the Vigilantes group who challenge Emma and Lyn directly about what they are doing with Vidalia's bar and building. This serious topic takes time to develop on the show, but it is counterbalanced from the beginning by the show's utter delight in its depiction of the sex-positive lifestyles of the two sisters.

At its simplest, "sex-positive" denotes consensual sex without judgment or shame. It relates to the term "sex positive feminism," which implies sexuality where women have agency. For "sex-positive," a Google search elicits "having or promoting an open, tolerant, or progressive attitude towards sex and sexuality."[19] And for "sex-positive feminism," a Google search elicits "centers on the idea that sexual freedom is an essential component of women's freedom."[20] These Google searches demonstrate commonly-held meanings and reflect what our students intend when they use these phrases. In our Recent TV Trends course, we've found that it is especially female students who are quick to note when a show is sex-positive, with one of their prime examples being *Fleabag* (BBC Three/BBC One: 2016–2019, Phoebe Waller-Bridge), which frankly presents the female protagonist's sexual activities. In *Vida*, it becomes apparent that the two sisters, Emma and Lyn, have agency and a wide spectrum of what they enjoy within the sexual arena. They also refrain from judging others' sexual interests or activities, except in cases where it represents a personal failing of some kind (and an example of this will be given later). In her *TV Guide* article "Starz's 'Vida' Is Plenty Sexy—But Every Graphic Moment Counts," Sadie Gennis states, "The show's portrayal of authentic, and quite graphic, sex—specifically queer, Latinx sex—is groundbreaking."[21] A hallmark of *Vida* is its incorporation of sex-positivity in a primary way within the story.

One of the possible critiques of *Vida*'s sexual content could be that it plays into stereotypical representations of Latinxs, and Latinas in particular. Isabel Molina-Guzmán states in her book *Latinas & Latinos on TV*: "Latina/o characters, however, are often characterized in stereotypical and mostly binary ways as the Latin lover or harlot, the dark lady or bandito, the female clown or male buffoon, and the señorita.... All the types are depicted as more sexual than their white counterparts except for the señorita archetype, who is often a character defined by her religious virtue and conservative sexual morality."[22] What's interesting is that the actress playing Lyn, Melissa Barrera, talks about how hard it is for her as a Latina to do the sex scenes on the show. She says, "But still, when we get to the first day that I have to do a nude scene, it was like, I wanted to cry all the time.... I don't know if it's a Latina thing. It's a shame thing that we've been taught. That it is shameful to show your body. That if you cover up, you're more worthy."[23] Frederick Luis Aldama and Christopher González make the point in their book *Reel Latinxs: Representation in U.S. Film & TV*, "No matter our massive variety as a people, we're generally mainstreamed into the hypersexual and exotic."[24] They make a particular case regarding the depiction of Latinas: "All this perpetuates a history of Latinas becoming sexual objects right before the public's eyes."[25] What makes this type of critique difficult to apply to *Vida* is that the female characters own their sexuality, and as Tanya Saracho puts it, *Vida* is a "Latinx female-gaze show."[26] In addition, the show knowingly comments on the act of fetishizing Latinas and doesn't ignore this concern. In "Episode #1.4," when Lyn first meets Jackson, a white man, in a coffee shop, she ends up going to his friend's house where he's staying. She greets the housekeeper, Aurora, in Spanish and his comment is "There is nothing sexier to me than when you guys roll your 'r's.'" Later, when all the partyers are lounging around the pool, a woman (later identified as Harper) says to Lyn, "I am obsessed with your eyebrows," and then she suggests that Jackson invite Lyn to Mammoth the next weekend, adding, "You don't understand. I'm in love with her." Finally, when the owner of the house throws up, Harper calls out, "Aurora! Charlie threw up again!" She then tells Lyn and Jackson that she feels bad that Aurora must keep cleaning it up. Jackson's reply is "Don't. That's what she's here for." When Lyn heads home, she's sitting on the bus a few rows behind Aurora. Tanya Saracho's comment is that Lyn is thinking, "We are the same thing to these people."[27] She is finally realizing that she isn't fitting in with white culture the way she believes she is. In this episode, the show acknowledges the damaging stereotypes and assumptions that result from a white gaze. But in most of the series, it is the Latinx gaze that predominates.

Despite its casual use, the term "sex-positive feminism" does have a specific origin and history. In her book *The Right to Sex: Feminism in the Twenty-First Century*, Amia Srinivasan provides the following summary: "Did porn kill feminism? That's one way of telling the story of the US women's liberation movement, which exploded with such joyous fury and seriousness of purpose in the late 1960s, yet within the space of a generation had become a fractured and worn thing. Debates about porn—is it a tool of patriarchy or a counter to sexual repression? A technique of subordination or an exercise of free speech?—came to preoccupy the women's liberation movement in the US, and to some degree the UK and Australia, and then to tear it apart."[28] This debate about whether to condemn or condone porn was interwoven with varying views on how sex itself fit within a feminist framework. It was Ellen Stein, who co-founded a radical feminist group called Redstockings in 1969, who clarified anti-sex and pro-sex feminist perspectives, culminating in a pivotal essay titled "Lust Horizons: Is the Women's Movement Pro-Sex?" that came out in 1981. Srinivasan explains, "Threading between the poles of pro-woman and anti-sex feminism, Willis led the way in the development of what came to be called 'pro-sex' or 'sex-positive' feminism."[29] Of course, currently, it is impossible to imagine limiting the availability of porn since internet porn has become ubiquitous and irreversibly part of our culture. In her book, Srinivasan turns her attention to the effect of porn on today's youth and states, "My students would not have stolen or passed around magazines or videos, or gathered glimpses here and there. For them sex was there, fully formed, fully interpreted, fully categorized—*teen, gangbang, MILF, stepdaughter*—waiting on the screen.... The psyches of my students are products of pornography. In them, the warnings of the anti-porn feminists seem to have been belatedly realized: sex for my students is what porn says it is."[30] Srinivasan relates asking her students an important question in her feminist theory course: "Does porn bear responsibility for the objectification of women, for the marginalization of women, for sexual violence against women? Yes, they said, yes to all of it."[31] As a result of these realities, Srinivasan reports that many young women are now identifying themselves as feminists.

An important point regarding the effects of porn is that many of today's young people believe that they are expected to be emotionally detached in their sexual lives. Srinivasan states, "My male students complained about the routines they were expected to perform in sex; one of them asked whether it was too utopian to imagine sex that was loving and mutual and not about domination and submission."[32] In her article "Will We Ever Figure Out How to Talk to Boys About Sex?" Peggy Orenstein, the author of *Girls & Sex* and *Boys & Sex*, echoes this point: "According to Andrew Smiler, a psychologist specializing in adolescent male behavior who surveyed over a hundred teen boys about dating and sex, most guys, in fact, prefer physical intimacy with someone they know, trust and with whom they feel comfortable. I found that to be true, too, though they seemed to view it as their personal quirk, not shared by their peers."[33] So, even though the desire for emotional connection to a sexual partner was prevalent, young men thought they were unusual in feeling that way. Michelle Goldberg, in her article "Why Sex-Positive Feminism Is Falling Out of Fashion" in *The New York Times*, states, "The word 'demisexual' refers to those attracted only to people with whom they share an emotional connection.... Now an aversion to casual sex has become a bona fide sexual orientation."[34] Goldberg's article advocates for a return to emotionally-based sex and partially blames sex-positive feminism for the lack of emotion: "Somehow, as sex positivity went mainstream and fused with a culture shaped by pornography, attention to emotion got lost." But is sex-positivity truly antithetical to emotional attachment? Not necessarily. And this becomes an essential element in the discussion of *Vida*.

Vida goes out of its way to expand sexual boundaries, defy expectations, and simply mix it up. Emma is queer; has sexual partners that are male, female, and non-binary; and has her own unique set of rules and desires. Lyn is straight (although she mentions some fluidity in her past) and has sex with men in all kinds of situations: wearing a dildo to screw a man, participating in an orgy, and eating a man's ass. As for the latter, which happens in "Episode #1.2," Melissa Barrera, the actress playing Lyn, didn't know what ass-eating was and called Saracho about it. Saracho's advice was to watch some porn.[35] The ass-eating moment happens when Lyn is with her San Francisco boyfriend, Juniper, in a hotel room in Los Angeles and he proceeds to break up with her. When he talks about finding closure, Lyn says, "Here's closure for you. You waited to dump me until after I ate your ass." Later, in the first episode of Season 2, Lyn participates in an orgy in the house of Jackson's friend, Charlie. We see a man going down on Lyn, but she brushes him away. Next, we see two women kissing and then a man pushes his body up against Lyn, as she casually hands him a condom. When the man lifts Lyn up and enters her, he decides to collapse onto the sofa with her. The result is that she pushes him off her. Another man comes up to Lyn and starts stroking her leg. She isn't interested and walks out of the room, just as one of the women throws up. Apparently in the script, this scene was written as "the world's saddest orgy."[36] Catalina Aguilar Mastretta, who directed this episode, remarks, "At this point in her life, Lyn is ready to move past this kind of shallow experience. You want the audience to realize with Lyn that she's a little bit better than this."[37] So a scene like this proves the sex-positivity of the series, in terms of the acceptance of all sexual practices where there is consent, but it also makes a statement about the lack of emotional attachment, or even genuine desire, among the people involved in this particular orgy. After Lyn walks out of the room, she says to another woman that she's done with all this, a point that is significant in her personal journey.

As for scenes that demonstrate the show's sex-positivity regarding Emma, we see her having her toe sucked by a non-binary partner in an erotically charged scene in "Episode #1.3" and then we see her push them over a table and finger them from behind. We later find out that the app hook-up is named Sam, played by queer writer Michelle Badillo.[38] Next, Emma aggressively pushes Sam down on the ground, removes her own panties, and sits on Sam's face. Emma is clearly the one in control and this is mirrored in her interactions with men as well. In "Episode #2.1," we see Emma packing up her toiletries in a hotel room as a man's hands reach around her. She asks why he isn't doing as he's told, and we see that it's one of the guys she worked with in Chicago. She then sits in a chair, wearing only a bra and panties, and tells him to take his clothes off. When he starts taking off his underwear, she tells him that she doesn't need all that today.

She takes off her panties and turns around, leaning on an armchair. He brushes her ass with his lips, and the scene cuts. Clearly, Emma intends to get what she wants from her sexual encounters. Even the scenes of Emma masturbating in "Episode #1.5" comment on the control that Emma seeks in her sexual life. The episode opens with Emma in her bedroom getting out a vibrator while hearing Eddy, her mother's widow, in the living room with a circle of women praying with rosary beads—all of which ends up being too distracting for Emma. One interpretation of the scene is that it illustrates the friction between Emma's sexual agency and the Catholic teachings of her childhood. But there is also more to it. At the end of the episode, we see that Emma is trying to masturbate again, but this time, she is distracted by the noise from the bar as Vidalia's friends give her the ultimate send-off. Emma finally starts crying, one of the few times since her mother died. In her *TIME* article "No Other Show Captures the Pleasures and Frustrations of Real Life Quite Like *Vida*," Judy Berman states, "I can't think of another series airing now that so freely depicts sex and sensuality without being exploitative or gratuitous; each of these scenes expresses more of what's going on behind each character's defense mechanisms than dialogue could ever reveal."[39] And that's the perfect way to describe what is happening in these scenes with Emma, especially since her defense mechanisms have seemed impenetrable up to this point. But through sexual activity, her inner emotions are revealed to the audience.

Increasingly, *Vida* becomes a fulfilling exploration of "story-progressing sex," a more desirable form of sexual depiction in narratives than "titillating sex," which can seem like soft porn clumsily inserted into an ongoing story. Story-progressing sex can also be more effective than "idealized sex," where sex is portrayed in overly romanticized and often vague ways, whether that's through the use of soft-focus or abstract shots of body parts. With story-progressing sex, the sexual interaction among the characters is depicted precisely, including sex acts that are specific and not generic. In addition, the depicted sex furthers the story and contributes to the development of the characters and the ongoing dynamic between those characters. This is similar to Len Abrahamson's approach to directing the sex scenes in *Normal People*, which in turn is an extension of the way Sally Rooney views sex as a dialogue between characters. As Sadie Gennis states in her *TV Guide* article, "And after all the praise for the graphic, in-your-face sex of Season 1, Saracho and her writers were mindful when crafting the new sex scenes that they remain authentic and story-driven at all times in the show's anticipated sophomore run."[40] What *Vida* offers is both sex-positivity and story-progressing sex.

One of the components of story-progressing sex is that it is usually tied to emotionally involved (rather than emotionally detached) sex, in

Chapter 5. Vida

large part because storytelling is typically dependent on the emotional interaction, as well as the deepening bonds, between characters. In the first season, *Vida* proclaims its sex-positivity through the variety of sexual behaviors that are portrayed, but it also includes sex scenes between characters who are developing intimate bonds with each other. In Season 1, both sisters start having sex with crushes from high school: Johnny (for Lyn) and Cruz (for Emma). In a SAG-AFTRA video with the cast of *Vida*, Stacey Wilson Hunt, the Hollywood editor for *New York Magazine* and *Vulture*, asserts that Johnny going down on Lyn in the pilot is a groundbreaking scene.[41] Lyn and Johnny proceed to have intercourse, all of which occur on the outdoor stairs leading down to the basement, and to top it off, it's during the reception at the bar after Vidalia's funeral. When they're done, Lyn says to Johnny, "Now back to the baby mama," referring to Karla, with whom Johnny came to the gathering. Johnny retorts, "She's not my baby mama. She's my fiancée." Lyn says, "That's what I meant." He says, "Oh, man, how could I fucking forget? Miss Superior Ass Lynda Hernández." With these lines of dialogue, we are witnessing a significant emotional exchange between Lyn and Johnny that has been generated by the sex they've just had. And then in the next episode, "Episode #1.2," Johnny tells Lyn, "But I shouldn't have gone to the *velorio* [funeral] because I should have remembered about you. I should have remembered that you'll always be a *mala hierba* [bad weed]." Even though Johnny is helplessly attracted to Lyn, he is also aware that she's oblivious to the havoc she's wreaking on the life he has carefully built. When they have sex again in "Episode #1.3," Johnny says to her, "I just mean you got some wild new tricks in your repertory. I like it. It's like the old Lyn, just like 2.0 and freaky. Your body, too. Like these." He sucks on one of her nipples. "I mean, I like them, I'm not going to lie, but also there was nothing wrong with the old ones either." Lyn gets up abruptly, puts on her dress, and leaves. Because Barrera's breast implants are noticeable in the nude scenes, it was a smart move for the show to acknowledge them. But this scene was about more than that. Toward the end of "Episode #1.3," Johnny takes Lyn to a look-out point at night, with the lights of L.A. below them. He talks about meeting Karla and how he got his life together because of her. Lyn says, "You could have just told me this in text. You didn't have to bring me to the most romantic parking spot in the city to break my heart." After he apologizes for the comment he made about her breasts, Johnny says, "I think you're the most beautiful thing that's ever walked the world and I didn't want you to go off thinking otherwise." Lyn is crying and says, "I didn't even want to get them done." Referring to Juniper, Johnny asks, "Did that asshole make you do it?" Lyn answers, "Not that asshole. But another asshole. And he didn't, like, force me. I just didn't know how to say no." As Tanya Saracho says, "This is the only thing that Lyn knows how to do—to jump from one guy to another."[42] As expected, Lyn and Johnny are soon drawn back together again, and Johnny breaks up with Karla. In "Episode #1.6," Lyn asks Doña Lupe, who lives in the building, to do a *limpia* (cleansing) for her. Lyn stands in the bathtub as Doña Lupe washes her and blows smoke around her. Later, Lyn takes off the white dress she was wearing and puts it in a bag. Doña Lupe says, "This bag contains *toda la porqueria* that I just removed from you ... the muck that is all the sorrow and doubt." Later in the episode, Lyn sees Karla crying after spilling her groceries, and then, when Lyn is talking to Johnny, he tells her that his family's auto shop is losing business because he broke up with Karla. He talks about wanting to get away from the neighborhood. Suddenly, she says, "I'm *la porqueria*." Afterward, Lyn confronts Doña Lupe: "What have you done to me?" Lyn continues to say that she broke up with Johnny and she doesn't even know why she did it. Doña Lupe says, "I only set you right. You set things straight." This is a turning point for Lyn, whom Emma describes as a "full-on agent of chaos" in "Episode #1.3." Although Lyn claims that drama just follows her around and she can't do anything about it, she gradually understands (over seasons 2 and 3) that she reaps what she sows.

As for Emma, her developing relationship with Cruz in the first season is an important first step in handling some of her personal issues. In "Episode #1.4," after Emma has been drinking and dancing with Cruz, she says something to her that's revealing and important to the overall story: "I never wanted to leave. Vidalia sent me away. You know that one day she found me with Lucy, this little girl that lived in the building and we were, I don't know, touching, I guess, kissing, and we were, like, eleven, and Vida freaked the fuck out. And there I went to live with *Abuelita* in south Texas." She was sent away a second time after Vidalia found her journal and her poems, which were all about Cruz. In this scene, Emma rationalizes it as her mother working out her gay shame by sending her away. Later in this episode, we see Cruz and Emma kissing passionately. Emma is feeling her up and then forcefully turns Cruz around and continues. Then, Cruz turns back to her and puts her fingers seductively in Emma's mouth. Everything seems fine, but then suddenly Emma collapses onto the floor. She has trouble breathing and her ears are ringing. When Cruz goes to get her some water, Emma sneaks out. One possible explanation for the collapse is that it was caused by Emma's conflicted feelings about Vidalia's death and the issues with the bar and the building. But a more likely explanation is that getting physically and emotionally closer to Cruz after confiding in her about her mother has made Emma's fear of intimacy come roaring back. Emma is clearly more comfortable when she is sexually detached. As we see the relationship between Emma and Cruz develop, there are some interesting moments that demonstrate Emma's unease with Cruz's growing familiarity. In "Episode #2.2," we see Emma and Cruz in the shower together. They try to have sex, but, as Emma says, "a shower thing never works." Then, Cruz gets out of the shower and pees on the toilet, which obviously annoys Emma. There is a change in their dynamic, however, in "Episode #2.3." We see Cruz kissing Emma's backside and then turn her around as she chooses a vibrator from four that are laid out. Emma moans with pleasure and says, "Go inside me ... wait, that's ... that's too much. Less, less. Fuck, I lost it," which becomes a relatable moment for many viewers. Cruz then goes down on Emma and brings her to orgasm. Afterward, Cruz summons the courage to ask Emma to accompany her to her *primo*'s (cousin's) wedding. Emma, feeling good, unexpectedly says "yes" and Cruz is pleased.

The wedding in this same episode ("Episode #2.3") is a pivotal scene. First, we see Julio and Luis, two white-clad Latino grooms dressed as *vaqueros* (cowboys) walk in, smiling and relaxed. Jenée LaMarque, the director of this episode, comments, "Just seeing this beautiful queer brown wedding, we all got kind of choked up when we saw the guys walk down the aisle."[43] After the ceremony, Cruz puts Emma on her lap when they are sitting at the table with Cruz's friends, Amanda and Tasha, and with a woman, Nico, who has just joined them. As Emma quickly gets off her lap, Cruz says, "She doesn't do public displays. I'm still working on her." Amanda says, "Oh, no, I get it. When I was a baby queer, I was all shifty in public too." Emma doesn't take this well, and yet the insinuation continues when Tasha later says, "The shifty never leaves the tourist," to which Emma retorts, "You didn't just call me a tourist." Nico contributes her opinion: "For real? I haven't had to deal with the concept of tourists since Shane was flipping bitches on *The L Word*." And, suddenly, we like Nico for coming to Emma's defense. When Tasha tells Emma that she passes, Nico says, "Oh, oh, so she should get an asymmetrical haircut or something, or a rattail to telegraph it to the world. Seriously, Emma, how else are queers supposed to announce themselves if not through the confines of the binary?" Emma says, "Thank you." And that's essentially the beginning of Emma and Nico. In coming up with the scene, Saracho remarks, "We need to have Emma be called a tourist and we just talk about this problem in our community that we police each other. Finally, it fit.... We had this wedding, a queer wedding, so it's like, 'How queer are you? How legit are you?'"[44] But the relationship with Cruz must come to an end before the relationship with Nico can truly get going. And Cruz delivers the final blow herself. Still at the table at the wedding, Cruz says, "Pretty Emma here chooses not to identify." When Amanda uses the term "baby queer" again, Lyn says to her,

"Stop saying baby queer. I'm sorry I don't abide by your dated categories of queers. I'm sorry that you think I'm confused or indecisive because I have a wide range of what I can get off to." Cruz interjects, "Now, that, getting off, I'll drink to that, and I'll drink to the little break-through we had this morning. Let's just say Baby Girl thawed. She just had to relax into it for once." And with that unpardonable breach of privacy, coupled with Cruz's condescending judgment, "Baby Girl" gets up and leaves. Emma and Nico end up talking outside and Emma invites her to come by the bar. In short order, Emma hires her as a bartender and as a consultant to develop the drinks and décor for the bar.

Besides the topic of internal policing in the queer community, *Vida* also deals with the dangers for queer people who are out in the straight world. A primary example involves Eddy, played by Ser Anzoategui, an actor who identifies as trans and non-binary. In "Episode #1.6," the finale of Season 1, Emma argues with Eddy about the bar, now called simply "Vida." (And, of course, it's symbolic that "*vida*" means "life." The bar is life, just as Vida gave Emma and Lyn life.) After the argument, Eddy ends up leaving and going with her friends to another bar. When a man harasses one of Eddy's lesbian friends, Eddy stands up to him and gets him to back down. Afterward, she's pumped up and orders a round of drinks for her friends. Later, when she goes to the bathroom, the man bursts through the door and severely beats her up. After Emma and Lyn visit Eddy in the hospital, finally acknowledging her publicly as their stepmother, Emma ponders whether Eddy has insurance to cover the hospital stay. When Lyn is astonished that this is what Emmy is thinking about, Emma replies, "No, Lyn, that's not the only thing I care about. What I care about is that I basically sent Eddy off to get beat unconscious and there's nothing I can do about that." It's a turnaround for Emma to understand the repercussions of her actions, which she often feels have been completely justifiable, even when they hurt other people. Emma says, "And I looked at [Vidalia's] broken wife today and I thought, God, that must've taken guts walking around this neighborhood together." Emma finally accepts that the bar is a haven for queer Latinas and voices her wish to do the bar right but better. And what follows is a gratifying scene of Emma and Lyn drinking on the roof of the building until sunrise, making their plans for the bar. Then, there's a cut to the little girl that Emma has been glimpsing throughout the first season, holding the hand of an unconscious Eddy in the hospital. We see Eddy's arm with the tattoo "Vidalia" across it. Then, we see the older version of Vidalia holding her hand. It's a fitting end to the first season. Saracho says, "We begin with Vida. We end with Vida."[45] Since the pilot showed a scene with Vidalia collapsing and then dying, it made sense to see this version of Vidalia at the end of Season 1, still watching over her love, Eddy.

Chapter 5. Vida

Another character worthy of discussion is Mari, who is Johnny's sister. She seems like a high school student, but she's actually 21 and she quit community college to have more time to take care of her father, her Ápa, who has health problems. She also works two jobs at the beginning of the series, one at a donut shop and the other at a nursing home. But her true passion is the Vigilantes, which, as already mentioned, is a community group that protests the gentrification, as well as the *gentefication*, of the neighborhood. Mari, who posts her videos under the name "*La Pinche Chinche*" (loosely translated as "The Fucking Nuisance"), is the very first character we see in the show. Saracho states, "We open with, thematically, with Mari, as the Greek chorus. She is the voice and soul of the neighborhood."[46] In "Episode #1.3," we see Mari with a guy she likes, Tlaloc, in the Vigilantes headquarters. First, he tells her that her hair is nice and then he kisses her. Then he unzips his pants and Mari goes down on him. He tells her, "You really know how to handle me, don't you?" and then, without Mari noticing, he takes out his phone and records it. Reflecting on this kind of scenario, Peggy Orenstein states, "In my own interviews with high school and college students conducted over the past two years, young men that I like enormously—friendly, thoughtful, bright, engaging young men—have 'sort of' raped girls, have pushed women's heads down to get oral sex, have taken a Snapchat video of a prom date performing oral sex and sent it to the baseball team. They all described themselves as 'good guys.' But the fact is, a 'really good guy' can do a really bad thing."[47] In *Vida*, the video gets out and Tlaloc claims to not know how it happened. In "Episode #2.2," when he is in Mari's bedroom with her, he talks to her about the video and says, "I was being a fucking gorilla." He continues with "You know how I feel about consent, right?" We assume that this is as unclear to Mari as it is to us since he hasn't spoken a word about consent up to this very moment. He then says, "Let's make it about you tonight." He takes off her pants and goes down on her, which proves to be a rare moment. By "Episode 2.6," he's back to the usual routine. Mari goes to his house to talk to him about the possibility of her going back to school, and his response is to kiss her, unzip his pants and lean back so she can give him a blowjob. Orenstein states a college sophomore told her, "Guys will say, 'A hand job is a man job, a blow job is yo' job.'"[48] It is important to point out that Mari is still a virgin, which we know because her best friend, Yoli (Elizabeth De Razzo), establishes that Mari still has her "V-card" at several points in the show. It is clear that Mari's sexual choices are influenced by the Christian traditions of her father and her community. The outcome of the situation with Tlaloc is that Johnny finds out about the video in "Episode #2.7" and beats Tlaloc up. When Mari rushes to Tlaloc's house to see how he is, he breaks up with her in short order. When Mari returns home, she is angry with Johnny about what he did to Tlaloc. Ápa overhears them and demands to see the video, which Johnny shows him. Ápa says to Mari, "I don't want to see you. You are not welcome here." So Mari receives the short end of every possible stick. At 21, she feels that she still needs to stay a virgin; she gets together with a man who is self-centered and primarily concerned with his own sexual needs; without her consent, the same man makes a video of her giving him a blowjob and the video gets out; he then breaks up with her because her brother has beaten him up; and, on top of it all, she loses the respect of her father and is kicked out of her home. Every man in this scenario has done her wrong. And much of it is the result of cultural and religious sensibilities concerning the rights of men to dictate the sexual behavior of women in the milieu that Mari has grown up in. Her situation presents the opposite of the sex-positivity enjoyed by the other characters on the show.

But Mari isn't the only woman to get involved with a problematic man. In Season 2, Lyn starts a relationship with Rudy, a Mexican American city councilman. The first time they have sex in "Episode #2.5," Lyn fakes an orgasm, only to find out that Rudy is somewhat soft and not really inside of her. She thinks the problem is with her, in that he doesn't find her attractive, and she is mortified. This is interesting for two reasons. First, Melissa Barrera is objectively quite beautiful, which she needs to be for the role, since the character of Lyn has been defined by her looks ever since she was a child. Second, Lyn immediately believes that the problem is with her, rather than assuming that there may be something going on with him. Rudy ends up reassuring Lyn that he thinks she's beautiful and then explains that the missionary position just doesn't turn him on. In this same episode, we find out more about how Lyn's self-perception was affected in childhood when she tells Doña Tita (an older family friend in the building) that her mother always told her, "Find a man, *mija* [my daughter]. That'll be the only way for you." Lyn says this in the context of feeling unable to be successful at anything in her life. This is belied in part by our witnessing Lyn's burgeoning expertise in managing the bar's entertainment, which also provides a reason for the many exquisite Latinx musical acts on the show. But Doña Tita reminds her that her mother did indeed give her something—she made sure that Lyn knew that she was a peacock. And Doña Tita tells her to use those feathers! By "Episode #2.6," we see Lyn wearing a dildo and screwing Rudy from behind, saying, "You like that, Senator Marquez?" Since he's a city councilman, she's stroking his ego by calling him a senator. She then does it too hard and he says, "Nice and easy." She slows down her thrust and then, in a teasing way, calls him "Mr. President." They're both obviously having fun with each other. In "Episode #3.1," Rudy says to her, "I'm so proud of you. So proud that

Chapter 5. Vida

I want to show you off." Lyn replies, "That's funny because being shown off is one of my favorite things." So, at this stage, they seem like a good match. Lyn is a peacock and Rudy wants a peacock. In addition, they are both adventurous sexually and seem to have a genuine rapport. In the same episode, Lyn and Rudy are having sex at his place, with him on top as he looks at himself in a mirror. Lyn starts to put a finger in his ass, but he says abruptly not to do that. When she says she's confused and points to the dildo lying on the floor, he says that he's okay with that because she's not looking right at him. In the same episode, another side of Rudy is revealed. Lyn has already had run-ins with his mother because she doesn't consider Lyn Mexican enough or worthy of her son. So, in this episode, Rudy encourages Lyn to let his mother help with the double quince Lyn is throwing for her friend Marcos (Tonatiuh). Rudy says, "Go borrow the centerpieces, babe. A little quality time between my two best girls would be good." The equation of his girlfriend with his mother is already somewhat suspect. It's also significant that the precious crystal punch bowl that Rudy's mother lends Lyn ends up getting broken at the party. Later in the episode, Rudy's mother tells Lyn, "I think it's good for a woman to entertain herself with work before marriage." And now it's clear that just as Mari's father is the upholder of everything traditional and patriarchal in Mexican culture, so is Rudy's mother, Silvia. In "Episode #3.5," Rudy tells Lyn at one of his political events (where his mother has already made Lyn cover up because she's not wearing a bra under a translucent blouse), "Let me do all the talking. You just smile pretty, like you always do." The culmination of this is a scene in "Episode #3.6," which starts on a photo of Rudy's mother. The camera then pans past the bed to Lyn kneeling and giving head to Rudy, who is sitting in a chair. Rudy says, "You really learned how I like it, *Mamita*. Learned how to get me ready for the day." His banter continues, and then he says, "I know *Mami*'s going to take you on a little shopping spree for bras later, but please don't bring up that punch bowl. If I have to hear one more thing about that fucking punch bowl...." Lyn lifts her head and says, "Okay, can we, like, not talk about your mother when your dick is in my mouth?" When Lyn gets up and starts getting dressed, Rudy comes up with the idea of her punishing him by peeing on him. When she doesn't respond well to this, Rudy says, "Hey, was that not cool to bring up? I was under the impression that we were comfortable enough that anything goes, as long as we consent, of course. Lyn, why are you acting so prissy and judgmental all of a sudden?" Lyn replies, "Okay, let's get one thing straight, Rudy. I don't care about you asking me to pee on you. It's what the peeing means to you." Lyn then draws the connection between his belief that getting peed on is a punishment and his "Mama Boy thing." Therefore, this scene clarifies that even though sex-positivity can mean being open to a wide range of sexual activities, it doesn't mean agreeing to everything. Lyn continues, "But, mainly, Rudy, what I didn't consent to was having your mom in here with us while I give you head. Literally." She gestures toward the photo of Silvia and the camera follows. "She has a fucking front-row seat." Lyn then says that she's breaking up with him. Rudy pleads with her, "We don't have to do the pee thing. We don't have to do anything you don't want to, ever." She replies, "But that's not really true, is it? Because I'll always end up doing whatever the fuck you want." And this brings up an interesting question. In her sexual activities, is Lyn servicing her male partners according to their dictates or is she demonstrating agency? Perhaps a bit of both. Yes, she may be caught up in doing what her lovers ask of her. On the other hand, she's certainly not passive and is clearly shown taking action in the sexual arena.

In terms of Emma's problematic interactions with men, there are two instances worth mentioning. The first occurs in "Episode #1.2" with Nelson, who wants to acquire the building for the Brobeck Group, which gave Vidalia a predatory second mortgage, with the result that now the debt is more than the building is worth. Nelson is Latino and grew up in the area, epitomizing the *gentefication* that Mari is so adamantly against. In this scene, Nelson is doing his best to convince Emma to sell the building. He puts his hand on her knee and says, "I want to take care of you here." Emma abruptly stands up and dumps a cup of hot coffee on his lap, saying, "I'll pay my mother's debt before I ever sell to you." As she leaves, he's covering up a hard-on and smiling wanly. Later, Lyn describes this as a "Me Too" moment for Emma. A different sort of scenario occurs with Baco, an ex-con who is doing work on the building. In "Episode #2.4," Emma tells Baco not to remove the graffiti from the bathrooms after all (since Nico has convinced her that it signals safety to the queer community) and then tells him to follow her to the office. The next thing we see is that she's sitting on him and getting off. So *Vida* turns the consent issue around in this instance by having the woman coerce a subordinate man to have sex with her. In "Episode #2.9," after having sex, Baco tells Emma that she doesn't even call him by his name but calls him Mr. Nava. She says that she's trying to be respectful. Baco replies, "You ain't respectful to me. You use me like a human dildo. And then when you're done with me, I'm just supposed to bow and say, 'Si, *patroncita*' and get lost." Emma says, "Oh, don't act like anyone forced you." Baco retorts, "See, that's something a shitty person would say. You're a shitty person, Emma, plain and simple. People aren't things you can just use and toss." By the next episode, "Episode #2.10," Emma shows up at his house, saying, "Baco, I behaved like a pig. And you were right to say it." She says that she has ended up in similar situations before but with people above her.

Chapter 5. Vida

Then she says, "This was different. And I feel like garbage." She apologizes to him, and he accepts it. Emma's remorse and recognition of her unfair conduct within the sexual arena clearly shows that she is growing as a person.

By the end of Season 3, we find out that Vidalia wasn't punishing Emma as a child by sending her away to her grandmother's but was actually protecting her from her father. We also get to meet the absent father, Victor, who has now re-entered their lives. He is a Christian preacher, and by "Episode #3.6," the finale of the series, he justifies taking them to court over the bar and the building with the condemnation, "It's clear that the perverted spirit of homosexuality that your mother left is still a curse on that place." Viewers now have more of an understanding of Emma's childhood and the homophobia she was exposed to through her father's religious convictions. It is further revealed that Victor beat Vidalia up when she tried to defend Emma after she was found with the little girl in the building. This revelation that Emma was being protected by her mother as a child offers closure at the end of the series because it demonstrates the importance of Emma having made this journey back home since one of the foundations of her personality had been that her mother had rejected her and her developing sexual identity. By the end of the series, she knows that her mother accepted her and loved her. One of the gratifying things about *Vida* is that, instead of ending on a cliffhanger as so many shows do, the story is wrapped up in a satisfying way. We also see that Emma becomes a kinder person through her association with Nico, whom Saracho imagined as her personal dream girl[49] and who is fittingly played by Roberta Colindrez. In "Episode #2.8," after Nico and Emma have an argument at the warehouse party, Emma says, "Every single person who violated my trust is no longer in my life. I don't come back from betrayal." And then, Nico holds out her hand, and truth be told, Roberta Colindrez has a sweet way of holding her hand out and inviting someone to take it, which Emma does. There are then several pivotal sex scenes between the two of them that demonstrate Emma's increasing ability to trust another human being. By "Episode #2.10," Nico is trying to convince Emma to be with her again and they steal a moment in the bar's bathroom on a busy night. Nico says, "I like you, Emma. I like you way too much for comfort. And you like me, too." Nico then kisses Emma's breasts and sucks on her nipples. When Nico starts to feel her up, Nico suddenly stops and smiles, saying that she should wash her hands because she was just recycling trash. It's a moment that makes the romance seem real. When the show cuts back to the scene, Nico and Emma are still in the bathroom. Emma reaches inside Nico's pants. They become passionate and Emma climaxes. Then, Nico sinks down into a squat with Emma straddling her. Nico says, "You gonna break out once I open that door?" Emma smiles and says, "Probably." It's an apt recognition of Emma's skittishness when it comes to relationships. Then, in "Episode #3.2," when they are in a bathtub together, Nico is lying down, and Emma is lying with her back on top of her. Nico is reaching her hands around to the front of Emma's body to stroke her and Emma appears to be enjoying a rare moment of uncomplicated contentment. So, unlike with Cruz, Emma finds out that it does work to have sex in a bathroom.

In *Vida*, the sisters' journeys are not the same. Emma must learn to open up to people and so it's important that she begin to trust Nico. Ironically, Lyn must do the opposite, learn to not give in to the man she loves but stand up for herself. In the finale of the show, "Episode #3.6," Lyn goes to Johnny, crying in distress about the bar. He says that he wishes he could fix it for her. They start kissing passionately. Lyn unzips her pants but then suddenly stops and says that they can't. Johnny reassures her that there's no Karla anymore. But he also hesitates and says that he doesn't want to be tossed aside again. She tells him that she wants to do it right. The point is that through the variety of sexual interactions on the show, the characters are both revealed and developed. Throughout *Vida*, the sex-positivity is heralded, but just as importantly, the sex scenes play a vital role in progressing the story.

Chapter 6

I May Destroy You
Overcoming Sexual Harm in a Drama

I May Destroy You is a 2020 limited series using a half-hour format created by Michaela Coel for BBC One and HBO that addresses sexual harm from the perspective of Arabella, a young, Black British woman. Michaela Coel wore many hats, including director (along with Sam Miller), executive producer, and lead actor, playing Arabella. Simon Maloney produced the first six episodes and Simon Meyers produced the last six episodes. The show was a tour de force and widely lauded. "*I May Destroy You* received an overwhelmingly positive critical reception, with BAFTA recognition [awards for Leading Actress, Direction, Writer, and Mini-Series], 98% approval on Rotten Tomatoes (at time of writing), and acclaim from around the world, with France's Le Monde declaring it a Top 10 TV show for 2020."[1] The series also won two Emmy awards, one for Outstanding Writing and one for Outstanding Music Supervision, as well as a Peabody Award, a GLAAD Media Award, an NAACP Image Award, two RTS Programme Awards and two Independent Spirit Awards. In her BBC Culture article, Leila Latif writes, "At number six in BBC Culture's poll of the 100 greatest TV series of the 21st Century, I May Destroy You is the most recent entry in the top 10 (having premiered in June 2020) and arguably both the most radical and of the 21st Century, in that no version of this show could have existed in the century, or even the decade, prior."[2] The show also presents a perspective that is rarely seen. Camilla Blackett, a Black British screenwriter, who has written for *Skins* in the UK and is working on a show for HBO, praises *I May Destroy You*, saying, "the thing that stood out to me was just how intrinsically [B]lack-British the show was…. It was our slang, our vernacular, our lived racial experience in what it is to live in this densely-populated multicultural postage stamp of land."[3] Since this show is primarily about Black British characters, only characters who aren't that will be identified by race, ethnicity, or national origin as needed within this chapter. Through this Black British perspective, the powerful voice behind the storytelling, and the candid discussion of sexual harm, there is a unique sensibility in *I May Destroy You* that establishes it as quite different from what has come before.

I May Destroy You fits well into the trend of "Sexual Candor" in that it was promoted as a drama that explores sexual consent. Just like *Vida*'s exploration of sex-positivity involves a frank examination of sex when there is consent, *I May Destroy You*'s exploration of sexual harm involves a frank examination of sex when there isn't consent. In this chapter, the term "sexual harm" will be used to cover the broad spectrum of consequences related to non-consensual sexual behavior that is depicted in *I May Destroy You*, some of which falls under legal definitions of sexual violence and some of which comprises ethical breaches. As a place to start, the National Health Service (NHS) in the UK states the following about consent for medical treatment: "For consent to be valid, it must be voluntary and informed, and the person consenting must have the capacity to make the decision."[4] These three basic conditions for valid consent fit sexual consent as well, but the complex ramifications of non-consensual sexual behavior require an articulation of finer points. A leaflet distributed by the NHS that explains sexual consent in legal terms (as defined by section 74 Sexual Offences Act 2003) includes a section on the "key issues for investigators and prosecutors," which are listed as "Capacity to consent; Freedom to consent; Steps taken to obtain consent; Reasonable belief in consent."[5] These categories are further explained as follows. "Capacity to consent" takes into consideration the state of the complainant, such as being drunk or drugged, having a mental health issue, or being asleep or unconscious. "Freedom to consent" includes factors such as the power dynamics in domestic violence cases or in other situations where the suspect is in a position of power over the complainant as well as whether the complainant was old enough to consent. "Steps taken to obtain consent" include asking the suspect how they ascertained that the complainant was in fact consenting. "Reasonable belief in consent" includes finding out whether the suspect ignored signs that the complainant didn't want to engage in sex as well as whether the complainant gave consent for all the sex acts that occurred or just for some. This overview of consent provides some background for many of the non-consensual acts that *I May Destroy You* explores.

In terms of the wide variety of paths that can be taken in response to sexual harm, Alexandra Brodsky states in her book *Sexual Justice*, "A common response to a public accusation of sexual violence is that the victim should have called the cops, as though a criminal trial were the only path to truth and justice. But sexual abuse is also a civil rights violation. Among other things, that means a victim can bring her own civil lawsuit, seeking monetary damages and policy changes."[6] Brodsky goes on to point out that many victims don't take the legal route at all, whether criminal or civil, but choose to file complaints with their human resources department at work or their Title IX coordinator at school. Amia Srinivasan in her book *The Right to Sex* makes the point that when these avenues fail, "women turn to the more diffuse punitive power afforded by social media."[7] Srinivasan also goes a step further and invites the reader to examine the broader ethics of sex: "The women in this [older feminist] tradition—from Simone de Beauvoir and Alexandra Kollontai to bell hooks, Audre Lorde, Catharine MacKinnon, and Adrienne Rich—dare us to think about the ethics of sex beyond the narrow parameters of 'consent.' They compel us to ask what forces lie behind a woman's *yes*; what it reveals about sex that it is something to which consent must be given; how it is that we have come to put so much psychic, cultural, and legal weight on a notion of 'consent' that cannot support it. And they ask us to join them in dreaming of a freer sex."[8] Similarly, *I May Destroy You* invites viewers to explore the broader ethics of sex but then specifically confronts the sexual harm that can occur precisely when people assume that "a freer sex" exists.

Beyond simply depicting a range of violations, *I May Destroy You* asks essential questions about the impact of sex without consent. Within more subtle situations, the question becomes how one processes a sexual encounter that one has engaged in willingly, only to find out later that one did so under false pretenses. Within more extreme situations of sexual violence, however, such as Arabella's rape after being drugged, the question becomes how one recovers from trauma to be able to fully participate in both sex and life again. What is distinctive in Arabella's primary storyline is that it is neither an account of rape victims who finally see their rapist brought to justice, such as in the devastating miniseries *Unbelievable* (Netflix: 2019, Susannah Grant, Ayelet Waldman, Michael Chabon), which is based on a true story, nor a story about women who become vigilantes seeking justice for rape victims, such as in the dark comedy *Sweet/Vicious* (MTV: 2016–2017, Jennifer Kaytin Robinson). Rather, it is about an individual, a writer who wants to honestly understand what has happened to her as well as to others who have had similar experiences. Dr. Kadian L. Pow, a Black feminist scholar studying racial representation and intersectionality, notes that the series is about "a victim reconciling with herself after this traumatic disruption, and finding real power again, making the journey more about an internal justice to the self."[9] Emily VanDerWerff states this about the series in her *Vox* review: "It never focuses on the crime when it can focus on the survivor."[10] The show's point of view comes from inside the experience, in large part because it reflects what happened to Coel herself. This is essential to what makes *I May Destroy You* feel authentic to viewers.

Even though there are a few depictions of Arabella having caring sex with her lover, Biagio (Moroccan-born Italian actor Marouane Zotti), most of the portrayals of sex in the show involve some form of assault or deception. Therefore, it can be quite a difficult show to watch. In her *New Yorker* article, Doreen St. Félix states, "In 'I May Destroy You,' violation is the omnipresent, cultural weather. Coel treats perpetrators with curiosity, and refuses to infantilize or pity the victims."[11] A bold approach is evident in the show, which reveals resonant details and psychological truths. Paapa Essiedu, who plays Kwame, states, "There's layers to this work, which means I think it will really benefit from rewatching. Because it's so direct and some of it is so hard to watch, sometimes your brain can't tolerate accessing the nuance that lies underneath it."[12] Understandably, the students in our Recent TV Trends course expressed difficulty with watching the material (which excluded the scenes of sexual assault but included references to it). At first, the prevalent sentiment was "This was uncomfortable," but then some students expressed, "But it was good that we saw it so we can think more about the topic." One student added, "I won't be watching any more of this show. I didn't enjoy it. But I'll never forget it." At the end of the term, on written assignments, several students stated views like "Everyone should probably see this." This progression in their views of the show demonstrated that some of the students were able to move beyond discomfort to the perception of value in understanding the larger topic of sexual harm and its ramifications. One student stated that she was able to watch the show because she understood that she was witnessing a fellow survivor trying to make sense of her own experience. Some of the lessons in presenting this show for us, as teachers, included that it was important to fully prepare students for what they were going to see; to give them choices for watching it on their own (rather than in class) or opting out altogether; and to make it clear that the primary story came out of Coel's processing of her own rape.

To be clear, there are many factors beyond the depictions of sexual harm that make *I May Destroy You* an absorbing and mesmerizing series. First, there is Arabella, often called Bella by her friends, who is captivating to watch because of Coel's dynamic portrayal. Second, there are Arabella's best friends, Terry and Kwame, who are wonderfully realized by Weruche Opia and Paapa Essiedu, respectively. Third, much of the show is visually arresting, such as the scenes in Italy throughout the show or the Halloween scenes in "Social Media Is a Great Way to Connect" (E9). Fourth, there is a palpable richness in the everyday lives of Arabella and her friends that keep the viewers actively engaged. Linda Holmes, reviewing the show for

Chapter 6. I May Destroy You

NPR, comments, "If you went in not knowing it was a story about sexual assault, you could watch most of the first episode as a day-in-the-life pilot for a quirky half-hour about a wandering millennial.... This is how you demonstrate that Arabella existed in full before she was assaulted."[13] The articulation of Arabella as a three-dimensional character and the show's exploratory approach makes viewers feel welcomed to come along for this no-holds-barred, complex journey.

Before *I May Destroy You*, Michaela Coel created the show *Chewing Gum* (E4: 2015–2017), which was adapted from her 2012 play *Chewing Gum Dreams*. It was her first foray into television. In *Vulture*, E. Alex Jung makes the point that even though Coel was having trouble properly structuring her scripts for a sitcom, it took a friend asking her how the script editor was helping her for Coel to even realize what a script editor was.[14] After some effort, she was then able to get the production company to hire one for her. Jung continues, "The show launched her career, but making it was marred by professional challenges that highlight the inevitably complicated dynamic of institutions trying to bring in 'outsiders'—people with no television experience whose very cachet comes from the fact that they don't look like you—without actually empowering them."[15] Even though the project came entirely from Michaela Coel in that she created it, wrote it, and starred in it, the production company declined to make her an executive producer. As a compromise, she was finally made a creative co-producer.[16] Coel discussed her experience working on *Chewing Gum* when she delivered the James MacTaggart Lecture at the 2018 Edinburgh International Film Festival, which was a notable event for a number of reasons. She was the first Black woman to ever deliver the James MacTaggart Lecture, and she chose to address the issues she had experienced as a Black woman in the industry. In describing the lecture, Jung states, "Instead of referring to something as 'racist,' she called it 'thoughtlessness'; she referred to underrepresented groups as 'misfits.' She is aware of the ways words like *racism* and *microaggression* have lost their power, so she searched for new ones that might make people listen."[17] Coel's lecture sent out further shock waves when she disclosed her sexual assault while working on Season 2 of *Chewing Gum*. She explained, "I was working overnight in the company's offices. I had an episode due at 7am. I took a break and had a drink with a good friend who was nearby. I emerged into consciousness typing season two, many hours later. I was lucky. I had a flashback. It turned out I'd been sexually assaulted by strangers."[18] She continued, "Like any other experience I found traumatic, it's been therapeutic to write about it, and actively twist the narrative of pain to one of hope, and even humor, and be able to share it with you, as part of a fictional drama on television because I think transparency helps."[19] Even though there are many similarities between what happened to Michaela Coel and what happens to Arabella Essiedu in the series, Coel's real life serves only as a springboard for creating the fictional show rather than as a blueprint. Coel states, "At some point, my life gets boring and isn't very televisual. And so then Arabella begins. Most of the show is fictional, so I don't even know if it legitimately falls under the category of autofiction."[20] But it is Coel's experience with assault and her continual process of recovery that informs the show's essential fiber and provides the necessary detail to make it feel grounded in reality.

When Coel was first pitching *I May Destroy You* in 2017, the exciting news was that she was offered $1 million by Netflix. When it became clear, however, that they were unwilling to give her even the smallest percentage of the copyright, she turned it down. She also realized that her CAA agents would have unfairly profited from the way the deal was packaged and so she walked away from them as well.[21] Bex Palmer writes, "Coel then pitched the show to Controller of BBC Drama, Piers Wenger. The next day, he agreed to everything Coel wanted, including retaining the rights to the show, full creative control, and a say on production, too."[22] The fact that the leadership at the BBC, and then later at HBO as well, gave Coel full creative control is what led to her vision being so exquisitely realized. Coel describes the writing of *I May Destroy You* as going up a mountain and opening herself up to the story that wants to be told. This process led to her writing 191 drafts, resulting in a show that both astounds and provokes. St. Félix notes, "But at its best this show is abrasively psychological; it is, as all good art can be, 'triggering,' because it sounds and feels and moves the way we do."[23] The show goes beyond demonstrating sexual violations on a surface level to become a deep dive into understanding the complex ramifications of sexual harm within the everyday lives of the characters.

There are a multitude of sexual consent scenarios explicated in the show, the first of which is introduced in "Eyes Eyes Eyes Eyes" (E1). As viewers, we see the situation develop from Arabella's perspective, so, just like her, we don't immediately understand that something bad has happened. After a new white acquaintance, David (Lewis Reeves), brings drinks to the table at Ego Death Bar, Arabella's friend, Simon (Aml Ameen), makes the toast, "Eyes, eyes, eyes, eyes," as they all look around the table into each other's eyes. The group includes Simon's Black American cousin, Derae (Ansu Kabia), and David's friend, Tariq (Chin Nyenwe), as well as Simon's lover, Alissa (Ann Akinjirin). Afterward, we see Arabella dancing and having a good time. Then, the sound becomes slightly distorted, and we see her become unsteady at the bar and then stumble toward the door. The next thing we see is her writing in her agents' office space and it's daylight. Everything seems normal. Then, she notices that her phone screen is cracked. Through quick shots, we surmise that she emails her pages by the deadline and goes home to shower. She then comes back to the office to discuss her work with her agents, Julian (Adam James) and Francine (Natalie Walter), both of whom are white and who seem dubious about her work. When they ask some questions, she realizes that she doesn't know what she has written and excuses herself to go to the toilet, where she quickly reads her pages. When she comes back, the cut on her forehead starts to bleed, prompting Julian to suggest, "Let's park this." At this point, the audience finally understands that something is wrong. (As an aside, these resonant details—regaining consciousness in the office, her phone being smashed, and her experience of writing material in a drug-induced fugue state—are all from Michaela Coel's own experience.)[24] After finishing the meeting with her agents, we then see Bella on the street, looking for the station. We hear overlapping and echoing sound that reflects her disorientation. Luckily, one of the fans of her first book, *Chronicles of a Fed-up Millennial*, comes up to her and helps her. When she's at home, her ears start to ring, and she gets a flash of a man thrusting. She is thoughtful for a moment and then simply says, "Hmm," which ends the episode. In "Someone Is Lying" (E2), much of the story is about Arabella trying to make sense of what happened that night and realizing that Simon's story doesn't hold up (which is explained only later in the series). One of the telling scenes is when Bella goes to the police station because she believes that she has witnessed someone else's assault. At first, she doesn't understand the way that Officer Funmi (Sarah Niles) is describing her experience, but more evidence becomes apparent. Besides her cracked phone screen and the gash on her head, she has bruises on her body and cuts on her knees. When she says that the man in the flashback doesn't seem like David, Officer Funmi says that if she's on the floor looking up, his nostrils would look bigger. Then, Officer Funmi asks what the man is looking at, and realizing that it was her, Arabella suddenly pulls her shirt over her face and starts crying. It's a heart wrenching moment when she realizes that she wasn't remembering someone else's assault but was remembering her own.

In the beginning of the show, there are other concerning behaviors surrounding sexuality that are woven into the story. In the first episode, we see Simon lying to his wife, Kat (Lara Rossi), about a potential threesome with Alissa, who is presumably a random hook-up from an app but who is actually Simon's lover of the past six months. Later, in "Don't Forget the Sea" (E3), we see a flashback of Arabella and Terry on their trip to Italy when they stay in a lovely apartment that Arabella labels as "expenses" to support her writing process. Excited about their grand adventure, they recite their mantra to each other: "Your birth is my birth. Your death is my death." They go out for a night on the town after buying drugs from the local drug dealer, who turns out to be Biagio. While Bella is dancing wildly at a club, Terry tells her that she's leaving, but Bella is too high to register what she's saying. Later, when Bella leaves the club, wasted and still looking for Terry, Biagio is the one who helps her get back to her apartment. In the meantime, Terry finds her own adventure, hooking up with two white Italian men, Giovanni and Luigi, who she thinks are strangers to each other. After their threesome, she looks through her bedroom window and sees them walking down the street together. There are several instances throughout the show of Terry bringing up this threesome proudly, including at an audition in Episode 1 and another time in Episode 11 to prove to Kai (Tyler Luke Cunningham), a trans man whom she has just met, that she's not a prude. She finally accepts that the two men knew each other and that she was set up to have this particular ménage á trois, which, in retrospect, she finds troubling. Dr. Pow states, "This was a great example of thinking one had consented to a fantasy one was in charge of, only to find out that one was the pawn. The ambiguity was in who owned the scenario."[25] Terry's experience highlights the need to make sure all factors have been disclosed when consenting to sexual interactions, whether with known partners or strangers, and in some cases, the need to ascertain who is controlling the situation.

The show continues its exploration of sexual harm with Kwame's experience in "That Was Fun" (E4). It starts with him talking to a casual acquaintance, Damon, who wants to learn from Kwame what it's like to live as a gay man. Kwame lets Damon know that his father is visiting from Ghana and doesn't approve of his lifestyle, so they can't go to his place. Then, they talk about what it's like being in London and Kwame says, "No one will throw me off a building or chase me with a stick." Kwame then asks Damon if he would be interested if he could find somewhere for them to be. The answer is yes, and they end up at the place of a Grindr hook-up, whose handle is hornyman808 and who says that he's from Nigeria. Kwame initially says that he's up for anything, but when the hook-up (who is called Malik in the subtitles) says that he wants to ride him bareback, Kwame says no, he doesn't do that. Malik respects what Kwame says, demonstrating that, at least at this juncture, he believes that he needs Kwame's consent before proceeding. After Damon decides to leave, Kwame and Malik continue to have sex. When they are done and Kwame is on his way out, Malik suddenly asks him to stay. He strips and tells Kwame to go on the bed, saying, "It's not sex." He then pushes Kwame down, forcibly holding him there, and humps him. Kwame struggles and tells him to get off of him, while Malik reaches climax. Malik then says nonchalantly, "What can I say, I'm a bad boy." At the end of the episode,

Chapter 6. I May Destroy You

Kwame is outside the apartment building, with tears rolling down his cheek. He calls Bella but just tells her that he's heading to bed. In "…It Just Came Up" (E5), Kwame still hasn't revealed what happened to him, even when he goes with Bella and Terry to the police station to hear the news about Bella's case. On the way out of the station, he is searching on his phone "Is non-consensual humping a crime?" and one of the things that comes up is "What is frotteurism?" Bella and Terry continue to look past Kwame's subdued mood. In "The Alliance" (E6), when Terry tries to get Kwame to pay attention to Arabella, Terry says, "So, no, she's not fine. She's vacant. She's empty. She's a shell of herself. She's dying inside. But if you aren't looking for it, you ain't going to see it." Since Terry doesn't know what happened to Kwame, but the viewers do, we feel both his pain and the sting of Terry's ironic statement. Tarana Burke, the founder of Me Too, has made it clear "men's first role in this movement is as survivors."[26] Overall, students found Kwame's experience to be a vital aspect of the show because many of them are well aware that women are not the only victims of sexual assault.

Later in Episode 5, Kwame finally decides to go to the police station to report what happened to him three weeks earlier. Whereas Arabella was treated sensitively by the police, Kwame is not. There is a decided lack of interest on the part of the Black, male police officer, which appears rooted in not taking the assault of one gay man by another gay man seriously, especially since it followed consensual sex. In trying to determine whether it was sexual assault or rape, the officer asks, "Did he penetrate you?" Kwame's answer is "Well, my trousers became very low at one point, so he might have, without going all the way in." In the ensuing conversation, the officer becomes clearly uncomfortable and says that there are machines out there to report things, and then, when he goes to ask a senior officer for advice, he leaves the door open, revealing a sign that states, "Keep this door closed. You're putting people in danger by leaving it open." Commenting on this scene, Paapa Essiedu, who plays Kwame, says, "Considering how male sexual assault is chronically underrepresented in the news, in TV, music, literature, that will obviously mean that those structures that are meant to protect those people aren't nourished and so those people are underserved. I think what we see with Kwame's story is quite a brutal examination of this."[27] In *Sexual Justice*, Alexandra Brodsky states, "Police officers are particularly unlikely to believe survivors who deviate from our popular model of the 'perfect victim'—generally, a white, heterosexual, cisgender, virginal, middle-class (or richer) woman, who was not drinking, using drugs, or selling sex, who did not know her assailant, and who fought to get away, ideally under the threat of some kind of weapon. Almost none of us are described by such a portrait. One 'requirement' alone knocks three-quarters of survivors out of the running: the vast majority know their abuser."[28] Brodsky paints a complex portrait of sexual harm in her book and explores possible ways for survivors to find justice, and if not that, then at least closure. What Brodsky explores in a factual way in print, Coel explores in a dramatized way on television.

Interestingly enough, the film *Promising Young Woman* (Focus Features, Universal Pictures: 2020, Emerald Fennell), which came out the same year as *I May Destroy You*, illustrates several of the points made in Brodsky's book, especially in regard to a white, heterosexual, cisgender, middle-class woman who is sexually assaulted but who still does not experience justice. The film tells the story of Cassie, who is seeking revenge for her friend, Nina, who committed suicide after being raped. Cassie wants everyone to answer for what happened: the men who witnessed the rape; the female friend, Madison, who got the video but did nothing; the female dean at the university who didn't take action; and the male lawyer who defended the case. One of the striking aspects of the film is the way in which various harmful attitudes about rape are woven into the story. At one point, Madison says, "If you have a reputation for sleeping around, then maybe people aren't going to believe you when you say something has happened." And Dean Elizabeth Walker says, "What would you have me do? Ruin a young man's life every time we get an accusation like this?" When Cassie confronts her boyfriend about his part in witnessing the rape, he says to her, "So, you're perfect, right? You've never done anything you're ashamed of?" And indeed, Cassie does seem to be perfect in every way, at least before she embarks on a path of vengeance. Of all of the differences between *A Promising Young Woman* and *I May Destroy You*, the most important one may be that Coel is not painting any of the survivors as being perfect. Whereas the general purpose of *Promising Young Woman* is to justify Cassie's actions as an avenging angel who punishes the wrongdoers, the purpose of *I May Destroy You* is to demonstrate that you don't have to be an angel to be considered a victim; revenge is not the way; and sometimes the best one can do for oneself is to find closure.

The sexual crime in *I May Destroy You* that comes closest to being resolved with a modicum of justice occurs in "That Was Fun" (E4), when Arabella's publisher suggests that one of their successful writers, Zain Sureen, help her finish her book. After trying to have a conversation about her work in a bar earlier, when Arabella is reminded of her spiked drink and suddenly has to leave, Zain ends up coming over to her place. When she asks about his background, he says "India," and they laugh because of a similar answer she gave earlier when she replied "Ghana" when he just wanted to know about her career background. When he tells her that he went to Cambridge, she's quite impressed. Then, Arabella brings up having sex and he asks if they should do that now. When they are in her bedroom, Zain asks if he can kiss her, and when she agrees and they kiss, she suddenly sees him in the tell-tale POV shot of the rapist. She moves away from him and takes a moment to smoke some weed. He asks if she is all right and whether he should go. So, again, just like with Malik, Zain seems sensitive at first to the need for consent. When they start to have sex, missionary style, Zain puts on a condom. He tells her to turn over and he then removes the condom (quite literally behind her back). Afterward, Zain says that he took the condom off because it got uncomfortable. He says, "I thought you could feel it." She is only mildly irritated and says that now she has to get the morning-after pill. Zain pays for it and all seems fine.

Arabella's revelation that all is not fine happens at the beginning of the next episode, "…It Just Came Up" (E5), when she wakes up next to Zain at his place. When he is in the shower, she starts listening to a podcast in which a woman is talking about a man secretly removing his condom. We hear the woman say, "There are actual Reddit forums where men share tips and tricks and even phrases, like he said to me, 'I thought you knew. You mean you didn't feel it?'" Suddenly, Arabella stands up and walks out of the apartment, wearing only a bra, panties, and Zain's shirt. Later in the same episode, Arabella gets confirmation from Officer Funmi that "secret condom removal" is indeed rape, a crime that is referred to as "stealthing." There are several instances of skillful writing in this episode that tease the audience with their ambiguity. Is Arabella making a Freudian slip or is she deliberately calling Zain out? The first one is when she is meeting with her agents, as well as Susy Henny (Franc Ashman), the head of the publishing company, who Bella is excited to find out is a Black woman. Sion, a young, white woman who works for the International Literary Summit, is also at the meeting. Arabella tells them, "I was raped. I reported it as soon as I found out, and luckily, I remember his face." She then says, "I even know his name, so…. Zain Sareen…." There's a pause, then a quick shot of Zain looking wide-eyed and one of Susy looking at him questioningly. Looking at Zain, Arabella continues, "Thank you so much. You've been so helpful." Then, looking at the others, she says, "Zain's been helping me finish my writing." The second instance is when Arabella and Zain are alone. He asks why she didn't tell him earlier about what happened to her. She replies, "I don't know. I guess I thought if we both knew you were a rapist, it might change us." He says, "What? What did you say?" She replies, "I thought if we both knew about the rapist, it might change us." These two moments foreshadow what finally happens when Arabella is at the International Literary Summit as one of the celebrated writers, along with Zain. After Terry gets stage fright and can't read the material,

Arabella finds herself on stage addressing the audience. First, she says thank you to her publisher and agents, and then she says, "Zain Sureen is a rapist. He took a condom off in the middle of having sex with me. He placated my shock and gaslighted me with such intention that I didn't have a second to understand the heinous crime that had occurred. I believe he is a predator. One woman has come forward and informed me of the same experience. So I'm not the first. If I don't take this opportunity to say this now, I certainly won't be the last. He is a rapist. Not rape-adjacent or a bit rapey. He's a rapist under UK law. If you're in the States, he's rape adjacent. If you're in Australia, he's a bit rapey." Terry then videos Zain's escape from the theater, which later becomes a meme, a prime example in the show of being shamed on social media as a substitute for the justice that victims of sexual assault are so often denied by the legal system. At the end of the episode when Arabella and Terry are sitting in a pub, staring at their phones, Sion pronounces, "You've literally broken the internet."

It is worth unraveling how Arabella comes to expose Zain's crime. Some of our students were confused about which woman came forward. In the previously mentioned meeting with the agents and publisher, the first hint that there was something between Zain and Sion is that he has trouble remembering her until she reminds him that she was at the British Library. There's a telling look when he registers exactly how he knows her. Then, at the reception before the Summit, after Sion asks Arabella about her connection to Zain, she says, "It's impossible to protect yourself from his nature. I know quite a few women who just..." Arabella finishes her statement: "couldn't." It is possibly too subtle for most viewers to catch that Arabella and Sion are talking about Zain's stealthing. In an interesting reversal, Arabella then imagines herself as the rapist, but in this version of the POV shot, she's smiling. The fact that she's smiling relates to an earlier scene of her doing yoga with Terry. Terry is nervous about presenting Arabella's writing at the Summit and Arabella tells her (while doing a difficult yoga pose of kneeling on her elbows with her hands on the floor), "All you have to do is breathe, assess the situation, assess the crowd, look them in the eyes, gather that strength and when you do, smile. Smile sweetly always and let it all flow, you know?" Finally, the way the sequence in the theater is structured makes it clear that Arabella did not initially plan on revealing Zain's crime at the Summit. The only reason Arabella ends up speaking at all is because Terry gets stage fright. In addition, Arabella has only just heard Sion's confirmation that Zain has done the same to her and other women. Therefore, it's clear that what Arabella says from the podium is not premeditated but only comes to her at the same time as that smiling image of herself. Through Arabella's words, it also feels like we're hearing the voice of Michaela Coel. Arabella has often seemed unsure up to this point, but now she's confident and firm, speaking with the commanding voice of an author.

Zain becomes an excellent example of the proverbial "promising young man" that many in our society have been so eager to protect and to which the title of the film *Promising Young Woman* refers. Zain went to Cambridge; he's a successful author; he's outwardly polite and considerate. In this show, however, with one public announcement, Arabella manages to ruin his reputation and diminish the threat level that he poses. He will now have a much harder time doing to other women what he did to Arabella and Sion. In contrast to this dramatization, Brodsky writes of a more typical situation, "I think often about an administrator at the prestigious Deerfield Academy who, according to a lawsuit filed against the school, told a young woman that the decision not to punish the boy who sexually assaulted her was based on 'the very difficult choice between a boy's future and her feelings.' As though only her *feelings* were at stake, and her own prospects—surely shaped by her assailant's continued presence in her small rural school—were of no consequence. As though only men get futures."[29] It is worth noting that Zain's future career might have been ruined as well by Arabella's revelations if Susy Henny hadn't found a way to keep publishing his work, albeit under a pseudonym. Although Arabella is initially thrilled that the "big boss" is Black, comparing Susy Henny to Obama, Dr. Pow points out that Henny's support of Arabella's rapist demonstrates that "Black women can't necessarily assume safety under other Black women in the industry."[30] Henny clearly cares more about her bottom line than she does about Arabella as a person. As for the practice of stealthing in the real world, Alexandra Brodsky is credited with bringing attention to it through her 2017 Yale University study, which spurred Assemblywoman Cristina Garcia to sponsor the bill that made stealthing a civil offense in California, allowing victims to sue for damages.[31] Stealthing appears to be a much more prevalent crime than one would suspect. "A study published in the journal Women's Health Issues in 2019 reported that 12 percent of women said that they had been a victim of stealthing. Another study that year found that 10 percent of men admitted to removing their condom during intercourse without their partner's consent."[32] Before seeing *I May Destroy You*, many viewers may have been unaware of stealthing as a crime. This points to the practical use of drama as a tool for bringing these issues to a broader audience.

Within the discussion of sexual harm, *I May Destroy You* also effectively explores the intersection of race, class, gender, and orientation. In her article in *The New York Times*, "'I May Destroy You' Imagines a Path Back from Sexual Assault," Salamishah Tillet, a Black American scholar and writer, describes her own experience with sexual assault: "In 1998, nearly two years after I was sexually assaulted and during the height of my depression, I'd spend hours imagining what I would do if ever saw my assailant again." It turned out that she never did see her assailant again and never experienced any sort of justice, much like Arabella in *I May Destroy You* and Coel in real life. In discussing Coel, Tillet states, "She also centers rape victims that have historically been treated as less worthy of support: Black women, those attacked while under the influence of drugs or alcohol, and in the case of Bella's friend, Kwame, Black queer men."[33] In regard to how the intersectionality of identities operates for Arabella, there is a telling sequence in "Happy Animals" (E7). In a meeting with her agents, Arabella reads the following from her writing: "Prior to being raped, I never took much notice of being a woman. I was busy being Black and poor. Daring to observe the hazard my gender may pose to my freedom and survival feels like a betrayal to the council flat I was born and raised in, where hardship was no respecter of genitals, and a little brother was as starved of food and love as his sister." This again feels like Michaela Coel's "writer" voice coming through and indeed it comes from her own experience while performing in a play, *Blurred Lines*, in 2014. Coel states, "This was a show about being a woman and I'd never considered any of these things…. When we discussed [the themes in it], I literally said, 'I really don't know. I'm busy being [B]lack and poor right now.'"[34] In terms of growing up poor, Michaela notes, "My family has rented our whole lives. You're always on fragile ground because it's not yours. It gives you a drive, an ambition, because nothing is certain."[35] Coel sees blessings in having had a background that gave her the drive to achieve and, no doubt, the courage to take the risks needed to create authentic work.

One of the many gifts of *I May Destroy You* is that it examines sexual harm not only from Arabella's perspective but from that of her friends, always keeping in mind the intersection of identities that influences the situations. In response to a question about talking to other survivors when writing the show, Coel states, "[My friends] began to share stories, because they knew what had happened to me."[36] In the same interview, when Coel is asked about the impact of the show, she replies, "I think that since the media has really even existed, it has dehumanized [B]lack people. In many ways, it's dehumanized and disempowered women. To be within the media, to challenge that, and to present us as fluid, multi-dimensional human people, just like everybody else, feels like a really amazing privilege."[37] Part of the brilliance of Coel's approach is that her work feels far from a polemic or even something meant to influence or convince. The voice of the show is never telling the audience how to feel, think, or judge. Rather, it is simply presenting what the characters experience in a forthright manner, even when they stumble.

Chapter 6. I May Destroy You

The fact that Coel's characters make their fair share of mistakes becomes an important aspect of *I May Destroy You*. When a show makes it clear that even its protagonists are guilty of wrongdoing, it communicates a certain fairness and attention to the truth. To start with, there is Biagio. Arabella appears to genuinely be in love with him, and when the viewers observe situations in which he is indeed kind and caring, we believe that her love is warranted. But when she first tries to tell him what happened to her (in Episode 5, when she is about to go into the Summit gathering), he admonishes her, saying she should watch her drink in a club. Later, when Biagio finds out that he must go to the police and give a DNA sample (as a consensual partner in Arabella's rape investigation), he is livid because, as a drug dealer, that's the last thing he wants to do. At the end of Episode 5, when they are FaceTiming on her laptop, Biagio screams at her, "You are fucking up my life!" Arabella gets upset and says, "Yeah, well, how the fuck do you think I feel with you telling me I've done something wrong, telling me there's something wrong with me, telling me what?" He comes back with "If you'd watched your drink, you wouldn't have been raped." She says, "I don't want to talk to you again," and slams her laptop shut. Besides blaming the victim, Biagio is also trying to enclose Arabella in a narrow world like his own, where he must be wary of other people. One of the reasons he likes Arabella is that she is different from him—trusting and open to others. Biagio is arguing that the only way to protect yourself is to be suspicious of everyone around you, and that is not the kind of life that Arabella wants to lead.

The next example of a character making mistakes involves Theo (Harriet Webb), whom Arabella knew as a teenager but meets again in the present time because Theo has formed a group for women who are survivors of sexual harm. In "The Alliance" (E6), during flashbacks with Teen Arabella (Danielle Vitalis) and Teen Terry (Lauren-Joy Williams), we see Teen Theo (Gaby French) during a sexual encounter with Ryan (Josiah Mutupa). At first, Theo is the one being taken advantage of because Ryan secretly videos her as he has sex with her from behind. Then, he treats her callously when she asks him to delete it. He says, "What did he give you? Is that how it works? He never said that. He just said you liked that kind of shit." She says, "But Dillan didn't try to take pictures." Ryan retorts, "I've seen it. So don't try it." As a token gesture, she gets money from him, and he records them having sex. Surreptitiously, she throws his phone out the window. But then to further get back at him, she falsely accuses him of raping her at knifepoint, to the point of cutting her legs to make it seem believable. This is an overt example of a false accusation, demonstrating something that many boys and men fear, although it's relatively uncommon in real life. In reference to false rape reports, Brodsky states, "all methodologically rigorous studies converge on rates between 2 and 8 percent of all rape reports, a range similar to that for other crimes."[38] An important factor, however, in this situation is race, since Theo is white and Ryan is Black. As a point of interest, in the report "Race and Wrongful Convictions in the United States," the following is stated: "Judging from exonerations, a [B]lack prisoner serving time for sexual assault is three-and-a-half times more likely to be innocent than a white sexual assault convict."[39] In addition, Brodsky states, "False rape allegations have long played an outsize role in the oppression of Black men."[40] In the situation in Episode 6, when the school administration springs into action to support Theo, Terry remarks, "White girl tears have high currency." But it turns out that there is proof that the encounter was consensual because Ryan had already sent a friend, Marcus, the pics. Armed with the photos, Arabella and Terry then go to the administrator's office to prove that Theo lied. Dr. Pow comments, "Theo's character demonstrates white women's tricky place in the race/gender matrix—as ones who possess both racial power and a femininity that is afforded protection, but who can also find themselves in positions of victimization. As a white girl, Theo uses that protected vulnerability for manipulation and power."[41] When Ryan is released and comes out of the building, his Black friends are all gathered around. He says, "You lot saved me, man." In a show of support, Terry proclaims, "This is the Alliance!" Later in the episode, Theo reveals to her aimable stepfather, Martin, that her mother made her lie about her father touching her when she was seven so that her mother could get custody. And so the episode ends on a glimpse into the forces that have shaped Theo's view of right and wrong in the sexual arena.

The wrongdoing of Terry and Simon is more subtle and interconnected. In Episode 3, when Terry leaves Arabella at the nightclub in Italy, Arabella gives her a hard time about it, but Terry's defense is that she told her she was leaving, even if she didn't register it. In "Happy Animals" (E7), when Simon and Terry are talking, he brings up that Terry told him to leave Arabella that night at Ego Death Bar, telling him that this is what Arabella does, the implication being that she was high, having a good time, and oblivious to everything else. Terry's counter is that Simon just wanted to be with his mistress. She also makes the point that she wasn't there and couldn't possibly have known what was going on. The difficulty is that once it is made clear in Episode 2 that Arabella was raped that night, Simon becomes cagey, not wanting to admit that he left her there by herself, which then makes it so much harder for Bella to figure out what happened that night. After this point, Bella decides to steer clear of Simon and many months go by. She finally gets him to tell the truth in "The Cause the Cure" (E10) when she goes to meet him to return his jacket, which he gave her that night and which she now has back since all the evidence from the case has been returned to her. From the conversation, it's clear that he has changed jobs and that he has separated from Kat. Suddenly, Arabella has a flash of him as the rapist in the same POV shot. After that, she tells him that she's sorry that she ever imagined that he had something to do with it. He tells her that if he didn't leave her that night, none of this would have happened. But he then goes on to imply that Terry was the one who forced him to lie and say that he stayed with her and that it was Terry who gave him approval to leave. Not realizing that Arabella doesn't know this version of the story, he says, "I'm glad she told you." When Arabella next sees Terry and says that she gave Simon back his jacket, Terry begins to apologize, but Arabella cuts her off and says, "You're amazing. Thank you for being an amazing friend." Since Terry has done everything that she possibly can to help Bella in her self-care goals since the rape happened, she has indeed been a good friend. But one can't help but think of Terry's actions as some form of atonement as well.

As for Arabella, her first wrongdoing is at Terry's birthday party in "Happy Animals" (E7). Thinking that it would be a fun prank, she locks Kwame in a room with Jamal because she thinks Kwame will be sexually interested in him. Instead, Kwame flashes back to when he was sexually assaulted (which Bella doesn't know about yet) and has an agonizing time before the door is finally opened. Dr. Pow makes the point that heterosexual women can sometimes show little regard for a gay man's vulnerability and can fail to understand the harm they are causing.[42] But it is in the next episode, "Line Spectrum Border" (E8), that transgressions of both Arabella and Kwame are more fully explored. Toward the beginning of the episode, Arabella and Terry are lingering in the waiting room of the police station because Arabella doesn't know what to do next after hearing that her rape case is no longer active. Finally, Bella tells Terry, "I need a plane ticket to Italy." After some initial hesitation, Terry provides this for her. We then see Bella at Biagio's apartment complex at night. She waits for someone to unlock the exterior gate so that she can slip in behind her, and she does the same with the locked door to the stairwell. She then finds the key to Biagio's apartment where she knows it's hidden. When Biagio comes into his place and suddenly sees her, he screams, "Bella, what the fuck are you doing here?" Then, more softly, he says, "Come here." They embrace and she says that she's sorry. They have a brief discussion, in which she tells him that she has stopped partying, drinking, and smoking. When he asks her to read what she has written on the pages she's holding in her hands, she demurs, which implies that she's not willing to fully open up to him, although she wants that from him. Then, she goes out front to meet the delivery boy with the pizza (which she ordered while waiting for Biagio).

When she comes back, Biagio has locked his apartment door. She tries to talk to him through the door, but there's no answer. Then she realizes that she's left her passport inside. But instead of letting her in, he just slides it out under the door. Then, she starts screaming at him and beating his door with all her strength. Coel's commentary on this sequence is "And actually, in that moment, the only scary person is Arabella. Arabella is the person that stole the key from under his mat, entered his house, and then basically suggested that she wasn't going to leave, without giving him any warning at all."[43] Finally, the door opens. He has a gun and tells her to get away from his door. Now he is the scary one and Arabella runs away from him.

Within the same episode, "Line Spectrum Border" (E8), we see that Kwame has decided to stay away from men after his sexual assault and decides to try women. He gets to know Nilufer, who is white, through an app and they go on a date. When they're walking down the street, she tells him, "I'm into guys with an edge. I'm into Black guys." Even though the implication is offensive that, somehow by definition, Black guys would have an edge, Kwame appears to brush it aside. When they go back to her place, she comes on strong, and they end up having sex. Kwame has flashes back to his assault, but this time, he sees himself in the position of the aggressor. Afterward, in casual conversation, Nilufer makes a homophobic remark and Kwame then tells her that he's gay. Nilufer becomes upset that he didn't tell her this before they had sex. Coel has this to say about it: "So it's all come kind of falling to pieces, his attempt to kind of explore his power and his sexual power and his sexual freedom which didn't have to be that way, but he didn't go about it the right way."[44] Dr. Pow comments that both Kwame and Nilufer are guilty of using each other to boundary cross, in that "white women have a history of using romantic proximity to Black men to transgress boundaries and self-explore."[45] The overall point is that in *I May Destroy You*, there is ample evidence to prove that almost everyone is capable of harming others within a sexual context. Even the title sequence of the show suggests this. "I May Destroy You," with the "You" frequently erased, indicates different readings of who the "I" and who the "You" are. Coel says, "Who is saying, 'I may destroy'? Is it Arabella? Is it the man that sexually assaulted her in Episode 1 who may destroy?"[46] In other words, "I" could be the assaulter and "You" the assaulted, or "I" could be the assaulted and "You" the assaulter. Either reading of the title makes sense within the show.

Returning to "Line Spectrum Border" (E8), there is a noteworthy sequence at the end that speaks to Arabella's state of mind. After fleeing from Biagio's apartment, she creeps through a locked gate to gain entrance to the beach. It's nighttime and she has no place to go. She also discovers that she has no international data and therefore can't call anyone for help. Then, it's morning and we see that Arabella has slept on the beach. We see her stand up and walk into the ocean, fully clothed, until she is submerged. Coel comments, "This is the moment where she gathers up the kind of darkness that she needs to overcome her trauma."[47] Coel also makes the point that it may seem like she wants to drown herself, but actually she's engaging in a ritual of baptism and rebirth. One way to read this scene is that it reflects Joseph Campbell's "The Adventure of the Hero," often referred to as the hero's journey, with its stages of Departure, Initiation, and Return. The scene of Arabella walking into the sea recalls the step of "The Belly of the Whale" at the end of the Departure stage, which Campbell writes this about, "the idea that the passage of the magical threshold is a transit into a sphere of rebirth is symbolized in the worldwide womb image of the belly of the whale. The hero, instead of conquering or conciliating the power of the threshold, is swallowed into the unknown, and would appear to have died."[48] This certainly fits with Arabella being under the water and appearing to drown. This moment also resonates as a "point of no return" in her journey, in that she has nowhere else to run or hide, and she must face the reality of her case being closed, Biagio having rejected her, and her own capacity for aggression. In the TV series *Joseph Campbell and the Power of Myth* (PBS: 1988, Joseph Campbell, Bill Moyers), Campbell states, "The whale represents the personification, you might say, of all that is in the unconscious. In reading these things psychologically, water is the unconscious."[49] And embracing the unconscious realm is also an important part of Bella's journey.

I May Destroy You has other connections with the hero's journey that are worth exploring. In the PBS series, Campbell comments, "The first stage in the hero adventure, when he starts off on adventure, is leaving the realm of light, which he controls and knows about, and moving towards the threshold."[50] In *I May Destroy You*, one could argue that the first step begins with Arabella's recognition that something bad has happened when she has a flash of the man's face as he is thrusting at the end of Episode 1. It is only in Episode 2 that she realizes that she was the one who was raped when Officer Funmi convinces her of this, at which point her world view is shattered and she leaves the realm of light (denoting that which is familiar and manageable). The step of "Crossing of the First Threshold" (still part of "Departure" stage) can be seen in Bella's calling out Zain in Episode 5, a significant move forward that demonstrates her ability to take action and, in so doing, also protect others. It's noteworthy that earlier in Episode 5, Bella goes to the hair salon and her hair stylist removes her wig, asking her, "The usual? Deep treatment and rebraiding?" Arabella asks her what she thinks, and then emerges with a shaved head, which is quite a departure from the pink wig she has been wearing. This striking change in her appearance reads as a symbol of transformation.

After the crucial "Belly of the Whale" step in Episode 8, Arabella is then propelled into the first step in the "Initiation" stage, "The Road of Trials," in "Social Media is a Great Way to Connect" (E9). In this episode, we see Arabella using social media to respond to others who have been sexually assaulted, which at first appears as both a heroic and personally positive path. And yet, it is demonstrated that this path is stressful for Bella and not aiding in her own recovery. Kwame shows that he is skeptical about the level of her involvement with people who follow her online when he's talking to Terry at a small distance from Bella. He mimics both sides of a conversation that she is having with someone who has approached her on the street: "'Thank you so much for reminding me of all the pain and frustration and that's all I can think about.' 'Oh, it's my pleasure. Make sure you tell your friends to follow me and make me more powerful.' 'Of course, you're my shero, consoler of the weak and avenger of the bad men.'" Kwame then yells at her, "Oi, Bells, can we go? This echo chamber is freezing." Later, we see more tension in the trio of friends when Kwame admits to his interaction with Nilufer, and Arabella immediately criticizes him: "You kind of had penetrative sex with someone under false pretenses." Arabella then goes on to insinuate that Kwame has made a "deceitful, destructive, narcissistic, sick, inconsiderate" mistake. Dr. Pow notes that "it's so pivotal that this polemic reaction comes right after the real life interaction with an online follower because it demonstrates an online righteousness and projection of her own devastation with Zain."[51] When Terry tries to defend Kwame, Bella discounts what she's saying. Bella then leaves her friends and retreats into her online world until the DMs are floating all around her in space, an evocative visual to make the point that she has become immersed in another plane of existence. This fits what Campbell states about this step: "Once having traversed the threshold, the hero moves in a dream landscape of curiously fluid, ambiguous forms, where he must survive a succession of trials."[52] Bella's DM-infused state of mind fits this description well.

Continuing his explanation of "The Road of Trials," Campbell states, "The hero is covertly aided by the advice, amulets, and secret agents of the supernatural helper whom he met before his entrance into this region."[53] This supernatural helper can be seen in Arabella's therapist, Carrie, whom she has indeed met before, in "That Was Fun" (E4). In that episode, Carrie tells Bella some of the symptoms of trauma, "high irritability, difficulty focusing, emotional numbing," and tells her to do relaxing, creative things with her friends like walks, yoga, and painting. Arabella begins to take self-care and her own recovery more seriously. In "The Alliance" (E6), she

Chapter 6. I May Destroy You

goes to Theo's group where she explains what has happened to her: "I had a not great experience, a drug-facilitated sexual assault. And I was trying to get back on track and then someone from my workplace sexually assaulted me. Someone said it was my fault and maybe it was, because twice, you know. I am here to learn how to avoid getting raped. There must be some way." By Episode 9, after being overwhelmed by her online world, she makes an emergency call to Carrie and goes to her place. Bella confesses that everything disturbing in her life ends up under her bed, including the investigation bags. In regard to this, Michaela Coel states, "and I'm constantly exploring the idea of going under, under the bed, under the sea,"[54] which symbolizes the unconscious. In Episode 9, Carrie helps Bella understand what is buried in her unconscious by drawing a diagram of what is and what is not Arabella, with a dividing line in between. Carrie says, "It happens more often than you might think. A line is drawn separating bad from good, friend from foe, men/women, Black/white, them/us, criminal/victim, God/devil. It helps us to deflect, avoid feelings like guilt, uncertainty, self-blame. These feelings are crucial in the stages of recovery. If we can't process and understand them, we can't process and understand ourselves." When Arabella is back in her bedroom, we see her take the prodigious step of deleting all of her social media accounts. She then dives under her bed so she can pull everything out, including the ultrasound of a fetus, a reminder of a long-ago abortion. When Terry and Kwame come to her place later, she apologizes to Kwame, saying that it was an intense day, and she also apologizes to him for locking him in the room with Jamal. At the end of the episode, Bella and Terry go through the investigation bags from her case and then go to Ego Death Bar to sit outside, on the lookout for David. Bella is no longer deflecting her own grief and is instead confronting her rape directly and trying to find closure.

The harsh reality of trying to find closure when there is no chance of achieving justice in sexual assault cases is amply portrayed in *I May Destroy You*. Arabella's case comes to nothing, and Kwame's case never gets started, even though he tries to report it to the police. In actuality, most survivors of sexual assault and rape have to rely on themselves to find closure. Brodsky writes, "Readers will remember that very few sexual assault reports lead to arrest (20 percent) or are referred to prosecution (4 percent). Even fewer—only about 2 percent—result in felony convictions. Reported sexual assaults are about three times less likely to result in convictions than nonsexual assaults and batteries. I find these numbers significant even though I don't see convictions as a true and straight forward measure of justice, given the horrors of incarceration and its incompleteness as a remedy for victims."[55] In her *Vox* article, "A different path for confronting sexual assault," sujatha baliga describes restorative justice as a process that "invites truth-telling on all sides by replacing punitive approaches to wrongdoing in favor of collective healing and solutions."[56] She goes on to state, "Most survivors are also looking for some indication that the person who harmed them truly understands what they've done and that they won't do it again."[57] But many survivors never have the hope of achieving this and this is clearly demonstrated in *I May Destroy You* with the sexual harm done to Arabella and Kwame.

The larger point in the show is to find ways to handle the trauma and fear after a sexual assault, including what stance to take regarding the perpetrator. When Coel was in the process of finding an ending for *I May Destroy You*, she was renting a cabin in Northern Michigan from a woman, Sally McCaughan, who recommended that she read Margaret Atwood's short story "Stone Mattress," which is about a woman who runs into a man who had sexually assaulted her years before. Jung writes, "Coel asked if it was going to end in murder, and—spoiler alert—McCaughan replied that it does. 'I'm kind of trying not to do that,' said Coel."[58] In the interview in *The Hollywood Reporter*, Coel asks, "Does it benefit you to see other people as complete and utter monsters, nothing but the devil inside of them? How does that help you sleep at night? How are you going to have empowerment in your life over the things people have done to you? That's the narrative I'm trying to correct."[59] And by the end, there is forgiveness in *I May Destroy You*. In "Would You Like to Know the Sex?" (E11), Arabella reaches out to Della Croy-Dickie, the author of *The Sundial* (a book she greatly admires), only to find out that the author is actually Zain. When he approaches her at an outdoor café, she says, "I'm not afraid of you. Because you're not under my bed. You're here with me, so you don't scare me." Zain says, "I don't want to scare you." Arabella says, "And I've gone underneath ... underneath into the darkness and that darkness is now in me ... looking at you, so I might seem a little bit more frightening than the last time you saw me." His response is "You were pretty frightening the last time I saw you." Surprisingly, she allows Zain to help her and even invites him into her home once more. When Zain is leaving after helping her organize her book, she says, "Thank you, Della." She then asks him to throw away the two bags of evidence on his way out, which is symbolically appropriate. He has helped her with her book and she has, in part, forgiven him—and now he will get rid of some of her baggage. It is clear that Arabella doesn't want to close her heart to others, including Zain, or be afraid. That's part of her recovery, to regain trust and let go of fear. It is only after Zain leaves and she's arranging the notes to put on the wall that Arabella finally remembers that night. She remembers being put in a cab and taken somewhere else. She remembers the bathroom and hitting her head. She remembers getting raped and David's accomplice, Tariq, watching the door. Viewed from the paradigm of the hero's journey, this is the step of crossing the return threshold, in that Arabella now fully knows her story and can tell her story to others.

From start to finish, *I May Destroy You* is framed as a story being written by its protagonist, Arabella. Just as Coel is fashioning a fictional story about her real experience, so too is her character, Arabella, but in her case, it's a book rather than a television show. The very first shot in "Eyes Eyes Eyes Eyes" (E1) is of Arabella's room with notes on the wall, which we later find out is how she is organizing the material with Zain's help in Episode 11. And by the last episode, "Ego Death" (E12), Arabella is ready to bestow her boon (her book) on the world. The name of both the bar and the episode, "Ego Death," again relates to the hero's journey. In the last step, "Freedom to Live," of the "Return" stage, Campbell describes the end of a Welsh tale about a hero, Gwion Bach: "Though he feared the terrible hag, he had been swallowed and reborn. Having died to his personal ego, he arose again established in the Self."[60] Campbell's explanation of the ego is as follows: "What I want, what I believe, what I can do, what I think I love, and all that. What I regard as the aim of my life and so forth. It might be too small. It might be that which pins you down."[61] Campbell makes the point that one must go beyond the limitations of the ego to realize the Self, which is the core of divinity in all people. In the same section in which Campbell discusses Gwion Bach, he also quotes *The Bhagavad Gita*: "Even as a person casts off worn-out clothes and puts on others that are new, so the embodied Self casts off worn-out bodies and enters into others that are new...."[62] Although this passage addresses reincarnation, an important component of Hindu belief, Campbell uses it as a metaphor for leaving one's former attitudes behind as one attains greater levels of awareness in the subsequent stages of a single lifetime. Eknath Easwaran, in the introduction to his translation of *The Bhagavad Gita*, explains the notion of Self: "In profound meditation, [ancient sages] found, when consciousness is so acutely focused that it is utterly withdrawn from the body and mind, it enters a kind of singularity in which the sense of a separate ego disappears. In this state, the supreme climax of meditation, the seers discovered a core of consciousness beyond time and change. They called it simply Atman, the Self."[63] In this final stage of the hero's journey, the hero must go beyond the ego to be reborn to the Self and then return to help others. Campbell states the following about the "Return" stage: "The full round, the norm of the monomyth, requires that the hero shall now begin the labor of bringing the runes of wisdom, the Golden Fleece, or his sleeping princess back into the kingdom of humanity, where the boon may redound to the renewing of the community, the nation, the planet, or the ten thousand worlds."[64] At the end of Episode 11 and into Episode 12, we see Arabella struggle with the best way to communicate what she has learned on her journey. Campbell comments on this process, "There must always remain, however, from the standpoint of normal waking consciousness, a certain baffling inconsistency between the wisdom brought forth from the deep, and the prudence usually found to be effective in the light world."[65] Arabella has gained spiritual understanding that will help her heal from trauma and will help others heal as well, but she needs to determine its form. When she comes back to the everyday world, she must find a way to connect what she has learned in the unconscious realm with that of the conscious realm of everyday life.

This has particular relevance in "Ego Death" (E12), as we see Arabella imagining what could happen if she were to encounter David again. We see her working through three scenarios that run the gamut from revenge to justice to forgiveness. Tillet comments, "By offering multifaceted endings, Coel gives victims of sexual assault, particularly Black women who have survived rape, some of the most radical and cathartic moments of television I have ever witnessed."[66] This episode is reminiscent of *Groundhog Day* (Columbia Pictures: 1993, Harold Ramis) in that the action keeps starting over, always beginning with the same close-up of Bella on the roof with her white flatmate and friend, Ben (Stephen Wight), tending his garden and commenting on a noisy bird. In Scenario #1, we see Arabella, Terry, and Theo set a trap for David (now going by Patrick), with Arabella saying, "Now we're going to give him a taste of his own medicine." The result is that he once again tries to rape Arabella (who is disguised in a blonde wig) in a bathroom stall. At the crucial moment, Bella goes from pretending to be drugged to looking him in the eye and saying, "The criminal always returns to the scene of the crime. But who's the criminal, you or me?" Immediately after this, Theo jabs a syringe in him, intending to knock him out. He ends up remaining conscious and they decide to follow him into the night. The end result is that Theo strangles him with Arabella's knickers, while Arabella punches and kicks him, finally realizing that he is dead. While it wouldn't seem believable for Bella to outright murder someone, it does seem plausible that between her and Theo, things could get out of hand. But what gives it away as a hypothetical scenario is the bus ride with David's corpse on the seat next to Arabella, his head leaning on her shoulder. Upon seeing his bloody face, a woman remarks, "Boys will be boys." Once home, Arabella pushes his corpse under her bed, takes off her wig and then writes a note and pins it to her wall. And thus, we have been presented with the revenge scenario, a nod to narratives like *Promising Young Woman*.

Chapter 6. I May Destroy You

In Scenario #2, Bella and Terry see David and Tariq (now going by Michael) in Ego Death Bar, and Bella immediately calls the police. But Terry reminds her that they need evidence and asks if she has a plan. When Arabella hesitates in giving an answer, Terry wonders why they've been coming here. Arabella exclaims, "Why have we been coming here? Because I'm deranged, Terry. You know that. That's never up for discussion. Why am I here? Because I'm fixated on the past, not a future in which I'm reunited with my raper." It turns out that Terry has a plan, and in this scenario, she gets Bella to do a lot of cocaine, so she won't be knocked out when she drinks the spiked cocktail. Terry distracts Tariq by sitting on him and gyrating, which is similar to Scenario #1. When Arabella confronts David when he's about to rape her, she says calmly, "You put something in my drink." He responds, "You knew all along and drank it anyway," and he proceeds to act meanly, calling her vicious names. Then, he imitates remembered voices, "Don't you tell anyone, David," "If you tell anyone, I'll kill you," and "You're fucking worthless." It becomes clear that Arabella is imagining a scenario in which he was abused as a child. Finally, they are in Bella's room, and he says that he did lots of therapy when he was in prison for rape. This is reflected in what baliga reports in her article: "Many men I've met in restorative justice circles in prisons speak about the sexual abuse they endured as children and how that unresolved trauma gave rise to their offending."[67] In this scenario, the officers come to Arabella's place and apprehend David. So there is sympathy in this scenario, and yet the inclusion of the police maintains the narrative of achieving justice through the law.

In Scenario #3, Bella and Terry are back at Ego Death Bar, but this time, Bella is opening the stalls in the bathroom and each one reveals a different compartment of sexual assault. We see the woman from the hospital, when Arabella was getting examined after the rape, and then we see Terry, Theo, and Arabella when they were teenagers. When present-day Arabella and Terry come out of the bathroom, the place is deserted, except for David sitting at the bar. Suddenly, it's opposite day, and Tariq is now gyrating for Terry. Bella is kissing David in a stall and then they are together in her bedroom with him on top and, surprisingly, it's loving. Then their positions change and she appears to be penetrating him from behind. She is enjoying each thrust and he moans in pleasure. Then, she wakes up next to him. He asks if she was hoping he would creep out in the night and she says, "No." He says he won't go until she tells him to. Then, she says, "Go." He leaves with the corpse of David from Scenario #1, which crawls out from under the bed. Arabella takes the note, "Ben-Garden," off the wall. At the end of the episode, we hear Ben say again, "It's such a loud bird" and then ask if Bella is going to do her bar-watch thing and she says, "I'm actually not going back." Terry comes over, and Bella shows her a copy of her book with the dedication to Terry. Then, the whole group (including Kai, the trans man, whom Terry is now dating) gathers to watch Terry's performance in her commercial. And finally, we see Sion introduce Arabella Essiedu's independently published book, *January 22* (which was the working title for the series and the date when Michaela Coel's rape occurred). We see a close-up of Arabella in the pink wig and then her running alongside the sea (symbolic of the unconscious) and then the typed word, End.

Joseph Campbell has this to say about coming back to the world to communicate what you have learned in the unconscious realm: "Freedom to pass back and forth across the world division, from the perspective of the apparitions of time to that of the causal deep and back—not contaminating the principles of the one with those of the other, yet permitting the mind to know the one by virtue of the other—is the talent of the master."[68] This applies not only to the fictional character Arabella but also to Michaela Coel. In the PBS series, Bill Moyers says to Joseph Campbell, "Unlike the classical heroes, we're not going on our journey to save the world, but to save ourselves." Campbell's rejoinder is "And in doing that, you save the world. I mean, you do. The influence of a vital person vitalizes, there's no doubt about it. The world is a wasteland. People have the notion of saving the world by shifting it around and changing the rules and so forth. No, any world is a living world if it's alive, and the thing is to bring it to life. And the way to bring it to life is to find, in your own case, where your life is, and be alive yourself, it seems to me."[69] And this is what Michaela Coel has done. One of the profound achievements of *I May Destroy You* is that it probes the typical stance of revilement and revenge. It demonstrates that we aren't required to hate, imprison, or kill in response to being abused, violated, or raped. But instead, we can arrive at a different response, possibly one involving empathy. It is this compassion that makes *I May Destroy You* soar and sets it apart from other shows that examine similar terrain. But it's the show's boldness, honesty, and depth that raise it to another level, independent of its subject matter. One can only hope that this impressive show leads to more like it in the future with other independent voices at their core.

IV

Retrospection

Chapter 7

Stranger Things
Exploring the Eighties Through Genre TV

When *Stranger Things*, created by the Duffer brothers, premiered on Netflix in July of 2016, it quickly became a success. While Netflix didn't originally release viewership numbers, ratings compiled by Symphony Advanced Media showed that the series averaged 14.07 million viewers in the 18–49 demographic its first 35 days, making it the third most-watched Netflix Original Series in that timeframe and demographic that year.[1] Only Season 1 of the relaunch of *Fuller House* (Netflix: 2016–2020, Jeff Franklin) and Season 4 of the popular *Orange Is the New Black* (Netflix: 2013–2019, Jenji Kohan) drew bigger numbers in their first 35 days.[2] This is remarkable for a show that audiences weren't familiar with and that initially had a modest marketing campaign. The story starts in the fictional town of Hawkins, Indiana, in the 1980s when a boy named Will Byers (Noah Schnapp) goes missing, and his mother Joyce (Winona Rider) enlists local police chief Jim Hopper (David Harbour) to help uncover his whereabouts. Soon, others are searching for Will, including his older brother Jonathan (Charlie Heaton) and his friends Mike Wheeler (Fin Wolfhard), Lucas Sinclair (Caleb McLaughlin), and Dustin Henderson (Gaten Matarazzo). Shortly after Will disappears, Barbara Holland (Shannon Purser), Barb for short, who is best friends with Mike's older sister Nancy (Natalia Dyer), also goes missing. Nancy teams up with Jonathan, to the initial chagrin of her boyfriend Steve Harrington (Joe Keery), to find her missing friend. They soon encounter supernatural forces and a mysterious girl called Eleven (Millie Bobby Brown) who has psychokinetic abilities. Together, they fight the Demogorgon, a supernatural humanoid monster from the Upside Down (an alternate dimension) and investigate what happened to Will and Barb. It's important to note that the main characters in the first two seasons of *Stranger Things* are all white, with the exception of Lucas, who is Black. Race goes largely unacknowledged on the show.

Chapter 7. Stranger Things

Stranger Things was created by brothers Matt and Ross Duffer, who also serve as executive producers along with Shawn Levy, Dan Cohen, Cindy Holland (2016), Jessica Mecklenburg (2016), Matt Thunell (2016), Karl Gajdusek (2016), Brian Wright (2016–2017), Iain Paterson (2017–present), and Curtis Gwinn (2022–present). After graduating from Chapman University's Dodge College of Film and Media Arts in 2007, the Duffer brothers went on to direct several short films and made their feature-length directorial debut with the horror film *Hidden* (Warner Bros. Pictures: 2015). The film was enough of a success that it led to them writing for the Fox TV series *Wayward Pines* (Fox: 2015–2016, Chad Hodge).[3] Despite their achievements, they were still relatively unknown at this point in their careers. The Duffer brothers pitched *Stranger Things* to more than 15 networks before finally securing a deal.[4] Executives were wary of the dark tone of the show, given that most of the main characters were children.[5] Netflix, on the other hand, saw its potential right away.[6] *Stranger Things* would go on to develop a devout fanbase and become one of Netflix's signature shows. It is also largely credited with sparking a renewed interest in eighties pop culture. Season 2 of *Stranger Things* premiered in 2017 and Season 3 premiered in 2019. Season 4 (broken up into two volumes and released five weeks apart) premiered in 2022 after several delays due to Covid-19. To date, Season 4 is the most-watched English-speaking series in the history of the streaming platform.[7] The Duffer brothers announced that there will be a Season 5 and that it will be the last.

Netflix launched in 1997 as a DVD rental and sales business, modeled after the e-commerce company Amazon (well before the days of Amazon Prime Video). It was the brainchild of Reed Hastings and Marc Randolph, who met while Randolph was working as a marketing director for Hasting's company, Pure Atria. Prior to Netflix, Hastings already had several successful start-ups on his resume, including various mail-order and direct-to-customer companies. Though brick-and-mortar video rental stores were quite popular with consumers, Netflix was able to highlight some of their shortcomings. Namely, consumers were plagued by deliberately understocked new releases and late fees. Netflix essentially made a profit the opposite way as their main competitors like Blockbuster. For a low monthly fee, subscribers could select the titles they wanted and have them sent directly to their home. After they finished watching the DVDs, they simply mailed them back. Unreturned DVDs meant that Netflix didn't have to pay for return shipping or send the next round of DVDs out. Most importantly, this new model eliminated late fees. It's important to note that Netflix invested in DVDs at a time when only 2 percent of American households even owned a DVD player.[8]

Their gamble paid off and DVDs took off in popularity soon after. By the year 2000, Netflix emerged as a legitimate competitor in the movie rental industry. But Blockbuster remained on top, in part, by earning roughly $800 million in late fees.[9] That year, Netflix also developed its personalized movie recommendation system, which would later become its trademark. Perhaps in response to the grip Blockbuster still had on the industry, Hastings and Randolph offered to sell Netflix to Blockbuster for $50 million. Blockbuster's then–CEO John Antioco turned the deal down.[10] This only galvanized Netflix more as it continued to gain traction with consumers. Facing pressure from both Netflix and Redbox, an automated video rental company, Blockbuster changed its lucrative late fee model and essentially copied Netflix. Though Blockbuster was initially plagued by technical issues that hindered their DVD-by-mail services, they still had the upper hand. One of their advantages was that customers had a choice of either mailing their DVDs back or returning them to their brick-and-mortar stores. They called this level of membership "Total Access." After an aggressive advertising campaign, things were finally looking up for Blockbuster, except for one problem: it was losing roughly $2 each time a Total Access member exchanged a DVD for a new one.[11] Blockbuster eventually had to raise prices and lost many customers in the process.[12] In 2007, Netflix approached Blockbuster yet again, this time with an offer to buy its online business at a price of $200 per subscriber (about $600 million).[13] The sale would mean that Netflix subscribers could return their rentals to Blockbuster stores. Thinking the offer was low, Blockbuster turned the deal down. John Antioco was ousted as CEO soon after over a dispute with board members about his bonus.[14] Also in 2007, the entertainment industry would be forever changed when Netflix introduced on-demand video streaming via the internet. Blockbuster countered by purchasing Movielink, which allowed patrons to rent and download movies from their online catalog. Despite the new strategy, problems persisted, and it eventually went back to a model that relied on a form of late fees for revenue. Blockbuster filed for chapter 11 bankruptcy in 2010, whereas Netflix thrived, and as of 2022, has 222 million subscribers.[15] In addition to its licensed content, it offers viewers a plethora of original shows and films. Although the streaming landscape is vastly different from when Netflix first offered streaming content and is much more crowded, Netflix remains number one. Since its inception, Netflix has shown a tremendous ability to adapt, thus retaining its crown.

Stranger Things proves to be an excellent example of the Retrospection trend. To be clear, retrospection in television predates the period covered in this book (2016–2020) and has been a component of every era of television. But *Stranger Things* is indicative of its increased use and higher level of sophistication, thus rising to the level of trend. While the term nostalgia denotes affection and longing for a time in the past, retrospection implies having both positive and negative recollections of a bygone era. In terms of positive depictions, *Stranger Things* certainly capitalizes on the 1980s nostalgia that has continued to rise in popularity over the past few years. This may be due to a cultural phenomenon known as the 30-year cycle, which predicts a renewed interest in cultural trends that existed 30 years prior (although to be fair, the exact length of the cycle is up for debate).[16] For example, the film *Back to the Future* (Universal Pictures: 1985, Robert Zemeckis) reflected a renewed interest in the 1950s as Marty McFly (Michael J. Fox) time travels from 1985 to 1955 and meets his parents.[17] The recent television landscape provides further evidence for the 30-year cycle theory. There are shows like *GLOW* (Netflix: 2017–2019, Liz Flahive, Carly Mensch) that take place in the eighties, relaunches like *Cobra Kai* (YouTube Red, Netflix: 2018–2023, Josh Heald, Jon Hurwitz, Hayden Schlossberg) that are based on eighties source material and continue the original story, and reboots like *MacGyver* (CBS: 2016–2021, Peter M. Lenkov) that are based on eighties source material but reinvent the original story. There are also shows like *I Am Not Okay with This* (Netflix: 2020, Jonathan Entwistle, Christy Hall) that take place in the modern day but have eighties references throughout. Other recent shows that take place in the eighties include (in chronological order by beginning year, and then alphabetically by title) *Everybody Hates Chris* (UPN, The CW: 2005–2009, Chris Rock, Ali LeRoi), *The Americans* (FX: 2013–2018, Joe Weisberg), *The Carrie Diaries* (The CW: 2013–2014, Amy B. Harris), *The Goldbergs* (ABC: 2013–2023, Adam F. Goldberg), *Halt and Catch Fire* (AMC: 2014–2017, Christopher Cantwell, Christopher C. Rogers), *Red Oaks* (Amazon Prime Video: 2014–2017, Gregory Jacobs, Joe Gangemi), *Show Me a Hero* (HBO: 2015, David Simon, William F. Zorzi), *Wet Hot American Summer: First Day of Camp* (Netflix: 2015, Michael Showalter, David Wain), *Dead of Summer* (Freeform: 2016, Edward Kitsis, Adam Horowitz, Ian Goldberg), *Snowfall* (FX: 2017–2023, John Singleton, Eric Amadio, Dave Andron), *Pose* (FX: 2018–2021, Ryan Murphy, Brad Falchuk, Steven Canals), *The Hardy Boys* (Hulu: 2020–present, Steve Cochrane, Jason Stone), and *BMF* (STARZ: 2021–present, Randy Huggins).

Much has been made of the nostalgia of *Stranger Things*, with countless articles, blogs, and videos dedicated to highlighting Easter eggs left by the Duffer brothers that reference eighties pop culture, so much so that we will not attempt to document them in this chapter. Rather, this chapter will assert that *Stranger Things* takes place in a world where filmmaker Steven Spielberg is the chief architect. To be clear, Spielberg's work does not necessarily capture the reality of many who lived through the 1980s. His films do much, however, to capture the cultural zeitgeist of the decade. The influence that Spielberg has had on *Stranger Things* is immeasurable. He is in the very DNA of the show. In an article in *The Guardian*, "The Duffer Brothers: 'Could we do what Spielberg did in the 80s and elevate it like he did?'" the Duffer brothers explain how *Stranger Things*, as we now know it, came to be. Ross Duffer is quoted as saying, "What Spielberg did in the 80s was he took these kind of B-movie ideas, like flying saucers or killer sharks, and he elevated it. In this new medium, can we go back and try and do a little of what he did, take something that's been relegated to being cheesy, and can you do an elevated version of that?"[18] In an interview published by *Quartz*, "Watch: The opening scene of 'Stranger Things' owes everything to 'E.T.,'" the author Ashley Rodriquez quotes *Stranger Things* director of photography Tim Ives as saying that his mantra for his work on the show is "What would Steven do?"[19] On his podcast, *Geek's Guide to the Galaxy*, critic Andrew Liptak calls the first season of the show "basically an eight-hour version of a Steven Spielberg movie."[20] Put simply, without Spielberg, there would be no *Stranger Things*.

In a *Deseret News* article, a Brigham Young University communications professor, Scott Haden Church, Ph.D., explains the appeal of a referential work like *Stranger Things* in a quote from Umberto Eco's essay "Casablanca: Cult Movies and Intertextual Collage," which analyzes the film *Casablanca* (Warner Bros. Pictures: 1942, Michael Curtiz). According to Eco, "Two clichés make us laugh, one hundred clichés move us."[21] Church continues, "If you just use one [cliché], then it feels contrived … but if you do all of them, together it becomes a masterpiece of referentiality.… These are tried and true techniques that resonate with people, and if you find a way to weave them all together and do a cohesive plot line, then it just wins you over."[22] Through its countless references to Spielberg and 1980s pop culture, *Stranger Things* proves the effectiveness of referentiality in television.

Out of all the Spielberg films that inspired *Stranger Things*, none is more obvious than the thriller *Jaws* (Universal Pictures: 1975). *Jaws* tells the story of police chief Martin Brody (Roy Scheider), shark hunter Quint (Robert Shaw), and oceanographer Matt Hooper (Richard Dreyfuss) as they set out to destroy a shark that's been terrorizing beachgoers. Days before its release and believing that they had a hit on their hands, Universal Pictures saturated television networks with ads for the film, which was unconventional at the time.[23] They also issued a wide release in hundreds of theaters, which was a tactic pioneered on the Francis Ford Coppola film *The Godfather* (Paramount Pictures: 1972) only a few years earlier and put into overdrive for *Jaws*.[24] The film smashed box office records and was described as a phenomenon. It also changed how studios thought

Chapter 7. Stranger Things 143

of the summer, as it was previously considered the off season and a time for studios to release their schlocky B-movies.[25] Lines stretched around the block with many moviegoers going back to see the film repeatedly. A few years later, the epic space opera *Star Wars* (20th Century–Fox: 1977), directed by George Lucas, would smash the box office records set by *Jaws*. Both *Jaws* and *Star Wars* were given the designation "blockbuster" and were substantially different from the New Hollywood films that preceded them.

As a brief explanation, New Hollywood began to emerge with breakout films in the 1960s like *Bonnie & Clyde* (Warner Bros., Seven Arts: 1967, Arthur Penn), *The Graduate* (Embassy Pictures: 1967, Mike Nichols) and *Midnight Cowboy* (United Artists: 1969, John Schlesinger). These films threatened to destabilize the Hollywood system and found audiences, in part, by not shying away from topics like violence and sexuality that would have been flagged by Hollywood censors just a few years prior. With the film *Easy Rider* (Columbia Pictures: 1969, Dennis Hopper), counterculture was put onscreen front and center and the era known as New Hollywood had officially begun. With New Hollywood, films were decidedly more gritty, subversive, and provocative. Taking their cue from other movements such as the French New Wave, they were also increasingly more innovative and spoke to a younger crowd. This was, in part, due to directors having an increased amount of control over their films.

By the late 1970s, New Hollywood began to crumble as the studios grew wary of the massive budgets and creative freedom demanded by directors. The national mood was also shifting again, with the general public wanting to feel good about America once more. This made audiences hungry for a new type of film and blockbusters fed that hunger. Studios also found that blockbusters were easily marketable (with cross promotions and merchandising), and though they had high production budgets, they were built for big box office returns. They also had short cinematic plots that could be summarized in one or two sentences, were usually science fiction, action, or horror films, and typically appealed to a young male crowd. Most importantly, the studios had regained control and were on the hunt for tent-pole films. As a result, films became less innovative and more formulaic. For better or worse, with the emergence of the blockbuster, the face of cinema was forever changed.

In particular, *Jaws* was the gamechanger that became the template for a new era of filmmaking that would define the eighties. It is therefore fitting that the impact of Spielberg's *Jaws* on *Stranger Things* is extensive. First, a comparison of the settings reveals similarities between *Jaws*' fictional Amity Island, off the coast of New England, and *Stranger Things*' fictional town of Hawkins, Indiana. When looking at Hawkins and Amity

Island, it's easy to draw a line from one to the other. At their core, they both show viewers a setting that offers wonder, adventure, and, yes, terror, from what feels to many like their own backyard. Of course, there are differences. Amity Island is more of a bustling beach town while Hawkins is landlocked. Still, we know the Duffer brothers were thinking of Amity Island in the early stages of developing *Stranger Things*. The show was originally going to take place in Montauk, New York, due to its similarities with Amity Island, but the location was later changed for practical reasons.[26] On a side note, they were also, in part, inspired by "the Montauk Project," which conspiracy theorists contend was a series of experiments conducted by the U.S. government in the area of psychological warfare.[27] At one point, the working title of the show was even *Montauk*.[28]

Other connections between *Jaws* and *Stranger Things* are evident in their marketing. In a promotion for *Stranger Things*, Netflix released a series of posters that pay tribute to the films that inspired the series, and not surprisingly, *Jaws* was one of the films selected. The original poster for *Jaws* depicts a woman swimming in the ocean with a giant shark lurking beneath her. Above her, in red, is the title, "Jaws," which compares to the top of the *Stranger Things* poster, which states in red, "Stranger Things." In the poster for *Stranger Things*, the Demogorgon takes the place of the shark, lurking in the Upside Down, as a ghostly figure walks above it. In between the two are the words "Don't go in the void," which echoes the tagline for *Jaws*, "You'll never go in the water again." On a side note, a *Jaws* poster can be seen in the Byers household as early as Season 2 and can be spotted throughout the series.

In addition, there are similarities between the shark in *Jaws* and the Demogorgon, the humanoid monster from the Upside Down, whose face opens like a flower in bloom to reveal its terrifying teeth. In an *Entertainment Weekly* article written by the Duffer brothers, titled "Stranger Things episode 6: How the Duffer Brothers created the monster," they write, "[the Demogorgon] is an interdimensional being that has more in common with the shark from Jaws than Pennywise [the evil clown] from It. When the monster enters our dimension, it's like a shark breaching the water."[29] Much like a shark, the Demogorgon is also attracted to blood. In "The Monster" (S1, E6) Jonathan and Nancy discuss the attributes of the Demogorgon. Nancy says, "it seems to hunt at night, like ... a lion or a coyote.... And remember at Steve's, when Barb cut herself?.... Sharks can detect blood in one part per million. That's one drop of blood in a million, and they can smell it from a quarter mile away." Nancy's analysis unmistakably illustrates the similarities between the Demogorgon and a shark. Finally, in Season 3, one of the primary antagonists is the mayor of Hawkins, Larry Kline (Cary Elwes), who becomes embroiled in a corruption scandal after unfairly giving land grants to the Starcourt company, which owns the local mall. We eventually find out the mall is a secret Soviet base. In *Jaws*, aside from the shark, the primary antagonist is Mayor Larry Vaughn (Murray Hamilton). Though not as maniacal as Larry Kane, Mayor Vaughn dismisses the shark attacks early on and refuses to close the beaches for fear that doing so would interfere with tourism revenue. The safety of the public is jeopardized as a result.

In terms of protagonists in *Stranger Things*, one of the outstanding ones is Chief of Police Jim Hopper, who oversees the safety and well-being of Hawkins. The character has several influences, including in Season 2 when Hopper wears a Hawaiian shirt as a nod to *Magnum P.I.* (CBS: 1980–1988, Donald P. Bellisario, Glen A. Larson). But the most apparent influence is Chief of Police Martin Brody in *Jaws*. Both Hopper and Brody seemingly landed carefree jobs in virtually crime-free towns after leaving New York City and their jobs in the NYPD. Even their police uniforms and vehicles are almost identical, though Brody's truck doesn't have a roof. In the pilot episode of *Stranger Things*, "The Vanishing of Will Byers," Hopper says the worst thing to happen in Hawkins "was when an owl attacked Eleanor Gillespie's head because it thought that her hair was a nest." In *Jaws*, Brody says, "I'm telling ya, the crime rate in New York will kill ya. There's so many problems, you never feel like you're accomplishing anything. Violence, rip-offs, muggings, kids can't leave the house, you gotta walk 'em to school. But in Amity, one man can make a difference. In twenty-five years, there's never been a shooting or murder in this town." Both have their amiable jobs disrupted when tragedy strikes. For Hopper, it is the disappearance of Will Byers. For Brody, it is a series of deadly shark attacks. On a side note, when Hopper types up the incident report for Will's disappearance, the close-up on his typewriter mirrors an early shot in *Jaws* when Brody types out the words "shark attack."

Both are also shaped by their fears and tragic pasts (albeit Hopper's backstory is much more tragic). For Hopper, it is the death of his daughter and the end of his marriage soon after. It is implied that he develops substance abuse problems as a method to cope. For Brody, it is his crippling fear of the water, presumably after a near-drowning experience. In both cases, the new tragedies they are forced to face resemble their own fears and traumas. In *Jaws*, we only get hints at how Brody's trauma impacts his life. While on the beach, an acquaintance named Harry (Alfred Wilde) comes up to him and says, "We know all about you, Chief. You don't go in the water at all, do you?" Brody responds with the non sequitur, "That's some bad hat, Harry," referring to his swimming cap. A little while later, when the shark attacks, we see Brody instinctively run toward the water, but he stops in his tracks as others rush past him to save their loved ones.

His fear of the water cripples his ability to take action. In *Stranger Things*, we get a much more in-depth look at Hopper's trauma and the toll it's taken on his life. In "The Nina Project" (S4, E5), while trapped in a Soviet prison, he tells former guard and fellow inmate Enzo (Tom Wlaschiha) about his experience working with the chemical Agent Orange while serving in the Vietnam War. Hopper talks about how, when he came back home, guys he had served with tried to have families, but their babies either died or had horrible birth defects. Hopper attributes this, and the eventual death of his own daughter, to their exposure to Agent Orange. He says, "The horror followed us, clung to us," and he concludes by saying, "Everyone I love, I hurt. See, I was wrong this whole time. I wasn't cursed; I am the curse." As a result of his trauma, Hopper feels responsible for the death of his daughter and thinks of himself as a liability to those around him.

In the opening minutes of the pilot episode of *Stranger Things*, it is clear that *E.T. the Extra-Terrestrial* (Universal Pictures: 1982, Steven Spielberg) is also a major influence on the show. The film is about a boy named Elliot (Henry Thomas) who forms a deep connection with an alien, who he calls E.T. (Matthew De Meritt), short for extra-terrestrial. When E.T.'s well-being becomes at risk, Elliot, his siblings, and friends embark on a mission to get E.T. home. Similar to Eliot's older brother Mike (Robert MacNaughton) and his friends playing *Dungeons & Dragons*, a fantasy role-playing game, at the beginning of *E.T. the Extra-Terrestrial*, we see Mike, Will, Dustin, and Lucas playing *Dungeons & Dragon* at the beginning of the pilot episode of *Stranger Things*. Both houses are set in suburbia, California and Indiana, respectively. Before *Stranger Things* even began production, the Duffer brothers used *E.T. the Extra-Terrestrial* to help develop their ideas for the show. According to an article they wrote for *Entertainment Weekly* titled "Stranger Things episode 5: The Duffer Brothers explain the show's soundtrack," they edited together footage from the film and others with synth-heavy music composed by John Carpenter.[30] According to them, "As soon as we heard John Carpenter's eerie synth drones play over shots from E.T., we got major goosebumps."[31] In addition to *E.T. the Extra-Terrestrial*, other Spielberg films not covered in this chapter that put kids front and center include *Indiana Jones and The Temple of Doom* (Paramount Pictures: 1984), *Hook* (TriStar Pictures: 1991), *Empire of the Sun* (Warner Bros. Pictures: 1987), and *Jurassic Park* (Universal Pictures: 1993). Throughout his career, Spielberg has been drawn to stories with young protagonists.

At its core, *Stranger Things* has a lot in common with *E.T. the Extra-Terrestrial*. Just as Elliot finds and bonds with E.T., an alien from another planet with telekinetic abilities, Mike finds and bonds with Eleven, a girl raised in a scientific lab with telekinetic abilities. E.T. takes refuge in

Elliot's house without his parents knowing, and Eleven takes refuge in Mike's household without his family knowing. *E.T. the Extra-Terrestrial* was also a major influence on how Millie Bobby Brown played Eleven. The Duffer brothers told her that they wanted the relationship between Mike and Eleven to resemble E.T and Eliot's relationship.[32] According to Brown, out of all the films she watched to prepare for her role in *Stranger Things*, *E.T. the Extra-Terrestrial* was her favorite.[33] At a closer glance, there are even some scenes in *Stranger Things* that are directly inspired by *E.T. the Extra-Terrestrial*. For example, when Elliot attempts to acclimate E.T. to his home by showing off his toy collection, among his action figures are the *Star Wars* characters Greedo, Lando Calrissian, and Boba Fett. In the *Stranger Things* episode, "The Weirdo on Maple Street" (S1, E2), when Mike is trying to acclimate Eleven, El for short, to his home, he shows her his toy collection, which includes the *Star Wars* character Yoda. In *E.T. the Extra-Terrestrial*, Elliot's sister Gertie (Drew Barrymore) dresses E.T. up in women's clothes, complete with a blonde wig, hat, dress, pearl necklace, and handbag. In the *Stranger Things* episode "The Body" (S1, E4), Mike, Dustin, and Lucas decide to sneak El into their school by dressing her in a pink dress and blonde wig with a jacket and tube socks. The purpose is so she can use the A.V. Club's Heathkit Ham Shack radio to better communicate with Will in the Upside Down, which can be likened to E.T. phoning home. Yet another example in *E.T. the Extra-Terrestrial* is when Eliot and Mike sneak E.T. out of the house on Halloween dressed as a ghost. In the *Stranger Things* episode "Trick or Treat, Freak" (S2, E2), El tries to convince Hopper to let her out of the house on Halloween because no one would recognize her if she's dressed like a ghost. When E.T. and El are left to their own devices in Eliot's and Mike's households, respectively, both develop an affinity for television. El's love of Eggo Waffles is even reminiscent of E.T.'s affinity for Reese's Pieces. Just like Reese's Pieces' popularity soared after *E.T. the Extra-Terrestrial* came out, so did the popularity of Eggo Waffles, with sales skyrocketing after Season 1 of *Stranger Things*. This illustrates the broader cultural impact of the show.

Beyond the above examples, there is a more general way in which *E.T. the Extra-Terrestrial* has influenced *Stranger Things*, in that the film encapsulated a certain sense of freedom that kids experienced in the eighties, specifically in suburban America. While many still bought into the idea of a nuclear family, the divorce rate peaked in 1981 and different types of family structures were becoming more common.[34] There was also the emergence of the "latchkey kid," which was a term used to describe kids who fended for themselves after school while their parents were still at work, since dual-income households were becoming more common.[35] Such arrangements gave kids a tremendous amount of freedom. In the age of smartphones, that feeling of freedom is often at odds with what kids experience today. In the book *Stranger Things and the '80s* by Joseph Vogel, Ross Duffer is quoted as saying, "We grew up without cellphones.... I don't know what it's like growing up now, but when we were kids, you go outside, you'd go into the woods behind your house, and your parents [couldn't] contact you. They don't know where you are. There was a sense of, 'What if we find a treasure map out here, and mobsters were after us, and we'd find a ship with gold?' It feels like now, it feels like your mom texts you that it's time for dinner—it might just take you right out of that."[36] In fact, some of the students in our Recent TV Trends course credit the freedom experienced by the young protagonists in *Stranger Things* as one of the main reasons for liking the show.

To many in the 1980s, suburbia was synonymous with the American dream. In a *Chicago Magazine* article titled "Were the Suburbs a Blip?" Edward McClelland writes, "The 1980s were the pinnacle of America's suburban era. Back then, nobody with money wanted to live in cities, which were seen as bankrupt relics of a lifestyle the country abandoned after World War II. In the '80s, moving to the suburbs meant you'd made it."[37] The idealization of suburbia was compounded by the growing idea that cities were dangerous. This was, in part, due to a large number of factories and plants in some areas closing.[38] The so-called "war on drugs" also gave rise to the idea of the "urban gangster pusher"[39] and the "predatory ghetto addict."[40] Government policies targeted inner-city drug dealers but did very little to crack down on suburban buyers who were fueling the illegal drug trade.[41] This, coupled with other factors like harsher sentences for crack users than cocaine users, meant that minority offenders were being incarcerated at alarming rates.[42] In suburbia, parents felt that they could leave their kids to their own devices.

One of the primary symbols of kids having agency in *Stranger Things* are the bicycles that are cherished by Mike, Will, Lucas, and Dustin. In the pilot episode, when Will goes missing, Hopper finds his bike abandoned off to the side of the road and comments, "[A] bike like this is a Cadillac to these kids." If Will abandoned it, obviously something very bad has happened to him. Throughout the series, we see Mike, Dustin, and Lucas zoom around Hawkins on their bikes fleeing from bad guys and trying to solve the mystery of what happened to Will, which is similar to Elliot, Mike, and their friends in *E.T. the Extra-Terrestrial* zooming around the suburbs on their bikes in an effort to save E.T. And it was indeed Spielberg in *E.T. the Extra-Terrestrial* who pioneered this "Kids on Bikes" subgenre.[43] Those who have seen the film will likely remember the iconic shot of Elliot riding his bike in midair with E.T. in the basket against the backdrop of a full moon. In this subgenre, bikes are a clear reminder of the agency that children and teens have within their stories. On a side note, the "Kids on Bikes" subgenre has seen a resurgence of late. For example, *Euphoria*, also covered in this book, features its young protagonists riding around on bicycles. However, it's *Stranger Things* that really rises to the level of *E.T. the Extra-Terrestrial* and introduces the subgenre to a new generation of viewers.

Another topic that is exemplified by both *E.T. the Extra-Terrestrial* and *Stranger Things* is the threat of governmental forces hanging over their suburban paradise, something which reflects actual concerns in the eighties. Just as Michael Myers silently terrorized suburbia in John Carpenter's horror slasher film *Halloween* (Compass International Pictures: 1978), a constant fear was lurking in suburbia's own finely manicured backyard. Several high-profile cases in the eighties that involved missing children caught the public's attention.[44] Also, each night, a 10:00 p.m. public service announcement ominously asked viewers, "Do you know where your children are?"[45] The United States was also in the midst of the Cold War (which wouldn't end until 1991) and there was constant fear that life could end any second due to nuclear war with the Soviet Union. The early eighties also saw the emergence of a mysterious illness, later identified as HIV/AIDS. Without the largely effective treatments that exist today, the virus was considered a death sentence for those who contracted it. Since gay men were one of the primary groups affected, fear of HIV/AIDS, coupled with President Reagan's initial refusal to publicly acknowledge it, often manifested itself as homophobia, leaving many to feel unsafe and ignored.

These negative aspects of the eighties are reflected in various ways on the show and are part of the show's intricate retrospection concerning the era. In *E.T. the Extra-Terrestrial* (as well as in *Jaws*), those in power prove that they cannot be trusted. Though more ignorant than malicious, the government agents and scientists do E.T. great harm. In *Stranger Things*, those in power prove to be destructive time and time again. Despite this, some characters, like Mike's father, Ted (Joe Chrest), are shown having a blind trust in the government that is to the point of being comical. In "The Bathtub" (S1, E7), when Mike and El are on the run from murderous government forces, Ted tells his wife that they must have trust, saying, "This is our government. They're on our side." The importance of individual freedom and a mistrust of governmental authority are two of the strongest themes in *Stranger Things*.

The final Spielberg film to discuss is *Close Encounters of the Third Kind* (Columbia Pictures: 1977), which is about a young boy named Barry Guiler (Cary Guffey) who is abducted by aliens. After the abduction, an electrician named Roy Neary (Richard Dreyfuss) investigates a power outage in the region. He soon encounters a UFO, which lightly burns one side of his face. After the encounter, he becomes obsessed with a vision of a mountain-like formation, as does Barry's mother, Jillian (Melinda Dillon), and a select group of people, presumably around the world. Once again, the influence of *Close Encounters of the Third Kind* on *Stranger Things* is evident to the viewer early on. Just as the film is about a boy, Barry, being abducted by aliens, the plot of season 1 of *Stranger Things* is set in motion by the disappearance of Will. Their mothers, Joyce and Jillian, respectively, are both portrayed as women who will stop at nothing to save their child. In addition, in *Close Encounters of the Third Kind*, we see Roy exhibit odd behavior, similar to Joyce's behavior in *Stranger Things*. In the film, Roy is sculpting a shape out of mashed potatoes that he has piled high on his plate, which is similar to the mountain-like formation. After seeing the shocked reaction of his family, he says, "Well, I guess you've noticed something a little strange with Dad. It's okay, though. I'm still Dad. I can't describe it. What I'm feeling. And what I'm thinking. This means something. This is important." In Season 1 of *Stranger Things*, Joyce is convinced that Will, who is trapped in the Upside Down, is trying to communicate with her through lights. As a result, she covers the inside of her house with colorful twinkle lights and paints the alphabet on the wall so Will can spell out words with the blinking lights. In a fight with her ex-husband, Lonnie (Ross Partridge), Joyce says, "Maybe I'm a mess. Maybe I'm crazy. Maybe I'm out of my mind, but God help me, I will keep these lights up until the day I die if I think there's a chance that Will's still out there." Both Roy and Joyce slowly appear to become unhinged, even though both are more in tune with what is actually happening than other characters around them. It should also be noted that, in *Close Encounters of the Third Kind*, the aliens use musical notes and blinking lights to communicate with the humans they encounter, similar to the twinkle lights used by Joyce to communicate with Will. Furthermore, both *Stranger Things* and *Close Encounters of the Third Kind* take place in Indiana, which was chosen by the Duffer brothers as a nod to the Spielberg film.[46] In Season 2 of *Stranger Things*, the comparison shifts and it's Will who resembles Roy when he becomes possessed by the Mind Flayer, a murderous entity from the Upside Down. In "Will the Wise" (S2, E4), Will frantically sketches out the underground tunnels the Mind Flayer uses to navigate Hawkins on seemingly hundreds of pieces of paper that span across the entire Byers residence, like Roy obsessively sculpting the mountain-like formation.

Will's first encounter with the Mind Flayer is a clear nod to *Close Encounters of the Third Kind*. In "Mad Max" (S2, E1), Will is in the bathroom at home when he hears a rumbling in the distance. As he exits the bathroom, the rumbling becomes more foreboding, and he sees red lights flashing through the front door. The door creeps open on its own to reveal the swirling wind and what appears to be red bolts of lightning lighting up the ominous sky. Through the clouds, Will can see the spider-like Mind Flayer looming over Hawkins. This scene is reminiscent of a scene in *Close Encounters of the Third Kind* when UFOs surround Barry's house. Just like Will, Barry is drawn to the door. When he opens it, a bright orange light comes flooding in and he is abducted soon after. In a YouTube video produced by *Wired*, the Duffer brothers elaborate on how Barry's abduction scene inspired the scene where Will sees the Mind Flayer. Matt Duffer says, "That was the sequence when we were kids and we saw *Close Encounters* for the first time that kind of stayed with us the most. So, when Will is first getting signals from the Upside Down in Episode 1 and he opens that door, that's a pretty direct homage to *Close Encounters*."[47] This scene is one of the most direct references to a Spielberg film within the entire series. A later scene, from "Suzie, Do You Copy?" (S3, E1), also resonates with *Close Encounters of the Third Kind*. Alone in his room, Dustin has just returned from summer camp thinking his friends have forgotten about him. Suddenly, his toys come to life and lead him to his living room where it is revealed that El is controlling them with her mind. She is there with Max (Sadie Sink), Lucas, Will, and Mike, who sneak up on him and blow party horns. Startled, Dustin sprays his can of Farrah Fawcett hairspray, recommended to him by Steve, in Lucas's face. Early on in *Close Encounters of the Third Kind*, Barry's toys come to life as a result of the alien presence and wake Jillian. In both scenes, a cymbal-banging toy monkey can be seen (and heard), and upon closer inspection, the toy monkeys appear to be identical.

Beyond these examples, the most meaningful way in which *Stranger Things* mirrors *Close Encounters of the Third Kind* is in its acknowledgment of childhood trauma. As previously mentioned, both *Close Encounters of the Third Kind* and Season 1 of *Stranger Things* center on an abduction. In *Stranger Things*, Will especially suffers from great physical and mental trauma while trapped in the Upside Down. His suffering only increases in Season 2 when he is possessed by the Mind Flayer. Dustin, Mike, and Lucas also struggle emotionally in the wake of their friend's disappearance, as do Joyce, Jonathan, and Nancy. Another character who suffers perhaps even more than Will is El, who at the beginning of Season 1 escapes from Hawkins National Laboratory. Dr. Brenner (Matthew Modine) oversees the lab responsible for experimenting on El, who refers to him as "Papa." It is a title he does not deserve. He is as cruel as he is conniving, and he exploits El's abilities while keeping her in untenable conditions. The whereabouts of El's biological parents are unknown until Season 2, and it is assumed that she was abducted. In the essay "Psychoanalytic Examination of Stranger Things' Eleven: Trials and Tribulations of Childhood Trauma on the 'Child-Hero,'" Chrisovolandou Gronowski writes, "From erratic responses of screaming, crying, and rocking herself, to constant hypervigilance and disturbing flashbacks of being dragged through hospital corridors only to be thrown in a small closet, Eleven's past continues to haunt her mind despite her physical escape from the laboratory at the beginning of the series. It can be argued that Eleven meets the majority of criteria for a Post-Traumatic Stress Disorder (PTSD) diagnosis and utilizes many defense mechanisms in order to cope with her trauma and potential disorder."[48]

Despite her mental health struggles, we see El not only cope but also begin to heal from the trauma she's endured. In the *Observer* article "Pop Psych: What Netflix's 'Stranger Things' Teaches Us About Childhood Trauma," author James Cole Abrams writes, "As [El] learns to trust her body and her presence in this world, so too does she learn to use her power for what she wants, rather than to be forced to perform others' will. And this in turn shows her a new world: whereas before her powers were linked to pain and isolation, as the series progresses they allow her to experience joy and community."[49] In a *Medium* article titled "'Stranger Things' Is an Amazing Depiction of Trauma," Gillian Branstetter elaborates further. She discusses how El begins to heal from the self-blame caused by her inadvertently creating the interdimensional window that allows the Demogorgon to enter the human world. She writes, "What makes Eleven so remarkable as an example of trauma ... are the hints at recovery the show gives us across its eight episodes. She not only becomes more confident and outspoken, but she also creates new associations between her actions and their consequences. So instead of fearing further experiments when using her abilities, Eleven is rewarded for them by her newfound friends with gratitude and amazement."[50] In Season 1, Episode 7, when El enters a makeshift deprivation chamber in an attempt to contact Will and Barb, who are believed to be stuck in the Upside Down, she sees Barb's dead body and screams. Joyce immediately comforts her and tells her, "It's okay." Speaking to the significance of that moment, Branstetter writes, "It's an extremely evocative and tear-jerking scene, bringing to life the power of love on a mind only fed abuse. Eleven's fear and alarm are settled by a simple message—*You're okay. You're okay* is perhaps the hardest lesson for trauma survivors to learn."[51] Not only does *Stranger Things* acknowledge childhood trauma, but in some cases, it also emphasizes the process of healing from it.

In Season 4, it's important to note that the main villain, Vecna (Jamie Campbell Bower), is clearly meant to be a manifestation of mental illness and trauma. Vecna is a humanoid monster in the Upside Down who invades the minds of those who have experienced previous traumas before killing them. His first victim, a popular cheerleader named Chrissy (Grace Van Dien), which also happens to be the name of the first shark victim in *Jaws*, had an eating disorder. His second victim, high school newspaper journalist Fred Benson (Logan Riley Benson), was involved in a car crash that killed another person. His third victim, high school basketball player Patrick McKinny (Myles Truitt), was presumably abused at home. Max is also targeted by Vecna due to the trauma caused by the death of her stepbrother Billy (Dacre Montgomery), who was killed by the Mind Flayer in the prior season. Nancy is also eventually targeted due to the guilt she feels over the death of Barb. In "Dear Billy" (S4, E4), when Vecna targets Max, she is sitting by herself at Billy's grave reading him a letter she wrote. In the letter, she expresses the guilt she feels for not saving him. In a *Radio Times* article, "How Stranger Things tackles depression is nothing short of extraordinary," Emma Clarke writes, "more often than not, those with mental illnesses feel as though they have to combat their thoughts, feelings and low mood alone. They think and believe things that other people cannot always understand or see themselves, and it can be all-consuming."[52] As it turns out, music can be used to break Vecna's trance and Max is eventually saved by listening to the song "Running Up That Hill (A Deal with God)" by Kate Bush.[53] After the show of support from her friends, Max begins to understand that she is not alone. On a side note, the song, originally released in 1985, once again demonstrates the cultural power of *Stranger Things* in that it rose all the way to number 1 on the Billboard Global 200 chart soon after the first volume of Season 4 of *Stranger Things* was released.[54]

In *Close Encounters of the Third Kind*, childhood trauma is less in the foreground as compared with *Stranger Things* but still very much present. Roy's obsession with the mountain-like formation causes him to have a complete mental breakdown. In the director's cut of the film, he sits in the shower fully clothed and drenched from the water, emotionally distraught. Shortly after being confronted by his wife, Ronnie (Teri Garr), their eldest son, Brad (Shawn Bishop), enters the bathroom and proceeds to slam the door open and shut, yelling "crybaby" over and over. The next morning, events culminate when Roy breaks a window to shovel dirt and other materials into their house in order to build a larger version of the mountain-like formation. His family watches helplessly and eventually leaves to stay with Ronnie's sister. Spielberg has been very candid about how his own childhood experiences have impacted his filmmaking. In the HBO documentary, *Spielberg* (2017, Susan Lacy), he recalls yelling, "Crybaby, you crybaby, you crybaby!" at his father the first time he saw him cry.[55] He was especially affected by his parents' divorce, and it should be noted that *Close Encounters of the Third Kind* ends with Roy abandoning his family. According to Spielberg, it was the combination of his parents' divorce and his experience making *Close Encounters of the Third Kind* that led him to make *E.T. the Extra-Terrestrial*. In an article that appeared in *The Wrap* by Adam Chitwood, Spielberg recalls saying to himself, "What if I turn my story about divorce into a story about children, a family, trying to fill the great need and creating such responsibility—a divorce creates great responsibility especially if you have siblings, we all take care of each other. What if Elliott, or the kid—I hadn't dreamed up his name yet—needed to, for the first time in his life, become responsible for a life form to fill the gap in his heart?"[56] At their heart, *Close Encounters of the Third Kind* and *E.T. the Extra-Terrestrial* reflect the very personal childhood experiences and traumas of Steven Spielberg. On a side note, these themes are explored by Spielberg in a much more personal way in his more recent film, *The Fablemans* (Universal Pictures: 2022).

There are several other Spielberg-directed films outside of *Jaws*, *E.T. the Extra-Terrestrial*, and *Close Encounters of the Third Kind* that have influenced *Stranger Things*. For example, in Season 2 of *Stranger Things*, the "Demodogs" (similar to the Demogorgon but with dog-like attributes) resemble the velociraptors in *Jurassic Park*. The first three *Indiana Jones* films (Paramount Pictures: 1981–1989) have also been a major influence, with the most obvious reference being Hopper's hat, which resembles the fedora worn by the adventuring archeologist Indiana Jones (Harrison Ford). Spielberg also produced or executive produced films that have been a major influence on *Stranger Things*. These films include *Poltergeist* (MGM/UA Entertainment Co.: 1982, Tobe Hooper), *Gremlins* (Warner Bros.: 1984, Joe Dante), *The Goonies* (Warner Bros. Pictures: 1985, Richard Donner), and the *Back to the Future* trilogy (Universal Pictures: 1985–1990, Robert Zemeckis).

Stranger Things also has many influences outside of Steven Spielberg. Other notable films include (in chronological order by year, and then alphabetically by title), but are not limited to, *The Exorcist* (Warner Bros.: 1973, William Friedkin), the original *Star Wars* trilogy (20th Century–Fox: 1977–1983, George Lucas, Irvin Kershner, Richard Marquand), *Alien* (20th Century–Fox: 1979, Ridley Scott), *Mad Max* (Warner Bros. Entertainment, Roadshow Entertainment, Metro-Goldwyn-Mayer: 1979, George Miller), *Altered States* (Warner Bros.: 1980, Ken Russell), *The Fog* (AVCO Embassy Pictures: 1980, John Carpenter), *Escape from New York* (AVCO Embassy Pictures: 1981, John Carpenter), *The Evil Dead* (New Line Cinema: 1981, Sam Raimi), *The Road Warrior* (Roadshow Film Distributors: 1981, George Miller), *Scanners* (New World, Mutual, Manson International: 1981, David

Cronenberg), *The Thing* (Universal Pictures: 1982, John Carpenter), *Risky Business* (Warner Bros.: 1983, Paul Brickman), *Ghostbusters* (Columbia Pictures: 1984, Ivan Reitman), *The Last Starfighter* (Universal Pictures: 1984, Nick Castle), *The Never Ending Story* (Warner Bros.: 1984, Wolfgang Petersen), *Red Dawn* (MGM/UA Entertainment Company: 1984, John Milius), *The Terminator* (Orion Pictures: 1984, James Cameron), *The Breakfast Club* (Universal Pictures: 1985, John Hughes), *Day of the Dead* (United Film Distribution Company: 1985, George A. Romero), *St. Elmo's Fire* (Columbia Pictures: 1985, Joel Schumacher), *Witness* (Paramount Pictures: 1985, Peter Weir), *Aliens* (20th Century–Fox: 1986, James Cameron), *The Princess Bride* (20th Century–Fox: 1987, Rob Reiner), and *Terminator 2: Judgement Day* (Tri-Star Pictures: 1991, James Cameron). Another important reference is the tabletop role-playing game *Dungeons & Dragons* (TSR, Wizards of the Coast: 1974–present, Gary Gygax, Dave Arneson), which is a major influence on *Stranger Things* and provides a framework and terminology to the strange events that have befallen Hawkins.

Stephen King also deserves special mention, as his influence on *Stranger Things* is second only to Spielberg's. Films based on his books that have inspired the series include *Carrie* (United Artists: 1976, Brian De Palma), *The Shining* (Warner Bros.: 1980, Stanley Kubrick), *Cujo* (Warner Bros., PSO International: 1983, Lewis Teague), *Firestarter* (Universal Pictures: 1984, Keith Thomas), and *Stand by Me* (Columbia Pictures: 1986, Rob Reiner), as well as the TV miniseries *It* (Warner Bros. Television Distribution: 1990, Tommy Lee Wallace, Lawrence D. Cohen). In addition, after watching the show, author Stephen King Tweeted, "Watching STRANGER THINGS is [like] watching Steve King's Greatest Hits. I mean that in a good way."[57] On a side note, Spielberg and the Duffer brothers recently announced that they will be collaborating on a project based on the Steven King and Peter Straub novel, *The Talisman*.

Stranger Things is also evolving. The Duffer brothers have been candid about how Season 4 is, in many ways, a departure from the seasons that came before it, and this applies to its primary film reference as well. In an *IndieWire* article written by Samantha Bergeson, "'Stranger Things 4' First Look: New Season Teases Serious 'Nightmare on Elm Street' Horror Vibes," Matt Duffer says, "They're not kids anymore—they really are full-blown teenagers.... That's why this season we leaned more into horror. We figured they should be in their own [version] of 'A Nightmare on Elm Street' basically."[58] The horror film, *A Nightmare on Elm Street* (New Line Cinema: 1984), was directed by Wes Craven.

Perhaps the biggest departure from the world of Spielberg is the music composed by Kyle Dixon and Michael Stein, who comprise the band

Survive. The synth-heavy score is vastly different from Spielberg's typical choice of music with collaborator John Williams and his orchestrations. The original music of *Stranger Things* is more in line with composers John Carpenter and Vangelis, or the band Tangerine Dream. However, on closer inspection, maybe the influence of Spielberg (and Williams) is present after all. In a *Sound on Sound* article written by Will Betts, "Scoring Stranger Things," Michael Stein is quoted as saying, "The Upside Down was a result of the directors requesting a 'monster theme.' The only reference was to have a signature similar to Jaws, in the sense of being something simple and yet easily recognizable. The backbone of this song is an eight-step sequence that utilizes only four 'notes.' When you hear it, you know it's referencing the monster, or the monster could be present."[59] John Williams composed the score for *Jaws*, including the famous musical motif for the shark. Even when not readily apparent, the DNA of Spielberg can be discovered in *Stranger Things*.

In conclusion, upon careful examination of *Jaws*, *E.T. the Extra-Terrestrial*, and *Close Encounters of the Third Kind*, among other films, it becomes clear that *Stranger Things* takes place in a world formed by the films of Steven Spielberg. These influences can be seen in the show's marketing, locations, characters, plot, music, cinematography, and set design. However, it's important to note that *Stranger Things* is not a carbon copy of the films that inspired it. In *Uncovering Stranger Things: Essays in Eighties Nostalgia, Cynicism and Innocence in the Series*, Jacopo Della Quercia writes, "*Stranger Things* is as much a celebration of Spielberg's movies as it is an inversion of them, which provides fantastic insight into why his films were so successful to begin with."[60] In *Jaws*, Brody has a loving and supportive family, whereas in *Stranger Things*, the death of Hopper's child and his broken marriage lead to substance abuse issues.[61] In *Close Encounters of the Third Kind*, the bright and colorful flashing lights of the spaceship illicit a feeling of awe, whereas in *Stranger Things*, the twinkle lights communicate how Will is alone and living in constant fear.[62] In *E.T. the Extra-Terrestrial*, E.T.'s powers are healing, whereas in *Stranger Things*, El's powers wreak havoc.[63] The Duffer brothers have used the building blocks of Spielberg's films to create a world and a story that, while familiar, feels fresh and new.

CHAPTER 8

Lovecraft Country

Exploring Our Racist Past through Genre TV

Lovecraft Country is a horror drama created by Misha Green that premiered in 2020 on HBO. Green expanded on Matt Ruff's 2016 novel of the same name by presenting a broader examination of the Black experience in America, particularly the effects of racism, both past and present. She got her start as a writer on shows such as *Sons of Anarchy* (FX: 2008–2014, Kurt Sutter) and *Heroes* (NBC: 2006–2010, Tim Kring) and then became a co-producer and writer for *Helix* (Syfy: 2014–2015, Cameron Porsandeh) and a co-creator (along with Joe Pokaski) and executive producer of *Underground* (WGN: 2016–2017). For *Lovecraft Country*, Green was not only the creator but was also the showrunner and one of the executive producers, along with Jordan Peele and J.J. Abrams. The series was produced by Monkeypaw Productions (Jordan Peele's company), Bad Robot Productions (J.J. Abrams and Katie McGrath's company), and Warner Bros. Television Studios. In explaining how the show came about, J.J. Abrams says, "We got to know Jordan Peele years ago before *Get Out*, and he brought us this book and asked if we'd want to collaborate with him on it.... It wasn't until we started working with Misha that it became clear just how potent this thing could be, because her vision of it was so powerful and so righteous."[1] The show proved to be both immensely popular and highly acclaimed. For the season finale in October 2020, *Variety* noted that "a total audience of 1.5 million tuned in on Sunday night across all platforms,"[2] which exceeded the audience for the Season 2 finale of *Succession* (HBO: 2018–2023, Jesse Armstrong) in October 2019, and came close to the 1.6 million viewers for the finale of *Watchmen* (HBO: 2019, Damon Lindelof) in December 2019. The *Variety* article continues, "'Lovecraft Country' is currently the number 1 show on HBO Max, per the streamer, and at this point its premiere is nearing 10 million viewers on the platform."[3] In addition, the first season of *Lovecraft*

Country received 18 Emmy nominations with two wins, one for Courtney B. Vance, who plays George, as Outstanding Guest Actor in a Drama Series, and the other for Outstanding Sound Editing for a Comedy or Drama Series (One Hour). *Rolling Stone*'s chief TV critic, Alan Sepinwall, stated, "*Lovecraft Country* was the year's most ambitious drama—and, at times, its best and most cathartic."[4] The two main actors, Jonathan Majors (playing Atticus Freeman) and Jurnee Smollett (playing Letitia Lewis), were also highly praised. Alan Sepinwall writes, "Jonathan Majors will be the show's big discovery (that is, if you haven't seen *Da 5 Bloods* or *The Last Black Man in San Francisco*)."[5] In regard to Jurnee Smollett, Daniel Fienberg, in his review for *The Hollywood Reporter*, states, "The ensemble is led by *Underground* veteran Smollett in her latest 'Why isn't she the biggest star in the land?' performance.... You can't take your eyes off her."[6] The performances, the exquisite production values, and the exciting drama made this show highly watchable. But it is the show's examination of the past, and its invitation to look at the present through the lens of the past, that makes it memorable and a sterling example of the Retrospection trend.

Misha Green's first objective with *Lovecraft Country* was to explore racism as a continuum throughout American history. Fienberg states, "*Lovecraft Country* is proudly comfort-resistant ... forcing viewers to interrupt their entertainment for regular confrontations with a past that's never too far in the past and nightmares that are hard to relegate to the realm of fiction."[7] In some ways, *Lovecraft Country* is similar to *Stranger Things*, which we covered in the previous chapter, in that it is a horror/sci-fi/fantasy drama that explores a bygone era and pays homage to 20th-century films. But an essential difference is that the retrospection in *Lovecraft Country* revolves around the perspectives of people of color who have been typically excluded from American history and media. *Lovecraft Country* tells the stories of mostly Black characters, but also one Asian character, by examining historical periods, primarily the 1950s, but also the 1920s. In addition, it includes real-life references to many decades in the past hundred years though visual imagery and spoken word segments, which create the sense of a journey through time. Green makes the point, "Even though it was set in the 1950s, it was important to make the show timeless.... This was not one place, one-time, one-person racism."[8] In his review in *Vulture*, Matt Zoller Seitz states, "It's impossible to watch episodes dealing with segregation, the white-supremacist attitudes and policies of certain rich Americans, and redlining practices in housing without thinking of their modern equivalents."[9] In "Sundown" (S1, E1), this concept is explicitly stated when Tic reads his father's letter aloud, saying, "I know that, like your mother, you think that you can forget the past. You can't. The past is a living thing."

Chapter 8. Lovecraft Country

In addition, the series endeavors to depict the racist horrors that Black people have endured in a way that isn't traumatizing for a Black audience and yet invites all viewers, regardless of race, to understand the crucial realities of the Black experience over time in America.

Misha Green's first objective is wedded to her second objective, which again originates with the source material. Matt Ruff's novel *Lovecraft Country*, which begins in 1954 (although the show begins in 1955), lays the groundwork for its Black characters to face the horrors of racism but then deftly intertwines that with their experience of the horrors of monsters, wizards, ghosts, and other supernatural beings. The book and the show's title refers to H.P. Lovecraft (1890–1937), the early 20th-century author known for creating the cosmic horror genre and for being racist, anti-Semitic, and xenophobic. "The racism of Howard Phillips Lovecraft was extreme even for its time, and like Ruff's novel, the series quotes from a particularly vile poem Lovecraft wrote in 1912, one with the title 'On the Creation of N—s' that only gets more racist from there."[10] In addition, "Lovecraft supported Adolf Hitler and believed lynchings were necessary to prevent interracial relationships…. [His] letters also include hate-fueled, racist language about Jewish, Chinese, Portuguese, Italian, and Latinx people as well as other racial and ethnic groups."[11] The premise of Matt Ruff's book relies on subverting the bigotry and racism of Lovecraft by using his brand of horror as a vehicle for Black protagonists to turn into heroes. In Salamishah Tillet's interview with Misha Green, she asks, "While Lovecraft himself wrote racist stories and letters, did you find it refreshing that Matt Ruff, who is a white author, tried to depict the multi-dimensionality of his Black characters in 'Lovecraft Country'?"[12] Green's response is "But, here's my thing: For a white writer *not* to be able to step into the shoes of people of color confuses me. That should be the default—many people of color have to step into the shoes of white people. Women have to step into the shoes of men."[13] Green clearly respected Matt Ruff's novel and said in another interview, "The book is a beautiful jumping off point, but we've got to do what the heart of the book is, which is … reclaiming genre spaces for people of color."[14] And this becomes the second main objective for Green, to reclaim genre spaces for people of color within this larger-than-life television show.

The "racism as horror" approach that Jordan Peele uses so effectively in *Get Out* (Universal Pictures: 2017) is also present in *Lovecraft Country*. Green states, "In horror, there's a level of anxiety that your life can be taken at any moment…. That's the Black experience."[15] Whereas *Get Out* stays within the logic of its constructed fictional world, *Lovecraft Country* branches out in many directions, including a connection with historical events as well as imaginative possibilities that are explored through fantasy and science fiction. It is important to recognize that the show was released in 2020, the year of the galvanized Black Lives Matter movement. Michael K. Williams, who played Montrose, said, "Had you told me that *Lovecraft* would be airing post George Floyd's murder, post Breonna Taylor's murder, I wouldn't have been able to fathom that. It was a blessing to have this piece of narrative, this piece of art to hold up a big mirror for us to look at ourselves and to see the timelines of how we got here."[16] And Green excels at bringing together a myriad of elements in *Lovecraft Country* to create a complex picture of "how we got here." Her approaches to exploring racism in *Lovecraft Country* can be categorized as follows:

1. Interweaving racist historical realities with the narrative
2. Using real-life sources for visual and aural commentary on racism
3. Immersing the viewer in the racist acts that threaten the characters
4. Emphasizing supernatural metaphors for racism

Each category will be discussed using examples from the first three episodes. One of the aims is to demonstrate that Green's approaches propel the show beyond the original source material. Some of this is because material resonates differently when it is actualized in an image/sound medium like television. For example, it is one thing to read about violence done to a character and quite another thing to see it happening to a human being on the screen. But most of what Green has accomplished is because she transformed the original material into something new.

(1) Interweaving Racist Historical Realities with the Narrative

Since most of the story takes place in Jim Crow America in the 1950s, a brief explanation is needed. The 1896 Supreme Court decision in *Plessy v. Ferguson* was significant in that it upheld racial segregation laws and established the "separate but equal" doctrine, which served to entrench racial injustice across the country. By the turn of the century, the vast collection of state and local laws that mandated racial segregation in the South became known as Jim Crow laws (named after an offensive Black minstrel character from 1828) and included the segregation of public schools, parks, and transportation as well as restaurants, theaters, restrooms, and drinking fountains. The laws permeated the culture and became a way of life that supported white supremacy by oppressing Black citizens. This led to not only de jure ("by law") segregation but also de

Chapter 8. Lovecraft Country

facto ("by fact") segregation, which continues until today as something that exists in reality even though it's not mandated by law. It's important to emphasize that Jim Crow laws extended beyond the South since similar laws existed in most states in America. This is particularly relevant to *Lovecraft Country* since it takes place in the Midwest and the Northeast.

There are two racist historical realities that the show introduces in "Sundown" (S1, E1), when we see Tic, his friend Leti, and his Uncle George travel from Chicago to fictional Ardham (equated with Lovecraft's Arkham) in Massachusetts to find Tic's father, Montrose. It is on this road trip that we are introduced to the frightening concept of "sundown towns." Green states, "If I wrote this horror movie talking about sundown towns where you can't be [B]lack after dark in America, people be like, 'OK, we get the metaphor,' and it's like, no, that's real."[17] To clarify, this trip would have entailed traveling through Indiana and Ohio in the Midwest and then through Pennsylvania and New York in the Northeast. The second historical reality is that *The Safe Negro Travel Guide* that George and Hippolyta published is based on *The Negro Motorist Green Book*, which Victor Hugo Green first published in 1936, starting with locations in New York City where Black people could feel safe. By 1939, the Green Book covered locations throughout the entire United States and continued until 1966.

In "Holy Ghost" (S1, E3), the show then takes on the topic of racism in regard to housing, a theme that was also covered a year later in *Them* (Amazon Prime Video: 2021, Little Marvin), when Leti buys a house in a white neighborhood. She and her boarders are harassed with continuous honking from bricks tied to car horns, signs that proclaim, "We Are a White Community, Undesirables Must Go," as well asdirect threats. In the episode, Leti's sister Ruby (Wunmi Mosaku) comments, "Here we go. I told you it was going to be Trumbull Park all over again." This is a reference to the Trumbull Park Homes Race Riots (1953–1954), which started when the Chicago Housing Authority (CHA) accidentally allowed a light-skinned Black woman, Betty Howard, to move into projects that were designated only for white people, having assumed that she was white. Every night for weeks, white crowds aimed fireworks, rocks, and racial slurs at the apartment that she and her husband, Donald Howard, occupied. After two months and much debate, the CHA agreed to move in 10 more Black families, which triggered yet another round of violence.[18] Another historical reference in Episode 3 is that the eight Black ghosts in Leti's house, who were brutally experimented on by Hiram Epstein, a white scientist, represent the long history of Black people who were experimented on against their will. A prime example is the Tuskegee experiment (1932–1972), in which Black men with syphilis were led to believe that they were being treated for the disease when they were actually being studied for the long-term effects of the disease, which involved going blind, passing syphilis on to their wives and subsequently their children, and dying prematurely. Another example of experimentation on Black people that is directly referenced in Episode 3 occurs with the names of three of the eight ghosts, Lucy, Betsey, and Anarcha, who were enslaved women in the mid–1800s who were operated on, without anesthesia, by white gynecologist J. Marion Sims.

Yet one more historical aspect of Episode 3 occurs when we see Dee in the attic using a Ouija board to play with Bobo and her other friends. It turns out that Bobo is the nickname for the real-life Emmett Till, who lived in Chicago and was brutally murdered at the age of 14 in 1955. In the attic scene, Bobo is wearing the same distinctive tie that Emmett wore in a well-known photograph. In reference to his fateful trip to Mississippi, Bobo asks, "Will I have a good time on my trip?" The Ouija board's answer is "NO." And in Episode 8, the funeral for Emmett Till takes place, which will be discussed later in this chapter. As background information, Emmett lived in Chicago, but he went to visit relatives in Mississippi in the summer of 1955. He was with his cousins and their friends when he decided to go alone into a country store. "There were no witnesses in the store, but Carolyn Bryant—the woman behind the counter—later claimed that he grabbed her, made lewd advances and wolf-whistled at her as he sauntered out."[19] Days later, the woman's husband, Roy Bryant, and his half-brother, J.W. Milam, brutally beat Emmett beyond recognition, gouged out his eye, shot him in the head, and threw his body (attached to a cotton gin fan with barbed wire) in the Tallahatchie River. Emmett's mother, Mamie Bradley, requested that his body be sent back to Chicago, where she had an open-casket funeral for all the world to see what the racist murderers had done to her son. Later, an all-white jury delivered a verdict of "not guilty" for Bryant and Milam. In his 2017 book *The Blood of Emmett Till*, Timothy B. Tyson stated that Carolyn Bryant (in a 2007 interview) recanted much of what she originally said. "'That part's not true,' she told Tyson, about her claim that Till had made verbal and physical advances on her."[20] Maya Phillips, in her *New York Times* article "The Unintended Racial Horror of *Lovecraft Country*," questions the way in which historical figures such as Emmett Till, as well as historical events, are woven into *Lovecraft Country* because she believes that they are tangential to the main action. She writes, "And yet, it doesn't take 'Lovecraft Country' long to cross the line between mining the past and exploiting it for the purposes of its convoluted fiction. The series shamelessly name-drops events and figures from Black history as if crossing off squares on a racial Bingo card."[21] Another way to view it, however, is that weaving these historical events and people into the show raises awareness of history, creates a realistic context for the fictional story, and supports the show's aim of exploring racism in a meaningful way.

(2) Using Real-Life Sources for Visual and Aural Commentary on Racism

Within *Lovecraft Country*, the use of historical photos and spoken word segments enhance the understanding of the Black experience as well as comment on racism over time. As an example, in Episode 1, we see George, Tic, and Leti drive by a recreation of the Margaret Bourke-White photo "At the Time of the Louisville Flood" (1937),[22] which features a billboard that proclaims "WORLD'S HIGHEST STANDARD OF LIVING" at the top, with the phrase "There's no way like the American Way" on the right, with an image of a white family happily driving in a car on the left. Then, in front of the billboard, there is a long line of tired-looking Black people, who are clearly not living the American dream. Kalina Ivanov, the production designer for *Lovecraft Country*, states, "The departure point [for the design] was the tremendous amount of research on Chicago and America in the 1950s. There is so much photography preserved from the period, with perhaps the most important being the work of Gordon Parks."[23] In Episode 1, we see a scene that references one of Gordon Parks' photos, "Untitled, Shady Grove, Alabama, 1956,"[24] when George, Tic, and Leti are sitting on a picnic table outside a segregated hamburger stand. Another Gordon Parks photo that was recreated in the show is titled, "Department Store, Mobile, Alabama, 1956."[25] The photo shows an elegantly dressed Black woman and a young girl (presumably her daughter) in front of a sign for the "Colored Entrance" to a department store. In the show, we see a similar mother and daughter as Tic, George, and Leti use a "Colored Entrance" to exit a department store. In a *New York Times* article, "Hidden in Plain Sight: The Ghosts of Segregation," the Seattle-based photographer and writer Richard Frishman makes it clear that the Jim Crow visuals from *Lovecraft Country* are still with us. One of his recent photos of Edd's Drive-In, located in Pascagoula, Mississippi, is similar to the Gordon Parks photo taken in Shady Grove, Alabama, and to the scene in *Lovecraft Country*. At the far right of the photo, there is a repurposed window that was formerly the "Colored" window. Frishman states, "Several years ago, I began to photographically document vestiges of racism, oppression and segregation in America's built and natural environments—lingering traces that were hidden in plain sight behind a veil of banality."[26] Frishman states, "when the telling traces are erased, the lessons risk being lost."[27] Both Richard Frishman and Misha Green are making sure to remind us. In addition to well-known photos used as source material for particular scenes, there are also instances of impressive recreations of historical environments on the show that used archival photos as references. A good example of this, which will be discussed later in the chapter, is in "Rewind 1921" (S1, E9) when the characters travel back in time to the Tulsa Race Massacre.

The soundtrack for *Lovecraft Country* is a marvelous testament to mixing disparate elements in order to achieve a singular effect. Green states, "On *Underground*, we had used contemporary music to pull you into the present.... So the next level of that came through this idea of what we called 'scource,' which is what we called found audio that we would use as score. That idea was really intriguing for me because it takes this show that's set in the 1950s, and pulls it out of time."[28] An excellent example of this happens in Episode 1 over a montage of Tic, George, and Leti's road trip. Without it being identified as such, we hear the beginning of James Baldwin's opening in a debate with William Buckley at Cambridge University in 1965. The topic was "Has the American Dream Been Achieved at the Expense of the American Negro?" The montage begins over a sign with an offensive sundown town warning, continues over a gas station scene where a teenage white boy makes monkey gestures at Tic, and comes to rest on an Aunt Jemima billboard. We then see Tic buy a rose from a Black woman with a baby and finally we see the scene that was recreated from the Margaret Bourke-White photo. James Baldwin's speech begins with "Good evening. I find myself, not for the first time, in the position of a kind of Jeremiah" and ends with "The Mississippi or the Alabama sheriff, who really does believe, when he's facing a Negro boy or girl, that this woman, this man, this child must be insane to attack the system to which he owes his entire identity. And on the other hand..." The speech then fades over a new scene of Leti sitting on the hood of Woody (George's wood-paneled Packard) with Tic washing up nearby and George looking at a map. Misha Green boldly weaves these historical moments into her fictional show without proclaiming what they are—leaving it up to the viewer to seek information about them.

Another example of "scource" is used at the end of "Whitey's on the Moon" (S1, E2) when Samuel Braithwhite, the white patriarch, is in the process of ritually killing Tic so he can open a portal to the Garden of Eden and achieve mortality. We hear the voice of Gil Scott Heron say that he has a poem here called "Whitey on the Moon," which is from his debut album in 1970, Small Talk at 125th and Lenox. Then we see the exterior of the Sons of Adam Lodge as the camera goes through a window to reveal Tic being led into the space. As the ritual begins, so does the poem, "A rat done bit my sister Nell. (with Whitey on the moon)"[29] and it continues with the narrator saying that he can't pay the doctor bills, his rent has gone up, there's nothing left in his paycheck after taxes, and yet Whitey is still on the moon. As the poem progresses, we see a suffering Tic in the center of the space, functioning as a lightning rod for both blue arc flashes and a golden inferno of light coming from the portal. Samuel has worked himself up into a frenzy as he shouts incantations in the language of Adam. It becomes clear that Samuel's quest to become immortal is equated with putting a white man on the moon (which happened in 1969 with the Apollo 11 mission) while the narrator of the poem is equated with Tic, who is just trying to save his loved ones and survive, but like other Black Americans, is being sacrificed for the ambitions of wahite people.

(3) *Immersing the Viewer in the Racist Acts That Threaten the Characters*

On the road trip in Episode 1, the trio soon arrives in Simmonsville, Massachusetts, and heads to what was Lydia's Diner but is now the Simmonsville Diner. When sitting at the table, Tic moves a vinyl tile on the floor and sees clearly that the place was burned, just as Leti comes running down the hall, yelling at the top of her lungs that they need to get out now. The implication is that "Aunt Lydia" was a white woman who served Black customers and, as a result, her business was burned. They pack into Woody and endure the harrowing experience of being shot at by white townspeople in a truck, with Leti driving at break-neck speed, swerving, and doing her best to outrun their attackers. George yells at her, "Dammit, girl, you're gonna crash us!" She yells back, "My name's not girl. It's Leticia Fuckin' Lewis." They escape and even brag about their adventure to Leti's brother, Marvin, who puts them up for the night. The next day, when they are searching for fictional Ardham (revealed to be near the actual city of Salem, Massachusetts, which is north of Boston), they encounter Sheriff Hunt. He uses racial slurs, insults them, and then threatens them with being hung if they don't leave Devon County (also fictional) before the sun sets—which will happen in seven minutes. He assures them that if they go above the speed limit, he will have to arrest them. Whereas Leti's challenge was to go as fast as possible, Tic's challenge is to go slowly and remain under the speed limit. At one point, he must handle being rear-ended by Sheriff Hunt while resisting George and Leti's urgent pleas to go faster. As they go over the train tracks and are finally out of the county, they breathe a sigh of relief, only to be met by four officers with their guns drawn. In the official HBO podcast for the show, *Lovecraft Country Radio*, Shannon Houston, a writer for the show, remarks, "Even after they successfully get to the county line in seven minutes ... it doesn't actually matter. You can't really win. And you still end up with your face in the mud and a gun to your head after following these ridiculous parameters."[30] As the sequence plays out, our protagonists are falsely accused of crimes they didn't commit and nearly murdered by law enforcement.

(4) Emphasizing Supernatural Metaphors for Racism

In "Sundown" (S1, E1) the danger of being out after dark in sundown towns is connected to Shoggoths coming out after sundown, just like vampires. In addition, a hard-to-miss metaphor occurs when the sheriff, a hideous racist, turns into a Shoggoth, a hideous monster. In "Whitey's on the Moon" (S1, E2), another significant example is that the magic of the Braithwhite family is equated with the power of white people in America. At one point in Episode 2, Tic says, "It seems the KKK isn't just *calling* themselves 'grand wizards' anymore," and in "Holy Ghost" (S1, E3), Montrose tells Tic, "You want us to tell them that wizards exist? Huh? That white folks got magic on their side too?" In Episode 2, there is also an extended metaphor that illustrates "the white gaze" when Tic, George, and Leti are each subjected to an illusion at the hands of the Braithwhites. During the ordeal, Leti is the least likely to know she's experiencing an illusion (at least until the end) because it's entirely possible that Tic could be in her room, whereas Tic is so engrossed in not dying at the hands of Ji-Ah (who we later find out he knew in Korea) that he doesn't have a chance to question whether she's real or not. It's only George, who has a romantic encounter with Tic's mother, Dora (Erica Tazel), who knows it's an illusion because Dora is dead. Nonetheless, he too experiences the emotions of the moment. In the *Lovecraft Country Radio* podcast on Episode 3, the point is made that the privacy of these moments is being violated by the surveillance of white people, because Leti, Tic, and George are all on display as entertainment for the white members of the Order of the Ancient Dawn.[31] After their illusions, when Leti and Tic are rattled by their experiences, George says calmly, "They want to make us crazy, terrorize us, make us scared." He then turns to Leti and says, "But Letitia Fuckin' Lewis don't get scared, do she?" Leti replies, "No, sir." It's a wonderful moment, like many others in the first two episodes, that endears the viewers to Uncle George.

There is another significant metaphor that occurs in Episode 3, which is identified by Richard Newby in his article in *The Hollywood Reporter*, "'Lovecraft Country': Black Spaces and Haunted Houses." He uses Tangina's line from *Poltergeist* (MGM/UA Entertainment Co., United

International Pictures: 1982, Tobe Hooper), "This house is clean," to ask whether a house built on racism can ever be clean. Even though the real estate mogul in *Poltergeist* makes a point of saying that the development was *not* built on a Native American burial ground, but rather on a regular cemetery, there are references to Native American burial grounds in both *The Amityville Horror* (American International Pictures: 1979, Stuart Rosenberg) and *The Shining* (Warner Bros., Columbia-EMI-Warner Distributors: 1980, Stanley Kubrick). This is significant because Misha Green used all three of these films as reference points for Episode 3. Newby asserts that these films and others that have used Native American burial grounds "have all hinged on these consequences of America's original sin. But rarely is the successive sin, the erasure of the burial grounds of Black people, examined in this light."[32] Jurnee Smollett, in an interview with Newby, says, "When you're brought to stolen land and are the descendants of stolen people, can you really belong?"[33] The eight Black ghosts, whose skeletons are in the basement of Leti's house, create a lasting metaphor about the racism that forms the foundation of American society.

Now that we've addressed Misha Green's approaches to exploring racism on *Lovecraft Country*, the next question is, given its serious and often disturbing subject matter, what makes this show so watchable? It's a truism that most people watch fictional television to escape reality. It's also the case that Black viewers (and others as well) often feel triggered or exhausted by stories that revolve around anti–Black racism. So how does a series creator provide meaningful commentary on reality while still making a show that is entertaining and attracts a large audience? Misha Green's answer is not only that she wanted to reflect what Matt Ruff did in his novel to reclaim genre spaces for people of color, but she wanted to expand upon it. She says, "I pitched a big show. I said we kind of want to go everywhere. We want to do all the genres. The sky's the limit, the moon's the limit, the next universe and the multi-verses are the limit."[34] To accomplish her goal of reclaiming genre spaces for people of color in a big way, Green's strategies were:

1. Referencing genre classics
2. Providing viewing pleasure
3. Centering the Black family
4. Creating mythic Black heroes

Each of these categories will be discussed using examples from the first three episodes. Again, the aim is to explore how these strategies move the show beyond what existed in the original novel. Going with the "travel" metaphor in *Lovecraft Country*, "genre" is the vehicle; the "exploration of racism" is the road; and "Black heroes" becomes the destination.

"Genre," as it is used in regard to television, is a way of classifying shows by a particular subject matter, form, or style. In the way that Green is using "genre," it means going beyond realistic fiction to incorporate the content and conventions of genres such as horror, action/adventure, science fiction, fantasy, etc. In discussing the use of genre to widen the appeal of a show, Green states, "I'd played with that on 'Underground'; that it was a heist movie but set in slavery times. That the people pursuing the heist happened to be enslaved people trying to steal back their most precious possession: their lives. I used the heist genre to appeal to people who thought, 'Ugh, I don't want to watch a slavery show.'"[35] Green's method of incorporating facets of genre stories on *Lovecraft Country* was to have a syllabus for each episode containing genre films and books that her writers needed to become familiar with so they could use them as references. In regard to the horror genre in particular, Green states, "But when I really started to think about this genre, I wondered, 'Why don't they have Black people, or why do the Black people have to die in the first 10 minutes?' So when I read Matt's book, I thought he beautifully reclaimed this genre space that hadn't been for people of color."[36] As a way to examine how films "hadn't been for people of color," it's worth examining the first four films in the *Alien* franchise (a mix of sci-fi and horror), especially since Green used *Aliens* (20th Century–Fox: 1986, James Cameron) as a reference for "Sundown" (S1, E1). Leti is similar to the tough and resilient Ripley (Sigourney Weaver), particularly when Leti runs to get flares from Woody and is pursued by Shoggoths, reminiscent of Ripley running from the alien creatures. It's important to note that all four original *Alien* films have only one Black main character, who is killed off sooner than comparable white characters. The actors and their characters are as follows: Yaphet Kotto as Parker in *Alien* (20th Century–Fox: 1979, Ridley Scott); Al Matthews as Sergeant Apone in *Aliens*; Charles S. Dutton as Leonard Dillon in *Alien*^{3} (20th Century–Fox: 1992, David Fincher); and Gary Dourdan as Christie in *Alien: Resurrection* (20th Century–Fox: 1997, Joss Whedon). In addition, when one examines the films used as references for the haunted house episode "Holy Ghost" (S1, E3), the same pattern holds true. For example, in *The Shining*, there is only one Black main character, Dick Hallorann (Scatman Crothers). The film even includes a sequence where Jack Torrance (Jack Nicholas) and Delbert/Charles Grady (Phillip Stone) call Hallorann the N-word. Given the film's structure, it would be reasonable to assume that Halloran would emerge as the hero. Even though he didn't know the family well, he cared enough to fly from Florida to Colorado to save them. Instead, Hallorann is summarily killed by Jack within minutes of arriving at the Overlook Hotel. It's important to note that in the novel, he survives, escaping with Jack's wife and son.

(1) Referencing Genre Classics

Misha Green made a point of providing what genre fans expect, which includes embedded references to genre classics. A wonderful example is the opening of the show, which is a virtuoso piece of television that combines references to numerous sources. After we see Tic fighting in the Korean War, the scene switches to a visually striking fantasy sequence that includes flying saucers and the tripods from H.G. Wells' 1898 novel *The War of the Worlds*. It continues with the swelling orchestration and soothing voice-over from *The Jackie Robinson Story* (Eagle-Lion Films: 1950, Alfred E. Green), "This is the story of a boy and his dream but more than that, it's the story of an American boy in a dream that is truly American." Then, a beautiful, red woman (Jamie Chung, who we later see playing Ji-Ah) descends from a spacecraft and sensually embraces Tic—a reference to Edgar Rice Burrough's 1917 novel *A Princess of Mars*. But young men in spring are thinking of ... baseball, or so the voice-over tells us. Next, we see Lovecraft's Cthulhu, which the VFX supervisor for the show, François Dumoulin, describes as "a giant squid with bat-wings."[37] Jackie Robinson takes a swing, dividing the Cthulhu in two, complete with gobs of bright green goo. He tells Tic, "I got you, kid." We then see the Cthulhu knit itself back together as Jackie prepares to take another swing—and then, the dream comes to an end as Tic wakes up on the bus to the faint sound of the song, "Sh-boom (Life Could Be a Dream)."[38]

(2) Providing Viewing Pleasure

As already explained, once the road trip begins in Episode 1, the audience witnesses countless acts of racism against the main characters, which culminate in George, Tic, and Leti being thrown face-down in the woods with guns pointed at their heads. Sheriff Hunt is just about to shoot them, when, lo and behold, a Shoggoth appears. As frightening as it is, our protagonists are saved by the mayhem that the Shoggoth causes. And for viewers, frankly, it's a relief. A Shoggoth is far better than the unrelenting grim realities that our protagonists have been facing, and that, in itself, is making a statement. Suddenly, the show becomes exciting, and in this moment, viewers can enjoy it as a fun piece of horror. There is also no confusion as to what's going on because Tic has conveniently explained to Leti just moments before that a Shoggoth is a Lovecraftian monster that is a "massive bubble blob with hundreds of eyes." This useful exposition illustrates an essential point about Green's storytelling, which is that she doesn't waste time with unnecessary mysteries because the show has a larger purpose, which is to explore racism. Another good example of this is when George, Tic, and Leti go to the village to begin their search for Tic's father, Montrose, and are led to a stone tower, which they immediately decide (correctly) is where Montrose is being held captive. And how fitting that Montrose, as a fan of *The Count of Monte Cristo* (the 1846 novel by Alexandre Dumas, a Black French author), would end up tunneling his way out of a dungeon in that stone tower.

In addition, viewing pleasure is provided through the many instances of Black joy throughout the show. On the simplest level, it would be hard to watch any show if it were unrelentingly grim and traumatizing. So some modicum of joy is needed for any show that is positioned to attract a larger audience, but the exploration of Black joy is particularly needed in this case to make it possible for a Black audience to continue watching. In the *Lovecraft Country Radio* podcast on Episode 3, Houston says that the writers tried to highlight Black joy in every episode. In Episode 1, it's the block party, when Ruby and Leti sing "Whole Lotta Shakin' Goin' On"[39] together on stage. In Episode 2, it's the opening of the episode with the theme song "Moving on Up"[40] from *The Jeffersons* (CBS: 1975–1985, Norman Lear, Don Nicholl, Michael Ross, and Bernie West) as we see an elated George perusing his new-found books and Leti trying on clothes that are part of her new wardrobe. And in Episode 3, it's the housewarming party, especially when Ruby sings "Is You Is or Is You Ain't My Baby,"[41] a question which is finally answered when Leti and Tic leave the party and get together in the bathroom upstairs. Their developing love story is also part of the viewing pleasure of the show.

(3) Centering the Black Family

If the characters in genre entertainment don't seem authentic, then it's hard for viewers to suspend disbelief and be drawn into what happens to them. And one of the best ways for viewers to get to know the characters is through witnessing the dynamics of their relationships. *Lovecraft Country* accomplishes this through an emphasis on the Black family. Green states, "At its core the show is a family drama. We had to dig into stuff that made us uncomfortable."[42] Two of the family relationships on the show that are explored in depth are (1) that of father and son, Montrose and Tic, and (2) that of two sisters, Leti and Ruby. In terms of the father and son dynamic, a crucial element is that Montrose beat Tic when he was growing up. We find out more about Montrose in later episodes which explains that as a Black gay man, he did what he had to do in order to survive and that some of those decisions molded who he became and how he treated his son. In Episode 8, Montrose tells a story from his childhood of a preacher who was found with a man and then sent to an asylum where "they cut half of his brain out." Having been exposed to those kinds of examples, Montrose said that he chose to have a life, one that included a wife and a child, because he believed that familial love was the strongest kind of love. He also talks about carving away all his soft parts to become tough. And this is what he thinks he is doing with Tic, removing his soft parts so he'll be a tougher (and more masculine) man and therefore safer in a society that is both racist and homophobic. But we see in the beginning episodes that Tic's resentment of his father spreads to his other relationships as well. In Episode 1, Tic gets angry with Uncle George, who is making excuses for Montrose because he feels that as the older brother, he should have protected Montrose from their father when they were kids. Tic says, "You ain't do shit to protect me. You regret that?" The accusation goes unanswered and is outweighed by how much Tic looks up to his Uncle George, clearly considering him as the preferable father figure, only to find out later that George may indeed be his father.

The relationship between the two sisters, Leti and Ruby, is chummy at times and fraught at other times, in large part because Leti is often irresponsible and Ruby often bails her out (sometimes literally). Michael K. Williams, who plays Montrose, says, "One of the things I love about episode one is the relationship between Leti and Ruby. That dynamic between Black women who are sisters, with different bodies and skin tones ... different fathers, that's a very real family dynamic in the Black community." And, certainly, colorism is explored on the show through Leti having lighter skin and demonstrably more advantages than Ruby. The fact that the sisters have different fathers and had different relationships with their mother is also shown to have contributed to the differences in their upbringing and the friction in their relationship. We can see that the result is that Ruby and Leti have taken different paths in their lives. Leti feels empowered to be a photographer, to have artist friends, and to be an activist, whereas Ruby is a rule-follower and dreams of finally having a sales job in a department store. In Episode 3, Leti and Ruby have a revealing argument about Leti buying the house with an inheritance from their mother (or so Leti believes at the time, although the money came from Christina). Ruby says to Leti, "Now you say you bought this house because you wanted to help our people. Well, it looks to me all you've done is move in your artist friends—and if you were half the sister that you claim you want to be, you would have split that money with me and Marvin, regardless of Mama's wishes. But you didn't." On the *Lovecraft Country Radio* podcast for Episode 3, Shannon Houston states, "And I think because of so many important conversations that we're having about colorism right now, particularly colorism in Hollywood, and the fact that we have, like, colorism deniers, or whatever you want to call them—that scene now has extra levels to it."[43] In discussing how a dynamic between a light-skinned sister and a dark-skinned sister plays out in real life, Houston says that people in the same family don't usually think of themselves in those terms. She also admits that at first she didn't want a light-skinned woman in the lead and they had a long conversation about it in the writers' room. Finally, she concluded, "It's not really how Black people see each other, right? It's about the white gaze."[44] Even though Houston ended up supporting the choices the show made (and particularly Smollett's brilliant performance), some critics still questioned it. Katrina Miller in her *Wired* article states, "viewers watch a familiar dynamic of desirability play out between the fair-skinned, slim-framed Leti and her darker-toned, heavier-set sister. The juxtaposition is predictable at best, but the show's writers never break free from this common depiction."[45] Whichever side one comes down on—that the show provides a forum for the discussion of colorism or that the show perpetuates the stereotypes associated with colorism—it is nonetheless useful to provoke a discussion about this issue.

(4) Creating Mythic Black Heroes

It's hard to watch historical shows that focus on the disempowerment of Black characters, even if the aim is to educate the audience about the bitter realities of the times being depicted. What makes this type of material bearable, however, is the emergence of Black heroes who find a way to fight back, resulting in empowering themselves and saving others. The making of heroes also involves exciting endeavors and triumphant moments—and, therefore, viewing pleasure. Within genre shows, there are even greater possibilities for creating Black heroes that achieve mythic status. Referencing more recent films with Black protagonists, such as Jordan Peele's *Get Out*, Tananarive Due reminds us in the documentary *Horror Noire: A History of Black Horror* (Shudder: 2019, Xavier Burgin), "We've shifted from being the focal point of the fear to being the heroes."[46] In "Sundown" (S1, E1), Tic tells the woman he met on the bus, "But I love pulp stories. I love that the heroes get to go on adventures in other worlds, defy insurmountable odds, defeat the monster, save the day. Little Negro boy from the South Side of Chicago don't notoriously get to do that." And yet, Tic does. Over the course of the show, his development as a hero happens with fits and starts, wins and losses. In "Whitey's on the Moon" (S1, E2), we see Tic willing to sacrifice his life in order to save those he loves, a decision which already makes him heroic. The outcome is that Leti lives but George dies. Since George doesn't die in the novel, it was a deliberate choice on Misha Green's part to remove Tic's father figure as a way to motivate him to achieve the next level of maturity he needed to become a mythic hero.

In terms of Leti, she quickly emerges as a woman of action, from driving the get-away car in Simmonsville, to making the run to Woody to get the flares, to swinging the bat into the cars in front of her house. But the pivotal moment that she ascends to the level of a hero is when she battles the ghost of Hiram toward the end of Episode 3. Against all odds, she perseveres, calling the eight ghosts to help her—as well as calling on Mama Oya, a deity in the Yoruba religion known for carrying souls to the afterlife. Mara Bachman, writing for *Screen Rant*, asserts, "When considering the mythological aspects of the African Goddess, it is clear that the entirety of 'Holy Ghost' is meant to frame Letitia as the physical manifestation of Mama Oya. When threatened, she brings a storm just like the Goddess is known for."[47] Leti is quite impressive, but she is flawed as well, something that is essential to the configuration of a modern-day hero. The most glaring evidence of this is in the way she takes advantage of her sister, Ruby.

Now that these points have been explained, we can use them to explore the remainder of the episodes chronologically, as well as examine other relevant topics along the way. As a place to start, there are further pertinent supernatural metaphors to discuss in "A History of Violence" (S1, E4). On the surface, this episode is a rousing adventure that recalls *The Goonies* (Warner Bros. Pictures: 1985, Richard Donner), *Indiana Jones and the Raiders of the Lost Ark* (Paramount Pictures: 1981, Steven Spielberg), and *Indiana Jones and the Last Crusade* (Paramount Pictures: 1989, Steven Spielberg). But under the surface, this episode comments on colonialism with the title referencing the history of violence inherent in the actions of white colonizers. After all, *Indiana Jones and the Raiders of the Lost Ark* starts with just that, "raiding" a temple in an "exotic land" and stealing a meaningful religious icon that belongs to a "primitive people" who the primary characters believe they can exploit with impunity.

In terms of references to *The Goonies*, *Lovecraft Country*'s use of the pirate ship in "A History of Violence" (S1, E4) puts us, as the viewers, in that same liminal space that *The Goonies* employs. How is it possible that the children in *The Goonies* go through a fireplace grate in the basement of a restaurant and end up in an immense underground space that is large enough to contain a pirate ship? And yet something similar happens in *Lovecraft Country*—under the Boston museum are comparable tunnels, cliffs, and labyrinths that eventually lead to a pirate ship. It is worth noting that there are also many references to *Indiana Jones and the Last Crusade*: the swinging blade across the path, the invisible plank across the abyss, the corpse-like knight that has been waiting for seven hundred years, and the focus on an adventurous son leading a reluctant father on a quest. We also come to understand that this underground labyrinth in Boston is directly connected to the sub-basement of Leti's house in Chicago, the former Winthrop house. The first clue is that Leti sees one of the dead intruders from her house floating in the water under the Boston Museum and another clue is that they "travel by elevator" from Boston back to the house in Chicago, which they also do in the final episode. Is this violation of physical laws too hard to accept within the story? No, not really, because we're in the land of the unconscious, the territory of fantasy and all that's buried in our psyches. The subterranean expanse represents the unconscious space of American culture, where the effects of white supremacy and the violence against those who are Indigenous and Black are clearly evident. It is part of the bedrock of our culture and what is inherent in the foundation of our media.

In "A History of Violence" (S1, E4), we also meet Yahima, an Indigenous character from Guyana who has the ability to help Tic translate Titus' pages from the *Book of Names* and thus acquire magical spells to fight the forces against him. Because we are told that Yahima's people understood the Language of Adam (and thus were able to help Titus with the translation of the *Book of Names*), the implication is that the Indigenous people from Guyana have a direct connection to the Garden of Eden. Yahima describes themselves as Two-Spirit, a term which can broadly mean having two genders, but which in this case specifically means being intersex, as evident in the introductory visuals of Yahima. Because Indigenous characters are rare in film and television, and "the number of Two-Spirit characters in media is practically non-existent,"[48] it seems as if the show is developing an exciting new character beyond the book. But to the dismay of the viewers, Yahima is killed by Montrose by the end of the episode. "Many saw it as yet another example of the tired 'bury your gays' trope, a common cliché in which LGBT+ characters are viewed as more expendable than their heteronormative counterparts."[49] Misha Green is credited with providing a thoughtful response to the criticism. On Twitter, she stated, "I wanted to show the uncomfortable truth that oppressed folks can also be oppressors. But I didn't examine or unpack the moment/portrayal of Yahima as thoroughly as I should have."[50] It was a missed opportunity to have a continuing Two-Spirit, Indigenous character on the show.

Green's response, however, alludes to the specific symbolic problem that arises when the character chosen to kill Yahima is Montrose. Within

"A History of Violence" (S1, E4), it appears that Yahima is meant to represent how white colonizers have treated Indigenous peoples in that their people were killed; they were held captive on a ship; they end up with no voice (other than that of a siren); and they have lost the connection to their land. But this analogy is subverted when it is Montrose, a gay Black man, who kills Yahima. Since there was some effort to explore the effects of colonization on Indigenous peoples in this episode, why would Green choose this particular story to make the point that the oppressed can also be oppressors? There's also the question of why Montrose chose this action in the first place. The simplest explanation is that he believes that he is protecting his son from the harmful effects of magic. He has already destroyed the *Bylaws & Precepts of the Order of the Ancient Dawn* as well as Titus' pages from the *Book of Names* that they received from Yahima. Therefore, in killing Yahima, he believes that he is destroying the only person able to translate the *Book of Names*, if indeed other pages were to be recovered. In addition, Ashley C. Ford comments that Montrose is thinking, "I have to protect my child from more otherness."[51] Richard Newby, writing for *The Hollywood Reporter*, also notes, "But on a deeper level, Montrose's actions could be viewed as a reflection of his own self-loathing, an attempt to destroy and bury a part of himself that goes against his upbringing and the idea of Black masculinity."[52] Whatever the interpretation, it remains an unresolved aspect of the story. It is also interesting that despite Montrose's many harmful actions, we don't think of him as a villain. In part, this is because he is so often driven by the fear instilled in him by the racism and homophobia he has endured, but mostly because he fundamentally loves his son, and he thinks he is doing right by him.

In terms of supernatural metaphors that address racism, one of the most direct ones is in "Strange Case" (S1, E5) when Ruby magically transforms into a white woman called Hillary. In the previous episode, we see that Ruby has gotten together with William, who the audience knows as the attractive white man from Ardham and who identifies himself as a close friend of Christina Braithwhite's. We see him at first listening to Ruby complain that another Black woman, Tamara, has gotten her coveted job at the Marshall Field's department store. William tells her that she should just apply anyway, but she assures him that there is no point, "because for us, it's a rat race to the finish line. And it's winner takes it all." Then she tells him, "If I was in your skin, I wouldn't even have to run." The mention of "skin" is apt because soon we see her changing her skin. The episode's title, "Strange Case," refers to *The Strange Case of Dr. Jekyll and Mr. Hyde*, the 1886 novel by Robert Louis Stevenson in which Dr. Jekyll creates an alter ego, Mr. Hyde, in order to act on his vices. The first time that we see Ruby transform into *her* alter ego, Hillary, she unwittingly awakens as a white woman and staggers out onto the street, disheveled and confused. Since she is acting oddly, she is surprised that she is treated with kid gloves by the Black people that she encounters. Even more telling is when she finds out that two white policemen believe her when she contradicts their accusation that a teenage Black boy, with whom she has collided, has molested her. We then realize that we have seen this white woman before— she was Dell, the racist groundskeeper in Ardham who got hit in the head with a shovel by Leti and who presumably died. Even though it isn't Ruby's choice to turn into a white woman this first time, it certainly is the second time when she goes for a pleasant stroll through William's neighborhood, dressed up and smiling. As we see her treated so kindly by the white people around her, we hear an excerpt of *for colored girls who have considered suicide / when the rainbow is enuf*, written from 1974 to 1976 by Ntozake Shange. There is a striking counterpoint between the words of the choreopoem calling for people to understand the struggle of Black girls and to treat them warmly, and the blissful experience that Ruby has when she is seen as a white woman. Lex Pryor in *The Ringer* states about Ruby, "Her newfound appearance provides her with access to the fruits of white womanhood in America; before she was a threat, now she is a prize to be protected."[53] Disguised as Hillary, Ruby proceeds to get her dream job at Marshall Field's and become Tamara's boss. She catches Tamara off guard when she notes that her hands are ashy or asks whether she took accounting courses at the Frederick Douglass Center, talking about things that a white woman wouldn't normally talk about and going out of her way to make Tamara's work life just that much harder. While incognito as Hillary, Ruby also hears how white people talk about Black people when she's with her fellow white saleswomen. During this episode, we witness yet another transformation—that of Montrose, and yet his isn't a supernatural change but an emotional one. After being brutally beaten by Tic, a reaction to Montrose's slaying of Yahima, a broken and bruised Montrose goes to Sammy and has perfunctory, loveless sex with him. We learn from Sammy's teasing friends that the two of them have never kissed. But later, when Montrose goes to a drag club, he kisses Sammy in public and decides to join the dancing, giving into the acceptance and exuberance that he feels all around him—another manifestation of Black joy on the show.

    The horror aspects of "Strange Case" (S1, E5), however, are encapsulated in the visceral scenes of Ruby bursting through the flesh of Hillary, which are gorefests of skin, blood, and tissue, as if to emphasize that crossing the boundary from white back to Black is a brutal process. Nicole Hill in her *Den of Geek* article states, "The first time Ruby emerges from her white body, she is literally cut out of it by William. She's both the newborn and the mutilated uterus that housed it, ripped, and ripped from."[54] This metaphor of birth, with its blood and pain, as well as the discarded afterbirth of the previous body, is a fitting one. And this first, difficult time becomes a Cesarean birth, assisted by William. It is only at the end of the episode that Ruby, like Dr. Jekyll, lets her alter ego get away with vice. First, Ruby witnesses the store manager, Paul, sexually assault and disparage Tamara, yelling, "You n—r bitch" when she bites him and runs away. Then, Ruby (disguised as Hillary) lures Paul into letting her tie him up and then rapes him with the heel of her stiletto. But she turns back into Ruby during the act because she wants him to see that it's a "n—r bitch" doing this to him. By the end of the episode, Ruby stumbles upon William transforming back into Christina and realizes that she has been duped by Christina all along. The continuation of this scene occurs in "I Am" (S1, E7) with Ruby finally demanding that Christina tell her the truth about everything. By "Jig-A-Bobo" (S1, E8), Ruby tells Leti, "And I finally got that job at Marshall Field's, and you know what I learned? I don't wanna be white." Lex Pryor explains Ruby's stance well: "what we see Ruby specifically struggle with is the fact that her new mien is little more than a veil to fool the world. And no matter how frequently she cocoons herself in it, her white skin will not change the terms of that world."[55] In Ruby's conversation with Leti, Ruby talks about being done with spaces that don't welcome her and wanting to create her own space, believing that Christina's promise of magic will make that possible for her.

In "Meet Me in Daegu" (S1, E6), the show expands the genre space for people of color by focusing on the story of Ji-Ah (Jamie Chung), a Korean woman Tic met when he was an American soldier fighting in the Korean War. It turns out that Ji-Ah is a kumiho, a nine-tailed fox spirit that is part of Korean legend, who seduces and kills men, taking their souls in the process. Through her bond with Tic, Ji-Ah becomes the one Asian character accepted into the group of Black characters by the end of the show. As a point of comparison, in *The Goonies*, there is a group of white characters with one Asian character, Data (played by the Vietnamese American actor, Ke Huy Quan). And in *Watchmen*, which includes an alternate history of the Vietnam War, there is Lady Trieu, who is half Vietnamese and half white (played by the Vietnamese-American actor, Hong Chau), who is the only Asian character among the rest of the Black and white main characters. It's a telling way to look at the inclusion of Asian characters in popular media as an outgrowth of the wars that the United States has fought. In response to a question about the reasons for choosing to do this episode, Shannon Houston responds that they wanted to explore America's global impact as well as get out of America for an episode to deal with the fact that Tic was a Korean War vet.[56]

In Episode 6, we soon discover that one of the significant parts of being a kumiho is that she absorbs the memories of the men she kills but has no memories of the woman that she once was, who was Soon-Hee's daughter, Ji-Ah, who was born out of wedlock. It is revealed that when Soon-Hee later married a man to regain her status in society, he continually raped her daughter, but she didn't intervene because she didn't want to lose her social standing. Finally, when Soon-Hee went to the Mudang, a shaman, to summon the kumiho to kill her husband, she essentially lost her now-grown daughter because the kumiho has taken her place. Soon-Hee understands that she will only get her daughter back when the kumiho has taken one hundred souls, and so she facilitates the killing, becoming hopeful once the ninety-ninth man has been killed. It becomes apparent that Ji-Ah, as the kumiho, is trapped in an endless cycle that she believes she cannot escape. Supporting this theme are the many references to Judy Garland, including excerpts of her films *Meet Me in St. Louis* (Loew's, Inc.: 1944, Vincente Minnelli), to which the title "Meet Me in Daegu" is referring, *Easter Parade* (Loew's, Inc.: 1948, Charles Walters), and *Summer Stock* (Loew's, Inc.: 1950, Charles Walters). We see how Ji-Ah loves these Judy Garland films, not only because she is learning how to seem like an alluring young woman, necessary as a kumiho, but also because she yearns for happiness. But what is most telling is the Judy Garland voice-over later in the episode, which is about her being deemed an unfit person, excerpted from the 1969 audiotapes that Garland made shortly before she died. Throughout her life, Judy Garland endured mental health and substance abuse issues that were initially caused by how she was controlled and mistreated when she started as a teenager in the film industry. Just as Garland felt she was judged as unfit, even though that was the result of others using her to get what they wanted, so too does Ji-Ah feel judged as being a monster, even though she was summoned by others to do their bidding. Within the episode, Tic is juxtaposed with Ji-Ah because he is in a similar situation as a soldier in Korea. During a search for Communist spies, he is ordered to shoot Ji-Ah's fellow nursing student as well as torture and kill her best friend. Ji-Ah tells him at one point, "We've both done monstrous things but that does not make us monsters." In the continuing action on the show, both Ji-Ah and Tic seek redemption for their past actions.

Ji-Ah is also the vehicle for exploring the nature of "destiny" within the show. From the first episode, we know of the prophecy that Tic will die, but it is only in Episode 6 that we understand that Ji-Ah has seen his death by looking into his mind as a kumiho. Before this, she has only seen a man's life through his memories, but with Tic, she sees his future as well because she manages to withdraw her fox tails in time so he doesn't die. At the end of the episode, when Ji-Ah sees the Mudang, her main concern is whether it's true, that Tic will die. The Mudang's response is that Ji-Ah hasn't yet become one with the darkness and that she will see many deaths before her journey is done. By the end of Episode 6, it is clear that Soon-Hee's daughter is gone and that the kumiho may want to keep it that way (by not killing the hundredth man) since she is forging her own path to personhood.

"I Am" (S1, E7) is different in tone from the rest of the episodes in that it is, on the whole, uplifting. Like the rest of the show, however, this sci-fi fantasy adventure is intent on expanding the genre space for people of color as well as including Black historical figures, providing viewing pleasure (with many examples of Black joy), and creating mythic Black heroes. This episode not only tells the story of a Black woman ascending to greatness but it also emphasizes the importance of Black women mentoring other Black women. The title is spelled with the period, so that it reads as a statement, possibly referring to the biblical term "Ego eimi" ("I am" in Koine Greek), which can be understood as another name for God. The episode embraces Afrofuturism, which Ytasha Womack, the author of *Afrofuturism: The World of Black Sci-Fi and Fantasy Culture*, defines as "a way of looking at the future and alternate realities through a Black cultural lens.... It is an artistic aesthetic, but also a kind of method of self-liberation or self-healing."[57] Womack also draws crucial comparisons between the Black experience and sci-fi, stating, "And many found the parallels between sci-fi themes of alien abduction and the transatlantic slave trade to be both haunting and fascinating. Were stories about aliens really just metaphors for the experience of [B]lacks in the Americas?"[58] Echoing this sentiment, Misha Green comments, "You watch all of these movies and it's set in the future and it's like white people are all subjugated to aliens, and you're like, 'This doesn't really seem like your story.'"[59] The story in Episode 7, however, changes the norm and brings together a Black woman's search for freedom with a sci fi journey to other multiverses.

At the beginning of Episode 7, Hippolyta has solved the puzzle of Horatio Winthrop's orrery, procuring both the mysterious key and the accompanying coordinates. On her drive to where the coordinates lead, we see Hippolyta have a bonding moment with a fellow traveler, who portrays the real-life Bessie Stringfield, the first Black woman to do a solo cross-country ride on a motorcycle. In addition, Hippolyta is listening to Josephine Baker's song "Piel Canela,"[60] foreshadowing that the renowned entertainer, an American-born Black woman who settled in France, will soon play a key role in the episode. When Hippolyta arrives at the observatory in Mayfield, Kansas, she starts the multiverse machine with the key and then does the necessary calculations, only to be interrupted by two policemen. After Tic arrives just in time to help her, she ends up killing one of the policemen in self-defense and getting sucked into the portal. She soon finds herself in a white, high-tech space, with no clothes on, and pink rectangles in her wrists. Immediately, we surmise that this must be the setting for an alien abduction story. When a being, who appears to be a tall, Black woman with an outsized Afro, enters the room, Hippolyta says, "Who are you? What are you?" The being replies, "I am." Hippolyta says, "You can't keep me here." The being replies, "You aren't in a prison." This is a significant interchange, which makes it clear that this isn't a story of Hippolyta being held captive but rather a story of liberation. In addition, many fans call the being "I am" because of her reply, but in the episode credits, she is called "Seraphina AKA Beyond C'est." Shannon Houston, who co-wrote the episode, simply calls her Beyond C'est, with c'est being a French phrase meaning "That is," and therefore, "Beyond C'est" is "Beyond That Is." But, of course, Beyond C'est is also a reference to Beyoncé, who has a connection to the show in other ways as well. For example, in "Holy Ghost" (S1, E3), when Leti uses a bat to smash the car windows, it references Beyoncé's video for "Hold Up."[61] Caryn James states in her *BBC Culture* article, "It isn't a stretch to see *Lovecraft Country* and Beyoncé's new visual album, *Black is King*, as similar in their aims, different though they are in style."[62] In addition, when Alan Sepinwall asked Misha Green where the idea came from for the spoken-word segments in the show, she said, "It was Beyoncé's *Lemonade* and *I Am Not Your Negro* at the same time."[63]

Both the viewing pleasure and the in-depth examination of the Black experience in "I Am" (S1, E7) begin when Beyond C'est finally says to Hippolyta, "Name yourself. Where do you want to be? Name it," Hippolyta's off-handed reply is "I want to be dancing on stage in Paris with Josephine Baker." And suddenly, she is. We see Hippolyta appreciating the wonder of it all and also baring her soul to Josephine, saying, "Now that I'm tasting it, freedom, like I've never known before, I see what I was robbed of back then. All those years, I thought I had everything I ever wanted, only to come here and discover that all I ever was, was the exact kind of Negro woman white folks wanted me to be. I feel like they just found a smart way to lynch me without me noticing the noose." It's a heart-wrenching sentiment that speaks of racism as something that one adapts to and which infiltrates one's self-perception, which becomes just another way of being controlled. In regard to ways in which Black women are often named by others, Aujanue Ellis, who plays Hippolyta, says, "All that stuff that is attached to us that has nothing to do with us.... We are constantly named. So much of our existence is about pushing that back, pushing it away."⁶⁴ On the *Lovecraft Country Radio* podcast on Episode 7, Ford and Houston talk about Josephine Baker as being an expat like so many Black Americans, including James Baldwin and Nina Simone, who had to leave the country to find themselves.⁶⁵ This episode goes one step further with Hippolyta becoming an expat of our version of reality. We then hear her say, "I am Hippolyta" three times and suddenly she's somewhere else. It is reminiscent of Dorothy in the film *The Wizard of Oz* (Loew's, Inc: 1939, Victor Fleming), who had the power all along to click her heels three times and go where she wanted to go. We then see Hippolyta in a circle of women, being taught to fight by Nawi. She gets better over time and finally wins against her teacher, earning a golden helmet from the Queen. Hippolyta then leads a group of female warriors to vanquish white Confederate soldiers on an African savannah, presenting an interesting confluence of symbolic messages. It's also important to know that in Greek mythology, Hippolyta was the daughter of Ares (the God of War) and Otrera (the founder of the Amazons), who then became Queen of the Amazons herself. But in this case, Hippolyta is a Dahomey Amazon, a name given to the female warriors of the Kingdom of Dahomey in Africa. They weren't disbanded until the 1900s, so they would have been contemporaneous with the Civil War. In addition, Nawi is the name of the last living Dahomey warrior, another nod to a real Black woman we see mentoring Hippolyta within the episode.

In the same episode, we then see the "Black family theme" being explored in the next part of Hippolyta's adventure. Hippolyta says, "I am Hippolyta, George's wife," and she finds herself in bed with George. After relaying some of her adventures, she tells him, "For so much of my life, I've been shrinking." And he admits that he let her shrink. He says, "I fell in love with you because you were so curious and I knew, deep down inside, that there was a discoverer in you." But he admits that he wanted a family and wanted her safe at home. It's important that the show acknowledges that Hippolyta was also held back by her husband. Then she says, "I am Hippolyta, discoverer." We then see Hippolyta and George in cool space suits, landing on another planet in a spaceship that looks like Woody. And so it is now Hippolyta (who wasn't allowed by George to do trips for the *Safe Negro Travel Guide*) who is taking him on a tour of another planet. They are welcomed by aliens, who give them tools to do their work as discoverers. We hear the voice of Sun Ra, recognized as one of the pioneers of Afrofuturism, from his 1974 film *Space Is the Place* (limited release: 1974, Plexifilm: 2003, John Coney), which begins, "I'm not real, I'm just like you. You don't exist in this society," and continues, "I come to you as the myth because that is what Black people are: myths." Then, we see Hippolyta as Orithyia Blue, just as Dee drew her mother for her comic book. And it turns out that Orithyia was also a Queen of the Amazons in Greek mythology. Finally, Hippolyta, although given the opportunity to integrate into the society of Beyond C'est, decides to be a mother and return to Dee. But back at the observatory, instead of seeing Hippolyta come out of the portal, we see Tic come out, and he's holding a book, *Lovecraft Country*, written by his son in the future. And one of the fun, meta moments in the show is in Episode 8 when Tic describes the book to Montrose: "Some of the details are different. Christina's a man. Uncle George survives Ardham. And Dee's a boy named Horace." He is describing the actual book *Lovecraft Country*, which Matt Ruff wrote. This also situates Misha Green's version of *Lovecraft Country* as taking place in just another 'verse in the multiverse.

For what it's worth, Hippolyta's journey in the show is a departure from the book in two primary ways. First, the book includes an evocative story from Hippolyta's childhood about naming Pluto by sending a letter from Harlem to an Arizona observatory. She is bested by the white granddaughter of a British head of Oxford's library, who arranges to telegraph the name to the observatory well before Hippolyta's letter arrives. The disappointment that Hippolyta feels as a child fuels her interest in one day becoming an astronomer and being able to name a planet. In the show, when Hippolyta is in the planetarium with Dee in Episode 4, she says that she named Hera's Comet, but the niece of an astronomer in Sweden got the credit. Dee's response is to yell out her mother's accomplishment to everyone gathered there. It's a nice but simple moment which doesn't have the same weight as the expanded story in the book. The second difference is that in the book, Hippolyta goes to a planet in another galaxy and meets Ida, a former servant of Hiram Epstein's in the 1920s. The action that follows may not serve a larger, thematic purpose like Hippolyta's sci-fi adventure in the show, but it does expand on Hippolyta's interests in outer space and becoming an astronomer. On the show, however, Hippolyta's multiverse adventure seems removed from traveling to other planets or galaxies (except for the fantastical journey to another planet at the end). Therefore, the vestiges of the original "astronomy" idea in the book seem somewhat out of place. If Hippolyta has been on another version of Earth, Earth 504, as she tells Dee in "Full Circle" (S1, E10), then why stick with the idea of the orrery, which is a depiction of a solar system with two suns? And why have Hippolyta go to an observatory (which implies looking out at space) unless the story will be about outer space? In addition, why have the multiverse machine in an observatory at all, when it could be housed anywhere? It seems to be an odd conflation of two different ideas. But if one looks past these few incongruencies, Episode 7 is a fulfilling adventure, a meaningful exploration, and a balm for the spirit.

In "Jig-A-Bobo" (S1, E8), we are confronted with another profound metaphor for the effects of racism when we see Dee (Hippolyta's and George's daughter) trying to escape from racial caricatures of Black girls, which are embodied in Topsy, a character from *Uncle Tom's Cabin* (the 1852 novel by Harriet Beecher Stowe, a white abolitionist), and Bopsy, an added character in the show. At the beginning of the episode, Dee is waiting with Atticus, Montrose, Leti, and Ruby in a crowd of people outside the church to view Emmett Till's body. The title of the episode refers to "jigaboo," a racial slur for a Black person, and "Bobo," Emmett's nickname. In response to a question about her decision to direct Episode 8, Misha Green replied, "It felt like a mixture of what I wanted to do, which is bring in a real-life historical event and then also do a genre story. It was also a very delicate one, with Emmett Till's legacy, so I just wanted to make sure we weren't tipping too far in any direction."[66] In that opening scene, Ruby says, "Maybe it wasn't a good idea to bring Dee." And Montrose says, "Ain't no getting around this. Every Negro's rite of passage in this country, child or not." To compound her grief, Dee is mourning the loss of her father, George, and feeling abandoned by her mother, who still hasn't returned. Unnoticed by the adults, she heads to the Broadway Penny Arcade, where we see her get angry at two Black girls she knows because they are laughing. She throws stones at them, yelling, "There ain't nothing to laugh about." As Dee continues on her way, Captain Lancaster and one of his cronies follow Dee into a gap between the houses and ask her about her comic book, *Orithyia Blue*, which was found under the dead cop in the observatory. When she isn't forthcoming, Lancaster does a spell and puts her in a chokehold. When she gasps, "I can't breathe," we are immediately reminded of George Floyd's murder by police. Lancaster then spits on her, leaving a sticky mess on her forehead. In the podcast discussing this episode, the co-hosts reference "The Talk" that Black parents have with their children about how to survive an encounter with the police.[67]

But the worst is yet to come as Lancaster's spell on Dee comes to fruition. She heads home, and when she is washing the spit off of her forehead in the bathroom, the book *Uncle Tom's Cabin* falls off the shelf and the cover changes to show a menacing Topsy. Later, when Dee is waiting on the train platform, she is pursued by a full-bodied Topsy (Kaelynn Harris), accompanied by Bopsy (Bianca Brewton). They are not only frightening but also unsettling as depictions of "pickaninnies," something which at first seems too politically incorrect to be depicted on a current TV show. As Nicole Hill states in her *Den of Geek* article, "Their wide mouths—big enough to eat watermelon and fried chicken—are carved into sinister smiles that expose jagged teeth. Their rhythmic movement is punctuated and animalistic. Their eyes glow. When they get close to Dee, their nails grow to talons.... They are made more frightening because they so accurately reflect the racist imagination they are a product of."[68] In one of many unnerving sequences, we see Dee riding her bike, trying to get away from Topsy and Bopsy, as we hear, "Stop Dat Knocking," a blackface minstrel song.[69] In the podcast on the episode, the co-hosts make the point that anytime you get mad as a Black girl, you become a stereotype. Ashley C. Ford adds, "I terrify people with my reasonable anger."[70] As Dee screams, riding her bike past Topsy and Bopsy, we hear Naomi Wadler, the 11-year-old who spoke at the March for Our Lives in 2018, "I am here today to acknowledge and represent the African American girls whose stories don't make the front page of every national newspaper, whose stories don't lead on the evening news." The decision from the outset to change George and Hippolyta's child from a son in the book to a daughter in the show was to bring attention to Black girls who are victims of violence in this country. At the end, when Dee is in the garage, Topsy and Bopsy get in, and Dee swings at them with a pipe. Montrose then arrives, and instead of asking her what's going on (since he can't see Topsy and Bopsy), he rushes toward her and holds her so that she can't defend herself anymore from them. Once again, Montrose, in trying to help, causes harm. But perhaps this also represents how parental figures may want to calm upset children, not seeing their difficulties, and end up taking away their defenses from the stereotypes they face.

At the beginning of "Rewind 1921" (S1, E9), we see Leti, Tic, Montrose, and Ruby trying to help a comatose Dee, who now has a withered arm where Topsy touched her. Hippolyta returns just in time to lend her energy for a temporary spell that Christina does for a price (Tic's assurance that he'll participate in her ritual on the autumnal equinox). They then arrive at a plan to use the multiverse machine to go back to the Tulsa Race Massacre in 1921 to get the *Book of Names* from Dora's family in order to help Dee. And so once again, a racist historical reality will be woven into the story. In real life, the Tulsa Race Massacre resulted in the destruction of the neighborhood of Greenwood, known as Black Wall Street, and the death of almost 300 people. The Massacre began because a 19-year-old Black man was accused of assaulting a 17-year-old white woman in an elevator, even though it's likely that all he did was trip and then grab her arm to catch his fall.[71] What followed his arrest were mobs of white people who attacked Black residents and destroyed the entire 35 blocks of the Greenwood neighborhood, resulting in the loss of 190 businesses.[72] They also looted and burned more than 1,470 homes, leaving 8,000 to 10,000 people homeless.[73] In the *Lovecraft Country Radio* podcast on Episode 9, Houston talks about how, in the writers' room, they agreed that nothing could be changed about the history of the Tulsa Massacre because it was important for it to stand.⁷⁴ The show faithfully depicts what happened, starting first with a prosperous Greenwood before the Massacre began. We see notable landmarks, such as the Stradford Hotel, one of the best hotels for Black Americans in the country, and the Williams Dreamland Theatre, the first movie theater for Black people in Tulsa.⁷⁵ Then, the episode shows us the nightmare of Greenwood in flames, with Black people being killed by white attackers, but also arming themselves and fighting back. In addition, the show depicts the historical reality that airplanes, flown by white pilots, dropped dynamite on the area from above.⁷⁶ In showing the Tulsa Race Massacre, *Lovecraft Country* has a connection with *Watchmen*, the acclaimed 2019 HBO series created by Damon Lindelof. Green states, "We learned about *Watchmen* doing Tulsa in the writers room. That became a big discussion that I quelled quickly. I was like, 'Tulsa is not one singular thing. What happened in Tulsa, what happens around America with these terrorist attacks on [B]lack communities, is a story that can be told multiple times.'"⁷⁷ And as the Langston League points out in its accompanying "Syllabus" for Episode 9 of *Lovecraft Country*, there were many times in the early 20th century that Black people were driven out of cities by white people. A sample of headlines from the newspaper articles they've collected include, "All Negroes Driven from Town in Riot" (Princess Anne, MD, 1934), "Negroes: All Driven from an Indiana Town by Mob" (Decatur, Indiana, 1902), "200 Negroes Driven from Nebraska City" (North Platte, NE, 1929), and "Negroes Drive: Five Cities Have Taken the Law Into Their Own Hands and Expelled Every Colored Person from Their Limits" (Pierce City, MO, 1901).⁷⁸ In addition, Florida's Rosewood Massacre in January 1923 resulted in the Black community of Rosewood being destroyed by a mob of several hundred white people, with the confirmed deaths of at least six Black people and two white people, but with larger estimations of 27 to 150 people killed.

Against the backdrop of the Tulsa Race Massacre, we see scenes of what happened that day with the teen versions of Montrose, George, and Dora. First, we see Montrose get beaten by his father for appearing effeminate and then we see him try to save his love interest, Thomas, who is destined to be killed by white attackers. Montrose tells Tic, "Thomas won't mean much. He's just the first in a long list of sacrifices I made to be your father." Tic manages to hold Montrose back since he believes that they shouldn't risk changing anything. And then, as they watch, Thomas is killed, and the teen versions of Montrose, George, and Dora are on the verge of being killed as well. When the mysterious stranger who swings a bat like Jackie Robinson (an established part of family lore) doesn't appear on cue, Tic steps in and realizes that it was him all along who saved them that day. Shannon Houston confirmed that the writers put in references to Jackie Robinson throughout the series because they knew they were heading to this moment in Episode 9.[79] In the meantime, Leti is in Dora's house, with Dora's grandmother, Hattie, asking her for the *Book of Names*. As the house starts to burn, Hattie wants to focus on saving her family, but Leti convinces her that she *will* be saving her family, just not the ones in this house. Since Leti is carrying Tic's baby boy, Hattie tells her, "When my great, great grandson's born, he will be my faith made flesh." Since Leti knows that she's invulnerable, she stays with Hattie to pray, and when Hattie begins to burn, we hear Sonja Sanchez's poem "Catch the Fire." In Steffan Triplett's *Vulture* article, he states, "This episode is a story about not just generational sacrifice, but generational relation. How we both extend from and reach back toward our ancestors.... What if the horrors of the past are not only a destructive fire, but one that drives us? 'The fire of living ... not dying,' as the poem suggests?"[80] Michael K. Williams, who played Montrose, said in an interview, "*Lovecraft* made me realize that I not only have trauma, my own personal life experiences, I also have blood trauma from my ancestors. *Lovecraft* reminded me that I stand on some really strong shoulders."[81] The image of Leti clutching the *Book of Names* as she walks through the fire captures what was lost and what has endured.

It is significant that two of the racist historical tragedies that are included in the show started because a Black male was accused of sexually assaulting a white female: Emmett Till's murder and the Tulsa Race Massacre. The protected nature of white women is addressed in several ways on the show, but the clearest example is the character Christina Braithwhite, who was changed from a man, Caleb Braithwhite, in the book. As if to acknowledge this gender swap, it's revealed at the end of Episode 5 that Christina has been transforming into William, her one-time lover who was "killed" by Lancaster, whose body lies in a coma in her basement. In the beginning, it is hard to determine Christina's intentions. She is first introduced in Episode 1 as an enigmatic woman who saves Tic and his companions twice: first, from the Simmonsville assailants by pulling her Bentley in front of their truck, and second, from the Sheriff and his deputies by releasing her Shoggoths to attack them. In Episode 2, she also serves the purpose of demonstrating that the Sons of Adam are not only racist but also sexist. She then saves Tic again by giving him the ring that thwarts Samuel Braithwhite's ritual to open a door to the Garden of Eden in order to achieve immortality. In the first two episodes, another reason that we don't see Christina as the villain is because we believe that Samuel Braithwhite is occupying that role. As his daughter, she seems subservient to him and not the one who has the power. When the Ardham Lodge burns and her father and the entire membership of the Order of the Ancient Dawn perish, we begin to wonder if this had been her plan all along. At the end of "Holy Ghost" (S1, E3), Christina tells Tic quite directly, after he is unable to shoot her or even move his body because of her magic, "And, Tic, really, you have to be smarter than this. You know you can't just go around killing white women." This emphasizes that she has the protection of both the invulnerability spell and being a white woman.

It finally becomes clear that Christina has been the snake in the grass (or Garden of Eden, if you will) all along. By Episode 8, we find out that she wants to sacrifice Tic for her own immortality ritual and she needed Leti to buy the house so she could get her hands on the orrery and thus the key to the multiverse machine so she could potentially find Horatio Winthrop's pages. And yet, she's a beautiful, cool villain who at times seems to care about Tic, as her distant cousin, and Ruby, as her lover. From another perspective, she also represents a white woman who seems helpful at first to Black people, but who, at the end of the day, isn't in their corner. In Episode 8, when Ruby comes to her, heartbroken over Emmett's death, Christina (as William) bathes her and they kiss. Ruby takes the potion and starts changing into the white woman, Hillary. While they are having sex, she sheds her white skin and becomes Ruby once more. She then says that she should have been on the South Side with her people today and she wonders whether Christina cares about a 14-year-old boy who was shot and beaten to death, finally saying, "I want you to feel what I feel right now." And then strangely, toward the end of the episode, Christina arranges to do just that. She pays two white men to beat her up, shoot her twice, and attach her to a cotton gin fan with barbed wire. She does a quick spell and then she's dumped into the water. She bursts out of the water onto the dock and rips open her clothes to look for her Mark of Cain, which ensures her invulnerability, and then she sobs. Are we supposed to think better of her because she re-enacted Emmett Till's murder on herself? She knows that she will end up unscathed. Did she do it just because Ruby said that she wished that Christina could feel how she feels about Emmett's death? In her *Wired* article, Katrina Miller comments on Christina's reenactment, "Maybe it's supposed to be cathartic, like some sort of revenge for the role a white woman had in Till's murder. But all it really does is show us in real time the horrific torture experienced by a 14-year-old boy, a unique iteration of the obsessive consumption of Black death."[82] In the final analysis, perhaps the show is trying to send the message that a white person can never fully experience what a Black victim of racism has endured, no matter what they do to achieve that understanding.

"Full Circle" (S1, E10) completes the journey of the show's Black heroes as well as provides more explorations of the Black family. The episode begins with Tic, Leti, Montrose, and Hippolyta bringing a still comatose Dee, who now looks exactly like Topsy and Bopsy, back home after their trip to 1921 Tulsa. By unbinding the *Book of Names*, Tic and Leti are able to go to the ancestral space and receive help from Hanna, Hattie, and Dora, the matrilineal line of Tic's ancestors. They save Dee, but her arm has become a dead limb and she can no longer draw. Dee is despondent and blames her mother for leaving her. In response, Hippolyta tells her about her adventures and then her decision to return and use all the wisdom she has gained in 200 years to help her daughter. This pattern of accusation and self-justification between a daughter who feels abandoned and a mother who needed time to find herself is a resonant theme. Another family relationship that is explored in Episode 10 is that of Leti and her sister, Ruby. When they meet at their mother's grave, Leti tells Ruby that they're going to use the *Book of Names* to do a binding spell against Christina and she needs Ruby's help in getting the bodily material needed from Christina. Ruby says, "You only wanna be my sister when you need something, Leti." It seems perfectly reasonable that Ruby doesn't want to help her. So Leti is surprised when Ruby shows up with the needed vial when they are all piling into Woody to drive to Ardham. There is a particularly memorable scene of everyone in the car (Tic, Leti, Montrose, Hippolyta, Dee, Ji-Ah, and Ruby) singing "Sh-Boom." In the *Lovecraft Country Radio* podcast on Episode 10, Ashley C. Ford points out that this is yet another moment of Black joy. When she asks Misha Green, who joined them for the podcast, why this was important, Green says that it's important to the full circle idea since "Sh-Boom" played in the first episode on the bus.[83] Kevin Wong in his Episode 10 Recap in *Gamespot* points out that this is the first indication that Ruby isn't really Ruby since she makes it clear in Episode 1 that she doesn't like the song.[84] And indeed, Ruby's true identity as Christina is revealed later when she and Leti are drawing protection symbols together at the top of the tower. Christina divulges that she caught Ruby trying to steal the potion and that it's Leti's fault that her sister is dead. This simple statement becomes an uncomfortable, off-screen end to a wonderful character beautifully portrayed by Wunmi Mosaku.

But Leti's journey to becoming a hero continues. After Christina (disguised as Ruby) throws Leti off the tower, she hits the ground on her back and appears to be dead. Christina proceeds to do the ritual, slashing Tic's arms and letting his blood pour over her. As Tic's essence goes into Christina, we see that Leti resurrects. She looks at her torso and confirms that she has the Mark of Cain again. It is later revealed (in the images that Ji-Ah sees at the end) that Christina, disguised as Ruby, murmurs an incantation after Leti falls, which is what gives her back her invulnerability. Green verifies that Christina did this to honor her promise to Ruby that she wouldn't harm Leti.[85] (Oddly, Christina is a person of her word, as proven throughout the show, but that certainly doesn't make her a good person.) After Leti resurrects, she runs to the ruins of the Ardham Lodge in time to tell Tic that she loves him before he dies. Even though her heart is broken, she doesn't give up. We see her plunge a sword through Christina from the back, chanting in the Language of Adam. Christina tells her that she's too late because she's immortal now. Christina removes the sword and the wound instantly begins to heal, but Leti keeps chanting. Christina says, "Give it up. The potion won't work because it didn't have my blood." Then, Hippolyta urges Ji-Ah to connect Christina's and Tic's bodies to make Leti's spell work. We see the Mudang's prophecy come true when Ji-Ah becomes one with the dark cloud emanating from Tic and then uses her fox tails to join Tic with Christina. Now that Ji-Ah has the ability to use her fox tails at will and help the group, she too is becoming a hero. As she absorbs the memories from both Tic and Christina, the audience catches glimpses of what they have missed, such as Christina discovering Ruby with the vial and Tic acquainting Dee with the Black Shoggoth. Through it all, we hear Leti's pleading incantations in the Language of Adam. Suddenly, all her perseverance pays off in an explosion of energy. The screen goes black and then we see Christina lying under the rubble, her face bloody, still muttering in the Language of Adam. She says, "You bound me from magic." Leti's reply is "Not just you. Every white person in the world." Leti then confirms, "Magic is ours now." And so Leti is a hero who does more than just save her loved ones from the villain; she also changes the balance of power on a grand scale. It's also noteworthy that Leti was resurrected from the dead not once but twice: the first time in Ardham after she is shot, and the second time when she is thrown off the tower. This is similar to Buffy in *Buffy the Vampire Slayer* (The WB: 1997–2003, Joss Whedon), who is resuscitated by Xander at the end of Season 1 and resurrected by her friends at the beginning of Season 6. With Leti, we understand that not even death can stop her. She is the hero who never gives up, from being the manifestation of Mama Oya to save the ghosts in the basement, to walking through the Tulsa fire with the *Book of Names*, and finally to defeating Christina and changing the world.

Dee's developing journey also bears mention. When Christina is stuck under the rubble at the end and cries for help, both Dee and the Black Shoggoth come. We then realize that Dee has acquired an impressive robotic arm, courtesy of her mother. Dee tells Christina, "You still haven't learned." She then uses her robotic hand to clutch Christina's neck and squeeze it until it bursts. Dee clearly has no illusions about what Christina has wrought upon her family. This may not be everyone's idea of justice, but one perspective is that Dee is doing what needs to be done, without quandaries or adult morals getting in the way. She has been toughened up in a short time, forged in the fire of incredible loss. In the *Lovecraft*

IV—Retrospection

Country Radio podcast on Episode 10, Misha Green says this about Dee: "She has the robotic arm, the militant mindset, and the Black Shoggoth."[86] In many ways, Dee is becoming her own version of a Dahomey Amazon. It is also worth noting that in DC comics, Wonder Woman is a warrior princess named Diana who is the daughter of Hippolyta, the Queen of the Amazons.

And now we come to the discussion of Tic as a hero. His journey in the finale starts with his time in the ancestral space. As he runs through the fire at the Ardham Lodge again, Hanna tells him, "The fire was my rage made manifest." But she says that she found a way to tame it and realized that magic was not something to fear but a gift to pass on. She gathers a ball of magical fire and hands it to him. When Tic tells Hanna that he unbound the *Book of Names* to save his cousin, Hanna's reply is "You gonna save 'em all." Then, Tic finds himself in his home, where he sees his mother Dora in the red glow of the fire. He embraces her and then puts his head in her lap, telling her, "I don't wanna die, Mama." She says, "I know, but if we ain't walking toward an altar to sacrifice ourself for something important, what is our purpose?" In an interview with *Rolling Stone*, Green says, "We talked a lot in the room about this idea of walking towards this hero's journey story, about destiny: You're the one, and you're meant to do something." This recalls Joseph Campbell's monomyth, which he applies to Jesus, Mohammed, Buddha, and others in his book *A Hero with a Thousand Faces*. And certainly, one aspect of this is that the hero sacrifices themselves to save others. In the final ritual scene, Tic is led to the contraption Christina has prepared and is strapped in, looking like Jesus on the cross. And indeed, his sacrifice is Christ-like but also specifically that of a Black martyr in its reference to the lynching of Black people in American history. In his book *The Cross and the Lynching Tree*, James H. Cone explains, "As Jesus was an innocent victim of mob hysteria and Roman imperial violence, many African Americans were innocent victims of white mobs, thirsting for blood in the name of God and in defense of segregation, white supremacy, and the purity of the Anglo-Saxon race."[87] After Tic is dead, Montrose goes to him and insists, just like a father would, that it's time to get up, that they have to go. Hippolyta gives Montrose his son's note, which includes the Dumas quote about those who have experienced the deepest grief being best able to experience supreme happiness. Over the scene of them carrying Tic's body, we hear the rest of the quote that references the familial pain and envisions a way to end the generational abuse: "Teach my son new ways of living, instead of repeating what we've been through." In the *Lovecraft Country Radio* podcast on Episode 10, Green says, "How dare I be from this long lineage of fighters and lovers and say I'm too afraid to make a difference?"[88] And with her

Chapter 8. Lovecraft Country

decision to change the ending of the book and have Tic sacrifice himself at the end, she is demonstrating what it means for a character to choose to make a difference.

If the situation at the end of the first season is that white people don't have magic anymore but Black people do, a fitting question is whether this was setting up a second season where the tables would be turned. Unfortunately, we won't ever know the answer, at least not through the show's continuation on HBO. Even though Misha Green worked with a group of writers to develop a bible for the second season, the second season was cancelled. Green gave hints about the second season on Twitter, including the title, *Lovecraft Country: Supremacy*, and a map of what looks like the United States but is now called the "Sovereign States of America," which is divided into four lands: the Tribal Nations of the West, the Whitelands, the New Negro Republic, and the Jefferson Commonwealth. Apparently, zombies are contained in the Whitelands region.[89] According to the Table of Contents for the second season bible, "The Old Generation" would be Leti and Tic, and "The New Generation" would be Dee and George (Tic's grown son) as well as new characters: Billie Baptiste, Wi Sapa ("Black Moon"), and Xochimitl (Flowered Arrow). Since this all sounds intriguing and the first season was so wildly successful, both critically and popularly, why was the second season cancelled? The reasons that were reported included that it would have been too expensive and that HBO wasn't on board with the vision.[90] But in James Andrew Miller's book *Tinderbox: HBO's Ruthless Pursuit of New Frontiers*, he states, "As gifted as Misha Green was artistically, HBO determined after a lengthy analysis that there were too many organizational behavior issues present. Several writers on the show refused to work with Green, blaming her for a toxic and hostile environment."[91] In talking about how she initially developed the writers' room, which consisted of Black men and women as well as one Asian man, Green said that she was seeking diverse and younger writers, and yet "they were really pushing upper-level writers."[92] In the same interview, she continues to say that Hollywood is "a monolith of white men."[93] It's hard to know exactly what happened, but one possibility is that digging for the truth might have been problematic for some of the writers. In a video interview with Green, she says, "every writer that came into the room, when I interviewed them, I said be prepared for therapy. We're gonna be excavating here. You're gonna feel uncomfortable a lot."[94] As another pertinent factor in the cancellation, *Lovecraft Country* started in 2017 before the merger with AT&T, under HBO chairman and CEO Richard Plepler, but by the time it came to a decision for greenlighting Season 2, that was up to HBO chief content officer Casey Bloys.[95] Interestingly enough, the deal that Misha Green made with Apple TV+

shortly after the cancellation of Season 2 brought her back to working with Richard Plepler, whose company Eden Productions has a five-year production deal with Apple TV+. Equally telling is that Misha Green's deal with Apple TV+ "reunites her with Apple's heads of worldwide video Zack Van Amburg and Jamie Erlicht, who previously ran 'Underground' producer Sony Pictures Television, as well as Apple's head of programming Matt Cherniss, who was president and general manager of WGN America and Tribune Studios."[96] One conjecture is that fans might even see a return of *Lovecraft Country* on Apple TV+.[97] Whether the show ever gets a second season or not, the first season stands as a triumph of the human spirit, a chance for the realities of the Black experience to predominate, and an opportunity for fans to revel in the expanded genre space for people of color.

Chapter Notes

Chapter 1

1. Sophie Gilbert, "The Dark Teen Show That Pushes the Edge of Provocation," *The Atlantic*, 19 June 2019, https://www.theatlantic.com/entertainment/archive/2019/06/euphoria-hbo-review-zendaya/591955/.
2. Emily VanDerWerff, "HBO's Euphoria is two shows in one. One is bad. The other could be good," *Vox*, 23 June 2019, https://www.vox.com/culture/2019/6/23/18701226euphoria-premiere-pilot-episode-1-recap-zendaya-hbo.
3. Rick Porter, "TV Long View: HBO's 'Euphoria' Audience Is Extremely Online," *The Hollywood Reporter*, 22 June 2019, https://www.hollywoodreporter.com/tv/tv-news/tv-long-view-hbos-euphoria-audience-is-extremely-online-1220360/.
4. Ibid.
5. Kim Lyons, "AT&T CEO John Stankey says it was 'time to unleash' Warner Media assets," *The Verge*, 24 May 2021, https://www.theverge.com/2021/5/24/22451111/att-ceo-stankey-unleash-assets-warnermedia-discovery-hbo.
6. Nicolas Vega, "HBO Max is just 'Max' now—here are the 4 things to know about the new streaming service," *CNBC*, 23 May 2023, https://www.cnbc.com/2023/05/23/hbo-max-is-now-just-max-what-you-need-to-know.html.
7. Edmund Lee and John Koblin, "HBO Must Get Bigger and Broader, Says Its New Overseer," *The New York Times*, 8 July 2018, https://www.nytimes.com/2018/07/08/business/media/hbo-att-merger.html.
8. Alison Herman, "'Euphoria' (and HBO) Want to Get a Rise Out of You," *The Ringer*, 14 June 2019, https://www.theringer.com/tv/2019/6/14/18677932/euphoria-review-drugs-sex-hbo.
9. Kalea Martin, "15 New and Classic High School TV Shows Available to Stream HBO Max Right Now," *Popsugar*, 30 March 2021, https://www.popsugar.com/entertainment/photo-gallery/48244019/image/48244062/Nancy-Drew. [AU: This link is to a different title]
10. Sharon Marie Ross, "Defining Teen Culture: The N Network," *Teen Television: Essays on Programming and Fandom*, ed. Sharon Marie Ross and Louisa Ellen Stein (Jefferson, NC: McFarland, 2008), 61. Print.
11. Marisa Meltzer, "When Brenda Walsh Was Young: The revolutionary first season of *Beverly Hills, 90210*," *Slate*, 7 December 2006, https://slate.com/culture/2006/12/the-revolutionary-first-season-of-beverly-hills-90210.html.
12. Ibid.
13. Sharon Marie Ross, "Defining Teen Culture: The N Network," *Teen Television: Essays on Programming and Fandom*, ed. Sharon Marie Ross and Louisa Ellen Stein (Jefferson, NC: McFarland, 2008), 62. Print.
14. Sofia Aguilar, "The Latinas of 'Euphoria' Leave Me Wanting More," *Latina Media Co.*, 2 March 2022, https://latinamedia.co/euphoria/.
15. Dana Goldstein and Billy Witz, "Abuse and Racism Accusations Bring '#MeToo Moment' to Northwestern," *The New York Times*, 28 July 2023, https://www.nytimes.com/2023/07/28/sports/ncaafootball/northwestern-sports-hazing.html.
16. Bryn Elise Sandberg, "'Euphoria'

Creator on Boundary-Pushing HBO Drama: 'We Didn't Want to Pull Any Punches,'" *The Hollywood Reporter*, 16 June 2019, https://www.hollywoodreporter.com/live-feed/euphoria-creator-boundary-pushing-hbo-drama-didnt-pull-punches-1218588.
17. Tim Goodman, "'Euphoria': TV Review," *The Hollywood Reporter*, 5 June 2019, https://www.hollywoodreporter.com/tv/tv-reviews/euphoria-review-1215681/.
18. Ibid.
19. "World Drug Report 2019," *United Nations Office on Drugs and Crime*, 26 June 2019, https://www.unodc.org/unodc/en/frontpage/2019/June/world-drug-report-2019_-35-million-people-worldwide-suffer-from-drug-use-disorders-while-only-1-in-7-people-receive-treatment.html.
20. Martha J. Ignaszewski, M.D., "The Epidemiology of Drug Abuse," *The Journal of Clinical Pharmacology* 61, Issue S2, pp. S10–S17, 15 August 2021, https://accp1.onlinelibrary.wiley.com/doi/full/10.1002/jcph.1937.
21. "World Drug Report 2019," *United Nations Office on Drugs and Crime*, 26 June 2019, https://www.unodc.org/unodc/en/frontpage/2019/June/world-drug-report-2019_-35-million-people-worldwide-suffer-from-drug-use-disorders-while-only-1-in-7-people-receive-treatment.html.
22. "Drug Use Among Youth: Facts and Statistics," *National Center for Drug Abuse Statistics*, 2023, https://drugabusestatistics.org/teen-drug-use/.
23. Tara Law, "What Euphoria Gets Right—and Wrong—About Teen Drug Use and Addiction," *Time*, 28 February 2022, updated 2 March 2022, https://time.com/6152502/euphoria-hbo-teenage-drug-use/.
24. Ibid.
25. Azeen Ghorayshi, "Report Reveals Sharp Rise in Transgender Young People in the U.S.," *The New York Times*, 10 June 2022, https://www.nytimes.com/2022/06/10/science/transgender-teenagers-national-survey.html.
26. Ariana Romero, "The Emmys Struck a Pose. The Trans TV Revolution Is Here," *Refinery29*, 16 July 2019, https://www.refinery29.com/en-us/2019/07/238021/pose-emmy-nominations-2019-best-transgender-television.
27. Reggie Ugwu, "Where 'Euphoria' Is Surprisingly Conservative," *The New York Times*, 30 July 2019, https://www.nytimes.com/2019/07/30/arts/television/euphoria-internet-relationships-conservative.html.
28. Emily VanDerWerff, "HBO's Euphoria is two shows in one. One is bad. The other could be good," *Vox*, 23 June 2019, https://www.vox.com/culture/2019/6/23/18701226euphoria-premiere-pilot-episode-1-recap-zendaya-hbo.
29. This article contains an interview with Linda Schuyler, the creator of *Degrassi*, in which she discusses their efforts to cast actors who were age-appropriate: Liz Shannon Miller, "Here's Why Degrassi Will Never Die (and No, It's Not Just Because of Netflix)," *IndieWire*, 18 July 2016, http://www.indiewire.com/2016/07/degrassi-creator-next-class-netflix-500-episodes-1201707118/.
30. Bryn Elise Sandberg, "'Euphoria' Creator on Boundary-Pushing HBO Drama: 'We Didn't Want to Pull Any Punches,'" *The Hollywood Reporter*, 16 June 2019, https://www.hollywoodreporter.com/live-feed/euphoria-creator-boundary-pushing-hbo-drama-didnt-pull-punches-1218588.
31. Emily VanDerWerff, "HBO's Euphoria is two shows in one. One is bad. The other could be good," *Vox*, 23 June 2019, https://www.vox.com/culture/2019/6/23/18701226euphoria-premiere-pilot-episode-1-recap-zendaya-hbo.
32. Doreen St. Félix, "'Euphoria' and the Flawed Art of Gen Z Prophesying," *The New Yorker*, 16 June 2019, https://www.newyorker.com/culture/on-television/euphoria-and-the-flawed-art-of-gen-z-prophesying.

Chapter 2

1. Ronan McGreevy, "'Chronic' RTÉ funding meant Normal People taken to BBC—Lenny Abrahamson," *The Irish Times*, 20 June 2020, https://www.irishtimes.com/culture/tv-radio-web/chronic-rt%C3%A9-funding-meant-normal-people-taken-to-bbc-lenny-abrahamson-1.4284610.
2. Ali Condon, "Normal People is a big hit with viewers as over 370,000 tune

in," *Extra.ie*, 5 May 2020, https://extra.ie/2020/05/05/entertainment/movies-tv/normal-people-big-hit-rte.

3. "How We Made *Normal People*: Complete Featurette Including Paul Mescal and Daisy Edgar-Jones," *BBC Three*, 16 August 2020, YouTube, https://www.youtube.com/watch?v=fNi2Upp WINk. Video.

4. Jen Chaney, "*Normal People* Is an Honest, Absorbing Love Story," *Vulture*, 28 April 2020, https://www.vulture.com/2020/04/normal-people-hulu-review.html.

5. Claire Armistead and Johanna Thomas-Corr, "'The stakes were really high': The stars bringing Sally Rooney's Normal People to TV," *The Guardian*, 12 April 2020 (modified 3 June 2020), https://www.theguardian.com/tv-and-radio/2020/apr/12/the-stakes-were-really-high-bringing-sally-rooney-normal-people-to-tv.

6. Will Tizard, "'Normal People' DP Suzie Lavelle on 'the Simplicity of Pure Storytelling,'" *Variety*, 3 October 2021, https://variety.com/2020/artisans/global/normal-people-suzie-lavelle-1234831663/.

7. James Poniewozik, "'Normal People' Review: Their Love Will Tear You Apart," *The New York Times*, 28 April 2020, https://www.nytimes.com/2020/04/28/arts/television/normal-people-review.html.

8. "Clubhouse Conversations—Normal People," Suzie Lavelle interviewed by Seamus McGarvey, *American Cinematographer*, https://ascmag.com/videos/clubhouse-conversations-normal-people. Video.

9. *Ibid.*

10. *Ibid.*

11. "How We Made *Normal People*: Complete Featurette Including Paul Mescal and Daisy Edgar-Jones," *BBC Three*, 16 August 2020, YouTube, https://www.youtube.com/watch?v=fNi2Upp WINk. Video.

12. Dwight Garner, James Poniewozik, Parul Sehgal, and Jennifer Szalai, "Bringing 'Normal People' to Sexy, Soundtracked Life," *The New York Times*, 15 May 2020, https://www.nytimes.com/2020/05/15/books/normal-people-sally-rooney-hulu-adaptation.html.

13. Jen Chaney, "*Normal People* Is an Honest, Absorbing Love Story," *Vulture*, 28 April 2020, https://www.vulture.com/2020/04/normal-people-hulu-review.html.

14. *Ibid.*

15. Claire Armistead and Johanna Thomas-Corr, "'The stakes were really high': The stars bringing Sally Rooney's Normal People to TV," *The Guardian*, 12 April 2020 (modified 3 June 2020), https://www.theguardian.com/tv-and-radio/2020/apr/12/the-stakes-were-really-high-bringing-sally-rooney-normal-people-to-tv.

16. *Ibid.*

17. "Clubhouse Conversations—Normal People," Suzie Lavelle interviewed by Seamus McGarvey, *American Cinematographer*, https://ascmag.com/videos/clubhouse-conversations-normal-people. Video.

18. Claire Armistead and Johanna Thomas-Corr, "'The stakes were really high': The stars bringing Sally Rooney's Normal People to TV," *The Guardian*, 12 April 2020 (modified 3 June 2020), https://www.theguardian.com/tv-and-radio/2020/apr/12/the-stakes-were-really-high-bringing-sally-rooney-normal-people-to-tv.

19. *Ibid.*

20. Anna Russell, "How 'Normal People' Makes Us Fall in Love," *The New Yorker*, 18 May 2020, https://www.newyorker.com/culture/on-television/how-normal-people-makes-us-fall-in-love.

21. *Ibid.*

22. Claire Armistead and Johanna Thomas-Corr, "'The stakes were really high': The stars bringing Sally Rooney's Normal People to TV," *The Guardian*, 12 April 2020 (modified 3 June 2020), https://www.theguardian.com/tv-and-radio/2020/apr/12/the-stakes-were-really-high-bringing-sally-rooney-normal-people-to-tv.

23. Sally Rooney, *Normal People* (London: Faber & Faber, 2018), 22. Print.

24. Anna Russell, "How 'Normal People' Makes Us Fall in Love," *The New Yorker*, 18 May 2020, https://www.newyorker.com/culture/on-television/how-normal-people-makes-us-fall-in-love.

25. Sally Rooney, *Normal People* (London: Faber & Faber, 2018), 51. Print.

26. *Ibid.*, 56.
27. *Ibid.*, 46.
28. Claire Armitstead and Johanna Thomas-Corr, "'The stakes were really high': The stars bringing Sally Rooney's Normal People to TV," *The Guardian*, 12 April 2020 (modified 3 June 2020), https://www.theguardian.com/tv-and-radio/2020/apr/12/the-stakes-were-really-high-bringing-sally-rooney-normal-people-to-tv.
29. Dwight Garner, James Poniewozik, Parul Sehgal, and Jennifer Szalai, "Bringing 'Normal People' to Sexy, Soundtracked Life," *The New York Times*, 15 May 2020, https://www.nytimes.com/2020/05/15/books/normal-people-sally-rooney-hulu-adaptation.html.

Chapter 3

1. Joe Otterson, "Donald Glover's 'Atlanta' to Stream on Hulu," *Variety*, 3 May 2017, https://variety.com/2017/tv/news/atlanta-donald-glover-hulu-1202407669/.
2. Kiersten Willis, "Donald Glover's 'Atlanta' Proves White People 'Don't Know Everything About Black Culture,'" *Atlanta Black Star*, 7 September 2016, https://atlantablackstar.com/2016/09/07/donald-glovers-atlanta-proves-white-people-dont-know-everything-about-black-culture/.
3. Donald Glover, "This Is America," mcDJ/RCA, 2018, written by Donald Glover and composed by Donald Glover, Ludwig Göransson, and Jeffery Lamar Williams. Song.
4. Travis M. Andrews, "Some took offense at Donald Glover's early work. He has evolved, but the Internet never forgets," *The Washington Post*, 15 May 2018, https://www.washingtonpost.com/news/arts-and-entertainment/wp/2018/05/15/some-took-offense-at-donald-glovers-early-work-he-has-evolved-but-the-internet-never-forgets/.
5. *This Changes Everything*, dir. Tom Donahue, Good Deed Entertainment, 2018. Film.
6. Peter White, "FX to Have a Majority of Diverse & Female Directors in 2021 as John Landgraf Lays Out Latest Diversity Data," *Deadline*, 27 August 2020, https://deadline.com/2020/08/fx-john-landgraf-diversity-data-directors-1203024974/.
7. Sandra Gonzalez, "After getting called out, FX overhauled its efforts to hire more diverse TV directors," *CNN*, 9 August 2016, https://money.cnn.com/2016/08/09/media/fx-female-directors/index.html.
8. Brian Boone, "Huge TV Shows That Totally Disappeared," *Looper*, 8 September 2020, https://www.looper.com/244616/huge-tv-shows-that-totally-disappeared/.
9. Isabel Molina-Guzmán, *Latinas & Latinos on TV: Colorblind Comedy in the Post-Racial Network Era* (Tucson: University of Arizona Press, 2018), 5. Print.
10. Kristen J. Warner, *The Cultural Politics of Colorblind TV Casting* (Oxfordshire: Routledge, 2015), 12. Print.
11. *Ibid.*, 2–5.
12. *Ibid.*, 13.
13. Stuart Jeffries, "Was this Britain's first black queen?" *The Guardian*, 11 March 2009, https://www.theguardian.com/world/2009/mar/12/race-monarchy.
14. Kalia Richardson, "Here's What to Know About 'Queen Charlotte: A Bridgerton Story,'" *The New York Times*, 11 May 2023, https://www.nytimes.com/2023/05/11/arts/television/queen-charlotte-bridgerton-history-shonda-rhimes.html.
15. Kristen J. Warner, *The Cultural Politics of Colorblind TV Casting* (Oxfordshire: Routledge, 2015), 13. Print.
16. Kristen J. Warner, "In the Time of Plastic Representation," *Film Quarterly*, 4 December 2017, https://filmquarterly.org/2017/12/04/in-the-time-of-plastic-representation/.
17. *Ibid.*
18. Kristen J. Warner, *The Cultural Politics of Colorblind TV Casting* (Oxfordshire: Routledge, 2015), 12. Print.
19. *Ibid.*, 147.
20. *Ibid.*
21. Dr. Darnell Hunt and Ana-Christina Ramón, "Hollywood Diversity Report 2021: Pandemic in Progress, Part 2: Television," *UCLA: College of Social Sciences*, 26 October 2021, https://socialsciences.ucla.edu/wp-content/uploads/2021/10/UCLA-Hollywood-Diversity-Report-2021-Television-10-26-2021.pdf.
22. *Ibid.*
23. "Being Seen On Screen: Diverse

Representation and Inclusion on TV," *Nielsen*, 2 December 2020, https://www.nielsen.com/us/en/insights/report/2020/being-seen-on-screen-diverse-representation-and-inclusion-on-tv/.

24. *Ibid.*
25. *Ibid.*
26. *Ibid.*
27. *Ibid.*
28. Tad Friend, "Donald Glover Can't Save You," *The New Yorker*, 26 February 2018, https://www.newyorker.com/magazine/2018/03/05/donald-glover-cant-save-you.
29. "Atlanta," *Rotten Tomatoes*, https://www.rottentomatoes.com/tv/atlanta.
30. Pilot Viruet, "'Atlanta' Is Great at Talking About Race Without Talking About Race," *Vice*, 28 September 2016, https://www.vice.com/en/article/7bm83a/atlanta-is-great-at-talking-about-race-without-talking-about-race.
31. *Ibid.*
32. Kristine Phillips, "Mike Pence links Trump's push for border wall to Martin Luther King, Jr.'s legacy," *Chicago Tribune*, 20 January 2019, https://www.chicagotribune.com/nation-world/ct-mike-pence-mlk-border-wall-20190120-story.html.
33. Melanie McFarland, "This Juneteenth, 'Atlanta' will give you all the insights you need on how America co-opts a holiday," *Salon*, 18 June 2021, https://www.salon.com/2021/06/18/juneteenth-atlanta-fx-holiday/.
34. Tad Friend, "Donald Glover Can't Save You," *The New Yorker*, 26 February 2018, https://www.newyorker.com/magazine/2018/03/05/donald-glover-cant-save-you.
35. Allison Samuels, "Rachel Dolezal's True Lies," *Vanity Fair*, 19 July 2015, https://www.vanityfair.com/news/2015/07/rachel-dolezal-new-interview-pictures-exclusive.
36. Denene Millner, "Why Rachel Dolezal Can Never Be Black," *NPR*, 3 March 2017, https://www.npr.org/sections/codeswitch/2017/03/03/518184030/why-rachel-dolezal-can-never-be-black.
37. *Ibid.*
38. *Ibid.*
39. Randee Dawn, "Setting the scene in 'Handmaid's Tale,' 'Atlanta' and more: Writers explain the draw of nominated episodes," *Los Angeles Times*, 17 August 2017, https://www.latimes.com/entertainment/envelope/la-en-st-key-scenes-writers-20170817-story.html.

40. Aisha Harris, "This Week's Atlanta Showed the Problem with Choosing Outrage at the Expense of Understanding," *Slate*, 12 October 2016, https://slate.com/culture/2016/10/atlantas-b-a-n-episode-critiques-p-c-outrage.html.

41. "New Analysis Shows Startling Levels of Discrimination against Black Transgender People," *National LGBTQ Task Force*, https://www.thetaskforce.org/new-analysis-shows-startling-levels-of-discrimination-against-black-transgender-people/.

42. Stereo Williams, "Hip-Hop's Transphobic OGs: Will the Rap Community Embrace Caitlyn Jenner?" *Daily Beast*, 6 June 2015, https://www.thedailybeast.com/hip-hops-transphobic-ogs-will-the-rap-community-embrace-caitlyn-jenner.

43. Bethonie Butlet, "An 'Atlanta' episode and Dave Chappelle's Netflix special show what has—and hasn't—changed in five years," *The Washington Post*, 15 October 2021, https://www.washingtonpost.com/arts-entertainment/2021/10/15/dave-chappelle-atlanta/.

44. *Ibid.*

45. Zach Sharf, "Donald Glover: Fear of 'Getting Cancelled' Is Resulting in 'Boring' Films and TV," *IndieWire*, 11 May 2021, https://www.indiewire.com/2021/05/donald-glover-cancel-culture-boring-movies-tv-1234636493/.

46. Dan Bernstein, "Sammy Sosa then and now: Former MLB star explains why his skin color is lighter since retirement," *The Sporting News*, 15 June 2020, https://www.sportingnews.com/us/mlb/news/sammy-sosa-skin-color-now/1aruhh5dunsn1llps943qzwlqk.

47. Beth Daley, "Women of color spend more than $8 billion on bleaching creams worldwide every year," *The Conversation*, 19 February 2021, https://theconversation.com/women-of-color-spend-more-than-8-billion-on-bleaching-creams-worldwide-every-year-153178.

48. "Vitiligo," *Mayo Clinic*, https://www.mayoclinic.org/diseases/conditions/vitiligo/symptoms-causes/syc-20355912.

49. Zeba Blay, "Hollywood Has a Colorism Problem, and the Conversation

keeps going nowhere," *Jezebel*, 7 October 2021, https://jezebel.com/hollywood-has-a-colorism-problem-and-the-conversation-1847817522.
50. *Ibid.*
51. "The Untold Truth of Teddy Perkins," *Looper*, 1 October 2018, *YouTube*, https://www.youtube.com/watch?v=EaPZMct-6_I. Video.
52. *Ibid.*
53. Angelica Jade Bastién, "In Its Second Season, Atlanta Used Horror to Explore Black Identity," *Vulture*, 18 May 2018, https://www.vulture.com/2018/05/atlanta-horror-second-two-black-identity.html.
54. *Ibid.*
55. *Ibid.*
56. "Why Donald Glover's Atlanta Feels So Weird," Thomas Flight, 28 March 2022, *YouTube*, https://www.youtube.com/watch?v=8rOU9wrEsoo&t=1s. Video.
57. Zack Sharf, "Lakeith Stanfield: 'I'm Kind of Mad' About Finding Out Teddy Perkins Is Donald Glover," *IndieWire*, 18 November 2020, https://www.indiewire.com/2020/11/lakeith-stanfield-mad-finding-out-donald-glover-teddy-perkins-1234599614/.
58. Merriam-Webster, https://www.merriam-webster.com/dictionary/surrealism.
59. Evan Higgins, "Atlanta's Surrealism Is What It Feels Like to Be Black," *Slate*, 27 February 2018, https://slate.com/culture/2018/02/atlantas-surrealism-and-the-black-experience-in-america.html.
60. Nathan Sharp, "Atlanta: The 10 Most Surreal Moments in the Show, Ranked," *Screen Rant*, 16 February 2021, https://screenrant.com/atlanta-surreal-moments/.
61. Evan Higgins, "Atlanta's Surrealism Is What It Feels Like to Be Black," *Slate*, 27 February 2018, https://slate.com/culture/2018/02/atlantas-surrealism-and-the-black-experience-in-america.html.
62. *Ibid.*
63. *Ibid.*
64. Malcolm Venable, "Why Donald Glover's Atlanta Is 'Twin Peaks with Rappers,'" *TV Guide*, 16 January 2016, https://www.tvguide.com/news/donald-glover-atlanta-twin-peaks-rappers/.
65. "Get Out, Atlanta, Sorry to Bother You, and the Afro-Surrealist Film Movement," *Surrealism Today*, 1 December 2021, https://surrealismtoday.com/the-afro-surrealist-film-movement/.
66. "Why Donald Glover's Atlanta Feels So Weird," Thomas Flight, *YouTube*, 28 March 2022, https://www.youtube.com/watch?v=8rOU9wrEsoo&t=1s. Video.
67. Norman Weiss, "Reservation Dogs was consistently great in its first season," *Primetimer*, 23 September 2021, https://www.primetimer.com/item/Reservation-Dogs-was-consistently-great-in-its-first-season-ElSZJ5.
68. Sandy Kim, "Donald Glover's Community: The comic turns his eye to his hometown—and black America—in Atlanta," *Vulture*, 22 August 2016, https://www.vulture.com/2016/08/donald-glover-atlanta.html.
69. *Ibid.*

Chapter 4

1. Myeisha Essex, "Ramy Youssef Jokes 'I Know You Guys Haven't Seen My Show' After First Golden Globe Win," *Entertainment Weekly*, 5 January 2020, https://www.etonline.com/ramy-youssef-jokes-i-know-you-guys-havent-seen-my-show-after-first-golden-globe-win-138856.
2. Sopan Deb, "'Ramy' Is a Quietly Revolutionary Comedy," *The New York Times*, 18 April 2019, https://www.nytimes.com/2019/04/18/arts/television/ramy-youssef-hulu.html.
3. "Being Seen on Screen: Diverse Representation and Inclusion on TV," *Nielsen*, 2 December 2020, https://www.nielsen.com/us/en/insights/report/2020/being-seen-on-screen-diverse-representation-and-inclusion-on-tv/.
4. *Ibid.*
5. *Ibid.*
6. *Ibid.*
7. Jaya Saxena, "Ramy Youssef Is Upending the First-Generation Narrative," *GQ*, 17 April 2019, https://www.gq.com/story/ramy-youssef-is-upending-the-first-generation-narrative.
8. *Ibid.*
9. *Ibid.*
10. Umber Ghatti, "Actor draws from Muslim-American identity in show exploring challenges of dual cultures," *Daily Bruin*, 10 September 2021, https://dailybruin.com/2019/04/11/

actor-draws-from-muslim-american-identity-in-show-exploring-challenges-of-dual-cultures.
11. Cortney Moore, "Hulu and the 5 things that set it apart from other streaming giants," *Fox Business*, 30 September 2019, https://www.foxbusiness.com/technology/5-things-to-know-about-hulu.
12. Todd Spangler, "Comcast Would Be Interested in Buying Hulu from Disney 'If It Was Up for Sale,' CEO Brian Roberts Says," *Variety*, 14 September 2022, https://variety.com/2022/digital/news/comcast-interested-buying-hulu-disney-ceo-brian-roberts-1235372543/.
13. Derek Walborn, "Hulu Improves to 41.6 Million Total Subscribers, Hulu Live TV Loses 200,000," *The Streamable*, 13 May 2021, https://thestreamable.com/news/hulu-q1-2021.
14. Jordan Moreau, "Zoë Kravitz Calls Out Hulu for Lack of Diverse Shows After 'High Fidelity' Cancellation," *Variety*, 8 August 2020, https://variety.com/2020/tv/news/zoe-kravitz-high-fidelity-hulu-diversity-1234729635/.
15. Dr. Darnell Hunt and Ana-Christina Ramón, "Hollywood Diversity Report 2020: A Tale of Two Hollywoods, Part 2: Television," *UCLA: College of Social Sciences*, 22 October 2020, https://socialsciences.ucla.edu/wp-content/uploads/2020/10/UCLA-Hollywood-Diversity-Report-2020-Television-10-22-2020.pdf.
16. Dr. Darnell Hunt and Ana-Christina Ramón, "Hollywood Diversity Report 2021: Pandemic in Progress, Part 2: Television," *UCLA: College of Social Sciences*, 26 October 2021, https://socialsciences.ucla.edu/wp-content/uploads/2021/10/UCLA-Hollywood-Diversity-Report-2021-Television-10-26-2021.pdf.
17. Sonia Rao, "Black TV writers have often felt like 'diversity decoration.' Now they're braced for another round of promises," *The Washington Post*, 1 July 2020, https://www.washingtonpost.com/arts-entertainment/2020/07/01/black-television-writers/.
18. Dr. Darnell Hunt and Ana-Christina Ramón, "Hollywood Diversity Report 2021: Pandemic in Progress, Part 2: Television," *UCLA: College of Social Sciences*, 26 October 2021, https://socialsciences.ucla.edu/wp-content/uploads/2021/10/UCLA-Hollywood-Diversity-Report-2021-Television-10-26-2021.pdf.
19. Ibid.
20. Kristen J. Warner, *The Cultural Politics of Colorblind TV Casting* (Oxfordshire: Routledge, 2015), 134. Print.
21. Ophira Eisenberg, "Ask Me Another: Ramy Youssef," *NPR*, 29 May 2020, https://www.npr.org/transcripts/864841785.
22. Sopan Deb, "'Ramy' Is a Quietly Revolutionary Comedy," *The New York Times*, 18 April 2019, https://www.nytimes.com/2019/04/18/arts/television/ramy-youssef-hulu.html.
23. Andrew Marantz, "Ramy Youssef's Sort-of-Sacred Standup," 15 April 2019, *The New Yorker*, https://www.newyorker.com/magazine/2019/04/22/ramy-yousefs-sort-of-sacred-standup.
24. Sopan Deb, "'Ramy' Is a Quietly Revolutionary Comedy," *The New York Times*, 18 April 2019, https://www.nytimes.com/2019/04/18/arts/television/ramy-youssef-hulu.html.
25. Matt Wilstein, "Why Muslim Comic Ramy Youssef Made His 9/11 Story About Masturbation," *The Daily Beast*, 16 April 2019, https://www.thedailybeast.com/the-last-laugh-podcast-why-muslim-comic-ramy-youssef-made-his-911-story-on-hulu-about-masturbation.
26. Derek Lawrence, "A golden match: Ramy Youssef and Mahershala Ali are each other's biggest fans," *Entertainment Weekly*, 19 May 2020, https://ew.com/tv/ramy-youssef-mahershala-ali-ramy-hulu/.
27. Mohammad Zaheer, "How Muslims Became the Good Guys On TV," *BBC*, 21 June 2019, https://www.bbc.com/culture/article/20190620-how-muslims-became-the-good-guys-on-tv.
28. Jack G. Shaheen, *The TV Arab* (Bowling Green: Bowling Green State University Popular Press, 1984), 4. Print.
29. Ibid., 7.
30. Jeffrey M. Jones, "Americans Felt Uneasy Toward Arabs Even Before September 11," *Gallup*, 28 September 2001, https://news.gallup.com/poll/4939/americans-felt-uneasy-toward-arabs-even-before-september.aspx.
31. Laura Durkay, "'Homeland' is the most bigoted show on television," *The Washington Post*, 2 October 2014,

https://www.washingtonpost.com/posteverything/wp/2014/10/02/homeland-is-the-most-bigoted-show-on-television/.

32. Michael Lipka, "Muslims and Islam: Key findings in the U.S. and around the world," *Pew Research Center*, 9 August 2017, https://www.pewresearch.org/facttank/2017/08/09/muslims-and-islam-key-findings-in-the-u-s-and-around-the-world/.

33. "Ramy Youssef—Telling an American Muslim's Story on 'Ramy,'" *The Daily Show with Trevor Noah*, Comedy Central, 26 August 2020, https://www.cc.com/video/wlouyz/the-daily-show-with-trevor-noah-ramy-youssef-telling-an-american-muslim-s-story-on-ramy. Video.

34. Omar Sanchez, "Why Ramy Youssef Doesn't Intend 'Ramy' to Represent Every Muslim Experience," *The Wrap*, 19 April 2019, https://www.thewrap.com/why-ramy-youssef-doesnt-intend-ramy-to-represent-every-muslim-experience/.

35. Alya Mooro, "Ramy Youssef Isn't Trying to Represent All Muslims, He Just Wants to Be Himself," *Shondaland*, 12 June 2020, https://www.shondaland.com/inspire/a32842712/ramy-youssef-ramy-season-2/.

36. WordData.info, https://www.worlddata.info/religions/islam.php#:~:text=Spread%20of%20Islam&text=Today%2C%20Islam%20is%20the%20second,has%20about%201.8%20billion%20followers.

37. Razan Mneimneh, "Muslim character in Grey's Anatomy took off her hijab ... and people lost it," *Step Feed*, 12 March 2018, https://stepfeed.com/muslim-character-in-grey-s-anatomy-took-off-her-hijab-and-people-lost-it-7785.

38. Mohammad Zaheer, "How Muslims Became the Good Guys On TV," *BBC*, 21 June 2019, https://www.bbc.com/culture/article/20190620-how-muslims-became-the-good-guys-on-tv.

39. Greg Evans, "Carlton Cuse Says 'Tom Clancy's Jack Ryan' Won't Demonize Islam; Unveil. Teaser Clip—NY Comic-Con Update," *Yahoo!*, 7 October 2017, https://www.yahoo.com/entertainment/tom-clancy-jack-ryan-amazon-224114302.html.

40. Nasim Pedrad, "Nasim Pedrad Fought to Play Herself—as a 14-Year-Old Boy," *Glamour*, 5 November 2019, https://www.glamour.com/story/nasim-pedrad-fought-to-play-herself-as-a-14-year-old-boy.

41. Sopan Deb, "'Ramy' Is a Quietly Revolutionary Comedy," *The New York Times*, 18 April 2019, https://www.nytimes.com/2019/04/18/arts/television/ramy-youssef-hulu.html.

42. *Ibid*.

43. Rebecca Patton, "Why Ramy Youssef Says 9/11 Made Him 'More Muslim,'" *Bustle*, 29 June 2019, https://www.bustle.com/p/in-ramy-youssefs-comedy-special-feelings-he-says-911-made-him-more-muslim-18153449.

44. Mohammad Zaheer, "How Muslims Became the Good Guys On TV," *BBC*, 21 June 2019, https://www.bbc.com/culture/article/20190620-how-muslims-became-the-good-guys-on-tv.

45. Margaretha A. van Es, "Van Es on Self-Representations of Muslim Women," *Palgrave Macmillan*, https://www.palgrave.com/gp/campaigns/internationalwomens-day/van-es-on-self-representations-of-muslim-women.

46. Jacques Brel, "Ne me quitte pas," La Valse à Mille Temps, Phillips, 1959, written and composed by Jacques Brel. Song.

47. Gazelle Emami, "There's Never Been a Show Like Ramy—How a weird, personal, sexually complicated, and yes, Muslim-American comedy, made it to TV," *Vulture*, 19 April 2019, https://www.vulture.com/2019/04/ramy-hulu-series-ramy-youssef-on-set.html.

48. *Ibid*.

49. Shamira Ibrahim, "What 'Ramy' Gets Wrong About Muslim Women," *The Atlantic*, 23 April 2019, https://www.theatlantic.com/entertainment/archive/2019/04/hulus-ramy-misses-mark-muslim-women/587722/.

50. Nailah Dean, "Why I'm Tired of Dating Ramy," *Muslim Girl*, 23 December 2020, https://muslimgirl.com/why-im-tired-of-dating-ramy/.

51. Scott Fontana, "Actor and Comedian with Muscular Dystrophy Works to Open Doors for More Disabled Stories," *Everyday Health*, 7 August 2020, https://www.everydayhealth.com/genetic-diseases/actor-and-comedian-with-muscular-dystrophy-works-to-open-doors-for-more-disabled-stories/.

52. Kristen Lopez, "Disability in

Television: Who Was the First Disabled Person You Saw on Television?" *IndieWire*, 13 August 2020, https://www.indiewire.com/2020/08/glee-star-trek-first-time-you-saw-disability-on-tv-1234571574/.

53. "Visibility of Disability: Answering the Call for Disability Inclusion in Media," *Nielsen*, 28 July 2021, https://www.nielsen.com/us/en/insights/article/2021/visibility-of-disability-answering-the-call-for-disability-inclusion-in-media/.

54. Michael Stahl, "How a Lifelong Friendship Led to Steve Way's Ramy Role," *Vulture*, 6 May 2019, https://www.vulture.com/2019/05/steve-way-ramy-stand-up-comedy-interview.html.

55. Maria Maddux, "Authentically Casting People with Disabilities and Talking About Sex: Why You Should Watch 'Ramy,'" *Virtual Research Center for the Americas*, 18 August 2020, https://www.olacolorado.org/post/authentically-casting-people-with-disabilities-and-talking-about-sex-why-you-should-watch-ramy.

56. "Visibility of Disability: Answering the Call for Disability Inclusion in Media," *Nielsen*, 28 July 2021, https://www.nielsen.com/us/en/insights/article/2021/visibility-of-disability-answering-the-call-for-disability-inclusion-in-media/.

57. "GLAAD's Where We Are on TV 2020–2021 Report: Despite Tumultuous Year in Television, LGBTQ Representation Holds Steady," *GLAAD*, 14 January 2021, https://www.glaad.org/releases/glaads-where-we-are-tv-2020-2021-report-despite-tumultuous-year-television-lgbtq.

58. "CDC: 1 in 4 U.S. adults live with a disability," *CDC*, 16 August 2018, https://www.cdc.gov/media/releases/2018/p0816-disability.html.

59. "Ramy Youssef—Telling an American Muslim's Story on 'Ramy,'" *The Daily Show with Trevor Noah*, Comedy Central, 26 August 2020, https://www.cc.com/video/wlouyz/the-daily-show-with-trevor-noah-ramy-youssef-telling-an-american-muslim-s-story-on-ramy. Video.

60. Matt Grobar, "Ramy Youssef on Depicting 'Anti-Blackness' in 'Ramy' Season 2: 'There's a Lot of Work to Do,'" *Deadline*, 30 June 2020, https://deadline.com/2020/06/ramy-creator-ramy-youssef-mahershala-ali-hulu-interview-news-1202955850/.

61. Caty Borum Chattoo and Lauren Feldman, *A Comedian and an Activist Walk Into a Bar: The Serious Role of Comedy in Social Justice* (Oakland: University of California Press, 2020), 7. Print.

62. David Marchese, "Ramy Youssef Is Not Using Comedy to Teach You About Muslims," *The New York Times*, 12 May 2020, https://www.nytimes.com/interactive/2020/05/12/magazine/ramy-youssef-interview.html.

63. Ibid.

64. Ibid.

Chapter 5

1. Nellie Andreeva, "Starz Greenlights Drama Series 'Vida' in Push to Attract Latino Viewers," *Deadline*, 13 September 2017, https://deadline.com/2017/09/starz-orders-vida-drama-series-veronica-osorio-melissa-barrera-to-star-push-latino-viewers-1202169060/.

2. Lesley Goldberg, "'Vida' to End with Season 3 on Starz," *The Hollywood Reporter*, 18 March 2020, https://www.hollywoodreporter.com/tv/tv-news/vida-end-season-3-starz-1285162/.

3. Maria Elena Fernandez, "What Hollywood Can Learn from Vida's All-Latina Directors," *Vulture*, 11 June 2019, https://www.vulture.com/2019/06/vida-season-2-tanya-saracho-latina-directors.html.

4. Pilot Viruet, "How Starz's 'Vida' Created a Safe Space to Explore Latinx and Queer Stories," *The Hollywood Reporter*, 4 May 2018, https://www.hollywoodreporter.com/tv/tv-news/how-starzs-vida-created-a-safe-space-explore-latinx-queer-stories-1107482/.

5. Ibid.

6. Ibid.

7. Maria Elena Fernandez, "What Hollywood Can Learn from Vida's All-Latina Directors," *Vulture*, 11 June 2019, https://www.vulture.com/2019/06/vida-season-2-tanya-saracho-latina-directors.html.

8. Mónica Marie Zorrilla, "Latinx TV Talent Still Largely Shunned by Hollywood, UCLA Diversity Report Indicates," *Variety*, 26 October 2021, https://variety.com/2021/tv/news/latinx-tv-talent-underrepresentation-hollywood-ucla-diversity-report-1235097213/.

9. *Ibid.*

10. "Vida Stars Melissa Barrera and Mishel Prada on Their Intimate Scenes on Latinx Show," *Cine Movie*, www.cinemovie.tv, accessed 21 January 2022. Video.

11. Pilot Viruet, "How Starz's 'Vida' Created a Safe Space to Explore Latinx and Queer Stories," *The Hollywood Reporter*, 4 May 2018, https://www.hollywoodreporter.com/tv/tv-news/how-starzs-vida-created-a-safe-space-explore-latinx-queer-stories-1107482/.

12. Tracy E. Gilchrist, "Vida Boldly Tackles Identity Policing Among Queer People," *Advocate*, 21 June 2019, https://www.advocate.com/television/2019/6/21/vida-boldly-tackles-identity-policing-among-queer-people.

13. *Ibid.*

14. Vanessa Erazo, "'Vida': Tanya Saracho on Colorism and the 'Authenticity Police,'" *The New York Times*, 22 May 2019, https://www.nytimes.com/2019/05/22/arts/television/vida-season-2-starz.html.

15. Jared Richards, "Vida: A shrewd, queer Latinx drama that's far too busy to explain everything to you," *The Guardian*, 7 January 2021, https://www.theguardian.com/culture/2021/jan/08/vida-a-shrewd-queer-latinx-drama-thats-far-too-busy-to-explain-everything-to-you.

16. Ludwig Hurtado, "What Happens When Latinx People Gentrify Latinx Communities," *Vice*, 31 January 2019, https://www.vice.com/en/article/mbynkq/what-happens-when-latinx-people-gentrify-latinx-communities.

17. *Ibid.*

18. Julia Barajas, "L.A.'s Eastside is a Latino 'Ellis Island.' But it's time for Hollywood to branch out," *Los Angeles Times*, 13 June 2021, https://www.latimes.com/entertainment-arts/tv/story/2021-06-13/latino-gap-netflix-gentefied-on-my-block-boyle-heights-east-la.

19. "Sex-positive" Google search—Oxford Languages, accessed 17 December 2021.

20. "Sex positive feminism" Google search—Google Arts & Culture, accessed 17 December 2021.

21. Sadie Gennis, "Starz's 'Vida' Is Plenty Sexy—But Every Graphic Moment Counts," *TV Guide*, 20 March 2019, https://www.tvguide.com/news/features/starz-vida-sex-scenes/.

22. Isabel Molina-Guzmán, *Latinas & Latinos on TV: Colorblind Comedy in the Post-Racial Network Era* (Tucson: University of Arizona Press, 2018), 15. Print.

23. Alicia Menendez, "VIDA's Melissa Barrera Embraces All Her Identities," *Latina to Latina*, Lantigua Williams & Co., 10 December 2018, LatinaToLatina.com.

24. Frederick Luis Aldama and Christopher González, *Reel Latinxs: Representation in U.S. Film & TV* (Tucson: University of Arizona Press, 2019), 18. Print.

25. *Ibid.*, 16.

26. Maria Elena Fernandez, "What Hollywood Can Learn from Vida's All-Latina Directors," *Vulture*, 11 June 2019, https://www.vulture.com/2019/06/vida-season-2-tanya-saracho-latina-directors.html.

27. "Vida: Inside the World—Episode 104," creator Tanya Saracho, Starz, 2018. Television.

28. Amia Srinivasan, *The Right to Sex: Feminism in the Twenty-First Century* (New York: Farrar, Straus and Giroux, 2021), 33. Print.

29. *Ibid.*, 81.

30. *Ibid.*, 41.

31. *Ibid.*, 40.

32. *Ibid.*

33. Peggy Orenstein, "Will We Ever Figure Out How to Talk to Boys About Sex?" *The New York Times*, 10 January 2020, https://www.nytimes.com/2020/01/10/opinion/sunday/boys-sex.html.

34. Michelle Goldberg, "Why Sex-Positive Feminism Is Falling Out of Fashion," *The New York Times*, 24 September 2021, https://www.nytimes.com/by/michelle-goldberg.

35. "Conversations with Vida," moderated by Stacey Wilson Hunt, Hollywood editor for *New York Magazine* and *Vulture*, SAG-AFTRA Foundation Conversations, 12 June 2018, *YouTube*, https://www.youtube.com/watch?v=5fRK5Pqr-rE, accessed 21 January 2022. Video.

36. Maria Elena Fernandez, "What Hollywood Can Learn from Vida's All-Latina Directors," *Vulture*, 11 June 2019, https://www.vulture.com/2019/06/vida-season-2-tanya-saracho-latina-directors.html.

37. *Ibid.*

38. Sadie Gennis, "Starz's 'Vida' Is Plenty Sexy—But Every Graphic Moment Counts," *TV Guide*, 20 March 2019, https://www.tvguide.com/news/features/starz-vida-sex-scenes/.
39. Judy Berman, "No Other Show Captures the Pleasures and Frustrations of Real Life Quite Like Vida," *Time*, 22 April 2020, https://time.com/5824773/vida-season-3-starz-review/.
40. Sadie Gennis, "Starz's 'Vida' Is Plenty Sexy—But Every Graphic Moment Counts," *TV Guide*, 20 March 2019, https://www.tvguide.com/news/features/starz-vida-sex-scenes/.
41. "Conversations with Vida," moderated by Stacey Wilson Hunt, Hollywood editor for *New York Magazine* and *Vulture*, SAG-AFTRA Foundation Conversations, 12 June 2018, YouTube, https://www.youtube.com/watch?v=5fRK5Pqr-rE, accessed 21 January 2022. Video.
42. "Vida: Inside the World—Episode 102," creator Tanya Saracho, Starz, 2018. Television.
43. Maria Elena Fernandez, "What Hollywood Can Learn from Vida's All-Latina Directors," *Vulture*, 11 June 2019, https://www.vulture.com/2019/06/vida-season-2-tanya-saracho-latina-directors.html.
44. Tracy E. Gilchrist, "Vida Boldly Tackles Identity Policing Among Queer People," *Advocate*, 21 June 2019, https://www.advocate.com/television/2019/6/21/vida-boldly-tackles-identity-policing-among-queer-people.
45. "Vida: Inside the World—Episode 106," creator Tanya Saracho, Starz, 2018. Television.
46. "Vida: Inside the World—Episode 101," creator Tanya Saracho, Starz, 2018. Television.
47. Peggy Orenstein, "It's Not That Men Don't Know What Consent Is," *The New York Times*, 23 February 2019, https://www.nytimes.com/2019/02/23/opinion/sunday/sexual-consent-college.html?action=click&module=RelatedLinks&pgtype=Article.
48. Peggy Orenstein, "When Did Porn Become Sex Ed?" *The New York Times*, 19 March 2016, https://www.nytimes.com/2016/03/20/opinion/sunday/when-did-porn-become-sex-ed.html?action=click&module=RelatedLinks&pgtype=Article.
49. Maria Elena Fernandez, "What Hollywood Can Learn from Vida's All-Latina Directors," *Vulture*, 11 June 2019, https://www.vulture.com/2019/06/vida-season-2-tanya-saracho-latina-directors.html.

Chapter 6

1. Bex Palmer, "How 'I May Destroy You' Got Made," *Backstage*, 14 June 2021, https://www.backstage.com/uk/magazine/article/how-i-may-destroy-you-got-made-73447/.
2. Leila Latif, "I May Destroy You and how it represents the future of TV," *BBC Culture*, 19 October 2021, https://www.bbc.com/culture/article/20211015-i-may-destroy-you-and-how-it-represents-the-future-of-tv.
3. *Ibid*.
4. NHS (National Health Service), "Overview—Consent," https://www.nhs.uk/conditions/consent-to-treatment/.
5. NHS (National Health Service), "Consent Information Leaflet," https://www.nhs.uk/aboutNHSChoices/professionals/healthandcareprofessionals/child-sexual-exploitation/Documents/Consent-information-leaflet.pdf.
6. Alexandra Brodsky, *Sexual Justice: Supporting Victims, Ensuring Due Process, and Resisting the Conservative Backlash* (New York: Metropolitan Books, 2021), 9. Print.
7. Amia Srinivasan, *The Right to Sex: Feminism in the Twenty-First Century* (New York: Farrar, Straus and Giroux, 2021), 22. Print.
8. *Ibid.*, xiii.
9. From feedback for this chapter provided by Dr. Kadian L. Pow, a lecturer in Sociology & Black Studies at Birmingham City University in the UK.
10. Emily VanDerWerff, "HBO's I May Destroy You might be the best TV show of the year," *Vox*, 7 August 2020, https://www.vox.com/culture/2020/8/7/21356216/i-may-destroy-you-hbo-review-michaela-coel.
11. Doreen St. Félix, "Michaela Coel's Chaos and Charisma in 'I May Destroy You,'" *The New Yorker*, 29 June 2020, https://www.newyorker.com/magazine/2020/07/06/michaela-coels-chaos-and-charisma-in-i-may-destroy-you.

12. Eleanor Stanford, "Paapa Essiedu Knows 'I May Destroy You' Is Hard to Watch," *The New York Times*, 6 July 2020, https://www.nytimes.com/2020/07/06/arts/television/paapa-essiedu-i-may-destroy-you.html?action=click&module=RelatedLinks&pgtype=Article.
13. Linda Holmes, "'I May Destroy You' Is HBO's New Unforgettable, Unmissable Drama," *NPR*, 7 June 2020, https://www.npr.org/2020/06/07/871472968/i-may-destroy-you-is-hbo-s-new-unforgettable-unmissable-drama.
14. E. Alex Jung, "Michaela the Destroyer," *Vulture*, 6 July 2020, https://www.vulture.com/article/michaela-coel-i-may-destroy-you.html.
15. Ibid.
16. "Michaela Coel/James MacTaggart Lecture/Edinburgh TV Festival 2018," *Edinburgh Television Festival*, 23 August 2018, YouTube, https://www.youtube.com/watch?v=odusP8gmqsg. Video.
17. E. Alex Jung, "Michaela the Destroyer," *Vulture*, 6 July 2020, https://www.vulture.com/article/michaela-coel-i-may-destroy-you.html.
18. "Michaela Coel/James MacTaggart Lecture/Edinburgh TV Festival 2018," *Edinburgh Television Festival*, 23 August 2018, YouTube, https://www.youtube.com/watch?v=odusP8gmqsg. Video.
19. Ibid.
20. Harper Lambert, "Michaela Coel Hopes 'I May Destroy You' Encourages Viewers to Change Their Self-Narratives," *The Hollywood Reporter*, 19 August 2021, https://www.hollywoodreporter.com/tv/tv-news/michaela-coel-i-may-destroy-you-emmys-1234998979/.
21. Caroline Framke, "How Michael Coel Processed Trauma and Fought to Own Her Story with 'I May Destroy You,'" *Variety*, 19 August 2020, https://variety.com/2020/tv/features/i-may-destroy-you-michaela-coel-1234739041/.
22. Bex Palmer, "How 'I May Destroy You' Got Made," *Backstage*, 14 June 2021, https://www.backstage.com/uk/magazine/article/how-i-may-destroy-you-got-made-73447/.
23. Doreen St. Félix, "Michaela Coel's Chaos and Charisma in "I May Destroy You,'" *The New Yorker*, 29 June 2020, https://www.newyorker.com/magazine/2020/07/06/michaela-coels-chaos-and-charisma-in-i-may-destroy-you.

24. E. Alex Jung, "Michaela the Destroyer," *Vulture*, 6 July 2020, https://www.vulture.com/article/michaela-coel-i-may-destroy-you.html.
25. From feedback for this chapter provided by Dr. Kadian L. Pow, a lecturer in Sociology & Black Studies at Birmingham City University in the UK.
26. Alanna Vagianos, "Tarana Burke: 'Me Too Is Not a Women's Movement,'" *HuffPost*, 24 April 2019, updated 10 May 2019, https://www.huffpost.com/entry/tarana-burke-me-too-not-womens-movement_n_5cc06af3e4b0764d31db5d88.
27. Eleanor Stanford, "Paapa Essiedu Knows 'I May Destroy You' Is Hard to Watch," *The New York Times*, 6 July 2020, https://www.nytimes.com/2020/07/06/arts/television/paapa-essiedu-i-may-destroy-you.html?action=click&module=RelatedLinks&pgtype=Article.
28. Alexandra Brodsky, *Sexual Justice: Supporting Victims, Ensuring Due Process, and Resisting the Conservative Backlash* (New York: Metropolitan Books, 2021), 54. Print.
29. Ibid., 25.
30. From feedback for this chapter provided by Dr. Kadian L. Pow, a lecturer in Sociology & Black Studies at Birmingham City University in the UK.
31. Isabella Grullón Paz, "California Makes 'Stealthing,' or Removing Condom Without Consent, Illegal," *The New York Times*, 8 October 2021 (updated 10 November 2021), https://www.nytimes.com/2021/10/08/us/stealthing-illegal-california.html.
32. Ibid.
33. Salamishah Tillet, "'I May Destroy You' Imagines a Path Back from Sexual Assault," *The New York Times*, 25 August 2020, https://www.nytimes.com/2020/08/25/arts/television/i-may-destroy-you-sexual-assault.html?action=click&module=RelatedLinks&pgtype=Article.
34. Olive Pometsey, "How Michaela Coel Transformed Her Trauma Into the Year's Best TV Show," *GQ*, 10 July 2020, https://www.gq.com/story/michaela-coel-i-may-destroy-you-interview.
35. E. Alex Jung, "Michaela the Destroyer," *Vulture*, 6 July 2020, https://www.vulture.com/article/michaela-coel-i-may-destroy-you.html.
36. Olive Pometsey, "How Michaela

Coel Transformed Her Trauma Into the Year's Best TV Show," *GQ*, 10 July 2020, https://www.gq.com/story/michaela-coel-i-may-destroy-you-interview.
37. *Ibid.*
38. Alexandra Brodsky, *Sexual Justice: Supporting Victims, Ensuring Due Process, and Resisting the Conservative Backlash* (New York: Metropolitan Books, 2021), 55. Print.
39. Samuel R. Gross, M. Possley, and K. Stephens, "Race and Wrongful Convictions in the United States," *The National Registry of Exonerations*, Newkirk Center for Science and Society, 2017, https://repository.law.umich.edu/cgi/viewcontent.cgi?article=1121&context=other.
40. Alexandra Brodsky, *Sexual Justice: Supporting Victims, Ensuring Due Process, and Resisting the Conservative Backlash* (New York: Metropolitan Books, 2021), 178. Print.
41. From feedback for this chapter provided by Dr. Kadian L. Pow, a lecturer in Sociology & Black Studies at Birmingham City University in the UK.
42. *Ibid.*
43. "Michaela Coel reacts to I May Destroy You scene/GQ Action Replay/British GQ," *British GQ*, 29 June 2020, *YouTube*, https://www.youtube.com/watch?v=GWNb6uGc748. Video.
44. *Ibid.*
45. From feedback for this chapter provided by Dr. Kadian L. Pow, a lecturer in Sociology & Black Studies at Birmingham City University in the UK.
46. "Michaela Coel reacts to I May Destroy You scene/GQ Action Replay/British GQ," *British GQ*, 29 June 2020, *YouTube*, https://www.youtube.com/watch?v=GWNb6uGc748, Video.
47. *Ibid.*
48. Joseph Campbell, *The Hero with a Thousand Faces*, Bollingen Series XVII, Third Edition (Novato, CA: New World Library, 2008), 74. Print.
49. "The Power of Myth—'The Hero's Adventure,'" Episode 1, *Joseph Campbell and the Power of Myth*, Bill Moyers, *PBS*, 1988, BillMoyers.com, https://billmoyers.com/series/joseph-campbell-and-the-power-of-myth-1988/. Video.
50. "The Power of Myth—'The Hero's Adventure,'" Episode 1, *Joseph Campbell and the Power of* Myth, Bill Moyers, *PBS*, 1988, BillMoyers.com, https://billmoyers.com/series/joseph-campbell-and-the-power-of-myth-1988/. Video.
51. From feedback for this chapter provided by Dr. Kadian L. Pow, a lecturer in Sociology & Black Studies at Birmingham City University in the UK.
52. Joseph Campbell, *The Hero with a Thousand Faces*, Bollingen Series XVII, Third Edition (Novato, CA: New World Library, 2008), 81. Print.
53. *Ibid.*
54. "Michaela Coel reacts to I May Destroy You scene/GQ Action Replay/British GQ," *British GQ*, 29 June 2020, *YouTube*, https://www.youtube.com/watch?v=GWNb6uGc748. Video.
55. Alexandra Brodsky, *Sexual Justice: Supporting Victims, Ensuring Due Process, and Resisting the Conservative Backlash* (New York: Metropolitan Books, 2021), 53. Print.
56. sujatha baliga, "A different path for confronting sexual assault," *Vox*, 10 October 2018, https://www.vox.com/first-person/2018/10/10/17953016/what-is-restorative-justice-definition-questions-circle.
57. *Ibid.*
58. E. Alex Jung, "Michaela the Destroyer," *Vulture*, 6 July 2020, https://www.vulture.com/article/michaela-coel-i-may-destroy-you.html.
59. Harper Lambert, "Michaela Coel Hopes 'I May Destroy You' Encourages Viewers to Change Their Self-Narratives," *The Hollywood Reporter*, 19 August 2021, https://www.hollywoodreporter.com/tv/tv-news/michaela-coel-i-may-destroy-you-emmys-1234998979/.
60. Joseph Campbell, *The Hero with a Thousand Faces*, Bollingen Series XVII, Third Edition (Novato, CA: New World Library, 2008), 209. Print.
61. "The Power of Myth—'The Hero's Adventure,'" Episode 1, *Joseph Campbell and the Power of Myth*, Bill Moyers, *PBS*, 1988, BillMoyers.com, https://billmoyers.com/series/joseph-campbell-and-the-power-of-myth-1988/. Video.
62. *Bhagavad Gita*, from the translation by Swami Nikhilananda (New York, 1944), 2:22–24, quoted in Joseph Campbell, *The Hero with a Thousand Faces*, Bollingen Series XVII, Third Edition (Novato, CA: New World Library, 2008), 206. Print.

63. Eknath Easwaran, *The Bhagavad Gita* (Tomales, CA: Nilgiri Press, 1985, 2007), 26. Print.
64. Joseph Campbell, *The Hero with a Thousand Faces*, Bollingen Series XVII, Third Edition (Novato, CA: New World Library, 2008), 167. Print.
65. *Ibid.*, 188.
66. Salamishah Tillet, "'I May Destroy You' Imagines a Path Back from Sexual Assault," *The New York Times*, 25 August 2020, https://www.nytimes.com/2020/08/25/arts/television/i-may-destroy-you-sexual-assault.html?action=click&module=RelatedLinks&pgtype=Article.
67. sujatha baliga, "A different path for confronting sexual assault," *Vox*, 10 October 2018, https://www.vox.com/first-person/2018/10/10/17953016/what-is-restorative-justice-definition-questions-circle.
68. Joseph Campbell, *The Hero with a Thousand Faces*, Bollingen Series XVII, Third Edition (Novato, CA: New World Library, 2008), 196. Print.
69. "The Power of Myth—'The Hero's Adventure,'" Episode 1, *Joseph Campbell and the Power of Myth*, Bill Moyers, PBS, 1988, BillMoyers.com, https://billmoyers.com/series/joseph-campbell-and-the-power-of-myth-1988/. Video.

Chapter 7

1. Daniel Holloway, "Stranger Things' Ratings: Where Series Ranks Among Netflix's Most Watched," *Variety*, 25 August 2016, https://variety.com/2016/tv/news/stranger-things-tv-ratings-netflix-most-watched-1201844081/.
2. *Ibid.*
3. Tom Huddlestron, Jr., "37-year-old brothers who created 'Stranger Things' got rejected by over 15 networks before Netflix said yes," *CNBC*, 11 December 2018, https://www.cnbc.com/2018/12/11/duffer-brothers-stranger-things-rejected-over-15-times-pre-netflix.html.
4. *Ibid.*
5. *Ibid.*
6. *Ibid.*
7. Natalie Andreeva, "'Stranger Things' Season 4 Final Viewership Comes Within Less Than 300M Hours of 'Squid Game' Record," *Deadline*, 2 August 2022, https://deadline.com/2022/08/stranger-things-season-4-final-viewership-squid-game-record-1235083997/.
8. Marjolein Oomen, "Netflix: How a DVD rental company changed the way we spend our free time," *BMI*, https://www.businessmodelsinc.com/exponential-business-model/netflix/.
9. Mae Anderson and Michael Liedtke, "Hubris—and late fees—doomed Blockbuster," *NBC News*, 23 September 2010, https://www.nbcnews.com/id/wbna39332696.
10. Mary Ellen Cagnassola and Lauren Giella, "Fact Check: Did Blockbuster Turn Down Chance to Buy Netflix for $50 Million," *Newsweek*, 11 March 2021, https://www.newsweek.com/fact-check-did-blockbuster-turn-down-chance-buy-netflix-50-million-1575557.
11. Tricia McKinnon, "8 Reasons Why Blockbuster Failed & Filed for Bankruptcy," *Indigo Digital*, 28 March 2022, https://www.indigo9digital.com/blog/blockbusterfailure.
12. *Ibid.*
13. Gina Keating, *Netflixed: The Epic Battle for America's Eyeballs* (New York: Portfolio/Penguin, 2012), 132. Print.
14. *Ibid.*
15. Fletcher Peters, "Netflix Tops 222 Million Subscribers Worldwide, Narrowly Missing Q4 Forecast," *Decider*, 20 January 2022, https://decider.com/2022/01/20/netflix-q4-subscriber-growth/.
16. "Eighties Nostalgia, Collective Memory, and the Thirty Year Cycle," *Catharsis*, 29 May 2019, https://www.catharsistheatre.com/the-name-of-action/2019/5/28/eighties-nostalgia-and-the-thirty-year-cycle.
17. *Ibid.*
18. Rebecca Nicholson, "The Duffer Brothers: 'Could we do what Spielberg did in the 80s and elevate it like he did?'" *The Guardian*, 14 October 2017, https://www.theguardian.com/tv-and-radio/ng-interactive/2017/oct/14/duffer-brothers-spielberg-80s-stranger-things.
19. Ashley Rodriguez, "Watch: The opening scene of 'Stranger Things' owes everything to 'E.T.,'" *Quartz*, 27 October 2017, https://qz.com/1112034/watch-how-stranger-things-nailed-its-1980s-homage-right-from-the-start/.
20. David Barr Kirtley, "The Stranger

Things Secret? It's Basically an 8-Hour Spielberg Movie," *Wired*, 12 August 2016, https://www.wired.com/2016/08/geeks-guide-stranger-things/.

21. Lottie Elizabeth Johnson, "Why do we like 'Stranger Things' so much? A BYU professor explains," *Deseret News*, 2 June 2019, https://www.deseret.com/2019/7/2/8935900/why-do-we-like-stranger-things-so-much-a-byu-professor-explains.

22. *Ibid*.

23. "Jaws—the monster that ate Hollywood," *Frontline*, WGBH educational foundation, https://www.pbs.org/wgbh/pages/frontline/shows/hollywood/business/jaws.html.

24. Tom Brueggemann, "'The Godfather' Helped Invent the Blockbuster, Even Before 'Jaws' and 'Star Wars,'" *Indie Wire*, 17 March 2022, https://www.indiewire.com/2022/03/the-godfather-invent-blockbuster-jaws-star-wars-1234602162/.

25. Luchina Fisher, "'Jaws' Turns 40: 5 Ways It Changed Movies Forever," *ABC*, 20 Junes 2015, https://abcnews.go.com/Entertainment/ways-jaws-changed-movies-forever/story?id=31366659.

26. Tom Reimann, "Everything You Didn't Know About Stranger Things," *Collider*, 30 May 2019, https://collider.com/galleries/everything-you-didnt-know-about-stranger-things/.

27. *Ibid*.

28. *Ibid*.

29. The Duffer Brothers, "Stranger Things episode 6: How the Duffer Brothers created the monster," *Entertainment Weekly*, 20 July 2016, https://ew.com/tv/2016/07/20/stranger-things-duffer-brothers-episode-6/.

30. The Duffer Brothers, "Stranger Things episode 5: The Duffer Brothers explain the show's soundtrack," *Entertainment Weekly*, 19 July 2016, https://ew.com/tv/2016/07/19/stranger-things-duffer-brothers-episode-5/.

31. *Ibid*.

32. Chelsey Stone, "The '80s Movie That Inspired Millie Bobby Brown's Eleven Will Make You Love 'Stranger Things' Even More," *Teen Vogue*, 17 August 2017, https://www.teenvogue.com/story/millie-bobby-brown-stranger-things-eleven-inspiration.

33. Ryan Northrup, "Millie Bobby Brown Names Favorite '80s Movie for Stranger Things Prep," *Screen Rant*, 2 June 2022, https://screenrant.com/stranger-things-millie-bobby-brown-et-inspiration/.

34. Amanda Robb, "Divorce, 1981-Style," *AARP*, August/September 2016, https://www.aarp.org/home-family/friends-family/info-2016/divorce-1980s.html.

35. Judy Mann, "The Lives of Latchkey Children," *The Washington Post*, 29 November 1985, https://www.washingtonpost.com/archive/local/1985/11/29/the-lives-of-latchkey-children/12712d60-ee0a-4844-a4ce-740bf0eaf3f9/.

36. Joseph Vogel, *Stranger Things and the '80s: The Complete Retro Guide* (U.S.A.: Cardinal, 2018), 88–89. Print.

37. Edward McClelland, "Were the Suburbs a Blip?" *Chicago Magazine*, 14 June 2019, https://www.chicagomag.com/city-life/June-2019/Were-the-Suburbs-a-Blip/.

38. *Ibid*.

39. Matthew D. Lassiter, *The Suburban Crisis: White America and the War on Drugs* (Princeton: Princeton University Press, 2023), 2–3. Print.

40. *Ibid*.

41. Jonathan Marshall, "How Our War on Drugs Shattered the Cities," *The Washington Post*, 17 May 1992, https://www.washingtonpost.com/archive/opinions/1992/05/17/how-our-war-on-drugs-shattered-the-cities/fb887f62-9efe-4c4a-82ac-a21bc30a769b/.

42. *Ibid*.

43. Glen Weldon, "Kids on Bikes: The Sci-Fi Nostalgia of 'Stranger Things,' 'Paper Girls' & 'Super 8,'" *NPR*, 27 July 2016, https://www.npr.org/2016/07/27/487602000/kids-on-bikes-the-sci-fi-nostalgia-of-stranger-things-paper-girls-super-8.

44. Joseph Vogel, *Stranger Things and the '80s: The Complete Retro Guide* (U.S.A.: Cardinal, 2018), 93–95. Print.

45. *Ibid*.

46. "Every Stranger Things Movie Reference Revealed by the Duffer Brothers (Seasons 1–3)," *Wired*, 25 July 2019, *YouTube*, https://www.youtube.com/watch?v=qGGc1wGmgbM. Video.

47. *Ibid*.

48. Chrisovolandou Gronowski, "Psychoanalytic Examination of Stranger

Things' Eleven: Trials and Tribulations of Childhood Trauma on the 'Child-Hero,'" *University of Hawaii at Hilo*, 2018, https://hilo.hawaii.edu/campuscenter/hohonu/volumes/documents/PsychoanalyticExaminationofStrangerThingsElevenTrialsandTribulationsofChildhoodTraumaontheChild-Hero.pdf.

49. James Cole Abrams, "Pop Psych: What Netflix's 'Stranger Things' Teaches Us About Childhood Trauma," *Observer*, 29 July 2016, https://observer.com/2016/07/pop-psych-what-netflixs-stranger-things-teaches-us-about-childhood-trauma/.

50. Gillian Branstetter, "'Stranger Things' Is an Amazing Depiction of Trauma," *Medium*, 20 July 2016, https://gillbranstetter.medium.com/stranger-things-is-an-amazing-depiction-of-trauma-6db931fec57.

51. *Ibid.*

52. Emma Clarke, "How Stranger Things tackles depression is nothing short of extraordinary," *Radio Times*, 31 May 2022, https://www.radiotimes.com/tv/sci-fi/stranger-things-4-max-depression-trauma-comment/.

53. Kate Bush, "Running Up That Hill (A Deal with God)," *The Hounds of Love*, EMI, 1985, written and composed by Kate Bush. Song.

54. Gary Trust, "Kate Bush's 'Running Up That Hill' Tops Both Billboard Global Charts," *Billboard*, 11 July 2022, https://www.billboard.com/music/chart-beat/kate-bush-running-up-that-hill-tops-both-billboard-global-charts-1235112654/.

55. *Spielberg*, dir. Susan Lacy, HBO, 2017. Film.

56. Adam Chitwood, "Steven Spielberg Explains How 'Close Encounters' and His Parents' Divorce Inspired 'E.T.,'" *The Wrap*, 22 April 2022, https://www.thewrap.com/steven-spielberg-et-close-encounters-of-the-third-kind-inspiration-interview/.

57. Lottie Elizabeth Johnson, "Why do we like 'Stranger Things' so much? A BYU professor explains," *Deseret News*, 2 June 2019, https://www.descret.com/2019/7/2/8935900/why-do-we-like-stranger-things-so-much-a-byu-professor-explains.

58. Charlie Heaton, "'Stranger Things 4' First Look: New Season Teases Serious 'Nightmare on Elm Street' Horror Vibes," *IndieWire*, 23 March 2022, https://www.indiewire.com/2022/03/stranger-things-season-4-first-look-horror-1234710421/.

59. Will Betts, "Scoring Stranger Things," *Sound on Sound*, March 2017, https://www.soundonsound.com/techniques/scoring-stranger-things.

60. Jacopo della Quercia, "Spielberg Things: The Nostalgic Heart of *Stranger Things*," *Uncovering Stranger Things: Essays on Eighties Nostalgia, Cynicism and Innocence in the Series*, ed. Kevin J. Wetmore, Jr. (Jefferson, NC: McFarland, 2018), 124. Print.

61. *Ibid.*, 115.
62. *Ibid.*, 116.
63. *Ibid.*, 119.

Chapter 8

1. James Andrew Miller, *Tinder Box: HBO's Ruthless Pursuit of New Frontiers* (New York: Henry Holt, 2021), 960. Print.

2. Will Thorne, "TV Ratings: 'Lovecraft Country' Finale Scares Up Series High Numbers," *Variety*, 20 October 2020, https://variety.com/2020/tv/news/lovecraft-country-finale-series-high-ratings-1234811369/.

3. *Ibid.*

4. Alan Sepinwall, "'Lovecraft Country' Creator Misha Green on Bold Storytelling and the Season Finale," *Rolling Stone*, 18 October 2020, https://www.rollingstone.com/tv-movies/tv-movie-features/lovecraft-country-creator-misha-green-interview-season-finale-1077047/.

5. Alan Sepinwall, "'Lovecraft Country': A Nightmare on Main Street," *Rolling Stone*, 7 August 2020, https://www.rollingstone.com/tv-movies/tv-movie-reviews/lovecraft-country-hbo-review-1038614/.

6. Daniel Fienberg, "'Lovecraft Country': TV Review," *The Hollywood Reporter*, 7 August 2020, https://www.hollywoodreporter.com/tv/tv-reviews/lovecraft-country-review-1306320/.

7. *Ibid.*

8. *Crafting Lovecraft Country*, special feature, executive producer John Wilhelmy, HBO, October 2020. Television.

9. Matt Zoller Seitz, "In Lovecraft

Country, Monsters Past and Present Converge," *Vulture*, 10 August 2020, https://www.vulture.com/news/tv-review/.

10. Laura Miller, "How Lovecraft Country Reappropriates H.P. Lovecraft's Notoriously Racist Creations," *Slate*, 7 August 2020, https://slate.com/culture/2020/08/lovecraft-country-hbo-series-racism-matt-ruff-novel.html.

11. Ariana Brockington, "This Is What Lovecraft Country Really Means," *Refinery29*, 16 August 2020, https://www.refinery29.com/en-us/2020/08/9959175/what-lovecraft-country-means-hp-racism.

12. Salamishah Tillet, "Living While Black in Lovecraft Country," *The New York Times*, 7 August 2020, https://www.nytimes.com/2020/08/07/arts/television/living-while-black-in-lovecraft-country.html.

13. Ibid.

14. *Lovecraft Country: Orithyia Blue and the Imagination of Diana Freeman*, special feature, writer and producer Scott McCulloch, HBO, 16 February 2021. Television.

15. Salamishah Tillet, "Living While Black in Lovecraft Country," *The New York Times*, 7 August 2020, https://www.nytimes.com/2020/08/07/arts/television/living-while-black-in-lovecraft-country.html.

16. James Andrew Miller, *Tinder Box: HBO's Ruthless Pursuit of New Frontiers* (New York: Henry Holt, 2021), 962. Print.

17. Liam Mathews, "Lovecraft Country's Misha Green Recommends These Books and Movies to Help Get the Full Show Experience," *TV Guide*, 14 October 2020, https://www.tvguide.com/news/lovecraft-country-books-movies-references/.

18. Bradford D. Hunt, "Trumbull Park Homes Race Riots, 1953–1954," *Encyclopedia of Chicago*, The Chicago Historical Society, 2005, http://www.encyclopedia.chicagohistory.org/pages/2461.html.

19. History.com Editors, "Emmett Till is murdered," *HISTORY*, A&E Television Networks, 2 February 2010, updated 12 January 2022, https://www.history.com/this-day-in-history/the-death-of-emmett-till.

20. Sheila Weller, "How Author Timothy Tyson Found the Woman at the Center of the Emmett Till Case," *Vanity Fair*, 26 January 2017, https://www.vanityfair.com/news/2017/01/how-author-timothy-tyson-found-the-woman-at-the-center-of-the-emmett-till-case?mbid=social_twitter.

21. Maya Phillips, "The Unintended Racial Horror of Lovecraft Country," *The New York Times*, 19 October 2020, https://www.nytimes.com/2020/10/19/arts/television/lovecraft-country-season-finale.html.

22. Margaret Bourke-White, "At the Time of the Louisville Flood," 1937, *MoMA*, https://www.moma.org/collection/works/46797. Photo.

23. Dapo, "Lovecraft Country Production Designer, Kalina Ivanov BTS on HBO Series," *IndieActivity*, https://www.indieactivity.com/lovecraft-country-production-designer-kalina-ivanov-bts-on-hbo-series/.

24. Gordon Parks, "Shady Grove, Alabama, 1956," *The Gordon Parks Foundation*, https://www.gordonparksfoundation.org/gordon-parks/photography-archive/segregation-in-the-south-1956. Photo.

25. Gordon Parks, "Department Store, Mobile, Alabama, 1956," *The Gordon Parks Foundation*, https://www.gordonparksfoundation.org/exhibitions/museum-exhibitions/a-choice-of-weapons?view=slider#2. Photo.

26. Richard Frishman, "Hidden in Plain Sight: The Ghosts of Segregation," *The New York Times*, 30 November 2020, https://www.nytimes.com/2020/11/30/travel/ghosts-of-segregation.html?campaign_id=2&emc=edit_th_20201201&instance_id=24596&nl=todaysheadlines&regi_id=75758980&segment_id=45733&user_id=e8f6ddcb0bccf40e24b3be3bbbbfc15f.

27. Ibid.

28. Richard Newby, "'Lovecraft Country': Inside the HBO Horror Drama's Chilling Premiere," *The Hollywood Reporter*, 16 August 2020, https://www.hollywoodreporter.com/tv/tv-news/lovecraft-country-series-premiere-explained-4046817/.

29. Alexis C. Madrigal, "Gil Scott-Heron's Poem, 'Whitey on the Moon,'" *The Atlantic*, 28 May 2011, https://www.theatlantic.com/technology/archive/2011/05/gil-scott-herons-poem-whitey-on-the-moon/239622/.

30. Ashley C. Ford and Shannon Hous-

ton, Episode 1, *Lovecraft Country Radio*, HBO/HBO Max, 16 August 2020-18 October 2020. Podcast.

31. Ashley C. Ford and Shannon Houston, Episode 2, *Lovecraft Country Radio*, HBO/HBO Max, 16 August 2020-18 October 2020. Podcast.

32. Richard Newby, "'Lovecraft Country': Black Spaces and Haunted Houses," *The Hollywood Reporter*, 1 September 2020, https://www.hollywoodreporter.com/tv/tv-news/lovecraft-country-black-spaces-and-haunted-houses-4053309/.

33. Richard Newby, "'Lovecraft Country': Jurnee Smollett on That Haunting Confrontation," *The Hollywood Reporter*, 30 August 2020, https://www.hollywoodreporter.com/tv/tv-news/lovecraft-country-jurnee-smollett-episode-three-4052619/.

34. *Lovecraft Country: Orithyia Blue and the Imagination of Diana Freeman*, special feature, writer and producer Scott McCulloch, HBO, 16 February 2021. Television.

35. Warner Media, "Q&A: Misha Green on All Things LOVECRAFT COUNTRY," media release, 6 August 2020, https://pressroom.warnermedia.com/us/media-release/hbo-0/lovecraft-country/qa-misha-green-all-things-lovecraft-country.

36. Salamishah Tillet, "Living While Black in Lovecraft Country," *The New York Times*, 7 August 2020, https://www.nytimes.com/2020/08/07/arts/television/living-while-black-in-lovecraft-country.html.

37. Thomas Bacon, "Lovecraft Country VFX Interview: François Dumoulin," *Screen Rant*, 12 September 2021, https://screenrant.com/lovecraft-country-vfx-francois-dumoulin-interview/.

38. The Chords, "Sh-Boom (Life Could Be a Dream)," Cat Records, 1954, Written by James Keyes, Claude Feaster, Carl Feaster, Floyd F. McRae, and William Edwards. Song.

39. Dave "Curlee" Williams, "Whole Lotta Shakin' Goin' On," 1955 (James Faye "Roy" Hall sometimes co-credited as songwriter). Song.

40. Ja'net DuBois with Jeff Barry, "Movin' on Up," theme song for *The Jeffersons* TV show (1975-1985). Song.

41. Louis Jordan and Billy Austin, "Is You Is or Is You Ain't My Baby," 1943. Song.

42. Warner Media, "Q&A: Misha Green on All Things LOVECRAFT COUNTRY," media release, 6 August 2020, https://pressroom.warnermedia.com/us/media-release/hbo-0/lovecraft-country/qa-misha-green-all-things-lovecraft-country.

43. Ashley C. Ford and Shannon Houston, Episode 3, *Lovecraft Country Radio*, HBO/HBO Max, 16 August 2020-18 October 2020. Podcast.

44. *Ibid*.

45. Katrina Miller, "No, Lovecraft Country Didn't Need a Second Season," *Wired*, 16 September 2021, https://www.wired.com/story/lovecraft-country-no-season-2/.

46. *Horror Noire: A History of Black Horror*, executive producers Robin R. Means Coleman, Ph.D., Tananarive Due, and Phil Nobile, Jr. Shudders, 2019.

47. Mara Bachman, "Lovecraft Country: Who Is Mama Oya? The African Goddess' Mythology Explained," *Screen Rant*, 3 September 2020, https://screenrant.com/lovecraft-country-episode-3-mama-oya-goddess-mythology/.

48. Nivea Serrao, "Lovecraft Country showrunner apologizes for having 'failed' queer indigenous character," *SYFY Wire*, 14 October 2020, https://www.syfy.com/syfy-wire/lovecraft-country-misha-green-failed-indigenous-two-spirit-representation.

49. Emma Powys Maurice, "Lovecraft Country creator admits she 'failed' iconic Indigenous two-spirit character Yahima," *PinkNews*, 13 October 2020, https://www.pinknews.co.uk/2020/10/13/lovecraft-country-hbo-misha-green-indigenous-two-spirit-yahima-death-backlash/.

50. *Ibid*.

51. Ashley C. Ford and Shannon Houston, Episode 4, *Lovecraft Country Radio*, HBO/HBO Max, 16 August 2020-18 October 2020. Podcast.

52. Richard Newby, "'Lovecraft Country' Star Michael K. Williams on Navigating Fear and the Past," *The Hollywood Reporter*, 13 September 2020, https://www.hollywoodreporter.com/tv/tv-news/lovecraft-country-michael-k-williams-4059531/.

53. Lex Pryor, "'Lovecraft Country' Recap: To Shape a Butterfly," *The Ringer*, 14 September 2020, https://www.theringer.com/tv/2020/9/14/21433073/lovecraft-country-episode-5-recap-skin-molting.

54. Nicole Hill, "Lovecraft Country:

What Ruby's Hillary Davenport Transformation Means," *Den of Geek*, 16 September 2020, https://www.denofgeek.com/tv/lovecraft-country-ruby-hillary-davenport-transformation/.

55. Lex Pryor, "'Lovecraft Country' Recap: To Shape a Butterfly," *The Ringer*, 14 September 2020, https://www.theringer.com/tv/2020/9/14/21433073/lovecraft-country-episode-5-recap-skin-molting.

56. Ashley C. Ford and Shannon Houston, Episode 6, *Lovecraft Country Radio*, HBO/HBO Max,16 August 2020–18 October 2020. Podcast.

57. Ytasha Womack, "Ytasha Womack—Afrofuturism Imagination and Humanity," *YouTube*, 14 June 2017. On p. 9 of Womack's book, *Afrofuturism: The World of Black Sci-Fi and Fantasy Culture*, Womack credits Ingrid LaFleur, an art curator and Afrofuturist, as saying, "I generally define Afrofuturism as a way of imagining possible futures through a [B]lack cultural lens." Ingrid LaFleur presented at the independently organized TEDx Fort Greene Salon in Brooklyn, New York.

58. Ytasha Womack, *Afrofuturism: The World of Black Sci-Fi and Fantasy Culture* (Chicago: Lawrence Hill, 2013), 17. Print.

59. Richard Newby, "'Lovecraft Country': Inside the HBO Horror Drama's Chilling Premiere," *The Hollywood Reporter*, 16 August 2020, https://www.hollywoodreporter.com/tv/tv-news/lovecraft-country-series-premiere-explained-4046817/.

60. Josephine Baker, "Piel Canela," Josephine Baker, Columbia, 1954, Written by Bobby Capo and Henri Lemarchand, Song.

61. Beyoncé, "Beyoncé—Hold Up (Video)," *YouTube*, 4 September 2016, https://www.youtube.com/watch?v=PeonBmeFR8o.

62. Caryn James, "Lovecraft Country is 'ambitious and unwieldy,'" *BBC Culture*, 6 August 2020, https://www.bbc.com/culture/article/20200806-lovecraft-country-is-ambitious-and-unwieldy.

63. Alan Sepinwall, "'Lovecraft Country' Creator Misha Green on Bold Storytelling and the Season Finale," *Rolling Stone*, 18 October 2020, https://www.rollingstone.com/tv-movies/tv-movie-features/lovecraft-country-creator-misha-green-interview-season-finale-1077047/.

64. Ashley C. Ford and Shannon Houston, Episode 9, *Lovecraft Country Radio*, HBO/HBO Max, 16 August 2020–18 October 2020. Podcast.

65. Ashley C. Ford and Shannon Houston, Episode 7, *Lovecraft Country Radio*, HBO/HBO Max, 16 August 2020–18 October 2020. Podcast.

66. Christina Radish, "'Lovecraft Country's Showrunner Answers Our Biggest Questions About That Bonkers Season 1 Finale," *Collider*, 18 October 2020, https://collider.com/lovecraft-country-hbo-finale-ending-explained/.

67. Ashley C. Ford and Shannon Houston, Episode 8, *Lovecraft Country Radio*, HBO/HBO Max, 16 August 2020–18 October 2020. Podcast.

68. Nicole Hill, "How Lovecraft Country Uses Topsy and Bopsy to Address Racist Caricatures," *Den of Geek*, 7 October 2020, https://www.denofgeek.com/tv/lovecraft-country-topsy-bopsy-uncle-toms-cabin-racist-caricatures/.

69. Peter Di-Sante, Brian Mark, David Van Veersblick, and Roger Smith, "Stop Dat Knocking," Song. *The Early Minstrel Show*, New World Records, 1998, written and composed by A.F. Winnemore, 1847. Song.

70. Ashley C. Ford and Shannon Houston, Episode 8, *Lovecraft Country Radio*, HBO/HBO Max,16 August 2020–18 October 2020. Podcast.

71. Yuliya Parshina-Kottas, Anjali Singhvi, Audra D.S. Burch, Troy Griggs, Mika Gröndahl, Lingdong Huang, Tim Wallace, Jeremy White, and Josh Williams, "What the Tulsa Race Massacre Destroyed," *The New York Times*, 24 May 2021, https://www.nytimes.com/interactive/2021/05/24/us/tulsa-race-massacre.html.

72. Lynn Weinstein, "Black Wall Street in Tulsa, OK Destroyed on 6/1/1921," *This Month in Business History*, Research Guides, Library of Congress, created July 2021, updated June 2022, https://guides.loc.gov/this-month-in-business-history/black-wall-street-destroyed.

73. Yuliya Parshina-Kottas, Anjali Singhvi, Audra D.S. Burch, Troy Griggs, Mika Gröndahl, Lingdong Huang, Tim Wallace, Jeremy White, and Josh Williams, "What the Tulsa Race Massacre Destroyed," *The New York Times*, 24 May 2021, https://www.nytimes.com/interactive/2021/05/24/us/tulsa-race-massacre.html.

74. Ashley C. Ford and Shannon Hous-

ton, Episode 9, *Lovecraft Country Radio*, HBO/HBO Max, 16 August 2020–18 October 2020. Podcast.

75. Yuliya Parshina-Kottas, Anjali Singhvi, Audra D.S. Burch, Troy Griggs, Mika Gröndahl, Lingdong Huang, Tim Wallace, Jeremy White, and Josh Williams, "What the Tulsa Race Massacre Destroyed," *The New York Times*, 24 May 2021, https://www.nytimes.com/interactive/2021/05/24/us/tulsa-race-massacre.html.

76. *Ibid.*

77. Alen Sepinwall, "'Lovecraft Country' Creator Misha Green on Bold Storytelling and the Season Finale," *Rolling Stone*, 18 October 2020, https://www.rollingstone.com/tv-movies/tv-movie-features/lovecraft-country-creator-misha-green-interview-season-finale-1077047/.

78. Dapo, "Lovecraft Country Production Designer, Kalina Ivanov BTS on HBO Series," *Indie Activity*, https://www.indieactivity.com/lovecraft-country-production-designer-kalina-ivanov-bts-on-hbo-series/.

79. Ashley C. Ford and Shannon Houston, Episode 9, *Lovecraft Country Radio*, HBO/HBO Max, 16 August 2020–18 October 2020. Podcast.

80. Steffan Triplett, "Lovecraft Country Recap: Home Runs on Their Heads," *Vulture*, 11 October 2020, https://www.vulture.com/article/lovecraft-country-recap-season-1-episode-9-rewind-1921.html.

81. James Andrew Miller, *Tinder Box: HBO's Ruthless Pursuit of New Frontiers* (New York: Henry Holt, 2021), 962. Print.

82. Katrina Miller, "No, Lovecraft Country Didn't Need a Second Season," *Wired*, 16 September 2021, https://www.wired.com/story/lovecraft-country-no-season-2/.

83. Ashley C. Ford and Shannon Houston, Episode 10, *Lovecraft Country Radio*, HBO/HBO Max, 16 August 2020–18 October 2020. Podcast.

84. Kevin Wong, "'Lovecraft Country Season 1 Finale' Easter Eggs and References in Episode 10, 'Full Circle,'" *Gamespot*, 19 October 2020, https://www.gamespot.com/gallery/lovecraft-country-season-1-finale-easter-eggs-and-references-in-episode-10-full-circle/2900-3605/#1. Accessed 9 July 2022.

85. Alan Sepinwall, "'Lovecraft Country' Creator Misha Green on Bold Storytelling and the Season Finale," *Rolling Stone*, 18 October 2020, https://www.rollingstone.com/tv-movies/tv-movie-features/lovecraft-country-creator-misha-green-interview-season-finale-1077047/.

86. Ashley C. Ford and Shannon Houston, Episode 10, *Lovecraft Country Radio*, HBO/HBO Max, August 2020–18 October 2020. Podcast.

87. James H. Cone, *The Cross and the Lynching Tree* (Maryknoll, NY: Orbis Books, 2011), 31. Print.

88. *Ibid.*

89. Nico Marrone, "Lovecraft Country Creator Shares Inside Look at Cancelled Season 2 Plans," *Screen Rant*, 14 July 2021, https://screenrant.com/lovecraft-country-season-2-story-plan-details-update/.

90. Megan Behnke, "Why Did HBO Cancel Lovecraft Country? New Book Makes Bold Claims," *CinemaBlend*, 24 December 2021, https://www.cinemablend.com/television/why-did-hbo-cancel-lovecraft-country-new-book-makes-bold-claims.

91. James Andrew Miller, *Tinder Box: HBO's Ruthless Pursuit of New Frontiers* (New York: Henry Holt, 2021), 963. Print.

92. Sam Briger, "'Lovecraft Country' Creator Aims to Reclaim the Horror Genre for People of Color." *NPR*, 30 March 2021, https://www.npr.org/2021/03/30/982668346/lovecraft-country-creator-aims-to-reclaim-the-horror-genre-for-people-of-color.

93. *Ibid.*

94. The A.V. Club, "SPOILERS/Lovecraft Country showrunner Misha Green on Indiana Jones and the dark truth of museums," *YouTube*, 7 September 2020, https://www.youtube.com/watch?v=Gufcp2G9K0g.

95. Meghan O'Keefe, "Is Cancelling 'Lovecraft Country' the Biggest Mistake HBO Has Ever Made?" *Decider*, 15 July 2021, https://decider.com/2021/07/15/lovecraft-country-hbo-mistake/.

96. Joe Otterson, "'Lovecraft Country' Creator Misha Green Sets Apple Overall Deal," *Variety*, 9 July 2021, https://variety.com/2021/tv/news/lovecraft-country-misha-green-apple-overall-deal-1235015943/.

97. Nico Marrone, "Lovecraft Country Creator Shares Inside Look at Cancelled Season 2 Plans," *Screen Rant*, 14 July 2021, https://screenrant.com/lovecraft-country-season-2-story-plan-details-update/.

Bibliography

Film

Spielberg. Dir. Susan Lacy. HBO, 2017. Film.
This Changes Everything. Dir. Tom Donahue. Good Deed Entertainment, 2018. Film.

Photography

Bourke-White, Margaret. "At the Time of the Louisville Flood, 1937." *MoMA*. https://www.moma.org/collection/works/46797. Accessed 10 April 2022. Photo.
Parks, Gordon. "Department Store, Mobile, Alabama, 1956." *The Gordon Parks Foundation*. https://www.gordonparksfoundation.org/exhibitions/museum-exhibitions/a-choice-of-weapons?view=slider#2. Accessed 10 April 2022. Photo.
Parks, Gordon. "Shady Grove, Alabama, 1956." *The Gordon Parks Foundation*. https://www.gordonparksfoundation.org/gordon-parks/photography-archive/segregation-in-the-south-1956. Accessed 10 April 2022. Photo.

Podcast

Ford, Ashley C., and Shannon Houston. Episodes 1–10, *Lovecraft Country Radio*. HBO/HBO Max, 16 August 2020–18 October 2020. Accessed 13 July 2022–20 July 2022. Podcast.

Print

Aldama, Frederick Luis, and Christopher González. *Reel Latinxs: Representation in U.S. Film & TV*. Tucson: University of Arizona Press, 2019. Print.
Brodsky, Alexandra. *Sexual Justice: Supporting Victims, Ensuring Due Process, and Resisting the Conservative Backlash*. New York: Metropolitan Books, 2021. Print.
Campbell, Joseph. *The Hero with a Thousand Faces*. Bollingen Series XVII, Third Edition. Novato, CA: New World Library, 2008. Print.
Chattoo, Caty Borum, and Lauren Feldman. *A Comedian and an Activist Walk Into a Bar: The Serious Role of Comedy in Social Justice*. Oakland: University of California Press, 2020. Print.
Cone, James H. *The Cross and the Lynching Tree*. Maryknoll, NY: Orbis Books, 2011. Print.
della Quercia, Jacopo. "Spielberg Things: The Nostalgic Heart of *Stranger Things*." *Uncovering* Stranger Things *: Essays on Eighties Nostalgia, Cynicism and Innocence in the Series*. Ed. Kevin J. Wetmore, Jr. Jefferson, NC: McFarland, 2018. Print.
Easwaran, Eknath. *The Bhagavad Gita*. Tomales, CA: Nilgiri Press, 1985, 2007. Print.
Fremon, David K. *The Jim Crow Laws and Racism*. Berkeley Heights, NJ: Enslow, 2015. Print.
Keating, Gina. *Netflixed: The Epic Battle for America's Eyeballs*. New York: Portfolio/Penguin, 2012. Print.

Lassiter, Matthew D. *The Suburban Crisis: White America and the War on Drugs*. Princeton: Princeton University Press, 2023. Print.
Molina-Guzmán, Isabel. *Latinas & Latinos on TV: Colorblind Comedy in the Post-Racial Network Era*. Tucson: University of Arizona Press, 2018. Print.
Packard, Jerrold M. *American Nightmare: The History of Jim Crow*. New York: St. Martins Griffin, 2002. Print.
Rooney, Sally. *Normal People*. London: Faber & Faber, 2018. Print.
Ross, Sharon Marie. "Defining Teen Culture: The N Network." *Teen Television: Essays on Programming and Fandom*. Ed. Sharon Marie Ross and Louisa Ellen Stein. Jefferson, NC: McFarland, 2008. Print.
Shaheen, Jack G. *The TV Arab*. Bowling Green: Bowling Green State University Popular Press, 1984. Print.
Srinivasan, Amia. *The Right to Sex: Feminism in the Twenty-First Century*. New York: Farrar, Straus and Giroux, 2021. Print.
Vogel, Joseph. *Stranger Things and the '80s: The Complete Retro Guide*. U.S.A.: Cardinal, 2018. Print.
Warner, Kristen J. *The Cultural Politics of Colorblind TV Casting*. Oxfordshire: Routledge, 2015. Print.

Song

Baker, Josephine. "Piel Canela." *Josephine Baker*. Columbia, 1954. Written by Bobby Capo and Henri Lemarchand.
Brel, Jacques. "Ne me quitte pas." *La Valse à Mille Temps*. Phillips, 1959. Written and composed by Jacques Brel. Song.
Bush, Kate. "Running Up That Hill (A Deal with God)." *The Hounds of Love*. EMI, 1985. Written and composed by Kate Bush. Song.
The Chords. "Sh-Boom (Life Could Be a Dream)." Cat Records, 1954. Written by James Keyes, Claude Feaster, Carl Feaster, Floyd F. McRae, and William Edwards. Song.
Di-Sante, Peter, Brian Mark, David Van Veersblick, and Roger Smith. "Stop Dat Knocking." *The Early Minstrel Show*. New World Records, 1998. Written and composed by A.F. Winnemore, 1847. Song.
DuBois, Ja'net, with Jeff Barry. "Movin' on Up." *The Jeffersons* (1975–1985). Song.
Glover, Donald. "This Is America." mcDJ/RCA, 2018. Written by Donald Glover and composed by Donald Glover, Ludwig Göransson, and Jeffery Lamar Williams. Song.
Jordan, Louis, and Billy Austin. "Is You Is or Is You Ain't My Baby." 1943. Song.
Williams, Dave "Curlee." "Whole Lotta Shakin' Goin' On." 1955. (James Faye "Roy" Hall sometimes co-credited as songwriter.) Song.

Television

Atlanta: Season 1. Creator Donald Glover. FX, 2016. Television.
Atlanta: Season 2. Creator Donald Glover. FX, 2018. Television.
Crafting Lovecraft Country. Special feature. Executive producer John Wilhelmy. HBO, October 2020. Television.
Euphoria: Season 1. Creator Sam Levinson. HBO, 2019. Television.
Euphoria: Special "Part 1: Rue." Creator Sam Levinson. HBO, 2020. Television.
Euphoria: Special "Part 2: Jules." Creator Sam Levinson. HBO, 2021. Television.
Euphoria Unfiltered: "Sn 1/Ep 2." Creator Sam Levinson. HBO, 2019. Television.
Euphoria Unfiltered: "Sn 1/Ep 4." Creator Sam Levinson. HBO, 2019. Television.
Grey's Anatomy: Season 14. Creator Shonda Rhymes. ABC, 2014. Television.
Horror Noire: A History of Black Horror. Executive producers Robin R. Means Coleman, Ph.D., Tananarive Due, and Phil Nobile, Jr. Shudders, 2019. Television.
I May Destroy You. Creator Michaela Coel. BBC One and HBO, 2020. Television.
Lovecraft Country. Creator Misha Green. HBO, 2020. Television.

Lovecraft Country: Orithyia Blue and the Imagination of Diana Freeman. Special feature. Writer and producer Scott McCulloch. HBO, 16 February 2021. Television.
Master of None: Season 1. Creators Aziz Ansari and Alan Yang. Netflix, 2015. Television.
Normal People. Miniseries. Creator Ed Guiney. BBC Three and Hulu, 2020. Television.
Ramy: Season 1. Creators Ramy Youssef, Ari Katcher, and Ryan Welch. Hulu, 2019. Television.
Ramy: Season 2. Creators Ramy Youssef, Ari Katcher, and Ryan Welch. Hulu, 2020. Television.
Stranger Things: Season 1. Creators the Duffer Brothers. Netflix, 2016. Television.
Stranger Things: Season 2. Creators the Duffer Brothers. Netflix, 2017. Television.
Stranger Things: Season 3. Creators the Duffer Brothers. Netflix, 2019. Television.
Stranger Things: Season 4 (Volume 1 and 2). Creators the Duffer Brothers. Netflix, 2022. Television.
Tom Clancy's Jack Ryan: Season 1. Creators Carlton Cuse and Graham Roland. Amazon Prime Video, 2018. Television.
"*Vida*: Inside the World—Episode 101." Creator Tanya Saracho. Starz, 2018. Television.
"*Vida*: Inside the World—Episode 102." Creator Tanya Saracho. Starz, 2018. Television.
"*Vida*: Inside the World—Episode 104." Creator Tanya Saracho. Starz, 2018. Television.
"*Vida*: Inside the World—Episode 106." Creator Tanya Saracho. Starz, 2018. Television.
Vida: Season 1. Creator Tanya Saracho. Starz, 2018. Television.
Vida: Season 2. Creator Tanya Saracho. Starz, 2019. Television.
Vida: Season 3. Creator Tanya Saracho. Starz, 2020. Television.

Video

The A.V. Club. "SPOILERS/Lovecraft Country Showrunner Misha Green on Indiana Jones and the Dark Truth of Museums." *YouTube*. 7 September 2020. https://www.youtube.com/watch?v=Gufcp2G9K0g. Accessed 8 July 2022. Video.
Beyoncé. "Beyoncé—Hold Up (Video)." *YouTube*. 4 September 2016. https://www.youtube.com/watch?v=PeonBmeFR8o. Accessed 31 August 2022. Video.
"Clubhouse Conversations—Normal People." Suzie Lavelle interviewed by Seamus McGarvey. *American Cinematographer*, June 30, 2020. https://ascmag.com/videos/clubhouse-conversations-normal-people. Accessed 10 December 2021. Video.
"Conversations with Vida." Moderated by Stacey Wilson Hunt, Hollywood editor for *New York Magazine* and *Vulture*. SAG-AFTRA Foundation Conversations, 12 June 2018. *YouTube*. https://www.youtube.com/watch?v=5fRK5Pqr-rE. Accessed 21 January 2022. Video.
"Every Stranger Things Movie Reference Revealed by the Duffer Brothers (Seasons 1–3)." *Wired*, 25 July 2019. *YouTube*. https://www.youtube.com/watch?v=qGGc1wGmgbM. Accessed 20 April 2022. Video.
"How We Made Normal People: Complete Featurette Including Paul Mescal and Daisy Edgar-Jones." *BBC Three*, 16 August 2020. *You Tube*. https://www.youtube.com/watch?v=fNi2UppWINk. Accessed 14 November 2021. Video.
LaFleur, Ingrid. "Visual Aesthetics of Afrofuturism." TEDx Fort Greene Salon, 25 September 2011. *YouTube*. https://www.youtube.com/watch?v=7bCaSzk9Zc. Accessed 14 September 2022. Video.
"Michaela Coel Reacts to I May Destroy You Scene/GQ Action Replay/British GQ." *British GQ*, 29 June 2020. *YouTube*. https://www.youtube.com/watch?v=GWNb6uGc748. Accessed 25 March 2022. Video.
"Michaela Coel/James MacTaggart Lecture/Edinburgh TV Festival 2018." *Edinburgh Television Festival*, 23 August 2018. *YouTube*. https://www.youtube.com/watch?v=odusP8gmqsg. Accessed 23 February 2022. Video.
"The Power of Myth—'The Hero's Adventure." Episode 1, *Joseph Campbell and the Power of Myth*. Bill Moyers. *PBS*, 1988. BillMoyers.com, https://billmoyers.com/series/joseph-campbell-and-the-power-of-myth-1988/. Accessed 13 May 2022. Video.

"Ramy Youssef—Telling an American Muslim's Story on 'Ramy.'" *The Daily Show with Trevor Noah*, Comedy Central, 26 August 2020. https://www.cc.com/video/wlouyz/the-daily-show-with-trevor-noah-ramy-youssef-telling-an-american-muslim-s-story-on-ramy. Accessed 19 August 2021. Video.

"The Untold Truth of Teddy Perkins." *Looper*, 1 October 2018. *YouTube*. https://www.youtube.com/watch?v=EaPZMct-6_I. Accessed 28 July 2022. Video.

"Vida Stars Melissa Barrera and Mishel Prada on Their Intimate Scenes on Latinx Show." *Cine Movie*. www.cinemovie.tv. Accessed 21 January 2022. Video.

"Why Donald Glover's Atlanta Feels So Weird." Thomas Flight, 28 March 2022. *YouTube*. https://www.youtube.com/watch?v=8rOU9wrEsoo&t=1s. Accessed 24 August 2022. Video.

Womack, Ytasha. "Ytasha Womack—Afrofuturism Imagination and Humanity." *YouTube*. 14 June 2017. https://www.youtube.com/watch?v=xlF90sXVfKk. Accessed 16 August 2022. Video.

Web Articles

Abrams, James Cole. "Pop Psych: What Netflix's 'Stranger Things' Teaches Us About Childhood Trauma." *Observer*, 29 July 2016. https://observer.com/2016/07/pop-psych-what-netflixs-stranger-things-teaches-us-about-childhood-trauma/. Accessed 1 June 2022.

Agard, Chancellor. "Atlanta Writer Stefani Robinson Breaks Down Alfred's Dark 'Woods' Adventure." *Entertainment Weekly*, 19 April 2018. https://ew.com/tv/2018/04/19/atlanta-stefani-robinson-woods/. Accessed 16 December 2021.

Aguilar, Sofia "The Latinas of 'Euphoria' Leave Me Wanting More." Latina Media Co., 2 March 2022. https://latinamedia.co/euphoria/. Accessed 9 July 2023.

Al-Ghamdi, Abdullah. "Lovecraft Country Was Canceled Due to Toxic Work Environment Alleges New Book." *Screenrant*, 24 November 2021. https://screenrant.com/lovecraft-country-canceled-toxic-work-environment-book-details/. Accessed 30 June 2022.

Anderson, Mae, and Michael Liedtke. "Hubris—and Late Fees—Doomed Blockbuster." *NBC News*, 23 September 2010. https://www.nbcnews.com/id/wbna39332696. Accessed 20 April 2022.

Andreeva, Nellie. "Hulu Reports Strong Start for 'Little Fires Everywhere,' Rise in Live News & Binge Viewing Amid COVID-19 Crisis." *Deadline*, 30 March 2020. https://deadline.com/2020/03/little-fires-everywhere-ratings-hulu-rise-in-live-news-binge-viewing-covid-19-crisis-keeping-up-with-the-kardashians-1202896063/. Accessed 16 July 2021.

Andreeva, Nellie. "Starz Greenlights Drama Series 'Vida' in Push to Attract Latino Viewers." *Deadline*, 13 September 2017. https://deadline.com/2017/09/starz-orders-vida-drama-series-veronica-osorio-melissa-barrera-to-star-push-latino-viewers-1202169060/. Accessed 30 August 2021.

Andreeva, Nellie. "'Stranger Things' Season 4 Final Viewership Comes Within Less Than 300M Hours of 'Squid Game' Record." *Deadline*, 2 August 2022. https://deadline.com/2022/08/stranger-things-season-4-final-viewership-squid-game-record-1235083997/. Accessed 1 September 2022.

Andrews, Travis M. "Some Took Offense at Donald Glover's Early Work. He Has Evolved, but the Internet Never Forgets." *The Washington Post*, 15 May 2018. https://www.washingtonpost.com/news/arts-and-entertainment/wp/2018/05/15/some-took-offense-at-donald-glovers-early-work-he-has-evolved-but-the-internet-never-forgets/. Accessed 23 December 2021.

Armitstead, Claire, and Johanna Thomas-Corr. "'The Stakes Were Really High': The Stars Bringing Sally Rooney's Normal People to TV." *The Guardian*, 12 April 2020 (modified 3 June 2020). https://www.theguardian.com/tv-and-radio/2020/apr/12/the-stakes-were-really-high-bringing-sally-rooney-normal-people-to-tv. Accessed 3 February 2021.

"Atlanta." *Rotten Tomatoes*. https://www.rottentomatoes.com/tv/atlanta. Accessed 24 September 2022.

Bachman, Mara. "Lovecraft Country: Who Is Mama Oya? The African Goddess'

Mythology Explained." *Screenrant*, 3 September 2020. https://screenrant.com/lovecraft-country-episode-3-mama-oya-goddess-mythology/. Accessed 1 July 2022.

Bacon, Thomas. "Lovecraft Country VFX Interview: François Dumoulin." *Screenrant*, 12 September 2021. https://screenrant.com/lovecraft-country-vfx-francois-dumoulin-interview/. Accessed 30 June 2022.

baliga, sujatha. "A Different Path for Confronting Sexual Assault." *Vox*, 10 October 2018. https://www.vox.com/first-person/2018/10/10/17953016/what-is-restorative-justice-definition-questions-circle. Accessed 26 February 2022.

Barajas, Julia. "L.A.'s Eastside Is a Latino 'Ellis Island.' But It's Time for Hollywood to Branch Out." *Los Angeles Times*, 13 June 2021. https://www.latimes.com/entertainment-arts/tv/story/2021-06-13/latino-gap-netflix-gentefied-on-my-block-boyle-heights-east-la Accessed 26 December 2021.

Bastién, Angelica Jade. "In Its Second Season, Atlanta Used Horror to Explore Black Identity." *Vulture*, 18 May 2018. https://www.vulture.com/2018/05/atlanta-horror-second-two-black-identity.html. Accessed 12 December 2021.

Behnke, Megan. "Why Did HBO Cancel Lovecraft Country? New Book Makes Bold Claims." *CinemaBlend*, 24 December 2021. https://www.cinemablend.com/television/why-did-hbo-cancel-lovecraft-country-new-book-makes-bold-claims. Accessed 30 June 2022.

"Being Seen on Screen: Diverse Representation and Inclusion on TV." *Nielsen*, 2 December 2020. https://www.nielsen.com/us/en/insights/report/2020/being-seen-on-screen-diverse-representation-and-inclusion-on-tv/. Accessed 12 December 2021.

Belle, Saidie. "Everything We Know About 'Atlanta' Seasons 3 and 4." *Thrillist*, 28 December 2021. https://www.thrillist.com/entertainment/nation/atlanta-season-3-season-4-preview. Accessed 22 December 2021.

Berman, Judy. "No Other Show Captures the Pleasures and Frustrations of Real Life Quite Like Vida." *Time*, 22 April 2020. https://time.com/5824773/vida-season-3-starz-review/. Accessed 17 December 2021.

Bernstein, Dan. "Sammy Sosa Then and Now: Former MLB Star Explains Why His Skin Color Is Lighter Since Retirement." *The Sporting News*, 15 June 2020. https://www.sportingnews.com/us/mlb/news/sammy-sosa-skin-color-now/1aruhh5dunsn1llps943qzwlqk. Accessed 5 January 2022.

Betts, Will. "Scoring Stranger Things." *Sound on Sound*, March 2017. https://www.soundonsound.com/techniques/scoring-stranger-things. Accessed 20 April 2022.

Blay, Zeba. "Hollywood Has a Colorism Problem, and the Conversation Keeps Going Nowhere." *Jezebel*, 7 October 2021. https://jezebel.com/hollywood-has-a-colorism-problem-and-the-conversation-1847817522. Accessed 24 September 2022.

Boone, Brian. "Huge TV Shows That Totally Disappeared." *Looper*, 8 September 2020. https://www.looper.com/244616/huge-tv-shows-that-totally-disappeared/. Accessed 24 September 2022.

Bowen, Sesali. "Don't Compare Atlanta's 'Teddy Perkins' to Get Out." *Refinery29*, 6 April 2019. https://www.refinery29.com/en-us/2018/04/195793/atlanta-fx-episode-6-black-horror. Accessed 16 December 2021.

Branstetter, Gillian. "'Stranger Things' Is an Amazing Depiction of Trauma." *Medium*, 20 July 2016. https://gillbranstetter.medium.com/stranger-things-is-an-amazing-depiction-of-trauma-6db931fec57. Accessed 20 April 2022.

Briger, Sam. "'Lovecraft Country' Creator Aims to Reclaim the Horror Genre for People of Color." *NPR*, 30 March 2021. https://www.npr.org/2021/03/30/982668346/lovecraft-country-creator-aims-to-reclaim-the-horror-genre-for-people-of-color. Accessed 22 July 2023.

Brockington, Ariana. "This Is What Lovecraft Country Really Means." *Refinery29*, 16 August 2020. https://www.refinery29.com/en-us/2020/08/9959175/what-lovecraft-country-means-hp-racism. Accessed 1 July 2022.

Brueggemann, Tom. "'The Godfather' Helped Invent the Blockbuster, Even Before 'Jaws' and 'Star Wars.'" *IndieWire*. 17 March 2022. https://www.indiewire.com/2022/03/the-god father-invent-blockbuster-jaws-star-wars-1234602162/. Accessed 20 April 2022.

Buddington, Erica. "Lovecraft Country Syllabus Ep. 9." *#Lovecraft Country: An Unofficial*

Syllabi, Langston League, 2020. https://langstonleaguellc.squarespace.com/popculturepd. Accessed 19 August 2022.

Butlet, Bethonie. "An 'Atlanta' Episode and Dave Chappelle's Netflix Special Show What Has—and Hasn't—Changed in Five Years." *The Washington Post*, 15 October 2021. https://www.washingtonpost.com/arts-entertainment/2021/10/15/dave-chappelle-atlanta/. Accessed 23 December 2021.

Cagnassola, Mary Ellen, and Lauren Giella. "Fact Check: Did Blockbuster Turn Down Chance to Buy Netflix for $50 Million." *Newsweek*, 11 March 2021. https://www.newsweek.com/fact-check-did-blockbuster-turn-down-chance-buy-netflix-50-million-1575557. Accessed 20 April 2022.

"CDC: 1 in 4 US Adults Live with a Disability." *CDC*, 16 August 2018. https://www.cdc.gov/media/releases/2018/p0816-disability.html. Accessed 19 August 2021.

Chaney, Jen. "Normal People Is an Honest, Absorbing Love Story." *Vulture*, 28 April 2020. https://www.vulture.com/2020/04/normal-people-hulu-review.html. Accessed 2 February 2021.

Chen, Lizzie. "Black Television Through the Years." Moody College of Communication at the University of Texas at Austin. https://moody.utexas.edu/news/black-television-through-years. Accessed 5 May 2021.

Chitwood, Adam. "Steven Spielberg Explains How 'Close Encounters' and His Parents' Divorce Inspired 'E.T.'" *The Wrap*, 22 April 2022. https://www.thewrap.com/steven-spielberg-et-close-encounters-of-the-third-kind-inspiration-interview/. Accessed 1 September 2022.

Clarke, Emma. "How Stranger Things Tackles Depression Is Nothing Short of Extraordinary." *Radio Times*, 31 May 2022. https://www.radiotimes.com/tv/sci-fi/stranger-things-4-max-depression-trauma-comment/. Accessed 1 September 2022.

Collazo, Richey. "Why You Shouldn't Be Supporting Atlanta, or Donald Glover." *Affinity*, 9 November 2016. http://affinitymagazine.us/2016/11/09/why-you-shouldnt-be-supporting-atlanta-or-donald-glover/. Accessed 14 October 2021.

Condon, Ali. "Normal People Is a Big Hit with Viewers as Over 370,000 Tune In." *Extra.ie*, 5 May 2020. https://extra.ie/2020/05/05/entertainment/movies-tv/normal-people-big-hit-rte. Accessed 25 June 2023.

Cooper, Brittney. "Hollywood's Post-Racial Mirage: How Pop Culture Got Gentrified." *Salon*, 25 March 2014. https://www.salon.com/2014/03/25/hollywoods_post_racial_mirage_how_pop_culture_got_gentrified/. Accessed 24 September 2022.

Crow, David. "Stranger Things 3: How Hawkins Found Its Jaws." *Den of Geek*, 4 July 2019. https://www.denofgeek.com/movies/stranger-things-3-jaws-mayor-hawkins/. Accessed 20 April 2022.

Crow, David. "Stranger Things Loves Close Encounters of the Third Kind." *Den of Geek*, 28 October 2017. https://www.denofgeek.com/movies/stranger-things-loves-close-encounters-of-the-third-kind/. Accessed 20 April 2022.

Cuffari, Steven. "Lovecraft Country: Hippolyta's Greek Name Origin Story Explained." *Screenrant*, 4 October 2020. https://screenrant.com/lovecraft-country-hippolyta-greek-origin-myth-name-meaning/. Accessed 30 June 2022.

Dailymail.com Reporter and Caters News Agency. "'Out-of-This World' Atlanta Spaceship Mansion Where Justin Bieber Used to Live Up for Rent at $20,000 a Month." *Daily Mail*, 25 October 2015. https://www.dailymail.co.uk/news/article-3288856/Out-world-Atlanta-spaceship-mansion-Justin-Bieber-used-live-rent-20-000-month.html. Accessed 28 November 2021.

D'Alessandro, Anthony. "'The Handmaid's Tale' Season 4 Premiere Is Most-Watched Hulu Original Ever—Update." *Deadline*, 6 May 2021. https://deadline.com/2021/05/the-handmaids-tale-season-4-premiere-is-most-watched-hulu-original-ever-1234750678/. Accessed 16 July 2021.

Daley, Beth. "Women of Color Spend More Than $8 Billion on Bleaching Creams Worldwide Every Year." *The Conversation*, 19 February 2021. https://theconversation.com/women-of-color-spend-more-than-8-billion-on-bleaching-creams-worldwide-every-year-153178. Accessed 12 December 2021.

Bibliography

Dapo. "Lovecraft Country Production Designer, Kalina Ivanov BTS on HBO Series." *Indie Activity*. https://www.indieactivity.com/lovecraft-country-production-designer-kalina-ivanov-bts-on-hbo-series/. Accessed 19 August 2022.

Dawn, Randee. "Setting the scene in 'Handmaid's Tale,' 'Atlanta' and More: Writers Explain the Draw of Nominated Episodes." *Los Angeles Times*, 17 August 2017. https://www.latimes.com/entertainment/envelope/la-en-st-key-scenes-writers-20170817-story.html. Accessed 23 December 2021.

Dean, Nailah. "Why I'm Tired of Dating Ramy." *Muslim Girl*, 23 December 2020. https://muslimgirl.com/why-im-tired-of-dating-ramy/. Accessed 16 July 2021.

Deb, Sopan. "'Ramy' Is a Quietly Revolutionary Comedy." *The New York Times*, 18 April 2019. https://www.nytimes.com/2019/04/18/arts/television/ramy-youssef-hulu.html. Accessed 19 August 2021.

Deininger, Keith. "Lovecraft Country: Biggest Differences Between the Book & HBO Show." *Screenrant*, 20 October 2020. https://screenrant.com/lovecraft-country-hbo-biggest-differences-book-show/. Accessed 30 June 2022.

"Drug Use Among Youth: Facts and Statistics." *National Center for Drug Abuse Statistics*, 2023. https://drugabusestatistics.org/teen-drug-use/. Accessed 8 July 2023.

The Duffer Brothers. "Stranger Things Episode 5: The Duffer Brothers Explain the Show's Soundtrack." *Entertainment Weekly*, 19 July 2016. https://ew.com/tv/2016/07/19/stranger-things-duffer-brothers-episode-5/. Accessed 20 April 2022.

The Duffer Brothers. "Stranger Things Episode 6: How the Duffer Brothers Created the Monster." *Entertainment Weekly*, 20 July 2016. https://ew.com/tv/2016/07/20/stranger-things-duffer-brothers-episode-6/. Accessed 2 February 2022.

Durkay, Laura. "'Homeland' Is the Most Bigoted Show on Television." *Washington Post*, 2 October 2014. https://www.washingtonpost.com/posteverything/wp/2014/10/02/homeland-is-the-most-bigoted-show-on-television/. Accessed 16 July 2021.

"Eighties Nostalgia, Collective Memory, and the Thirty Year Cycle." *Catharsis*, 29 May 2019. https://www.catharsistheatre.com/the-name-of-action/2019/5/28/eighties-nostalgia-and-the-thirty-year-cycle. Accessed 20 April 2022.

Eisenberg, Ophira. "Ask Me Another: Ramy Youssef." *NPR*, 29 May 2020. https://www.npr.org/transcripts/864841785. Accessed 16 July 2021.

Emami, Gazelle. "There's Never Been a Show Like Ramy—How a Weird, Personal, Sexually Complicated, and Yes, Muslim-American Comedy, Made Tt to TV." *Vulture*, 19 April 2019. https://www.vulture.com/2019/04/ramy-hulu-series-ramy-youssef-on-set.html. Accessed 19 August 2021.

Eng, Joyce. "How FX boss Improved Diversity in TV After a 'Good, Swift Kick in the Butt.'" *TV Guide*, 6 April 2018. https://www.tvguide.com/news/fx-john-landgraf-diversity-tv/. Accessed 22 December 2021.

England, Jenna. "Black Faces, White Masks—Race in 'The Good Place.'" *Medium*, 6 February 2020. https://popoff.us/black-faces-white-masks-race-in-the-good-place-fff9c60c5778. Accessed 29 July 2023.

Erazo, Vanessa. "'Vida': Tanya Saracho on Colorism and the 'Authenticity Police.'" *The New York Times*, 22 May 2019. https://www.nytimes.com/2019/05/22/arts/television/vida-season-2-starz.html. Accessed 17 December 2021.

Essex, Myeisha. "Ramy Youssef Jokes 'I Know You Guys Haven't Seen My Show' After First Golden Globe Win." *Entertainment Weekly*, 5 January 2020. https://www.etonline.com/ramy-youssef-jokes-i-know-you-guys-havent-seen-my-show-after-first-golden-globe-win-138856. Accessed 9 August 2021.

Evans, Greg. "Carlton Cuse Says 'Tom Clancy's Jack Ryan' Won't Demonize Islam; Unveil. Teaser Clip—NY Comic-Con Update." *Yahoo!*, 7 October 2017. https://www.yahoo.com/entertainment/tom-clancy-jack-ryan-amazon-224114302.html. Accessed 9 August 2021.

Fernandez, Maria Elena. "What Hollywood Can Learn from Vida's All-Latina Directors." *Vulture*, 11 June 2019. https://www.vulture.com/2019/06/vida-season-2-tanya-saracho-latina-directors.html. Accessed 17 December 2021.

Fienberg, Daniel. "'Lovecraft Country': TV Review." *The Hollywood Reporter*, 7 August

2020. https://www.hollywoodreporter.com/tv/tv-reviews/lovecraft-country-review-1306320/. Accessed 30 June 2022.

Fisher, Luchina. "'Jaws' Turns 40: 5 Ways It Changed Movies Forever." *ABC*, 20 Junes 2015. https://abcnews.go.com/Entertainment/ways-jaws-changed-movies-forever/story?id=31366659. Accessed 2 February 2022.

Framke, Caroline. "Donald Glover Has Always Had an Eye for the Surreal. With FX's Atlanta, He Might Have Perfected It." *Vox*, 2 November 2016. https://www.vox.com/culture/2016/11/2/13492830/atlanta-fx-donald-glover-surrealism. Accessed 16 December 2021.

Framke, Caroline. "How Michael Coel Processed Trauma and Fought to Own Her Story with 'I May Destroy You.'" *Variety*, 19 August 2020. https://variety.com/2020/tv/features/i-may-destroy-you-michaela-coel-1234739041/. Accessed 22 January 2022.

Friedman, Gabe. "Why Jews Should Watch 'Ramy,' a New Hulu Show About a Millennial Muslim." *Jewish Telegraphic Agency*, 23 April 2019. https://www.jta.org/2019/04/23/culture/why-jews-should-watch-ramy-a-new-hulu-show-about-a-millennial-muslim. Accessed 5 August 2021.

Friend, Tad. "Donald Glover Can't Save You." *New Yorker*, 26 February 2018. https://www.newyorker.com/magazine/2018/03/05/donald-glover-cant-save-you. Accessed 15 January 2022.

Frishman, Richard. "Hidden in Plain Sight: The Ghosts of Segregation." *The New York Times*, 30 November 2020. https://www.nytimes.com/2020/11/30/travel/ghosts-of-segregation.html?campaign_id=2&emc=edit_th_20201201&instance_id=24596&nl=todaysheadlines&regi_id=75758980&segment_id=45733&user_id=e8f6ddcb0bccf40e24b3be3bbbbfc15f. Accessed 30 November 2020.

Garner, Dwight, James Poniewozik, Parul Sehgal, and Jennifer Szalai. "Bringing 'Normal People' to Sexy, Soundtracked Life." *The New York Times*, 15 May 2020. https://www.nytimes.com/2020/05/15/books/normal-people-sally-rooney-hulu-adaptation.html. Accessed 19 May 2020.

Geiser, Bradley. "'I Spy' Was the First American TV Show Featuring a Black Actor in a Lead Role." *Showbiz CheatSheet*, 27 November 2020. https://www.cheatsheet.com/entertainment/i-spy-was-the-first-american-tv-show-featuring-a-black-actor-in-a-lead-role.html/. Accessed 5 May 2021.

Gennis, Sadie. "Starz's 'Vida' Is Plenty Sexy—But Every Graphic Moment Counts." *TV Guide*, 20 March 2019. https://www.tvguide.com/news/features/starz-vida-sex-scenes/. Accessed 4 April 2022.

"Get Out, Atlanta, Sorry to Bother You, and the Afro-Surrealist Film Movement." *Surrealism Today*, 1 December 2021. https://surrealismtoday.com/the-afro-surrealist-film-movement/. Accessed 24 September 2022.

Ghatti, Umber. "Actor Draws from Muslim-American Identity in Show Exploring Challenges of Dual Cultures." *Daily Bruin*, 10 September 2021. https://dailybruin.com/2019/04/11/actor-draws-from-muslim-american-identity-in-show-exploring-challenges-of-dual-cultures. Accessed 19 October 2021.

Ghorayshi, Azeen "Report Reveals Sharp Rise in Transgender Young People in the U.S." *The New York Times*, 10 June 2022. https://www.nytimes.com/2022/06/10/science/transgender-teenagers-national-survey.html. Accessed 8 July 2023.

Gilbert, Sophie. "The Dark Teen Show That Pushes the Edge of Provocation." *The Atlantic*, 19 June 2019. https://www.theatlantic.com/entertainment/archive/2019/06/euphoria-hbo-review-zendaya/591955/. Accessed 8 August 2019.

Gilchrist, Tracy E. "Vida Boldly Tackles Identity Policing Among Queer People." *Advocate*, 21 June 2019. https://www.advocate.com/television/2019/6/21/vida-boldly-tackles-identity-policing-among-queer-people. Accessed 30 August 2021.

"GLAAD's Where We Are on TV 2020–2021 Report: Despite Tumultuous Year in Television, LGBTQ Representation Holds Steady." *GLAAD*, 14 January 2021. https://www.glaad.org/releases/glaads-where-we-are-tv-2020-2021-report-despite-tumultuous-year-television-lgbtq. Accessed 9 August 2021.

Goldberg, Lesley. "'Vida' to End with Season 3 on Starz." *The Hollywood Reporter*, 18

March 2020. https://www.hollywoodreporter.com/tv/tv-news/vida-end-season-3-starz-1285162/. Accessed 17 December 2021.

Goldberg, Michelle. "Why Sex-Positive Feminism Is Falling Out of Fashion." *The New York Times*, 24 September 2021. https://www.nytimes.com/by/michelle-goldberg. Accessed 20 December 2021.

Goldstein, Dana, and Billy Witz. "Abuse and Racism Accusations Bring '#MeToo Moment' to Northwestern." *The New York Times*, 28 July 2023. https://www.nytimes.com/2023/07/28/sports/ncaafootball/northwestern-sports-hazing.html. Accessed 19 August 2023.

Gonzalez, Sandra. "After Getting Called Out, FX Overhauled Its Efforts to Hire More Diverse TV Directors." *CNN*, 9 August 2016. https://money.cnn.com/2016/08/09/media/fx-female-directors/index.html. Accessed 12 December 2021.

Goodman, Tim. "'Euphoria': TV Review." *The Hollywood Reporter*, 5 June 2019. https://www.hollywoodreporter.com/tv/tv-reviews/euphoria-review-1215681/. Accessed 8 August 2019.

Gottlieb, Meryl. "Here Are the References to '80s Movies in Netflix's Great New Show 'Stranger Things.'" *Insider*, 29 July 2016. https://www.businessinsider.com/references-made-in-stranger-things-side-by-side-comparison-2016-7. Accessed 20 April 2022.

Grobar, Matt. "Ramy Youssef on Depicting 'Anti-Blackness' in 'Ramy' Season 2: 'There's a Lot of Work to Do.'" *Deadline*, 30 June 2020. https://deadline.com/2020/06/ramy-creator-ramy-youssef-mahershala-ali-hulu-interview-news-1202955850/. Accessed 9 August 2021.

Gronowski, Chrisovolandou. "Psychoanalytic Examination of Stranger Things' Eleven: Trials and Tribulations of Childhood Trauma on the 'Child-Hero." *University of Hawaii at Hilo*, 2018. https://hilo.hawaii.edu/campuscenter/hohonu/volumes/documents/PsychoanalyticExaminationofStrangerThingsElevenTrialsandTribulationsofChildhoodTraumaontheChild-Hero.pdf. Accessed 20 April 2022.

Gross, Samuel R., M. Possley, and K. Stephens. "Race and Wrongful Convictions in the United States." *The National Registry of Exonerations*, Newkirk Center for Science and Society, 2017. https://repository.law.umich.edu/cgi/viewcontent.cgi?article=1121&context=other. Accessed 11 June 2022.

Harris, Aisha. "This Week's Atlanta Showed the Problem with Choosing Outrage at the Expense of Understanding." *Slate*, 12 October 2016. https://slate.com/culture/2016/10/atlantas-b-a-n-episode-critiques-p-c-outrage.html. Accessed 15 January 2022.

Hastings, Reed. "CEO Reed Hastings on How Netflix Beat Blockbuster." *Marketplace*, 8 September 2020. https://www.marketplace.org/2020/09/08/ceo-reed-hastings-on-how-netflix-beat-blockbuster/. Accessed 20 April 2022.

Heaton, Charlie. "'Stranger Things 4' First Look: New Season Teases Serious 'Nightmare on Elm Street' Horror Vibes." *IndieWire*, 23 March 2022. https://www.indiewire.com/2022/03/stranger-things-season-4-first-look-horror-1234710421/. Accessed 1 September 2022.

Hedash, Kara. "Stranger Things: Every Jaws Easter Egg & Reference." *Screenrant*, 16 September 2020. https://screenrant.com/stranger-things-jaws-easter-eggs-references/. Accessed 20 April 2022.

Hedash, Kara." Stranger Things: The Spielberg Character That Joyce Byers Was Modeled After." *Screenrant*, 23 May 2020. https://screenrant.com/stranger-things-joyce-influence-spielberg-close-encounters-roy/. Accessed 20 April 2022.

Herman, Alison. "'Euphoria' (and HBO) Want to Get a Rise Out of You." *The Ringer*, 14 June 2019. https://www.theringer.com/tv/2019/6/14/18677932/euphoria-review-drugs-sex-hbo. Accessed 4 July 2021.

Higgins, Evan. "Atlanta's Surrealism Is What It Feels Like to Be Black." *Slate*, 27 February 2018. https://slate.com/culture/2018/02/atlantas-surrealism-and-the-black-experience-in-america.html. Accessed 15 January 2022.

Hill, Nicole. "How Lovecraft Country Uses Topsy and Bopsy to Address Racist Caricatures." *Den of Geek*, 7 October 2020. https://www.denofgeek.com/tv/lovecraft-country-topsy-bopsy-uncle-toms-cabin-racist-caricatures/. Accessed 14 July 2022.

Hill, Nicole. "Lovecraft Country: What Ruby's Hillary Davenport Transformation Means." *Den of Geek*, 16 September 2020. https://www.denofgeek.com/tv/lovecraft-country-ruby-hillary-davenport-transformation/. Accessed 14 September 2022.

History.com Editors. "Emmett Till Is Murdered." *HISTORY*, A&E Television Networks, 2 February 2010. Updated 12 January 2022. https://www.history.com/this-day-in-history/the-death-of-emmett-till. Accessed 26 February 2022.

"The History of Homelessness." *Harbor Interfaith Services*. https://www.harborinterfaith.org/ homelessness/history-causes/. Accessed 15 July 2023.

Holloway, Daniel. "'Stranger Things' Ratings: Where Series Ranks Among Netflix's Most Watched." *Variety*, 25 August 2016. https://variety.com/2016/tv/news/stranger-things-tv-ratings-netflix-most-watched-1201844081/. Accessed 1 June 2022.

Holmes, Linda. "'I May Destroy You' Is HBO's New Unforgettable, Unmissable Drama." *NPR*, 7 June 2020. https://www.npr.org/2020/06/07/871472968/i-may-destroy-you-is-hbo-s-new-unforgettable-unmissable-drama. Accessed 24 January 2022.

Hough, Q.V. "Lovecraft Country: What Is the Poem in Episode 2?" *Screenrant*, 30 August 2020. https://screenrant.com/lovecraft-country-hbo-whitey-moon-poem-explained/. Accessed 1 July 2022.

Huddlestron, Tom, Jr. "37-Year-Old Brothers Who Created 'Stranger Things' Got Rejected by Over 15 Networks Before Netflix Said Yes." *CNBC*, 11 December 2018. https://www.cnbc.com/2018/12/11/duffer-brothers-stranger-things-rejected-over-15-times-pre-netflix.html. Accessed 20 April 2022.

Hunt, Bradford D. "Trumbull Park Homes Race Riots, 1953–1954." *Encyclopedia of Chicago*, The Chicago Historical Society, 2005. http://www.encyclopedia.chicagohistory.org/pages/2461.html. Accessed 9 August 2022.

Hunt, Darnell, Dr., and Ana-Christina Ramón. "Hollywood Diversity Report 2020: A Tale of Two Hollywoods, Part 2: Television." *UCLA: College of Social Sciences*, 22 October 2020. https://socialsciences.ucla.edu/wp-content/uploads/2020/10/UCLA-Hollywood-Diversity-Report-2020-Television-10-22-2020.pdf. Accessed 9 August 2021.

Hunt, Darnell, Dr., and Ana-Christina Ramón. "Hollywood Diversity Report 2021: Pandemic in Progress, Part 2: Television." *UCLA: College of Social Sciences*, 26 October 2021. https://socialsciences.ucla.edu/wp-content/uploads/2021/10/UCLA-Hollywood-Diversity-Report-2021-Television-10-26-2021.pdf. Accessed 23 December 2021.

Hurtado, Ludwig. "What Happens When Latinx People Gentrify Latinx Communities." *Vice*, 31 January 2019. https://www.vice.com/en/article/mbynkq/what-happens-when-latinx-people-gentrify-latinx-communities. Accessed 26 December 2021.

Ibrahim, Shamira. "What 'Ramy' Gets Wrong About Muslim Women." *The Atlantic*, 23 April 2019. https://www.theatlantic.com/entertainment/archive/2019/04/hulus-ramy-misses-mark-muslim-women/587722/. Accessed 9 August 2021.

Ignaszewski, Martha J., M.D. "The Epidemiology of Drug Abuse." *The Journal of Clinical Pharmacology* 61, Issue S2, pp. S10–S17, 15 August 2021. https://accp1.onlinelibrary.wiley.com/doi/full/10.1002/jcph.1937. Accessed 8 July 2023.

Jackson, Dan. "Why Black Justin Bieber on 'Atlanta' Was So Damn Funny." *Thrillist*, 27 September 2016. https://www.thrillist.com/entertainment/nation/atlanta-justin-bieber. Accessed 18 November 2021.

Jackson, Leigh-Ann. "'Atlanta' Season 2, Episode 3: It's Michael Vick." *The New York Times*, 15 March 2018. https://www.nytimes.com/2018/03/15/arts/television/atlanta-season-2-episode-3-recap.html. Accessed 5 December 2021.

James, Caryn. "Lovecraft Country Is 'Ambitious and Unwieldy.'" *BBC Culture*, 6 August 2020. https://www.bbc.com/culture/article/20200806-lovecraft-country-is-ambitious-and-unwieldy. Accessed 1 July 2022.

"Jaws—the Monster That Ate Hollywood." *Frontline*, WGBH educational foundation. https://www.pbs.org/wgbh/pages/frontline/shows/hollywood/business/jaws.html. Accessed 1 September 2022.

Jeffries, Stuart. "Was This Britain's First Black Queen?" *The Guardian*, 11 March 2009. https://www.theguardian.com/world/2009/mar/12/race-monarchy. Accessed 23 July 2023.

Johnson, Lottie Elizabeth. "Why Do We Like 'Stranger Things' So Much? A BYU Professor

Bibliography

Explains." *Deseret News*, 2 June 2019. https://www.deseret.com/2019/7/2/8935900/why-do-we-like-stranger-things-so-much-a-byu-professor-explains. Accessed 20 April 2022.

Jones, Jeffrey M. "Americans Felt Uneasy Toward Arabs Even Before September 11." *Gallup*, 28 September 2001. https://news.gallup.com/poll/4939/americans-felt-uneasy-toward-arabs-even-before-september.aspx. Accessed 8 August 2021.

Jordan, Mike. "What Donald Glover's 'Atlanta' Unapologetically Shows Us About Our City." *Thrillist*, 7 September 2016. https://www.thrillist.com/entertainment/atlanta/atlanta-donald-glovers-fx-show-nails-the-city. Accessed 14 October 2021.

Jung, E. Alex. "Michaela the Destroyer." *Vulture*, 6 July 2020. https://www.vulture.com/article/michaela-coel-i-may-destroy-you.html. Accessed 22 January 2022.

Kariuki, Patrick. "How and When Did Netflix Start? A Brief History of the Company." *MUO*, 22 October 2021. https://www.makeuseof.com/how-when-netflix-start-brief-company-history/. Accessed 20 April 2022.

Khan, Mariam. "From Mute to Menacing: Why TV's Portrayal of Muslims Still Falls Short." *The Guardian*, 15 October 2020. https://www.theguardian.com/tv-and-radio/2020/oct/15/why-tvs-portrayal-of-muslims-still-falls-short-ramy-bodyguard. Accessed 5 August 2021.

Khomami, Nadia. "Kate Bush Reaches UK No 1 with Running Up That Hill After 37 Years." *The Guardian*,17 June 2022. https://www.theguardian.com/music/2022/jun/17/kate-bush-uk-no-1-running-up-that-hill. Accessed 1 September 2022.

Kim, Sandy. "Donald Glover's Community: The Comic Turns His Eye to His Hometown—and Black America—in Atlanta." *Vulture*, 22 August 2016. https://www.vulture.com/2016/08/donald-glover-atlanta.html. Accessed 23 December 2021.

Kirtley, David Barr. "The Stranger Things Secret? It's Basically an 8-Hour Spielberg Movie." *Wired*, 12 August 2016. https://www.wired.com/2016/08/geeks-guide-stranger-things/. Accessed 20 April 2022.

Lambert, Harper. "Michaela Coel Hopes 'I May Destroy You' Encourages Viewers to Change Their Self-Narratives." *The Hollywood Reporter*, 19 August 2021. https://www.hollywoodreporter.com/tv/tv-news/michaela-coel-i-may-destroy-you-emmys-1234998979/. Accessed 24 January 2022.

Latif, Leila. "I May Destroy You and How It Represents the Future of TV." *BBC Culture*, 19 October 2021. https://www.bbc.com/culture/article/20211015-i-may-destroy-you-and-how-it-represents-the-future-of-tv. Accessed 24 January 2022.

Law, Tara. "What Euphoria Gets Right—and Wrong—About Teen Drug Use and Addiction." *Time*, 28 February 2022, updated 2 March 2022. https://time.com/6152502/euphoria-hbo-teenage-drug-use/. Accessed 8 July 2023.

Lawrence, Derek. "A Golden Match: Ramy Youssef and Mahershala Ali Are Each Other's Biggest Fans." *Entertainment Weekly*, 19 May 2020. https://ew.com/tv/ramy-youssef-mahershala-ali-ramy-hulu/. Accessed 19 August 2021.

Lee, Edmund, and John Koblin. "HBO Must Get Bigger and Broader, Says Its New Overseer." *The New York Times*, 8 July 2018. https://www.nytimes.com/2018/07/08/business/media/hbo-att-merger.html. Accessed 14 July 2021.

Lipka, Michael. "Muslims and Islam: Key Findings in the U.S. and Around the World." *Pew Research Center*, 9 August 2017. https://www.pewresearch.org/fact-tank/2017/08/09/muslims-and-islam-key-findings-in-the-u-s-and-around-the-world/. Accessed 9 August 2021.

Littleton, Cynthia. "How Rebecca Campbell Rose from Local TV to Become Disney's New Streaming Boss." *Variety*, 20 May 2020. https://variety.com/2020/tv/news/rebecca-campbell-disney-kevin-mayer-direct-to-consumer-international-1234611583/. Accessed 16 July 2021.

Lopez, Kristen. "Disability in Television: Who Was the First Disabled Person You Saw on Television?" *IndieWire*, 13 August 2020. https://www.indiewire.com/2020/08/glee-star-trek-first-time-you-saw-disability-on-tv-1234571574/. Accessed 8 August 2021.

Lyons, Kim. "AT&T CEO John Stankey Says It Was 'Time to Unleash' WarnerMedia Assets." *The Verge*, 24 May 2021. https://www.theverge.com/2021/5/24/22451111/att-ceo-stankey-unleash-assets-warnermedia-discovery-hbo. Accessed 14 July 2021.

Bibliography

Maas, Jennifer. "We Asked Donald Glover's Old Comedy Team, Derrick, Who Was Funniest—Turns Out Stephen Glover Is." *The Wrap*, 28 February 2018. https://www.thewrap.com/derrick-comedy-donald-glover-stephen-atlanta/. Accessed 14 October 2021.

Maddux, Maria. "Authentically Casting People with Disabilities and Talking About Sex: Why You Should Watch 'Ramy.'" *Virtual Research Center for the Americas*, 18 August 2020. https://www.olacolorado.org/post/authentically-casting-people-with-disabilities-and-talking-about-sex-why-you-should-watch-ramy. Accessed 9 August 2021.

Madrigal, Alexis C. "Gil Scott-Heron's Poem, 'Whitey on the Moon.'" *The Atlantic*, 28 May 2011. https://www.theatlantic.com/technology/archive/2011/05/gil-scott-herons-poem-whitey-on-the-moon/239622/. Accessed 10 August 2022.

Magnum, Trey. "RJ Walker, Who Plays Clark County on 'Atlanta,' Proves That Like His Character, There's More Than Meets the Eye." *Shadow and Act*, 29 March 2018. https://shadowandact.com/rj-walker-clark-county-atlanta-interview. Accessed 28 November 2021.

Mama, Heran. "To Not Be Stunted On: How 'Atlanta' Makes Biting, but "Woke" Plot Lines Hysterical." *Medium*, 25 April 2018. https://medium.com/@heranmamo/to-not-be-stunted-on-how-atlanta-makes-biting-but-woke-plot-lines-hysterical-fabb6ed42b1a. Accessed 5 December 2021.

Mann, Judy. "The Lives of Latchkey Children." *The Washington Post*, 29 November 1985. https://www.washingtonpost.com/archive/local/1985/11/29/the-lives-of-latchkey-children/12712d60-ee0a-4844-a4ce-740bf0eaf3f9/. Accessed 20 April 2022.

Marantz, Andrew. "Ramy Youssef's Sort-of-Sacred Standup." *The New Yorker*, 15 April 2019. https://www.newyorker.com/magazine/2019/04/22/ramy-youssefs-sort-of-sacred-standup. Accessed 16 July 2021.

Marchese, David. "Ramy Youssef Is Not Using Comedy to Teach You About Muslims." *The New York Times*, 12 May 2020. https://www.nytimes.com/interactive/2020/05/12/magazine/ramy-youssef-interview.html. Accessed 19 August 2021.

Marrone, Nico. "Lovecraft Country Creator Shares Inside Look at Cancelled Season 2 Plans." *Screenrant*, 14 July 2021. https://screenrant.com/lovecraft-country-season-2-story-plan-details-update/. Accessed 18 July 2022.

Marshall, Jonathan. "How Our War on Drugs Shattered the Cities." *The Washington Post*, 17 May 1992. https://www.washingtonpost.com/archive/opinions/1992/05/17/how-our-war-on-drugs-shattered-the-cities/fb887f62-9efe-4c4a-82ac-a21bc330a769b/. Accessed 2 July 2023.

Martin, Kalea. "15 New and Classic High School TV Shows Available to Stream HBO Max Right Now." *Popsugar*, 30 March 2021. https://www.popsugar.com/entertainment/photo-gallery/48244019/image/48244062/Nancy-Drew. Accessed 7 July 2021.

Mathews, Liam. "Lovecraft Country's Misha Green Recommends These Books and Movies to Help Get the Full Show Experience." *TV Guide*, 14 October 2020. https://www.tvguide.com/news/lovecraft-country-books-movies-references/. Accessed 1 July 2022.

Maurice, Emma Powys. "Lovecraft Country Creator Admits She 'Failed' Iconic Indigenous Two-Spirit Character Yahima." *PinkNews*, 13 October 2020. https://www.pinknews.co.uk/2020/10/13/lovecraft-country-hbo-misha-green-indigenous-two-spirit-yahima-death-backlash/. Accessed 4 July 2022.

McClelland, Edward. "Were the Suburbs a Blip?" *Chicago Magazine*, 14 June 2019. https://www.chicagomag.com/city-life/June-2019/Were-the-Suburbs-a-Blip/. Accessed 20 April 2022.

McKinnon, Tricia. "8 Reasons Why Blockbuster Failed & Filed for Bankruptcy." *Indigo Digital*, 28 March 2022. https://www.indigo9digital.com/blog/blockbusterfailure. Accessed 1 September 2022.

Meltzer, Marisa. "When Brenda Walsh Was Young: The Tevolutionary First Season of *Beverly Hills, 90210*." *Slate*, 7 December 2006. https://slate.com/culture/2006/12/the-revolutionary-first-season-of-beverly-hills-90210.html. Accessed 14 June 2020.

Menendez, Alicia. "VIDA's Melissa Barrera Embraces All Her Identities." *Latina to Latina*, Lantigua Williams & Co., 10 December 2018. LatinaToLatina.com. Accessed 15 December 2021.

Bibliography

Merriam-Webster. https://www.merriam-webster.com/dictionary/surrealism. Accessed 15 January 2022.

Miller, Katrina. "No, Lovecraft Country Didn't Need a Second Season." *Wired*, 16 September 2021. https://www.wired.com/story/lovecraft-country-no-season-2/. Accessed 1 July 2022.

Miller, Laura. "How *Lovecraft Country* Reappropriates H.P. Lovecraft's Notoriously Racist Creations." *Slate*, 7 August 2020. https://slate.com/culture/2020/08/lovecraft-country-hbo-series-racism-matt-ruff-novel.html. Accessed 6 August 2020.

Miller, Liz Shannon. "'Atlanta': Donald Glover Wants You to Feel What It's Like to Be Black." *IndieWire*, 9 August 2016. https://www.indiewire.com/2016/08/donald-glover-atlanta-fx-hiro-murai-trump-1201714877/. Accessed 16 December 2021.

Miller, Liz Shannon. "Here's Why Degrassi Will Never Die (and No, It's Not Just Because of Netflix)." *IndieWire*, 18 July 2016. http://www.indiewire.com/2016/07/degrassi-creator-next-class-netflix-500-episodes-1201707118/. Accessed 3 April 2018.

Millner, Denene. "Why Rachel Dolezal Can Never Be Black." *NPR*, 3 March 2017. https://www.npr.org/sections/codeswitch/2017/03/03/518184030/why-rachel-dolezal-can-never-be-black. Accessed 24 September 2022.

Mneimneh, Razan. "Muslim Character in Grey's Anatomy Took Off Her Hijab ... and People Lost It." *Step Feed*, 12 March 2018. https://stepfeed.com/muslim-character-in-grey-s-anatomy-took-off-her-hijab-and-people-lost-it-7785. Accessed 19 August 2021.

Moore, Cortney. "Hulu and the 5 Things That Set It Apart from Other Streaming Giants." *Fox Business*, 30 September 2019. https://www.foxbusiness.com/technology/5-things-to-know-about-hulu. Accessed 16 July 2021.

Moore, Sam. "How Donald Glover's Surrealism Makes 'Atlanta' a Work of Art." *NME*, 3 April 2018. https://www.nme.com/blogs/tv-blogs/atlanta-donald-glover-season-two-robbin-season-surrealism-work-of-art-surreal-2273547. Accessed 18 November 2021.

Mooro, Alya. "Ramy Youssef Isn't Trying to Represent All Muslims, He Just Wants to Be Himself." *Shondaland*, 12 June 2020. https://www.shondaland.com/inspire/a32842712/ramy-youssef-ramy-season-2/. Accessed 19 August 2021.

Moreau, Jordan. "Zoë Kravitz Calls Out Hulu for Lack of Diverse Shows After 'High Fidelity' Cancellation." *Variety*, 8 August 2020. https://variety.com/2020/tv/news/zoe-kravitz-high-fidelity-hulu-diversity-1234729635/. Accessed 16 July 2021.

"New Analysis Shows Startling Levels of Discrimination Against Black Transgender People." *National LGBTQ Task Force*. https://www.thetaskforce.org/new-analysis-shows-startling-levels-of-discrimination-against-black-transgender-people/. Accessed 24 September 2022.

Newby, Richard. "'Lovecraft Country': Black Spaces and Haunted Houses." *The Hollywood Reporter*, 1 September 2020. https://www.hollywoodreporter.com/tv/tv-news/lovecraft-country-black-spaces-and-haunted-houses-4053309/. Accessed 14 July 2022.

Newby, Richard. "'Lovecraft Country': Jurnee Smollett on That Haunting Confrontation." *The Hollywood Reporter*, 30 August 2020. https://www.hollywoodreporter.com/tv/tv-news/lovecraft-country-jurnee-smollett-episode-three-4052619/. Accessed 14 July 2022.

Newby, Richard. "'Lovecraft Country' Star Michael K. Williams on Navigating Fear and the Past." *The Hollywood Reporter*, 13 September 2020. https://www.hollywoodreporter.com/tv/tv-news/lovecraft-country-michael-k-williams-4059531/. Accessed 11 July 2022.

NHS (National Health Service). "Consent Information Leaflet." https://www.nhs.uk/aboutNHSChoices/professionals/healthandcareprofessionals/child-sexual-exploitation/Documents/Consent-information-leaflet.pdf. Accessed 8 June 2022.

NHS (National Health Service). "Overview—Consent." https://www.nhs.uk/conditions/consent-to-treatment/. Accessed 8 June 2022.

Nicholson, Rebecca. "The Duffer Brothers: 'Could We Do What Spielberg Did in the 80s and Elevate It Like He Did?'" *The Guardian*, 14 October 2017. https://www.theguardian.com/tv-and-radio/ng-interactive/2017/oct/14/duffer-brothers-spielberg-80s-stranger-things. Accessed 1 June 2022.

Northrup, Ryan. "Millie Bobby Brown Names Favorite '80s Movie For Stranger Things Prep."

Screenrant, 2 June 2022. https://screenrant.com/stranger-things-millie-bobby-brown-et-inspiration/. Accessed 1 September 2022.

Obenson, Tambay. "'Lovecraft Country' Review: HBO Tackles Racism with Confounding Jim Crow-Era, Genre-Bending Drama." *IndieWire*, 16 August 2020. https://www.indiewire.com/2020/08/lovecraft-country-review-hbo-1234579616/. Accessed 1 July 2022.

Ocana Perez, Damarys. "8 Boundary-Breaking Black TV Shows." *History*, 1 February 2021. https://www.history.com/news/black-tv-shows-culture. Accessed 5 May 2021.

O'Keefe, Meghan. "Is Cancelling 'Lovecraft Country' the Biggest Mistake HBO Has Ever Made?" *Decider*, 15 July 2021. https://decider.com/2021/07/15/lovecraft-country-hbo-mistake/. Accessed 1 July 2022.

Oomen, Marjolein. "Netflix: How a DVD Rental Company Changed the Way We Spend Our Free Time." *BMI*. https://www.businessmodelsinc.com/exponential-business-model/netflix/. Accessed 1 September 2022.

Orenstein, Peggy. "It's Not That Men Don't Know What Consent Is." *The New York Times*, 23 February 2019. https://www.nytimes.com/2019/02/23/opinion/sunday/sexual-consent-college.html?action=click&module=RelatedLinks&pgtype=Article. Accessed 30 December 2021.

Orenstein, Peggy. "When Did Porn Become Sex Ed?" *The New York Times*, 19 March 2016. https://www.nytimes.com/2016/03/20/opinion/sunday/when-did-porn-become-sex-ed.html?action=click&module=RelatedLinks&pgtype=Article. Accessed 30 December 2021.

Orenstein, Peggy. "Will We Ever Figure Out How to Talk to Boys About Sex?" *The New York Times*, 10 January 2020. https://www.nytimes.com/2020/01/10/opinion/sunday/boys-sex.html. Accessed 12 January 2020.

Otterson, Joe. "Donald Glover's 'Atlanta' to Stream on Hulu." *Variety*, 3 May 2017. https://variety.com/2017/tv/news/atlanta-donald-glover-hulu-1202407669/. Accessed 24 September 2022.

Otterson, Joe. "'Lovecraft Country' Creator Misha Green Sets Apple Overall Deal." *Variety*, 9 July 2021. https://variety.com/2021/tv/news/lovecraft-country-misha-green-apple-overall-deal-1235015943/. Accessed 1 July 2022.

Palmer, Bex. "How 'I May Destroy You' Got Made." *Backstage*, 14 June 2021. https://www.backstage.com/uk/magazine/article/how-i-may-destroy-you-got-made-73447/. Accessed 24 January 2022.

Parshina-Kottas, Yuliya, Anjali Singhvi, Audra D.S. Burch, Troy Griggs, Mika Gröndahl, Lingdong Huang, Tim Wallace, Jeremy White, and Josh Williams. "What the Tulsa Race Massacre Destroyed." *The New York Times*, 24 May 2021. https://www.nytimes.com/interactive/2021/05/24/us/tulsa-race-massacre.html. Accessed 16 August 2022.

Patton, Rebecca. "Why Ramy Youssef Says 9/11 Made Him 'More Muslim.'" *Bustle*, 29 June 2019. https://www.bustle.com/p/in-ramy-youssefs-comedy-special-feelings-he-says-911-made-him-more-muslim-18153449. Accessed 16 July 2021.

Paz, Isabella Grullón. "California Makes 'Stealthing,' or Removing Condom Without Consent, Illegal." *The New York Times*, 8 October 2021, updated 10 November 2021. https://www.nytimes.com/2021/10/08/us/stealthing-illegal-california.html. Accessed 26 February 2022.

Perez, Sarah. "Hulu Restructures Under Disney, CEO Randy Freer Departs." *TechCrunch*, 3 February 2020. https://techcrunch.com/2020/02/03/hulu-restructures-under-disney-ceo-randy-freer-departs/. Accessed 14 October 2021.

Peters, Fletcher. "Netflix Tops 222 Million Subscribers Worldwide, Narrowly Missing Q4 Forecast." *Decider*, 20 January 2022. https://decider.com/2022/01/20/netflix-q4-subscriber-growth/. Accessed 20 April 2022.

Pfeiffer, Sacha. "'Ramy' Is About One Millennial American Muslim—and Everyone's Racist Uncles." *NPR*, 21 April 2019. https://www.npr.org/2019/04/21/715290814/ramy-is-about-one-millennial-american-muslim-and-everyone-s-racist-uncles. Accessed 5 August 2021.

Phillips, Maya. "The Unintended Racial Horror of Lovecraft Country." *The New York*

Times, 19 October 2020. https://www.nytimes.com/2020/10/19/arts/television/lovecraft-country-season-finale.html. Accessed 22 November 2020.

Pometsey, Olive. "How Michaela Coel Transformed Her Trauma Into the Year's Best TV Show." *GQ*, 10 July 2020. https://www.gq.com/story/michaela-coel-i-may-destroy-you-interview. Accessed 30 January 2022.

Poniewozik, James. "'Normal People' Review: Their Love Will Tear You Apart." *The New York Times*, 28 April 2020. https://www.nytimes.com/2020/04/28/arts/television/normal-people-review.html. Accessed 5 February 2021.

Poniewozik, James. "Review: In 'Vida,' Home Is Where the Gentrification Is." *The New York Times*, 2 May 2018. https://www.nytimes.com/2018/05/02/arts/television/vida-starz-review.html. Accessed 17 December 2021.

Porter, Rick. "'Ramy' Renewed for Season 3 on Hulu." *The Hollywood Reporter*, 9 July 2020. https://www.hollywoodreporter.com/tv/tv-news/ramy-renewed-season-3-hulu-1302672/. Accessed 16 July 2021.

Porter, Rick. "TV Long View: HBO's 'Euphoria' Audience Is Extremely Online." *The Hollywood Reporter*, 22 June 2019. https://www.hollywoodreporter.com/tv/tv-news/tv-long-view-hbos-euphoria-audience-is-extremely-online-1220360/ Accessed 4 July 2021.

Pryor, Lex. "'Lovecraft Country' Recap: To Shape a Butterfly." *The Ringer*, 14 September 2020. https://www.theringer.com/tv/2020/9/14/21433073/lovecraft-country-episode-5-recap-skin-molting. Accessed 11 July 2022.

Radish, Christina. "'Lovecraft Country's Showrunner Answers Our Biggest Questions About That Bonkers Season 1 Finale." *Collider*, 18 October 2020. https://collider.com/lovecraft-country-hbo-finale-ending-explained/. Accessed 8 July 2022.

Randolph, Marc. "He 'Was Struggling Not to Laugh': Inside Netflix's Crazy, Doomed Meeting with Blockbuster." *Vanity Fair*, 17 September 2019. https://www.vanityfair.com/news/2019/09/netflixs-crazy-doomed-meeting-with-blockbuster. Accessed 1 June 2022.

Reed, Sabrina. "Ramy Season 3 Is Not Coming to Hulu in April 2021." *Fansided*, 15 April 2021. https://hiddenremote.com/2021/03/31/ramy-season-3-not-coming-hulu-april-2021/. Accessed 5 August 2021.

Reimann, Tom. "Everything You Didn't Know About Stranger Things." *Collider*, 30 May 2019. https://collider.com/galleries/everything-you-didnt-know-about-stranger-things/. Accessed 20 April 2022.

Richards, Jared. "Vida: A Shrewd, Queer Latinx Drama That's Far Too Busy to Explain Everything to You." *The Guardian*, 7 January 2021. https://www.theguardian.com/culture/2021/jan/08/vida-a-shrewd-queer-latinx-drama-thats-far-too-busy-to-explain-everything-to-you. Accessed 17 December 2021.

Richardson, Kalia. "Here's What to Know About 'Queen Charlotte: A Bridgerton Story.'" *The New York Times*, 11 May 2023. https://www.nytimes.com/2023/05/11/arts/television/queen-charlotte-bridgerton-history-shonda-rhimes.html. Accessed 23 July 2023.

Robb, Amanda. "Divorce, 1981-Style." *AARP*, August/September 2016. https://www.aarp.org/home-family/friends-family/info-2016/divorce-1980s.html. Accessed 20 April 2022.

Rodriguez, Ashley. "Donald Glover's 'Atlanta' Brilliantly Plays with Race and Class in TV Commercial Parodies." *Quartz*, 12 October 2016. https://qz.com/807375/in-fxs-atlanta-donald-g.lover-brilliantly-plays-with-race-and-class-in-tv-commercial-parodies/. Accessed 28 November 2021.

Rodriguez, Ashley. "Watch: The Opening Scene of 'Stranger Things' Owes Everything to 'E.T.'" *Quartz*, 27 October 2017. https://qz.com/1112034/watch-how-stranger-things-nailed-its-1980s-homage-right-from-the-start/. Accessed 1 June 2022.

Romero, Ariana. "The Emmys Struck a Pose. The Trans TV Revolution Is Here." *Refinery29*, 16 July 2019. https://www.refinery29.com/en-us/2019/07/238021/pose-emmy-nominations-2019-best-transgender-television. Accessed 30 June 2021.

Russell, Anna. "How 'Normal People' Makes Us Fall in Love." *The New Yorker*, 18 May 2020. https://www.newyorker.com/culture/on-television/how-normal-people-makes-us-fall-in-love. Accessed 3 February 2021.

St. Félix, Doreen. "'Euphoria' and the Flawed Art of Gen Z Prophesying." *The New Yorker*,

16 June 2019. https://www.newyorker.com/culture/on-television/euphoria-and-the-flawed-art-of-gen-z-prophesying. Accessed 8 August 2019.

St. Félix, Doreen. "Michaela Coel's Chaos and Charisma in 'I May Destroy You.'" *The New Yorker*, 29 June 2020. https://www.newyorker.com/magazine/2020/07/06/michaela-coels-chaos-and-charisma-in-i-may-destroy-you. Accessed 24 January 2022.

Sanchez, Omar. "Why Ramy Youssef Doesn't Intend 'Ramy' to Represent Every Muslim Experience." *The Wrap*, 19 April 2019. https://www.thewrap.com/why-ramy-youssef-doesnt-intend-ramy-to-represent-every-muslim-experience/. Accessed 9 August 2021.

Sandberg, Bryn Elise. "'Euphoria' Creator on Boundary-Pushing HBO Drama: 'We Didn't Want to Pull Any Punches.'" *The Hollywood Reporter*, 16 June 2019. live-feed/euphoria-creator-boundary-pushing-hbo-drama-didnt-pull-punches-1218588. Accessed 15 April 2020.

Saxena, Jaya. "Ramy Youssef Is Upending the First-Generation Narrative." *GQ*, 17 April 2019. https://www.gq.com/story/ramy-youssef-is-upending-the-first-generation-narrative. Accessed 8 August 2021.

Schwartz, Matthew S. "Disney Officially Owns 21st Century Fox." *NPR*, 20 March 2019. https://www.npr.org/2019/03/20/705009029/disney-officially-owns-21st-century-fox. Accessed 22 December 2021.

Scott, Fontana. "Actor and Comedian with Muscular Dystrophy Works to Open Doors for More Disabled Stories." *Everyday Health*, 7 August 2020. https://www.everydayhealth.com/genetic-diseases/actor-and-comedian-with-muscular-dystrophy-works-to-open-doors-for-more-disabled-stories/. Accessed 16 July 2021.

Seitz, Matt Zoller. "In Lovecraft Country, Monsters Past and Present Converge." *Vulture*, 10 August 2020. https://www.vulture.com/news/tv-review/. Accessed 1 July 2022.

Sepinwall, Alan. "'Lovecraft Country': A Nightmare on Main Street." *Rolling Stone*, 7 August 2020. https://www.rollingstone.com/tv-movies/tv-movie-reviews/lovecraft-country-hbo-review-1038614/. Accessed 1 July 2022.

Sepinwall, Alan. "'Lovecraft Country' Creator Misha Green on Bold Storytelling and the Season Finale." *Rolling Stone*, 18 October 2020. https://www.rollingstone.com/tv-movies/tv-movie-features/lovecraft-country-creator-misha-green-interview-season-finale-1077047/. Accessed 10 July 2022.

Serrao, Nivea. "Lovecraft Country Showrunner Apologizes for Having 'Failed' Queer Indigenous Character." *SYFY Wire*, 14 October 2020. https://www.syfy.com/syfy-wire/lovecraft-country-misha-green-failed-indigenous-two-spirit-representation. Accessed 4 July 2022.

Sharf, Zach. "Donald Glover: Fear of 'Getting Cancelled' Is Resulting in 'Boring' Films and TV." *IndieWire*, 11 May 2021. https://www.indiewire.com/2021/05/donald-glover-cancel-culture-boring-movies-tv-1234636493/. Accessed 15 January 2022.

Sharp, Nathan. "Atlanta: The 10 Most Surreal Moments in the Show, Ranked." *ScreenRant*, 16 February 2021. https://screenrant.com/atlanta-surreal-moments/. Accessed 15 January 2022.

Sippell, Margeaux. "Former 'Ramy' Staff Writer Says No Women Writers Were Asked Back for Season 2." *Yahoo Life*, 18 September 2019. https://www.yahoo.com/lifestyle/former-ramy-staff-writer-says-221838371.html. Accessed 8 August 2021.

Soloski, Alexis. "Gods, Monsters and H.P. Lovecraft's Uncanny Legacy." *The New York Times*, 7 August 2020. https://www.nytimes.com/2020/08/07/arts/television/hp-lovecraft.html. Accessed 22 November 2020.

Spangler, Todd. "Comcast Would Be Interested in Buying Hulu from Disney 'If It Was Up for Sale,' CEO Brian Roberts Says." *Variety*, 14 September 2022. https://variety.com/2022/digital/news/comcast-interested-buying-hulu-disney-ceo-brian-roberts-1235372543/. Accessed 18 September 2022.

Srihari, Prahlad. "How Ramy Offers a Refreshing but Flawed Representation of the Muslim Experience in America." *Firstpost*, 2 September 2020. https://www.firstpost.com/entertainment/how-ramy-offers-a-refreshing-but-flawed-representation-of-the-muslim-experience-in-america-8777791.html. Accessed 5 August 2021.

Stahl, Michael. "How a Lifelong Friendship Led to Steve Way's Ramy Role." *Vulture*, 6 May

2019. https://www.vulture.com/2019/05/steve-way-ramy-stand-up-comedy-interview.html. Accessed 19 August 2021.

Stahler, Kelsea. "Lovecraft Country's Soundtrack Boasts Blues Classics & a Few Truly Momentous Speeches." *Refinery29*, 19 October 2020. https://www.refinery29.com/en-us/2020/08/9963453/lovecraft-country-soundtrack-songs-list-season-1#slide-1.

Stanford, Eleanor. "Paapa Essiedu Knows 'I May Destroy You' Is Hard to Watch." *The New York Times*, 6 July 2020. https://www.nytimes.com/2020/07/06/arts/television/paapa-essiedu-i-may-destroy-you.html?action=click&module=RelatedLinks&pgtype=Article. Accessed 22 January 2022.

Stone, Chelsey. "The '80s Movie That Inspired Millie Bobby Brown's Eleven Will Make You Love 'Stranger Things' Even More." *Teen Vogue*, 17 August 2017. https://www.teenvogue.com/story/millie-bobby-brown-stranger-things-eleven-inspiration. Accessed 20 April 2022.

Tan, Marcus. "The Downfall of Blockbuster." *Medium*, 8 March 2021. https://medium.com/an-idea/the-downfall-of-blockbuster-da69f6c8a536#:~:text=At%20its%20peak%20in%20the,over%20%24900%20million%20in%20debt. Accessed 20 April 2022.

Tharpe, Frazier. "'Atlanta' Star Khris Davis Reveals Tracy's Waves Were a Weave." *Complex*, 8 March 2018. https://www.complex.com/pop-culture/2018/03/atlanta-robbin-season-tracy-khris-davis-interview. Accessed 16 December 2021.

Thorne, Will. "Ramy Youssef on 'Never Being Afraid to Get Political' with Season 2 of His Self-Titled Hulu Series." *Variety*, 28 May 2020. https://variety.com/2020/tv/news/season-2-hulu-ramy-youssef-1234617986/. Accessed 8 August 2021.

Thorne, Will. "TV Ratings: 'Lovecraft Country' Finale Scares Up Series High Numbers." *Variety*, 20 October 2020. https://variety.com/2020/tv/news/lovecraft-country-finale-series-high-ratings-1234811369/. Accessed 1 July 2022.

Tillet, Salamishah. "'I May Destroy You' Imagines a Path Back from Sexual Assault." *The New York Times*, 25 August 2020. https://www.nytimes.com/2020/08/25/arts/television/i-may-destroy-you-sexual-assault.html?action=click&module=RelatedLinks&pgtype=Article. Accessed 22 January 2022.

Tillet, Salamishah. "Living While Black in Lovecraft Country." *The New York Times*, 7 August 2020. https://www.nytimes.com/2020/08/07/arts/television/living-while-black-in-lovecraft-country.html. Accessed 22 November 2020.

Tizard, Will. "'Normal People' DP Suzie Lavelle on 'the Simplicity of Pure Storytelling.'" *Variety*, 3 October 2021. https://variety.com/2020/artisans/global/normal-people-suzie-lavelle-1234831663/. Accessed 3 October 2021.

Triplett, Steffan. "Lovecraft Country Recap: Home Runs on Their Heads." *Vulture*, 11 October 2020. https://www.vulture.com/article/lovecraft-country-recap-season-1-episode-9-rewind-1921.html. Accessed 14 July 2022.

Trust, Gary. "Kate Bush's 'Running Up That Hill' Tops Both Billboard Global Charts." *Billboard*, 11 July 2022. https://www.billboard.com/music/chart-beat/kate-bush-running-up-that-hill-tops-both-billboard-global-charts-1235112654/. Accessed 10 July 2023.

Turchiano, Danielle. "'Pose' and 'Lovecraft Country' Bosses Break Down 'Decentralizing White Men' in Their Narratives." *Variety*, 3 June 2021. https://variety.com/2021/tv/features/pose-lovecraft-country-decentralizing-white-male-stories-1234970965/. Accessed 1 July 2022.

Ugwu, Reggie. "Where 'Euphoria' Is Surprisingly Conservative." *The New York Times*, 30 July 2019. https://www.nytimes.com/2019/07/30/arts/television/euphoria-internet-relationships-conservative.html. Accessed 6 August 2019.

Vagianos, Alanna. "Tarana Burke: 'Me Too Is Not a Women's Movement.'" *HuffPost*, 24 April 2019, Updated 10 May 2019. https://www.huffpost.com/entry/tarana-burke-me-too-not-womens-movement_n_5cc06af3e4b0764d31db5d88. Accessed 26 February 2022.

van Es, Margaretha A. "Van Es on Self-Representations of Muslim Women." *Palgrave Macmillan*. https://www.palgrave.com/gp/campaigns/international-womens-day/van-es-on-self-representations-of-muslim-women. Accessed 18 September 2022.

VanDerWerff, Emily. "FX's Atlanta Is a Terrific Comedy—and the Best New Show of the

Fall." *Vox*, 6 September 2016. https://www.vox.com/2016/9/6/12777632/atlanta-review-fx-donald-glover-best-new-tv-shows. Accessed 16 December 2021.

VanDerWerff, Emily. "HBO's Euphoria Is Two Shows in One. One is Bad. The Other Could Be Good." *Vox*, 23 June 2019. https://www.vox.com/culture/2019/6/23/18701226/euphoria-premiere-pilot-episode-1-recap-zendaya-hbo. Accessed 15 April 2020.

VanDerWerff, Emily. "HBO's I May Destroy You Might Be the Best TV Show of the Year." *Vox*, 7 August 2020. https://www.vox.com/culture/2020/8/7/21356216/i-may-destroy-you-hbo-review-michaela-coel. Accessed 30 January 2022.

Variety500. "John Landgraf." *Variety*. https://variety.com/exec/john-landgraf/. Accessed 22 December 2021.

Vega, Nicholas. "HBO Max Is Just 'Max' Now—Here Are the 4 Things to Know About the New Streaming Service." *CNBC*, 23 May 2023. https://www.cnbc.com/2023/05/23/hbo-max-is-now-just-max-what-you-need-to-know.html. Accessed 29 June 2023.

Venable, Malcolm. "Why Donald Glover's Atlanta Is 'Twin Peaks with Rappers.'" *TV Guide*, 16 January 2016. https://www.tvguide.com/news/donald-glover-atlanta-twin-peaks-rappers/. Accessed 15 January 2022.

Viruet, Pilot. "'Atlanta' Is Great at Talking About Race Without Talking About Race." *Vice*, 28 September 2016. https://www.vice.com/en/article/7bm83a/atlanta-is-great-at-talking-about-race-without-talking-about-race. Accessed 12 December 2021.

Viruet, Pilot. "How Starz's 'Vida' Created a Safe Space to Explore Latinx and Queer Stories." *The Hollywood Reporter*, 4 May 2018. https://www.hollywoodreporter.com/tv/tv-news/how-starzs-vida-created-a-safe-space-explore-latinx-queer-stories-1107482/. Accessed 30 August 2021.

"Visibility of Disability: Answering the Call for Disability Inclusion in Media." *Nielsen*, 28 July 2021. https://www.nielsen.com/us/en/insights/article/2021/visibility-of-disability-answering-the-call-for-disability-inclusion-in-media/. Accessed 19 August 2021.

"Vitiligo." *Mayo Clinic*. https://www.mayoclinic.org/diseases-conditions/vitiligo/symptoms-causes/syc-20355912. Accessed 15 January 2022.

Walborn, Derek. "Hulu Improves to 41.6 Million Total Subscribers, Hulu Live TV Loses 200,000." *The Streamable*, 13 May 2021. https://thestreamable.com/news/hulu-q1-2021. Accessed 19 August 2021.

Warner, Kristen J. "In the Time of Plastic Representation." *Film Quarterly*, 4 December 2017. https://filmquarterly.org/2017/12/04/in-the-time-of-plastic-representation/. Accessed 28 June 2023.

Warner Media. "Q&A: Misha Green on All Things LOVECRAFT COUNTRY." Media release, 6 August 2020. https://pressroom.warnermedia.com/us/media-release/hbo-0/lovecraft-country/qa-misha-green-all-things-lovecraft-country. Accessed 18 July 2022.

Weinstein, Lynn. "Black Wall Street in Tulsa, OK Destroyed on 6/1/1921." *This Month in Business History*, Research Guides. Library of Congress, created July 2021, updated June 2022. https://guides.loc.gov/this-month-in-business-history/black-wall-street-destroyed. Accessed 19 August 2022.

Weiss, Norman. "Reservation Dogs Was Consistently Great in Its First Season." *Primetimer*, 23 September 2021. https://www.primetimer.com/item/Reservation-Dogs-was-consistently-great-in-its-first-season-ElSZJ5. Accessed 24 September 2022.

Weldon, Glen. "Kids on Bikes: The Sci-Fi Nostalgia of 'Stranger Things,' 'Paper Girls' & 'Super 8.'" *NPR*, 27 July 2016. https://www.npr.org/2016/07/27/487602000/kids-on-bikes-the-sci-fi-nostalgia-of-stranger-things-paper-girls-super-8. Accessed 1 June 2022.

Weller, Sheila. "How Author Timothy Tyson Found the Woman at the Center of the Emmett Till Case." *Vanity Fair*, 26 January 2017. https://www.vanityfair.com/news/2017/01/how-author-timothy-tyson-found-the-woman-at-the-center-of-the-emmett-till-case?mbid=social_twitter. Accessed 10 August 2022.

White, Peter. "FX to Have a Majority of Diverse & Female Directors in 2021 as John Landgraf Lays Out Latest Diversity Data." *Deadline*, 27 August 2020. https://deadline.com/2020/08/fx-john-landgraf-diversity-data-directors-1203024974/. Accessed 15 January 2022.

Wilhelmi, Jack. "Lovecraft Country: True History of Trumbull Park (& What It's Like

Today)." *Screenrant*, 5 September 2020. https://screenrant.com/lovecraft-country-true-story-trumbull-park-explained/. Accessed 30 June 2022.

Williams, Stereo. "Hip-Hop's Transphobic OGs: Will the Rap Community Embrace Caitlyn Jenner?" *Daily Beast*, 6 June 2015. https://www.thedailybeast.com/hip-hops-transphobic-ogs-will-the-rap-community-embrace-caitlyn-jenner. Accessed 23 December 2021.

Willis, Kiersten. "Donald Glover's 'Atlanta' Proves White People 'Don't Know Everything About Black Culture.'" *Atlanta Black Star*, 7 September 2016. https://atlantablackstar.com/2016/09/07/donald-glovers-atlanta-proves-white-people-dont-know-everything-about-black-culture/. Accessed 12 December 2021.

Wilstein, Matt. "Why Muslim Comic Ramy Youssef Made His 9/11 Story About Masturbation." *The Daily Beast*, 16 April 2019. https://www.thedailybeast.com/the-last-laugh-podcast-why-muslim-comic-ramy-youssef-made-his-911-story-on-hulu-about-masturbation. Accessed 9 August 2021.

Wong, Kevin. "'Lovecraft Country Season 1 Finale' Easter Eggs and References in Episode 10, 'Full Circle.'" *Gamespot*, 19 October 2020. https://www.gamespot.com/gallery/lovecraft-country-season-1-finale-easter-eggs-and-references-in-episode-10-full-circle/2900-3605/#1. Accessed 9 July 2022.

"World Drug Report 2019." *United Nations Office on Drugs and Crime*, 26 June 2019. https://www.unodc.org/unodc/en/frontpage/2019/June/world-drug-report-2019_-35-million-people-worldwide-suffer-from-drug-use-disorders-while-only-1-in-7-people-receive-treatment.html. Accessed 8 July 2023.

Zaheer, Mohammad. "How Muslims Became the Good Guys on TV." *BBC*, 21 June 2019. https://www.bbc.com/culture/article/20190620-how-muslims-became-the-good-guys-on-tv. Accessed 9 August 2021.

Zorrilla, Mónica Marie. "Latinx TV Talent Still Largely Shunned by Hollywood, UCLA Diversity Report Indicates." *Variety*, 26 October 2021. https://variety.com/2021/tv/news/latinx-tv-talent-underrepresentation-hollywood-ucla-diversity-report-1235097213/. Accessed 3 January 2022.

Index

A24 8
Abrahamson, Lenny 30, 31, 32, 35, 36, 47, 100
Abrams, J.J. 157
Afrofuturism 179, 182
Afrosurrealism 72
Alien 154, 168
Alien Resurrection 168
Alien³ 168
Aliens 155, 168
Altered States 154
American Horror Story 53
The Americans 53, 141
The Amityville Horror 167
The Amos 'n' Andy Show 54
Antioco, John 140
Apple TV+, examination of 191–192
Arab and Muslim representation 79
Asian representation 75, 77, 177–178
Assassination Nation 8
Atlanta 4, 5, 52–73, 77, 82, 89, 90

Back to the Future (film) 141
Back to the Future (film trilogy) 154
Baker, Josephine 179, 181
Baldwin, James 164, 181
Baraka, Amiri 72
Barry 88
BBC One and HBO, partnership 111, 116
BBC Three and Hulu, partnership 30
Betty 11
Beverly Hills, 90210 12, 34
Beyoncé 180
Bieber, Justin 59, 60
bike riding 16–17
Black representation 54–55
blockbuster (era) 143
Blockbuster (store) 139, 140
Blurred Lines 124
BMF 141
Bonnie & Clyde 143
Bourke-White, Margaret 163, 164

The Breakfast Club 68, 155
Bridgerton (novel series) 56
Bridgerton (TV show) 56
Buffy the Vampire Slayer 28, 189

Camp 53
Campbell, Joseph 129–130, 133–134, 136, 190
Carpenter, John 146, 149, 156
Carrie 155
The Carrie Diaries 141
Casino 21
"Catch the Fire" 186
Chad 81–82
Chance 30
Chapelle, Dave 66
Chewing Gum (TV show) 115
Chewing Gum Dreams (play) 115
The Chi 72
childhood trauma 151–154
Close Encounters of the Third Kind 149–151, 153, 154, 156
The Closer 66
Clueless 34
Cobra Kai 141
Coel, Michaela 111, 114, 115, 116, 117, 120, 122, 124, 125, 128, 129, 131, 132, 133, 134, 136
color-conscious casting 55, 57, 77
colorblind casting 56, 57, 77
colorism 67, 171–172
Comedy Central Presents 53
Community 52, 53, 88
The Cosby Show 55
The Count of Monte Cristo 170
Cujo 155

Da 5 Bloods 158
Dahomey Amazon 181, 190
Dawson's Creek 28
Day of the Dead 155
Dead of Summer 141

233

Deadwood 92
Degrassi: The Next Generation 12, 26
Derrick Comedy 52
Devious Maids 92
Diallo, Nkechi Amare 64–65; *see also* Dolezal, Rachel
A Different World 55
Diner 8
disabled representation 86–88
Disney, examination of 53–54, 76
Dixon, Kyle 155
Dogg, Snoop 66
Dolezal, Rachel 64–65; *see also* Diallo, Nkechi Amare
drug addiction 14–16
Dublin Murders 30
Due, Tananarive 172
Duffer, Matt 139, 151, 155
Duffer, Ross 139, 142, 148, 150
Duffer brothers 138, 139, 141, 142, 144, 146, 147, 155, 156
Dungeons & Dragons 146, 155

East Side West Side 55
Easter Parade 178
Easy Rider 143
Eggo waffles 147
Empire of the Sun 146
Escape from New York 154
E.T. the Extra-Terrestrial 146, 147, 148, 149, 154, 156
Euphoria (2012–2013) 8
Euphoria (2019–present) 4, 8–29, 31, 149
Everybody Hates Chris 141
The Evil Dead 154
The Exorcist 154

Family Matters 55
femininity, throwback 21–22
Firestarter 155
Fleabag 88, 96
Floyd, George 160, 183
The Fog 154
for colored girls who have considered suicide / when the rainbow is enuf 176
The Fresh Prince of Bel-Air 55
Friday Night Lights 22
frotteurism 119
Fuller House 138
FX, examination of 53–54

Gambino, Childish 53
Generation 11
gentrification and *gentefication* 95, 105
Get Out 63, 67, 69, 157, 159, 172
Ghostbusters 155
Gilmore Girls 28

Girls 78
Glover, Donald 52–53, 58, 59, 62, 63, 64, 65, 66, 67, 69, 70, 71, 72, 73, 88, 90
GLOW 141
The Godfather 142
The Goldbergs 141
Good Morning, Vietnam 8
The Good Place 55–56
The Goonies 173, 177
Gossip Girl (2007–2012) 11, 34
Gossip Girl (2021–2023) 11
The Graduate 143
Green, Misha 157, 158, 159, 160, 161, 163, 164, 167, 168, 169, 170, 174, 175, 179, 180, 183, 185, 188, 190, 191
Gremlins 154
Grey's Anatomy 80, 81, 82
Groundhog Day 134
Guava Island 53

half-hour format for drama 31–32, 62, 92, 111
Halloween 149
Halt and Catch Fire 141
The Handmaid's Tale 74
The Harder They Fall 67
The Hardy Boys 141
Hastings, Reed 139, 140
HBO, examination of 10–11, 191
Heathers 34
Helix 157
Heroes 157
the hero's journey 129–130, 133–134, 136, 190
Hidden 139
High Fidelity 76
Hippolyta, in Greek mythology 181
His Dark Materials 31
HIV/AIDS 149
Homeland 79, 80
Homicide: Life on the Street 8, 57
Hook 146
Horror Noire: A History of Black Horror 172
How to Get Away with Murder 92
Hulu, examination of 74, 75–76

I Am Not Okay with This 141
I May Destroy You 4, 5, 111–136
I Spy 55
Indiana Jones (film trilogy) 154
Indiana Jones and the Last Crusade 173
Indiana Jones and the Raiders of the Lost Ark 173
Indiana Jones and the Temple of Doom 146
Insecure 78
The Invisible Man 69

"Is You Is or Is You Ain't My Baby" 170
It 155
It's Always Sunny in Philadelphia 53
Ives, Tim 142

Jack Ryan (novel series) 81
The Jackie Robinson Story 169
Jackson, Michael 67, 68
Jaws 142–144, 145, 146, 149, 153, 156
The Jeffersons 55, 170
Jenner, Caitlyn 63, 64, 65, 66
Jim Crow laws, explanation of 160–161
Joseph Campbell and the Power of Myth 129
Julia 55
Juneteenth 60, 61
Jurassic Park 146, 154
Justified 53

Kids 9
kids on bikes subgenre 148–149
King, Martin Luther, Jr. 61
King, Stephen 155
Kravitz, Zoë 76

The L Word 94
Landgraph, John 54
Langston League 185
The Last Black Man in San Francisco 158
The Last Starfighter 155
The Late Show with Stephen Colbert 74
Latinx representation 75, 77, 92–95, 96–97
Lavelle, Suzie 30–31, 32, 35
The League 53
Legion 53
Levinson, Sam 8, 9, 12, 13, 14, 16, 26
The Lion King 53
Little Fires Everywhere 74
The Little Stranger 30
Living Single 55
Looking 92
Lovecraft, H.P. 159, 161, 169
Lovecraft Country (novel) 157, 159, 167, 168, 173, 174, 182, 184, 186, 191
Lovecraft Country (TV show) 4, 157–192
Lovecraft Country: Supremacy 191

MacGyver 141
Mad Max 154
Magnum P.I. 145
Mama Oya 173, 189
Martin 55
Martin Luther King, Jr., Day 61
masculinity, toxic 19–20
Master of None 81, 82
Mean Girls 34

Meet Me in St. Louis 178
mental health issues 14, 17
Midnight Cowboy 143
Miller, D. Scot 72
Misery 69
Mo 81
"Moving on Up" 170
My So-Called Life 28

Nawi (Dahomey Amazon) 181
"Ne Me Quitte Pas" (Don't Leave Me) 84
The Negro Motorist Green Book 161
Netflix, examination of 139, 140
The Never Ending Story 155
New Hollywood 143
A Nightmare on Elm Street 155
Nip/Tuck 53
Nope 63
Normal People (novel) 30, 32, 33, 36, 38, 40, 42, 43, 47
Normal People (TV show) 4, 30–49, 92, 100

The O.C. 11, 25
The Office 88
Orange Is the New Black 138
Orithyia, in Greek mythology 182
Oz 8

Parks, Gordon 163
Parks and Recreation 88
Peele, Jordan 63, 157, 159
Pence, Mike 61
PEN15 76
"Piel Canela" 179
plastic representation 56
Plessy v. Ferguson 160
Poltergeist 154, 166–167
Pose 54, 141
post-racial TV 55–56
Pretty Little Liars 11
The Princess Bride 155
A Princess of Mars 169
Promising Young Woman 120, 123, 134
Psycho 69
Pulp Fiction 71

Queen Charlotte 56
Queer as Folk (1999–2000) 94
Queer as Folk (2000–2005) 94
queer representation 17–18, 93–94, 102–104

Rain Man 8
Ramy 4, 5, 74–90
Ramy Youssef: Feelings 74
Randolph, Marc 139, 140

Red Dawn 155
Red Oaks 141
Reese's Pieces 147
Reservation Dogs 72, 76
Rhimes, Shonda 56
Ripper Street 30
Rise Again: Tulsa and the Red Summer 62
Risky Business 155
Riverdale 25
Room 30
Rooney, Sally 30, 32, 33, 35, 100
Roots 55
Rosewood Massacre 185
RTÉ 30
Ruff, Matt 159, 167, 168, 182
"Running Up That Hill (A Deal with God)" 153

St. Elmo's Fire 155
Sanford and Son 55
Saracho, Tanya 92, 93, 94, 95, 97, 99, 100, 102, 103, 104, 105, 109
Saved by the Bell 87
Scandal 28
Scanners 154
See Dad Run 74
Se7en 27
Sex Education 13
sex positive feminism 96–100
sex-positivity 20, 96, 98–99, 107–108
sexting and explicit material, weaponization of 25
sexual consent, explanation 112
"Sh-Boom (Life Could Be a Dream)" 169, 188
Sherlock 30
The Shield 53
The Shining 155, 167, 168
Show Me a Hero 141
Simone, Nina 181
Six Feet Under 92
skin bleaching 67
Skins 13
Sleeper Cell 79
Snowfall 141
Solo: A Star Wars Story 53
Sons of Anarchy 53, 157
The Sopranos 92
Sosa, Sammy 67
Soul Train 55
Space Is the Place 181
Spielberg 153
Spielberg, Steven 141–142, 146, 150, 151, 153–154, 155, 156
Stand by Me 155
Star Wars (film) 143, 147

Star Wars (film trilogy) 154
STARZ, diverse voices 92–93
stealthing 121–123
Stein, Michael 155
"Stone Mattress" 132
"Stop Dat Knocking" 184
story-progressing sex 100
The Strange Case of Dr. Jekyll and Mr. Hyde 175
Stranger Things 4, 138–156, 158
Stratford Hotel 185
Stringfield, Bessie 179
suburbia 148
Succession 30, 157
Summer Stock 178
Sun Ra 181
surrealism 70, 71–72
Survive 156
Sweet/Vicious 113

The Talisman 155
Tangerine Dream 156
Taylor, Breonna 160
The Terminator 155
Terminator 2: Judgment Day 155
Them 162
The Thing 155
30 Rock 52, 88
30-year cycle 141
This Changes Everything 54
"This Is America" 53
Till, Emmett 162, 183, 186, 187
Tom Clancy's Jack Ryan (TV show) 80–81, 82
trans representation 17–18
Transparent 89
transphobia 65–66
transracial identity 64–66
True Blood 28
True Romance 22
Trumbull Park Homes Race Riots 161
Trump, Donald 61
Tulsa Race Massacre 184–186
Tuskegee experiment 161
24 79, 80
Twin Peaks 71
Two-Spirit representation 174
Tyrant 79

Unbelievable 113
Uncle Tom's Cabin 183
Underground 157, 192
Us 63

Van Dusen, Chris 56
Vangelis 156
Veronica Mars 34

Vida 4, 92–110, 112
Vikings 31

Wadler, Naomi 184
The War of the Worlds 169
war on drugs 148
Watchmen 157, 184
Wayward Pines 139
We Are Who We Are 11–12
Weirdo 53
Wet Hot American Summer: First Day of Camp 141
Whatever Happened to Baby Jane? 69

"Whitey's on the Moon" 164–165
"Whole Lotta Shakin' Goin' On" 170
Williams, John 156
Williams Dreamland Theatre 185
The Wire 57, 92
The Wizard of Lies 8
The Wizard of Oz 181
Woke 76
Wonder, Stevie 68
Wonder Woman 190

Youssef, Ramy 74–75, 77, 78, 79–80, 81, 82, 83, 84–85, 86, 88, 89, 90

www.ingramcontent.com/pod-product-compliance
Ingram Content Group UK Ltd.
Pitfield, Milton Keynes, MK11 3LW, UK
UKHW041942140426
52171PUK00014B/616